THE FIRST XI
2ND EDITION

WINNING
ORGANISATIONS
IN AUSTRALIA

HUBBARD · SAMUEL · COCKS · HEAP

1807
WILEY
2007

John Wiley & Sons Australia, Ltd

First published 2007 by
John Wiley & Sons Australia, Ltd
42 McDougall Street, Milton Qld 4064

Offices also in Sydney and Melbourne

Typeset in Berkeley LT 11.2/13.7 pt

© G.&J. Hubbard Services P/L, Delyth Samuel, ERU Consulting and Productive Workplaces P/L 2007.

The moral rights of the authors have been asserted

National Library of Australia Cataloguing-in-Publication data:

The first XI : winning organisations in Australia.

   2nd ed.
   Bibliography.
   Includes index.
   ISBN 9780731405619.

   ISBN 0 7314 0561 7.

   1. Organizational effectiveness. 2. Success in business - Australia. 3. Management - Australia. I. Hubbard, Graham.

658.400994

All rights reserved. Except as permitted under the *Australian Copyright Act 1968* (for example, a fair dealing for the purposes of study, research, criticism or review), no part of this book may be reproduced, stored in a retrieval system, communicated or transmitted in any form or by any means without prior written permission. All inquiries should be made to the publisher at the address above.

Cover image ©Photolibrary/Workbook, Inc.

Wiley bicentennial logo: Richard J Pacifico

Extracts from *Brambles: Working its Way around the World* by Edna Carew, reproduced with the permission of Brambles
Extracts from *Built to Last: Successful Habits of Visionary Companies* by Jim Collins and Jerry I Porras, published by Century Business Books and reprinted with permission
Extracts from *The Detailed Westfield Story: The First 40 Years* ©Westfield Group
Extracts from 'The way we work' reproduced with the permission of Rio Tinto
Lend Lease 'Beliefs' ©Lend Lease Corporation
'What we stand for' reproduced with the permission of Macquarie Bank

The Sydney Morning Herald is a registered trademark of John Fairfax Publications Pty Ltd.
The Age is a registered trademark of The Age Company Ltd.
For advertising inquiries for Fairfax Books please contact:
VIC: Steve Berry 03 9601 2232
NSW: Sophie Leach 02 9282 3582

Printed in Australia by McPherson's Printing Group

10 9 8 7 6 5 4 3 2 1

Disclaimer
The material in this publication is of the nature of general comment only, and does not represent professional advice. It is not intended to provide specific guidance for particular circumstances and it should not be relied on as the basis for any decision to take action or not take action on any matter which it covers. Readers should obtain professional advice where appropriate, before making any such decision. To the maximum extent permitted by law, the authors and publisher disclaim all responsibility and liability to any person, arising directly or indirectly from any person taking or not taking action based upon the information in this publication.

Contents

Foreword v

Preface vii

About the authors xi

1 'Winning' organisations in Australia: a journey, not just an outcome 1
2 Effective execution 21
3 Perfect alignment 47
4 Adapt rapidly 81
5 Clear and fuzzy strategy 113
6 Leadership, not leaders 137
7 Looking out, looking in 171
8 Right people 201
9 Manage the downside 235
10 Balance everything 263
11 How does 'Australia' make it different? 287
12 Strategy over time: the strategic cycle in Australia 311
13 The First XI: where are they now? 335
14 Comparing our findings with other studies 373
15 Starting your organisation on a winning journey 391

Appendix A: winning organisation brief biographies 409

Appendix B: minor studies 437

Appendix C: winning organisations in Australia—selected survey questions 445

Bibliography 449

Index 453

Acknowledgements

This project would not have been possible without the support of many people, all of whom played important roles in putting the pieces of this jigsaw puzzle together for both editions. We thank them all.

To Mt Eliza Business School for providing research funding and time to develop this project. To the Adelaide Graduate School of Business at the University of Adelaide for research support for the second edition.

For assistance with our research and findings: Murray Ainsworth, Sara Allen, Sajid Anwar, Gail Avard, Robert Belleville, Carole Christopherson, Peta Cohen, Ray Cotsell, Feng Fu, Lynette Francis, John Harvey, Terry Heap, Isaac Hinton, Les Howard, Lan Huong, Andrew Hubbard, Judy Hubbard, Michael Hubbard, Trish Johnston, Shahebaz Khan, Josephine Maio, Gerry Moriarty, Bruce McKern, Paul Mills, Judith Mitchell, Margaret Nash, Leeanne O'Connor, Gary Pemberton, Jerry Porras, Helen Quinn, Janette Quinn, Michael Regan, Pi-Shen Seet, Graeme Stanway, Adam Steen and Mark Suares.

To all those respondents who answered the initial questionnaires and to our MBA and executive students who assisted us with our initial search for possible winning organisations.

To our interviewees and their organisations for providing their time and assistance: Michael Angwin, Margaret Armstrong, Fiona Balfour, Roger Bamber, Tom Barlow, Robin Batterham, Gail Burke, Robert Burns, Matthew Butlin, Peter Callender, David Clarke, Roger Corbett, Leigh Clifford, Barry Cusack, Ron Cutler, Bev Davis, Douglas Davis, Belinda de Rome, Geoff Dixon, Andrew Downe, Tim Duncan, Kim Edwards, Paul Edwards, David Forsyth, Peter Hanley, Ian Head, Bryan Hood, Peter Hughes, Mark Johnson, John Jeffrey, Hayden Kelly, Michelle Knight, Narendra Kumar, Megan Lane, Stuart Lee, Charlie Lenegan, Michael Lin, Andrew Lockwood, Matthew Loughnan, Ian MacDonald, Peter McKinnon, Garth McKenzie, Sandra McPhee, Roland Matrenza, Nick Minogue, Nicholas Moore, Allan Moss, Kristine Neill, Alan Oster, Ross Pinney, Brandon Phillips, Bob Prowse, Gary Reid, Michael Rocca, Mark Ryan, Bill Scales, Richard Sheppard, Michael Sharp, Michael Sharpe, Greg Smith, Brad Soller, John Stanhope, Peter Stansfeld, John Staite, Les Strong, Brian Thomas, David Turner and Phil Young.

For assistance with publication: all the team at Wiley.

Foreword

The First XI deals with an important question in management—in fact, some would say the most important question—namely what are the ingredients for sustained above-average performance in an organisation? This is a quest I refer to as the management equivalent of the search for the Holy Grail, for two reasons.

First, the search is extremely difficult. Only few firms achieve sustained above-average performance. Numerous studies have found that only about 5 per cent of firms achieve consistent above-average returns for 10 to 15 or so years. Graham Hubbard and his colleagues examined 199 firms before identifying 11 that met their sustained success criteria. Successful firms have to overcome powerful forces, such as competition, inertia, hubris and ageing, that wear down the above-average performer over time.

Second, the search is like that for the Holy Grail because finding success ingredients is extremely valuable. Pay, options or share values, self-esteem and recognition flow to the executives in consistent above-average performers. Conversely, below-average performers often find their tenure shortened and their job frustrating.

The book's value is not only in tackling the question, but in doing so from a uniquely Australian perspective. The success literature is well populated by stories about US icons such as General Electric, Microsoft, Proctor & Gamble and McDonald's. There is far less serious writing about Australian success stories such as Westfield, Macquarie Bank, Woolworths and Brambles. Hence, the book fills an important gap.

While *The First XI* seeks the Holy Grail, it does so in a realistic way. Specifically, it:

▶ recognises the long time frames required to fundamentally improve a large organisation. None of these companies were built or transformed in one- to two-year periods. Rather, five- to 10-year (and sometimes longer) periods of stable and consistent leadership seem to be needed

▶ appreciates that the success formulae put forward are at best a general guide. For example, one key requirement is to have the 'right people'. But what makes a person 'right'? The answer proposed is a fit with culture and strategy, plus the 'right attitude'. How are these attributes defined and applied? Despite the inclusion of significant case material and examples from the 11 firms, there are no easy answers

▶ is not obsessed with one measure, such as total returns to shareholders. Instead, a balanced scorecard is used, which may well be better aligned with the multiplicity of stakeholders and demands now being made of major organisations and their leaders. It also allows the study to include interesting not-for-profit organisations such as the Salvation Army.

Although *The First XI*'s findings are broadly consistent with other work on this subject, it highlights an aspect not widely commented on—managing risk and downsides. My own experience is that people find this difficult and unpleasant, preferring to grow rather than to contract, to buy rather than to sell and to reward rather than to punish.

Management of large complex organisations is still a discipline in its infancy, still part art, part science, part instinct and part logic. Learning from experience—one's own and others—is thus critical, and that ultimately is what this book is about.

Frederick G Hilmer
Vice chancellor
University of New South Wales

Preface

Since the first edition of *The First XI* was published, we have been very pleased by the response to our 'Australian' research on winning organisations. It has been enthusiastically received and it 'jells' with all the senior managers who are exposed to it. It resonates, confirms, inspires and raises other questions we had not thought of.

During this period, our winning organisations have experience a wide variety of circumstances. We wondered—and people wanted to know—what has happened to these organisations and why? Are they still winners?

They've also asked us, 'How do we get started ourselves?' And we've asked ourselves, 'Is Australia still different?' and how does the concept of the strategic cycle in Australia that we introduced in the first edition explain some of these events.

In this second edition, we've addressed all these issues and updated all the chapters, refining the text and ideas to reflect our experience between 2001 and 2006. We've added many new examples to the chapters so that readers, including owners of the first edition, will gain greatly from reading this new edition.

We're also thrilled to have Fairfax as a co-branding partner for the book. Reflecting our faith in the quality and value of the work, Fairfax's support gives further credibility to our findings.

We're just as excited by this edition as the first one! We continue to reflect on the findings, the practices and the organisations. There's a lot more to be done, but we hope you will enjoy this second edition.

The genesis of this project was in 1992 when Graham Hubbard accepted a visiting professorship position at the University of Minnesota. Frustrated with the inability of both MBAs and executives in Australia to be able to classify or determine which organisations were performing well, he began researching how organisations actually measured 'performance'.

Over the next three years, through three empirical research projects in the US and then back in Australia, Graham concluded that 'performance' was little understood, even within organisations. Yet, for a strategist, organisational performance is the key result area. Organisational performance simply must be understood if we are to highlight 'high-performing' organisations and try to understand what makes them tick.

In 1994, *Built to Last* was published. Following the 1982 publication of *In Search of Excellence*, this book focused Graham's mind. Reinforced by a client company that was also galvanised by *Built to Last*'s findings, Graham wanted to conduct a 'built to last' for Australia to answer three burning questions:

1 Which were the high-performing organisations in Australia?

2 What were the organisational practices that set them apart?

3 How is being 'high-performing' different in Australia?

The opportunity to pursue the idea did not come until 1999, when Graham moved to Mt Eliza Business School and got support from the School to begin this project. The research team was then developed. Delyth and Simon joined the project on graduating from the MBA program. Delyth's background in technology, innovation and international competitiveness and Simon's in marketing and consulting complemented Graham's expertise in strategic management and accounting. Graeme, with 20 years' practical experience in technology, executive roles, operations and change management, joined Mt Eliza Business School and the project shortly afterwards. The team was deliberately structured to include people from a variety of backgrounds, with wide experience and strong opinions, yet who were team players.

We believe this project goes a long way towards providing answers to the three questions. We have identified nine principles of organisational life that lead to 'winning'. We believe these principles, if applied properly to most organisations, would see an enormous improvement in the quality of organisational outcomes in Australia.

Indeed, further, we believe that we know what is needed to be a winner. But how difficult it is to apply it!

The 11 organisations identified here, the 'First XI', are not the only 'winning organisations' in Australia. Indeed, we feel major sectors of Australian organisational life—all except the public-listed sector—are under-represented. But at least we have made a start and found, tested and highlighted some organisations grown in Australia that have succeeded over long periods.

We hope the principles and the specific examples from the winning organisations identified here will provide leadership teams and individual leaders with the inspiration and a practical framework for improving their organisational practice, and consequently their organisational performance.

But we warn readers—this book is not about easy fixes. The ideas here are complex. They take time to develop, to implement and to realise. Becoming a winning organisation is not something that happens in 12 months, or even in several years. It takes time. It is difficult. But it can be done. And it can be done by any organisation, wherever it begins its life and whatever industry it is in. There is hope! Do you want to commit yourself and your organisation to pursue 'winning'?

We believe that the principles of 'winning' are pretty timeless! There are differences between our findings and those of *In Search of Excellence*, *Built to Last* and *Good to Great*, but the similarities are much greater than the differences. And virtually none of the fads are important or recognised in these principles.

This book captures the fundamental drivers of sustainable winning organisations, so that the lessons learned from them can be adapted by others. In this way, we hope that more organisations in Australia will be successful so our people, communities and society will prosper and share in the wealth and knowledge that follow success.

Graham Hubbard
Delyth Samuel
Graeme Cocks
Simon Heap
January 2007

About the authors

Graham Hubbard

Graham Hubbard is Professor of Strategic Management at the University of Adelaide, where he teaches on local and international MBA programs and undertakes and supervises research in the area of strategic management. He is the author or co-author of 13 books mainly in the areas of strategy, concentrating particularly on strategy in the Australian context. Graham consults widely and has written many case studies, mainly on Australian organisations. He has also taught at the University of Minnesota and Cranfield University overseas, and at Melbourne, Monash, RMIT, Deakin and Swinburne universities in Australia. Graham can be contacted at <graham.hubbard@adelaide.edu.au>.

Delyth Samuel

Delyth Samuel is Chief Examiner for the CPA professional qualifications capstone module 'Business Strategy and Leadership'. She is a board member of the International Fibre Centre (IFC), and she supervises and examines industry projects for the Mt Eliza Centre for Executive Education at Melbourne Business School. Delyth's business career includes key roles in textile manufacturing, a teaching role and R&D program management in textile manufacturing, and a business product development and commercialisation role with the School of Enterprise at the University of Melbourne. She is highly regarded for her project and business planning expertise. Her current role focuses on the design, development and delivery of educational programs for the university and corporate clients. Delyth can be contacted at <d.samuel@soe.unimelb.edu.au>.

Graeme Cocks

Graeme Cocks is Associate Professor of Strategic and Operations Management at Melbourne Business School and the Mt Eliza Centre for Executive Education. He specialises in business integration, operations management, project management, performance measurement and technology transfer. Combining an academic career with several CEO, executive and international management positions in a broad range of public and private enterprises, he has held business and research positions in Australia, Canada, England and the US. Graeme has also published and presented widely in international scientific and management journals and forums. He has been a consultant to many Australian and overseas corporations, including Telstra, ICI (UK), AMP, Olin Corporation (US) and Canada Westinghouse. Graeme can be contacted at <g.cocks@mbs.edu>.

Simon Heap

Simon Heap is a best-selling author and management consultant based in Melbourne. He has been a disciple of 'winning' from an early age, initially in international sport through his membership of the Australian national ski team, then later in business. He currently advises for ERU Consulting Group and is a consultant to organisations globally on how to improve their performance. Simon is also engaged on a permanent retainer by Fastline Group, a global distributor of racing go-karts and accessories, for which he advises on organisational strategy and systems, mergers, acquisitions and leadership. Visit Simon at <www.simonheap.com>.

1 'Winning' organisations in Australia: a journey, not just an outcome

The aims of this book

Despite the tremendous amount of media coverage of business in Australia, there is little agreement about which are the best organisations in Australia and what practices they have followed to become the best. In these times, when organisations face an increasingly turbulent international world of competition, Australian businesspeople and Australian organisations need to know and understand how to win, and win in the long term, not just how to shine briefly and then fade away.

The first edition of this book set out to answer three questions:

1 Which are the 'winning' organisations in Australia?

2 What do they do to be winners?

3 How is 'winning' different in Australia?

The response from business professionals to the first edition was overwhelmingly enthusiastic. Finally, they said, there is a book about winning practice in Australia, a book that relates to Australian conditions and includes examples we can relate to. This response has been consistent over the five years since the first edition was published that we have been presenting and talking about the findings from our research.

This second edition retains the original aims and material, but seeks to answer three additional questions:

1. What has happened to the 'First XI' team of organisations that we chose to represent Australia back in 2000? Are they still continuing to perform? If not, why is this the case?
2. What does the strategic cycle in Australia—a concept we briefly touched on in the first edition—look like?
3. How can my organisation get started on the winning journey?

We consider how the 11 organisations we analysed have performed in the five years since our original research ended—that is, between 2001 and 2006. We show how your organisation—whatever type and size it is—can begin the journey towards winning and, in doing so, contribute to improved organisational performance and outcomes for Australia. Your organisation, too, can be chosen in the 'First XI'!

From this book, you will come to understand what it takes to be a winning organisation in Australia, and discover how your organisation can take these ideas and apply them directly, quickly and effectively. If more organisations seek out the recipe for winning, we'll have better organisational performance, and better organisations, in Australia. And that will be good for everybody—shareholders, employees, customers, governments, suppliers, managers and local communities. It's not easy, but it *is* possible.

However, the questions are difficult and the answers have taken some time to develop. In this chapter, we explain how we went about addressing the first set of questions. We take you on our original three-year journey to find and understand the answers.

As a result of the research we also explode some myths that exist—the common practices organisations are following that *do not* lead to success. Then we provide detailed discussion of the *winning wheel framework* we have developed to explain winning in Australia. Using specific examples from the 'First XI' winning organisations, we explain the elements of the winning wheel. We also explain how winning is different in Australia and why. We show that organisations undergo a *strategic cycle*—each stage of which requires different sets of capabilities for success.

Beginnings of the project

This project began in the late 1980s, when several strategists in Australia began to think about what organisations had to do to succeed in Australia and whether and how that was different from other countries.

In the early 1990s, three key developments provided the foundations for this project (see figure 1.1).

Figure 1.1: the foundations of the research

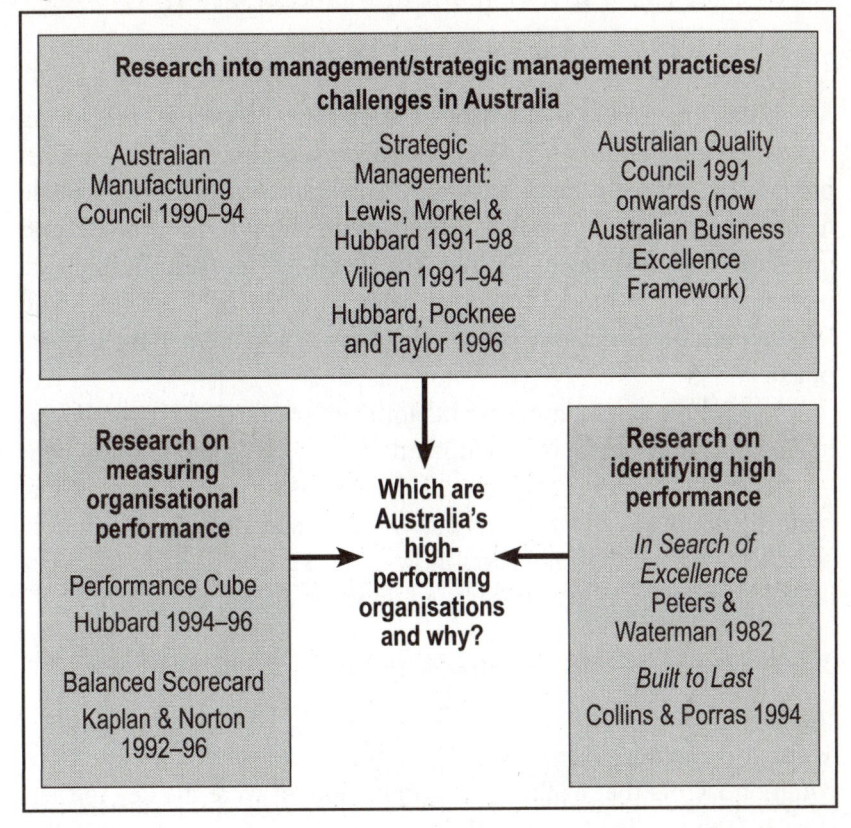

```
┌─────────────────────────────────────────────────────────────┐
│  Research into management/strategic management practices/   │
│                    challenges in Australia                   │
│                                                              │
│   Australian          Strategic         Australian Quality  │
│   Manufacturing      Management:         Council 1991       │
│   Council 1990-94    Lewis, Morkel &     onwards (now       │
│                      Hubbard 1991-98     Australian Business│
│                                          Excellence         │
│                      Viljoen 1991-94     Framework)         │
│                                                              │
│                      Hubbard, Pocknee                        │
│                      and Taylor 1996                         │
└─────────────────────────────────────────────────────────────┘
                              │
   ┌──────────────┐           ▼            ┌──────────────┐
   │ Research on  │     Which are          │ Research on  │
   │  measuring   │     Australia's        │ identifying  │
   │organisational│──▶     high-       ◀───│     high     │
   │ performance  │     performing         │ performance  │
   │              │     organisations      │              │
   │ Performance  │     and why?           │ In Search of │
   │    Cube      │                        │  Excellence  │
   │   Hubbard    │                        │   Peters &   │
   │   1994-96    │                        │ Waterman 1982│
   │              │                        │              │
   │  Balanced    │                        │ Built to Last│
   │  Scorecard   │                        │  Collins &   │
   │ Kaplan &     │                        │ Porras 1994  │
   │   Norton     │                        │              │
   │   1992-96    │                        │              │
   └──────────────┘                        └──────────────┘
```

1 *Developing organisational management principles for Australia*

During the 1990s a series of authors and groups wrote about the Australian business landscape and also wrote case studies of Australian organisations. These works provided general frameworks for strategic management and some detailed examples of successful role models. The Australian Manufacturing Council produced *The Global Challenge* in 1990 and *Leading the Way* in 1992 to indicate generally how Australian organisations might compete and what the challenges were for them. Lewis, Morkel and Hubbard (1991–98), Viljoen (1991–94), and Hubbard, Pocknee and Taylor (1996) were some who developed early comprehensive Australian strategic management texts for business executives.

During this period, too, Australian organisations were turning to the quality movement to understand and absorb its principles and apply them to organisational processes, in order to contend with international competitors. The Australian Quality Council produced a framework for assessment for the Australian Quality Awards, which helped many organisations improve their processes.

2   Changing how to measure organisational performance

At about this time, the balanced scorecard model of measuring organisational performance was developed by Kaplan and Norton. This provided a four-sector method of measuring performance—measuring financial, market, internal efficiency, and long-term growth and innovation performance—rather than simply measuring financial performance. The model was favourably received by managers, who felt it represented what was intuitively important to them in managerial practice.

Around the same time, insights into empirical research conducted in Australia and overseas by Hubbard (1996) led to the development of the 'performance cube' model for assessing the organisational performance of any organisation in any industry at any time. The model provided a way of thinking about how to measure 'success' for all types of organisations, not just those listed on the sharemarket.

3   Using empirical evidence to assess winning organisations overseas

In 1994 Collins and Porras published *Built to Last*, which identified 18 high-performing companies (17 from the US plus Sony) and the common factors that Collins and Porras thought were the key to their success.

An important element that gave the book credibility was that it started with CEOs' opinions of high-performing companies, then used rigorous analysis to test these opinions and to analyse the common factors associated with that group of companies. This book excited Australian executives who read it. It seemed to hit a lot of the key issues that managers felt were important but that were too subtle to be picked up in standard management literature.

Built to Last advanced Peters and Waterman's seminal 1982 book *In Search of Excellence*, which also identified a group of excellent American companies and their key management practices. *Built to Last*'s methodology was clearly laid out, it appeared to be based on objective evidence and it appeared to be very thorough, with the authors and their large research team having spent six years on the work.

Assessing winning organisations in Australia

These three developments provided the foundations for this project. What was still missing was an Australian equivalent to *Built to Last* or *In Search of Excellence*. Which companies in Australia might qualify for such a list? Were their practices similar to or different from those in the US studies? What made it more difficult was that, whenever we asked managers which were the best performing companies in Australia, we received three consistent responses:

▶ They found it difficult to make the assessment at all. Typical replies were 'What do you mean by "best"?' or 'We don't know'.

▶ Their choices were very wide-ranging and subject to considerable dispute with their peers. That is, the organisations chosen by some were regarded by others as poor performers—and there was no easy way to resolve these anecdotal views.

▶ Many of the companies identified were well-known American examples, such as Microsoft, General Electric, McDonald's and Disney, not local organisations.

The questions still remained: how could Australian managers learn from their own role models, facing an Australian environment? Is Australia just the same as overseas? If it is not, how is 'winning' different in Australia? We simply had no well-researched information or even general anecdotal agreement.

The project begins

In 1999, this project formally began at Mt Eliza Business School (which has subsequently merged with Melbourne Business School at the University of Melbourne). Its aims were:

▶ To identify organisations operating in Australia that were considered to be high performing, or 'winning' over the long term.

▶ To understand what the common characteristics were for these organisations.

Our research methodology

Our methodology followed that of Collins and Porras where feasible and appropriate. In addition, we gathered and analysed a substantial body of literature on 'successful' companies that had been developed using a variety of methodologies. This literature and its findings are summarised in chapter 14. While these provided some insights, we felt that the Collins and Porras work used a superior methodology and was practical to follow.

Initially, we surveyed CEOs of the 1000 largest organisations in the country, asking them to identify 'winning' organisations. We believed that they were in the best position to be aware of other organisations and to be able to assess their performance. We also sought the opinions of executives on public senior management courses at Mt Eliza Business School. We were interested in all types of organisations — listed, private, government, non-profit and subsidiaries of overseas organisations.

In seeking nominations, we defined 'winning' as being 'extremely successful over long periods of time'. We defined 'success' generally as 'using a balanced scorecard approach'. To qualify for assessment, organisations had to be in existence for at least 20 years and had to have had more than one CEO. This ensured that the organisation would have endured both good and bad economic cycles and minimised the possibility that the success of the organisation might be due simply to the original founder or CEO.

From this survey in 1999 to 2000, 199 organisations were nominated. We chose the 14 organisations that were most nominated for our initial analysis, as there seemed to be a clear break point between these organisations and the next group.

We first analysed the financial statements and the share price performance (where relevant) of the organisations over 20 years (1981 to 2000) to ensure that financial performance both in accounting and sharemarket terms was above average, taking into account the type of industry. Two of the organisations were eliminated at this stage — though popular, their financials simply did not stand up.

Using a balanced scorecard/performance cube approach to assess performance more widely, we analysed the annual reports of the selected organisations over the 20-year period to get a wider perspective on performance and to try to understand the key factors that had led to that performance. We attempted to understand each organisation's financial and market position, internal efficiency and effectiveness, and ability to grow and develop, taking account of the type of organisation, its industry and its position. Three of us read every company annual report in detail — over 6000 pages of reading each — to ensure that we captured all the key issues over the long time span we were covering.

The team that undertook this work was deliberately chosen to have a wide variety of experience and backgrounds. Consequently, getting agreement about both the organisation's performance and the key factors for success was challenging, but the team's diversity was an undoubted strength. At the end of this process, we eliminated another organisation from the sample. While its financial and market positions were very good, the organisation had been in turmoil for some years and it appeared to be 'stuck' in terms of leadership and strategy, while employees were damning in their criticism of its internal processes.

Evidence of success

Although we then chose the winning organisations on the basis of their balanced scorecard and performance cube rather than their financial performance, the latter is the only common measure we can use to give you an idea of their performance.

Figure 1.2 shows what would have happened if you had invested $1 in each of the listed organisations and left it there for 20 years, compared with $1 invested in the All Ordinaries Accumulation Index. It shows that the investment would have grown to $42 550 while the Accumulation Index would have grown to $14 650, outperforming the index by almost three times!

Figure 1.2: sharemarket performance for the winning organisations, 1980–2001

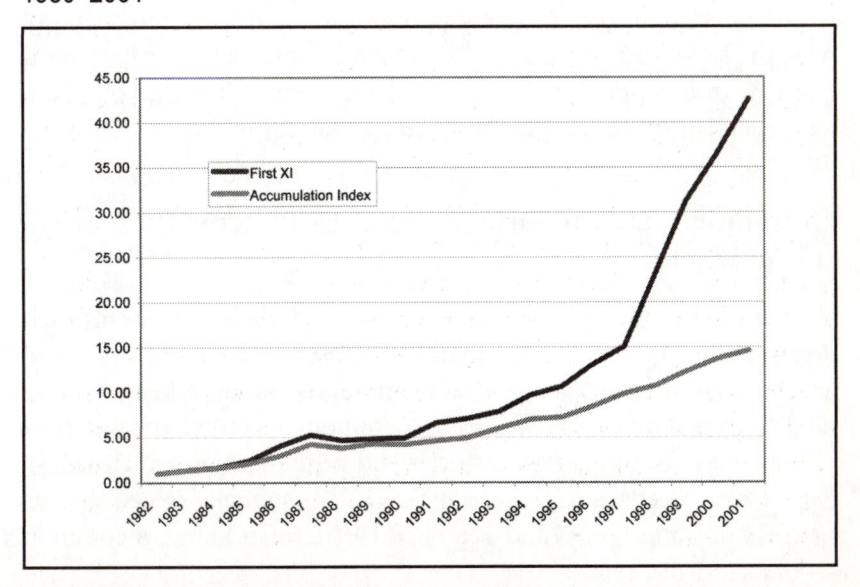

In one respect, we were not able to follow the *Built to Last* methodology. We did not identify comparative organisations for the winning organisations. While it would have been possible to do this for some of the winning organisations, it would not have been possible to do so for quite a few in such a small market as Australia. Consequently, we omitted this step. However, having the findings of *Built to Last* and *In Search of Excellence* enabled us to compare our findings to other world-renowned studies.

Having satisfied ourselves from the outside that the remaining organisations were worthy candidates for the title of 'winning organisations', in the second half of 2001 we contacted them to seek interviews. We wished to interview key executives who had been with the organisation for long periods and who represented a variety of different perspectives. We also sought out books, case studies and other significant analyses of the organisations, particularly those that had a historical or long-term perspective. Interviews generally lasted one hour and were attended by at least two members of the research team, again to ensure that different views were covered, opinions were agreed on and to act as a double-check on the information recorded.

Not all the organisations were cooperative at this stage, as several were caught up in major organisation- and industry-changing events such as the airline industry upheaval, the turmoil that followed the events of 11 September 2001, global mergers and CEO changes. So we used our networks to identify other people who could give us insights on the organisation, either from their past employment in or consulting experiences with it.

At no stage in the interview process did we divulge our views of what the key factors were thought to be. All interviews and discussions began with a simple but fundamental question: 'What do you think have been the causes of success for [organisation] in the long term?'

From individual organisation success to generic success factors

Having agreed among ourselves on the key factors for success for each organisation, we then met to find—if possible—a common set of generic success factors across the organisations. Some of the team were doubtful that any factors would be 'common', given the great variety of organisations, industries, histories and positions studied. However, over several meetings during the research, we gradually agreed that, as both Collins and Porras and Peters and Waterman found, a common set of factors did exist.

We subsequently checked this set of factors against each organisation to be confident that each factor did apply. After we had completed our work, we compared our factors to those chosen by Collins and Porras to see the degree of similarity—and the differences. See chapter 14 for a comparison of our findings with those of Collins and Porras and with other important studies about the elusive nature of 'winning'.

Finally, we also discussed for each organisation—and overall—what factors, if any, were unique to the Australian environment. Did it make any difference that the organisations developed in Australia, or are the factors for success common across countries? Chapter 11 addresses what makes 'winning' different in Australia.

Notes of caution

We strike three notes of caution at this point. First, like Collins and Porras, we do not claim that these are the only 'winning' organisations in Australia. Interestingly, some of these organisations were not well known to us at the start of the research. If we were making our own choices, other organisations might have been included. But this, of course, would have made our findings very subjective. Instead, we took the nominations of the experienced CEOs and senior managers as our base data set. So organisations that were not selected by a sufficient number of CEOs were not analysed further.

Second, all the winning organisations are large and all but one are listed on the stock exchange. Size and being listed on the exchange attracts publicity and makes information about organisational performance easier to come by and to assess by outsiders. However, we are sure that there are other organisations that would qualify as winning organisations. Private companies, not-for-profits, government enterprises and subsidiaries of overseas corporations are under-represented or absent. We believe they were not widely nominated because their long-term stories are not well enough known or widely enough understood. Indeed, we hope that one of the outcomes of our work will be further well-researched pursuit and identification of other 'winning' organisations that will show how to be successful in Australia.

Third, we do not claim that these 'winning' organisations have not made mistakes. Indeed, at any particular time we expect that at least one or two will be facing significant challenges. This was the case throughout the study period and the subsequent five years. No organisation is perfect. All organisations, even winning ones, go backwards at some point.

What we *do* claim is that the principles for winning organisations will hold true into the future. As such, we believe that an organisation that practises these principles over the long term will be well placed to succeed, whatever its industry. The organisations identified here, having been winning organisations for a long period, are more likely to be able to recover from setbacks or challenges than new organisations that have never faced adversity or change.

Nevertheless, just because an organisation is identified as a long-term high performer does not guarantee that it will remain so forever. Decline and failure are as much a part of the market system as growth and success. Organisations that forget this, or that grow complacent, eventually reap their just desserts. In chapter 12 we analyse what has happened to the 'First XI' since they were selected. Have they followed the principles? Do they still belong in the 'First XI'? What mistakes have the organisations made and how are they addressing them?

What 'winning' is *not* about

During the course of our research, we found that a number of ideas that are widely held to be important for success in the business community simply did not feature in the practices of the winning organisations, in terms of making a difference. We want to explode these myths before we start. They are:

1 'Winning' is *not* about vision and mission statements

For strategists, this is an extremely disconcerting finding. Most organisations seem to have at least one of these statements, if not more than one of both (different mission and vision statements in different divisions or departments).

Only one of our winning organisations even had one of them at the end of the initial analysis period. In 2006, only one had a vision statement and only four had mission statements. In no case in our original research was the mission or vision pointed out to us as an important element of success, or in any explanation of the strategy of the organisation. Yet many firms spend hundreds of hours and thousands of dollars generating these statements that have become perceived as necessary for a 'real' organisation.

Why did they not feature here? First, we are not saying that 'strategy' is not important, only that vision and mission *statements* are not. Second, vision and mission statements are extremely varied in practice. There is little agreement among strategists or businesspeople about exactly what should go into each, or even if there should be one or both. No wonder they have little impact! Third, they have become increasingly long and/or bland. As such, they are neither memorable nor unique, which is exactly what they were designed to be!

In summary, you may be wasting your time and money developing these statements. Having a clear strategy is important, but it doesn't have to be put into a vision or mission statement.

2 Winning is *not* about Big Hairy Audacious Goals

Collins and Porras (1994) found that Big Hairy Audacious Goals (BHAGs) were one of the key principles for their winning organisations. They said:

> A BHAG should fall well outside the comfort zone. People in the organization should have reason to believe they can pull it off, yet it should require heroic effort and perhaps even a little luck...A BHAG should be so bold and exciting in its own right that it would continue to stimulate progress even if the organization's leaders disappeared... (p. 112)

We did not find a single BHAG in our winning organisations. Research done at Telstra that looked at appropriate leadership styles for Australian organisations found that Australians want clear guidelines and directions about where they and the organisation are heading. They also want a reason that has social and moral implications—a cause—for why the organisation is moving in that direction. Without this clear view, the study concluded that people will not become committed to and involved with the organisation. The study also found that Australians are innately insecure. Together, these two findings suggest that Australians will not identify with BHAGs, which are too confronting and carry too high a risk of failure.

3 Winning is *not* about great breakthrough ideas

Unlike US organisations cited in *Built to Last*, such as Boeing, IBM, Motorola, Sony or 3M, none of our organisations succeeded simply on the basis of a single 'breakthrough' idea. Our winning organisations are mainly in low-tech and mature industries. While there is a great deal of innovation in these organisations, none is based on 'one big idea' or 'one big innovation'. Winning is the outcome of a lot of decisions and activities, not one, and not just luck.

4 Winning is *not* about charismatic or high-profile leaders

Our bet is that you will be able to name less than half of the CEOs of our winning organisations. Further, we will be surprised if you can name any person who has been a CEO of some of them, regardless of when that was! (See appendix A for lists of all the CEOs.)

Why is this? Despite the personalisation of large organisations over the last 10 to 15 years, publicity has not had a lot to do with 'winning'. Instead it has more to do with activity (for example, acquisitions, growth, scandals, large losses, changes, or an outspoken leader). Much publicity does not investigate how well the organisation is doing, only that it has done something or said something. All three of the organisations we rejected had extremely high public profiles. We surmised that they were considered to be 'winning' simply because they were changing a lot.

While organisation success or failure is often attributed to the CEO, the reality is that in truly winning organisations there are whole groups of people, coupled with systems and processes, that are difficult, even boring, or impossible to write about in the popular press. Winning organisations are about much more than an individual leader, attractive though charismatic CEOs are to us all.

5 Winning is *not* about profits alone

There is a strong body of business opinion that profits and profitability alone are what counts in the end. We reject this argument. While the winning organisations are profitable (or, in the case of the non-profit, it covers its costs each year), and often highly so, they are not the most profitable organisations, even in the longer term. In a survey by A.T. Kearney (Kavanagh, 2001), none of the winning organisations were in the top 10 for average shareholder return over the previous five years, but all of them were in the top 50. This shows that their financial performance is very good, but not the absolute best. Winning is about more than profits.

The reason for this is that profitability is only one of the measures of organisational performance. In line with the balanced scorecard/ performance cube approach, naturally the winning organisations do well on the financials, but they also have to do well in regard to customers, efficiency, development, employees and key stakeholders. Financial performance is important but it is not the sole way to judge how well an organisation is doing. All-round, long-term performance is what matters.

6 Winning is *not* about formal organisational structure

A great deal of space is devoted in management courses to the correct structure for an organisation. One of the first solutions normally proposed for an organisation in trouble is 'restructure'. One model of strategic success has three elements—strategy, structure and process. Yet neither our findings nor those of Collins and Porras or others conclude that structure is an important element for success. Not one organisation mentioned structure as a cause of success. In fact, structure only appeared as a constraint to operation (for example, as silos that impeded information flows or as bureaucracy, creating barriers that were unnecessary).

How can so many people be so wrong? Of course, it helps if you have a good structure that is consistent with, and aligned to, the goals of the organisation. But you can also succeed without it. There is a useful saying: 'Good people can get around a bad structure. A good structure can't make bad people good'.

Structures in winning organisations are being constantly changed to cope with new projects starting and old ones stopping. Promotions, external changes, innovation and new organisational themes were other causes for structural change.

So, if you are thinking about structure as a key part of your change process, or as a way to solve the problems of your organisation or create a winning organisation, we suggest you think again.

7 Winning is *not* about marketing promotion

This is another very uncomfortable conclusion, but this is what the evidence tells us. Ask yourself the question, 'If an organisation had poor products and services over the long term, but great marketing promotion, would it succeed?' We doubt it.

Naturally, marketing promotion helps. But it seems that understanding the customer, innovation, alignment and execution matter a lot more. The product has to be right before you put it into a nice package and promote it. As a consequence, organisations can waste a lot of marketing expenditure if the products and services being marketed simply don't deliver. Here is another way in which organisations may need to rethink what they need to do to become winners—get the products and services right first, then apply good marketing.

8 Winning is *not* about high pay levels

Recently there has been a great increase in the attention given to the incentive role of pay for staff. Intriguingly, we found that the winning organisations were quite inconsistent in regard to their positions on the importance of pay. Some made it clear that they were not high payers, simply trying to be at or around the average. Others, which did aim to get the best people, were often prepared to pay for them, in the belief that the true cost of the best people was actually much lower than it seemed due to their efficiency or innovative skills. What did seem to matter to them was the fixed/variable ratio of pay and the ability to link individual performance to variable compensation.

We found that people were very committed to their organisations, to the 'cause' of the organisation. Staff turnover at all organisations was considered to be low. Consequently, pay was not the determinant of performance it often appears to be.

Of course, it also helps if the organisation is successful! Working for a successful organisation is likely to be more rewarding than working for a losing one.

'Winning' in Australia: the 'winning wheel' framework

From the 199 organisations nominated by CEOs and senior managers, we analysed 14 in detail and selected 11 as winning organisations. This may seem a small number, but Collins and Porras included only 18 in their original study from the US—a country around 10 times the size of Australia. Collins' (2001) more recent study of underperforming listed companies that have turned themselves around and performed well for at least 15 years—*Good to Great*—was released during our research period. It included only 11 companies, so we feel that our number is in the ballpark, and there is a risk if a very small number is used that the findings will be biased by the specifics of those few organisations.

The 11 organisations chosen as a result of the three years of research involved in this specific project are shown in table 1.1.

Table 1.1: winning organisations in Australia

Organisation	Services/operations
Brambles	Diversified industrial services
Harvey Norman	Discount specialist retailer
Lend Lease	Property developer and manager, and property investment management
Macquarie Bank	Specialist banking and funds management services
National Australia Bank	Retail bank
Qantas Airways	Airline
Rio Tinto	Diversified resource explorer, miner and developer
The Salvation Army*	Religious welfare agency
Telstra	Telecommunications
Westfield	Shopping centre developer
Woolworths	Discount retailer

*The Salvation Army divides Australia into two independent territories—Southern (Vic., Tas., SA, WA, NT) and Eastern (ACT, NSW, Qld). Our analysis relates primarily to the Southern territory.

Appendix A outlines a brief history of each of these organisations. In business terms, it is a very diverse group:

▶ While 10 of them are well-known listed public companies, one is a church that is known and respected for its welfare agency activities.

▶ Two of the organisations represent privatisations of government-owned enterprises (Telstra and Qantas), an area not generally regarded as a source of well-run organisations.

▶ Two of the organisations are subsidiaries of overseas organisations (Rio Tinto, which was CRA until Rio Tinto reacquired it in 1995, and the Salvation Army, which represents two geographical branches of the global organisation).

▶ Most of the products and services are in 'basic' industries, with only Telstra and perhaps Westfield and Qantas benefiting from being in significant growth industries during the period.

All this suggests that it is the organisations themselves, not their industries, which are the underlying causes of their success.

So what are the key elements that this unusual collection of winning organisations does differently? We found nine elements that they shared (see figure 1.3 on page 18 for the 'winning wheel' framework).

1 *Effective execution*—These organisations do what they say they will. They deliver results—on time and within budget. They are efficient. They are rigorous. They do not cross-subsidise underperforming business units. How simple, but how different.

2 *Perfect alignment*—In order to achieve effective execution, these organisations' systems, procedures, people and leaders are all aligned, almost perfectly, or the organisations believe they can achieve perfect alignment. And they are able to deliver the same products and services, consistently, over and over again.

3 *Adapt rapidly*—However, these organisations do not simply provide the same products and services over and over again. As organisations grow and develop, they must change. They adapt themselves, and do it rapidly. This adaptation is necessary to allow for externally induced changes in the environment, as well as internally induced changes from continuous improvement or innovations. The specific types of changes are influenced by their position in the strategic cycle (a concept we explain in detail in chapter 12).

4 *Clear and fuzzy strategy*—Yes, that's right. Strategy is both clear and fuzzy. The general direction is clear, but some of the specifics at the edges are fuzzy. Opportunities (externally focused) that fit within the general direction and, particularly, with the values and culture, can be taken. But the strategy is also clear about what should not be done (perfect alignment) and is quick to adapt to any strategic mistakes that are made.

5 *Leadership, not leaders*—Perhaps surprisingly, leadership did not instantly identify itself as one of the key elements, because, as we have noted earlier, few leaders of our winning organisations were or are charismatic. But we could not get away from the conclusion that leadership is one of the keys. It is often the decisions of the leaders that start the journey, but it is not a single charismatic leader whose own actions are the cause of the success. While there are plenty of examples here of

individual leaders who have had a significant influence on their organisations, it is the actions leadership takes *as a group* to build the organisation, not the personalities of the individual leaders, that are critical.

6 **Looking out, looking in**—While these organisations are internally aligned and execute to deliver results, they are equally externally focused. They are looking outwards all the time. Customers matter to them. They have networks. They manage relationships outside the organisation. They know their place in the value chain and understand how value is created, not only by them, but by others in the chain. These external activities and orientation are critical to their overall success.

7 **Right people**—Despite the common mantra 'people are our greatest asset', we did not find that the *best* people are necessarily hired. What is important is to get the *right* people—the people who fit into the particular system with its specific culture and values. We also found that the people invariably have a fierce pride in what their organisation is doing. They feel they are working for a cause, not just holding down a job. They are committed to the goals and culture of the organisation. However, they don't jump up and down and shout this out loud. While they are committed and proud, they are actually quite reluctant to demonstrably show this.

8 **Manage the downside**—While the organisations grow rapidly and innovate significantly, they all regard themselves as cautious and conservative! This is because, while they take risks, they evaluate the risks well, plan for them and take actions to minimise those risks to themselves, rather than simply reducing the amount of risk.

9 **Balance everything**—Combining the above eight elements is very difficult. Some seem contradictory. Yet that is exactly what these organisations do. They 'balance' everything. It is not either/or. It is both, or all elements, everything together: and, and, and. Achieving this balance is what enables execution to occur—it all comes together, at the right time. And that's what makes them winning organisations.

Figure 1.3 (overleaf) shows how the framework fits together. The elements of the 'winning wheel' are connected together to make the wheel work, and steer and roll the organisation toward its goals. There is no 'start' or 'finish' to the wheel. All elements are important and necessary for long-term success. The wheel also shows the central role of effective execution. We see this as both an element of the framework—the process—and also as representing the results of the framework—the outcome.

Figure 1.3: the winning wheel framework for organisational success in Australia

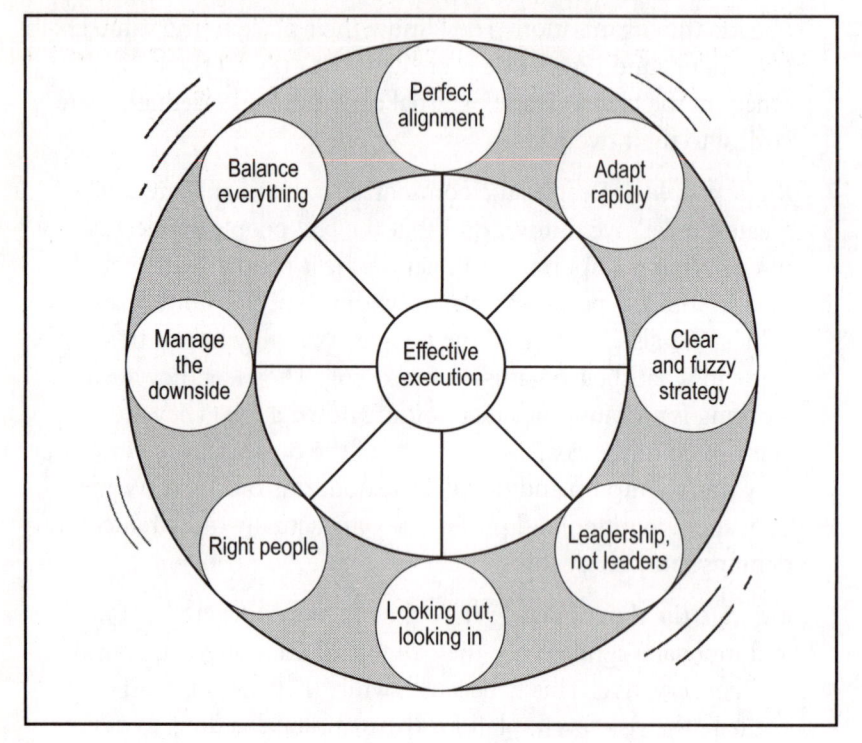

[Figure 1.3: A circular wheel diagram with "Effective execution" at the centre, surrounded by eight elements: Perfect alignment, Adapt rapidly, Clear and fuzzy strategy, Leadership, not leaders, Looking out, looking in, Right people, Manage the downside, Balance everything.]

The rest of the book

In the chapters that follow, we take each of these nine elements of the winning wheel and discuss them in detail, using examples from each of the winning organisations to demonstrate how the framework works.

Then in chapter 11, we'll look at how being an Australian-based organisation affects the development of the organisation, compared with our general assumptions about successful organisations. We'll further explore this concept in chapter 12 when we develop the strategic cycle for Australian organisations, showing the steps these organisations have gone through as they have developed.

In chapter 13, we'll explore what has happened to the winning organisations since we completed our research in 2000. We'll consider what they have done and how they have performed since they have been in our spotlight. Do they still deserve to be 'First XI' organisations? We remind you, though, this book is about the principles of winning rather than any specific set of organisations. There are always new high-performing organisations ready to step into the 'First XI' team.

In chapter 14, we'll compare our findings to other major studies to see to what extent our findings support or differ from those of other acclaimed studies.

Finally, in chapter 15, we give you perhaps the most important chapter—how your organisation can start the journey to become a winning organisation and to become a First XI organisation.

2 Effective execution

Do what you say
Deliver results on time
and within budget

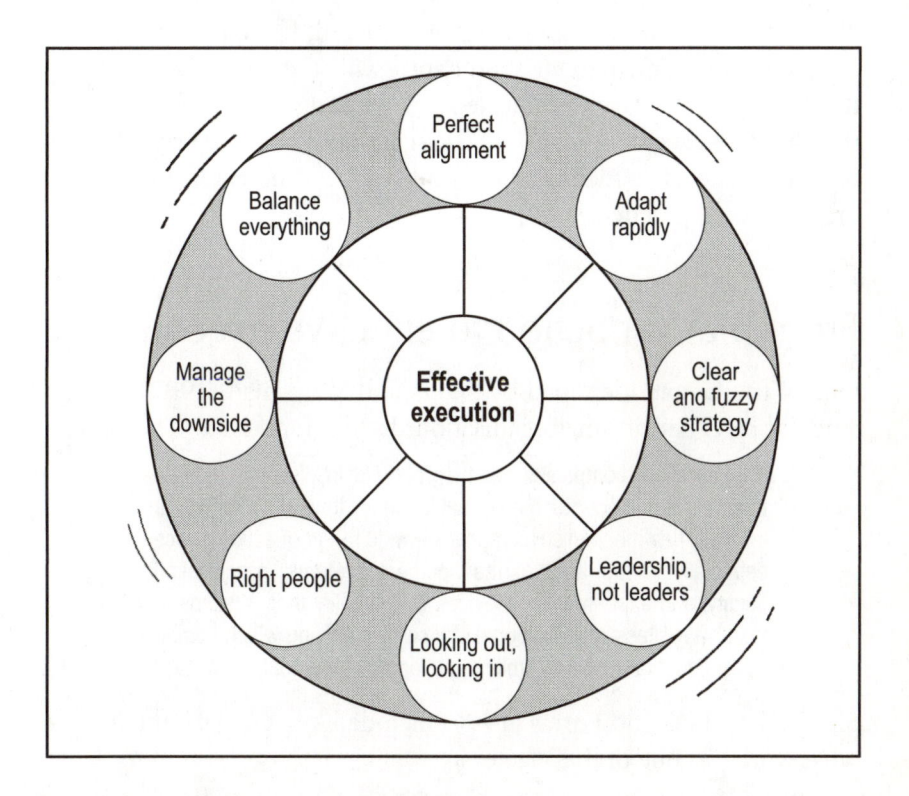

Figure: Effective execution framework — Perfect alignment, Adapt rapidly, Clear and fuzzy strategy, Leadership, not leaders, Looking out, looking in, Right people, Manage the downside, Balance everything.

From the framework developed in chapter 1 (see figure above), you're probably wondering why we would start with execution, when this appears to be one of the last elements, perhaps even the end result of all the other elements.

We asked ourselves the same question. Originally, we planned to start this book with leadership. But as we asked ourselves the question, 'What really makes the First XI organisations different from others?', we realised that it was the results that occurred, the results that they delivered, that was the difference—they get the score on the board. We chose these organisations on the basis of their results. And it is effective execution that enables them to deliver these results. That is what makes them different.

In everyday dealings with all types of organisations, one thing stands out fairly consistently. Most organisations disappoint their stakeholders by their failure to deliver what they say, what they promise, what they promote and market. Organisations that *effectively execute*, that do what they say, that deliver results, stand out from the crowd. So we begin our discussion of the nine elements of the framework with 'effective execution'.

In this chapter, we'll start by examining how our characterisation of 'effective execution' is similar to, but different from, previous similar research. The main part of the chapter will then be taken up with discussing the key factors that lead to winning organisations having the ability to execute. Finally, we'll discuss how winning organisations handle mistakes, which also appears to be different from normal organisational practice.

From bias for action to effective execution

One of the factors identified by Peters and Waterman (1982) in their study of high-performing organisations is 'bias for action'. They say:

> The excellent companies seem to abound in distinctly individual techniques that counter the normal tendency toward conformity and inertia. Their mechanism comprises a wide range of action devices, especially in the area of management systems, organisational fluidity, and experiments—devices that simplify their systems and foster a restless organisational stance by clarifying which numbers really count or arbitrarily limiting the length of the goal list (p. 121).

Similarly, Collins and Porras (1994) included 'try a lot of stuff and see what works' as one of their factors:

> We were struck by how often they made some of their best moves not by detailed strategic planning, but rather by experimentation, trial and error, opportunism, and—quite literally—accident (p. 141).

> If you add enough branches to a tree (variation) and intelligently prune the deadwood (selection), then you'll likely evolve into a collection of healthy branches well positioned to prosper in an ever-changing environment. (p. 146)

But our view of these ideas is subtly different. It is not simply about 'action' for action's sake. It is not about 'experimenting' for experimenting's sake. It is about action and experimentation to execute, to do what you say, to deliver results.

The winning organisations say what they are going to do and then do it. And they keep doing it, again and again. This is quite frightening for most organisations, because saying what you are going to do sets an expectation and a target—did you achieve what you said you would? For most organisations, this invites an assessment of failure. For winning organisations, however, it provides the opportunity to demonstrate success. For instance:

- Brambles announced in 1984, when its profit was $33 million, that it wished to add $100 million within five years, which it did.
- Harvey Norman announces each year how many stores it will open in the next year, and it does so.
- Macquarie planned to become the first new entrant to receive a full banking licence when the industry was deregulated and opened more than six months before any other new entrant.
- NAB announced the cost/sales ratio it planned to achieve, which was well below that of its competitors, and achieved it.
- Rio Tinto consistently brings mines into production on time and on budget (see illustration 2.1 overleaf).
- Woolworths announced in 1999 that the cost savings it expected from its long-term Project Refresh would be $100 million per annum. In 2000, it announced that it expected savings to increase to $134 million per annum by 2002–03. In 2005 it announced that total cumulative savings from the project had reached $3.6 billion and it expected to save $8 billion by 2008.

A Woolworths executive summarised Woolworths' approach to delivering results:

> We are successful because we have an execution culture... The job is a repetitive process so we have to do the same job today and tomorrow and tomorrow. We have to do it consistently, but get better each year and find scope for improvement... We are very focused. We have targets and budgets. This is a numbers game.

The First XI

We understand customer needs. This is a simple business. We are not cutting edge in market research or information technology but we do seem to understand what customers need. We get this by talking to them and passing that information up the chain. This is part of our culture.

To cope with varying demand, we use a lot of casual staff and kids at the checkout, which is where much of the contact between Woolworths and its customers takes place. We have high turnover with this type of staff, but we rely on their interactions with the customer.

Illustration 2.1: Rio Tinto on time and on budget

Throughout CRA/Rio Tinto's annual reports for the period we studied, there were consistent references to its ability to complete projects on time and on budget. These included:

1982	Blair Athol first coal shipment on schedule.
1983	Tarong first coal deliveries ahead of schedule, Blair Athol first steaming coal ahead of schedule.
1984	Argyle diamond development activity on schedule and within budget.
1985	Blair Athol (Phase II) constructed below budget.
1986	Argyle diamond mine completed on schedule and within budget.
1992	Peak gold mine completed on schedule and within budget.
1993	Channar iron ore mine development on schedule.
1994	Weipa bauxite dump station on schedule and under budget.
1995	Boyne Island aluminium smelter on schedule.
1997	Boyne Island completed six months ahead of schedule and on budget.
1998	Yandicoogina iron ore mine five months ahead of schedule and under budget.
2003	Hail Creek coking coal mine on budget and ahead of schedule.
2004	Comalco alumina refinery shipped first product months ahead of schedule.
2005	Whole range of projects on budget and ahead of schedule, including Robe River's West Angelas iron ore mine.

Larry Bossidy, former General Electric senior executive and Allied Signal CEO, has written a book just on execution (Bossidy, Charan and Burck, *Execution: The Discipline of Getting Things Done*, 2002). He says:

> Companies are less than they could be because of poor execution. The gap between promise and delivery is widespread and clear ... No company can deliver on its commitments or adapt well to change unless it can practice the discipline of execution at all levels ... If you don't know how to execute, the whole of your effort as a leader will always be less than the sum of its parts. (Ch. 1)

There is no magic formula here, nothing that is a single, unique management tool. Execution is the difference. These organisations do what they say ... and they say what they are going to do. Just do it.

'Results' means a balanced scorecard approach

When we talk about results, we remind you that this does not mean simply profits or return on equity (ROE). Doing what you say and delivering results applies for all stakeholder groups — not only shareholders, but also customers (which is how market share is gained), suppliers, employees and others.

Of course, in business, 'results' that favour one group may well be at the expense of other groups. The 'balanced' nature of winning means though that results must not be seen just from a financial perspective. All stakeholder groups need to benefit. Rio Tinto published its 'statement of business practice' — 'The way we work' — on its website (in 22 languages) to show how it addressed this issue. It was a much broader statement than a normal vision or mission statement and covered several different stakeholder groups. It included the following statements (which can be measured):

- deliver superior returns to shareholders over time
- long term and responsible approach to the Group's business
- work as closely as possible with our host countries and communities, respecting their laws and customs
- we seek to contribute to sustainable development
- the health and safety of our employees is our first priority
- we employ local people at all levels and ensure fair and equitable transfer of benefits and enhancement of opportunities.

Robert Wilson, former executive chairman at Rio Tinto, emphasised how this statement worked:

> It was produced after a lengthy, iterative dialogue within the company worldwide to identify and consolidate our own best performance and practice... It was then submitted to the Board for consideration.
>
> Why did we go this way round?... We wanted a wide sense of ownership of the policy, a feeling amongst our management that 'this is a statement of our principles', not something imposed on them. The difficulty is in achieving effective implementation, especially where policies relate to 'values' which are personal as well as corporate. We saw the process of consultation as an important step towards commitment. Values need to be shared rather than imposed from outside. For this reason, I favour the notion of companies expressing their own principles in their own way, and being prepared to stand by them and be judged by them. The result is likely to be more coherent and consistent implementation. (Wilson, 1999)

How do winning organisations execute to deliver results?

So what is it that winning organisations do to facilitate execution and the delivery of results? In addition to the other major elements of the framework, we found seven specific factors that directly contribute to delivering results (see figure 2.1). They are:

▶ clear processes
▶ operational and technical efficiency
▶ taking personal responsibility
▶ good management control systems
▶ rigorously measuring performance
▶ handling mistakes positively
▶ no cross-subsidisation of business units.

These factors are linked with each other, as well as being causal factors for execution. Let's explore how this works.

Clear processes

The first factor in helping execution is having clear processes. Knowing what you are supposed to do — having clear processes — is an important ingredient for delivering outcomes. Having structures that support these processes and delegating the authority and responsibility to carry out the processes—and make decisions quickly in borderline or grey area cases—supports the completion of the organisation's tasks and activities.

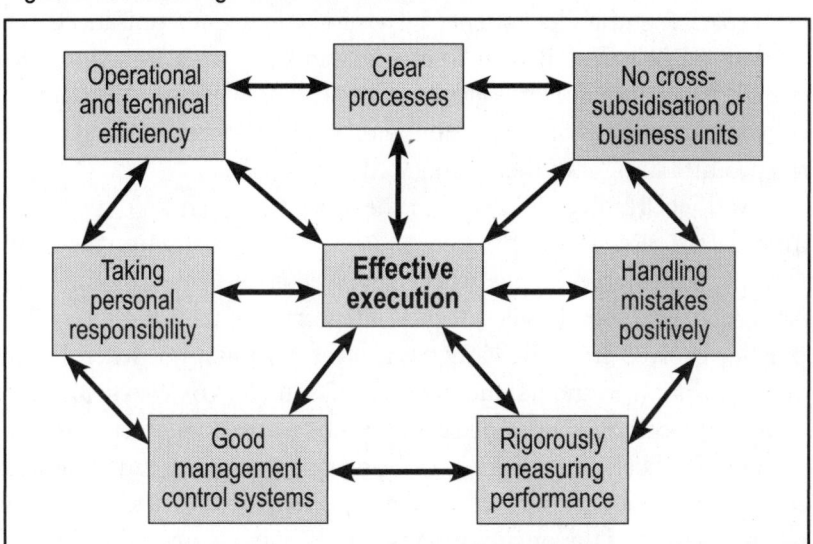

Figure 2.1: achieving effective execution

```
┌─────────────────────────────────────────────────────────┐
│  Operational        Clear           No cross-           │
│  and technical  ↔   processes   ↔   subsidisation of    │
│  efficiency                         business units      │
│                                                         │
│  Taking             Effective       Handling            │
│  personal       ↔   execution   ↔   mistakes            │
│  responsibility                     positively          │
│                                                         │
│  Good               Rigorously                          │
│  management     ↔   measuring                           │
│  control systems    performance                         │
└─────────────────────────────────────────────────────────┘
```

But what does a 'clear process' look like? The specifics of 'clear processes' and the associated structures and responsibilities vary greatly from one organisation to another. For instance, the Salvation Army has the most formally structured approach to clear processes among the winning organisations. This comes from the 'army' or military set of values within the organisation. Structure and discipline are considered highly valuable. The Salvation Army has processes for everything, including such issues as entry into new countries, annual staff appointments, and church and service reviews. In the case of staff appointments, all staff receive a letter at the end of October telling them where they will be going the following January. Everyone knows what is happening and when.

Woolworths is similarly highly structured, as it depends on repetitive consistency in transacting many small items to achieve its results. Early in its history Woolworths developed detailed operating manuals that were referred to as the Bibles. They covered every aspect of Woolworths' operations. They were regarded as encyclopedias of detail and were constantly updated to ensure they reflected best practice.

But 'clear processes' does not mean simply, or always, having highly structured and mechanistic processes. At Harvey Norman, 'clear process' occurs through the decisions about what items to purchase. The buying committee, which meets to decide what product range to purchase, includes representatives of the franchisees/sellers, as well as the head office purchasing function. This process overcomes a key problem in most retail organisations where the buyers and sales force are separate and independent. In a regular retail organisation, the buyer is all powerful. Buyers 'know best' and buy what they think the market will want without consulting the sellers. At Harvey Norman, in contrast, the sellers order directly with their suppliers for delivery of the product straight to their franchised premises.

Westfield resolves its issues in the same way each time, in a very informal process. A meeting (ironically named a formal action meeting) is called, at which everyone who is involved and affected by the issue is present. Everyone is able to, and is expected to, have their say. This practice evolved from the early days of the organisation, when Frank Lowy and John Saunders, the joint 50–50 founders of Westfield, used to always meet together to discuss issues before making decisions.

Westfield believes it has a big advantage in having all functions and activities represented and getting all perspectives on the issue, especially when so much of the organisation is vertically integrated and so is 'in-house'. At the end of a meeting a decision is made. While the process is 'democratic' during the meeting, if an impasse is reached the CEO(s), will decide. Originally, when an impasse was reached, Lowy and Saunders would step outside to confer. A decision would be made and brought back to the meeting. While the individual meetings are long, the decision-making process is quick compared to the conventional method of a series of cascading meetings with different parties and different perspectives at each meeting.

What is implicit in 'clear processes' is that people accept the process and the outcomes. Whether the process is highly structured or highly democratic, acceptance by those who form part of the process and who must make the process and decisions work is critical. We'll address this more fully in 'Taking personal responsibility'.

Operational and technical efficiency

Of course, it is not enough just to have 'clear processes' to get execution. Bureaucracies have clear processes—these organisations need to be efficient too! The second contributor to achieving effective execution is being efficient, in both an operational and a technical sense. Keeping costs down and changing systems over time to meet different circumstances are other aspects of achieving efficiency (see figure 2.2).

Figure 2.2: factors affecting efficiency

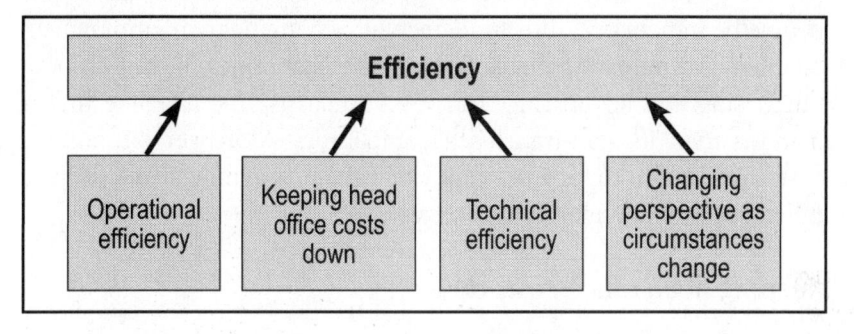

```
                        Efficiency
           ↑          ↑          ↑          ↑
    Operational   Keeping head  Technical   Changing
    efficiency    office costs  efficiency  perspective as
                  down                      circumstances
                                            change
```

Operational efficiency

Operational efficiency is the use of operating systems that work to achieve their expected objectives, which could be related to cost, quality, speed or service. For the Salvation Army, where every dollar contributed and used on administration is a dollar that cannot be used on providing services to the needy, having efficient administration is important for relative success. The Salvation Army has a very low administrative cost ratio (around 12 cents of every dollar raised is spent on administration, less than its competitors). Of course, one way in which the Salvation Army achieves this is through the use of volunteers and low-paid employees, but its competitors also have access to similar volunteer or low-paid structures.

Harvey Norman achieves operating efficiency completely differently. Buying committees representing individual franchisees determine what products will be purchased centrally. Harvey Norman representatives then negotiate with suppliers in conjunction with franchisees to determine buying prices and deals, though individual franchisees can also negotiate their own deals. Harvey Norman franchisees own their own business, which is a separate legal entity for each franchisee, employ their own staff, and order and own their own stock. Information is centralised so that individual franchisees have the benefit of a large system, while Harvey Norman has the benefit of centralised control and comparison of information. Cash management and control is also centralised.

Franchisees obtain finance from a Harvey Norman subsidiary as part of their franchise arrangements and they benefit from generic Harvey Norman advertising, negotiated at bulk rates centrally. However, they place and pay for their own local advertising. Harvey Norman franchisees achieve higher levels of earnings due to the fact that they run their own business and monitor costs very closely. By having its people be franchisees, thus fundamentally changing their employment contract and motivation, and through the economies of scale in both purchasing and advertising, Harvey Norman is able to make higher margins than its non-franchised competitors. Moreover, purchasing costs are thought to be 4 per cent lower than its competitors—a huge difference in a low-margin business.

Keeping head office costs down

One aspect of operational efficiency is keeping head office costs down, particularly for diversified corporations. During our research interviews, we were surprised by the relatively low-key head offices and the modest quality of the offices that most of these winning organisations had. For instance:

▶ Woolworths and Harvey Norman are renowned for their low-cost head offices. Harvey Norman is in Homebush, an outer working-class suburb of Sydney. Woolworths' head office was in a low-quality building above one of its modest city stores in Sydney, but in 2005 it moved to Bella Vista, an outer suburb more than an hour's drive out of the Sydney CBD. While its new head office is large and spacious, its cost is no more than was the collection of business-unit office buildings that it has brought together under one roof.

▶ John Menadue, CEO of Qantas in the mid 1980s, moved the Qantas head office from the centre of Sydney to the airport, to link it more closely with operations.

▶ Rio Tinto split its divisions off from the head office and forced them to move away so that they focused more on the business and less on head office politics.

Commenting on his attitude to head office costs, Gerry Harvey said:

> The rent here is very cheap. It's in my nature to be frugal with money...I don't have this great urge to have these things. In a perverse sort of way I would feel better in a housing commission home with no furniture. (Condon, 2002)

Technical efficiency

Efficiency is not just about low absolute operating costs. Using better quality technical systems can result in more efficient outcomes, in terms of delivering results.

For example, Qantas is a high-quality full service brand and knows it cannot compete with the cost structures of Asian international competitors (or, now, its domestic low-cost competitors, including its own Jetstar brand). So 'efficiency' for Qantas is primarily about technical efficiency—safety, yield management systems, reservation systems, operational logistics, booking systems, customer service, customer relationship management, plane turnaround times, lost luggage and so on. This can be matched against Qantas' value proposition of high-quality customer service, which requires different measurements of 'efficiency' than does a value proposition of low cost, which aims to minimise cost per kilometre flown.

Rio Tinto aims to achieve operational efficiency using an almost completely opposite approach. Rio Tinto believes that hiring the very best people with good remuneration will be more than repaid through the resulting high levels of innovation and productivity, which will enable Rio Tinto to deliver low-cost operating mines. In general, Rio Tinto will not start a mine unless it is in the bottom quartile of world operating costs, yet it does this while employing well-rewarded people.

Lend Lease's approach is similar to Rio Tinto's. It seeks high-quality people, high-quality design, high-quality project management approaches, high-quality materials and high-quality partners in order to get high-quality buildings—efficiently.

Changing perspectives on operating and technical efficiency

Of course, should the external environment change, the concepts of technical and operating efficiency may need to change too. For instance, during the 1970s and 1980s Rio Tinto (then called CRA) was very much focused on technical efficiency, without great concern for its commercial results. It believed that the resources slump, which was caused by the OPEC cartel-inspired oil price crisis that began in the early 1970s, would eventually end and that high global resources demand growth would return. This did not happen. Instead, the world became much more efficient at resource use. Eventually, in the early 1990s CRA came to realise that it needed to make a more reasonable

ROE, and not just be a very technically efficient miner. A Rio Tinto executive said:

> Return on capital is much more important than we appreciated. Business is not just cost control and operating efficiency. Our previous 'Rolls Royce' approach to mine production systems was not necessary in all areas.

Beginning with one very troublesome project—the Marandoo iron ore mine in the Pilbara, which was commissioned in 1992—CRA found that it needed to substantially reduce costs to make the project viable. It found that it could cut 30 per cent off its capital costs by applying much more rigorous financial analysis—primarily its focus had been on technical analysis—without affecting the technical efficiency of the operation. Applying this type of logic to all other future capital—and operating—investments, Rio Tinto has subsequently greatly improved its financial performance, despite the low growth and low prices in resources that existed for long periods during the 1980s and 1990s.

Telstra is another organisation that has been focused on technical efficiency for most of its life. As the setter of industry technical standards in its old role as the government-owned monopoly provider, Telstra provided high technical standards for the whole Australian telecommunications system. In recent years, however, due to the change in its ownership and the fall-off in industry growth rates, it has had to rebalance its focus to become much more commercially oriented.

Taking personal responsibility

Of course, many organisations have good processes and good technical and operating systems that can provide efficient operations. Yet somehow they rarely work to the degree they should. Why is that?

The third important factor for getting outcomes from a system is the way that people in the system behave. Results cannot be delivered simply by having a great system. People are needed to operate the system or to use the system's outputs. So the attitudes that people take to the system will significantly affect the outcomes from the systems—and the results that will be delivered.

To achieve effective execution, people need to take responsibility for the performance of the organisation, or at least their part of it. Is that the case in your organisation? Who is 'responsible'? What happens if results don't meet expectations? Usually the answer in most organisations is 'not much'. So is it any real surprise that plans do not actually come to fruition?

An important factor in people taking responsibility is open and direct feedback from management during planning and execution about what is working and what is not.

Most organisations don't take plans seriously. They are seen as mere guides to get the action started, and no-one necessarily feels personally committed or personally responsible for them.

By contrast, people in winning organisations will do almost anything to make the outcome occur, once it has been approved. At Lend Lease, Brambles and Macquarie, there is a feeling that, once the project has been approved, the organisation trusts and empowers the people responsible to get the results that they have said will occur. They have created little business units within the large organisation (see the 'No cross-subsidisation' section for a detailed discussion) and provided opportunities for their people to take action. And the people have great incentives to deliver—personal financial gain, the opportunity for promotion and personal satisfaction from being responsible and achieving results. As a result, responsible managers (and people) work incredibly hard to overcome any unforeseen difficulties to ensure that the projected outcomes occur.

As one ex-Lend Lease executive said:

> It was an exciting opportunity to be there (straight out of university). You were able to be a decision-maker. It was not about the pay. It was about the opportunities, about career development.

A similar approach exists at Macquarie. A person whose project is approved through the Macquarie system knows that they are expected to achieve the approved outcomes. They know their personal performance will be evaluated against the achievement or otherwise on that project. Further, they know that their remuneration will significantly depend on that evaluation, so they have a very large personal incentive to ensure that the project meets its projected targets (see chapter 8 for a discussion on incentive systems).

At organisations like Telstra, the Salvation Army and Woolworths, this responsibility is generated more through the pride, commitment and the 'cause' that people feel about providing a valued community service. At Telstra, people (still) feel a responsibility for the quality of the whole Australian telecommunications system and to make sure it works well. Telstra people feel responsible for restoring service of the *system*, even though it is no longer responsible for the whole system. At the Salvation Army, people feel a great desire to help others, particularly those less fortunate than themselves and particularly in emergency situations, such as the Bali bombings, the Asian tsunami, bushfires, cyclones and floods. At Woolworths, people feel that they act as the agent for the customer in securing food and other products at good prices. Woolworths says:

> Everything we do is driven by a commitment to providing customers with the freshest produce, the best prices and the best possible service.
>
> As the 'Fresh Food People'... we have made it our mission to source the very best farmers and growers Australia has to offer. We also continue to offer an extensive range of affordable, everyday grocery items from trusted and well-known brands.
>
> Our staff are passionate about customer service. We strive to help our customers enjoy fresh, healthy food whenever possible... <www.woolworths.com.au>

Good management control systems

To check whether they have clear processes that are efficiently undertaken by responsible people, winning organisations need good management control systems. Controls begin during the planning and approval process. Illustration 2.2 highlights the Lend Lease system of management controls in some detail.

It is much easier to measure project performance directly in an organisation like this than it is in an organisation like a bank, where 'performance'—say for a loan or a customer—may not be clear for several years. On the other hand, each project is unique, so the chance of failure is much higher, as precedent is of limited value in projects.

Control systems are very different at Qantas, as its activity is based on a very large number of much smaller transactions that must be managed for success. Qantas regards its revenue/yield management system as one of the causes of its success (though this is only a relatively recent development, so it can only be the cause of recent success, not of how Qantas managed to be a winning organisation prior to this period). Its yield management systems enable Qantas to continuously change the variety and quantity of fares available on every flight, based on actual bookings received. Particular fares can be and are closed off or opened up instantly by the system if demand changes warrant this. In an era of internet bookings, of 24/7 open systems, this is necessary. While these sudden changes are frustrating for potential passengers who are waiting, planning or comparing fares and suddenly find fares are not available, it simply reflects demand from other passengers who are satisfied!

> **Illustration 2.2: management control systems in project approval at Lend Lease**
>
> Lend Lease's business is heavily project based and the company is credited with introducing most of the major elements of project management used in Australia. It is very difficult to get a project approved at Lend Lease, because:
>
> - an enormous amount of due diligence is required to be undertaken in order to understand all the risks
> - it must be clear that the project has drawn on existing expertise and experience within Lend Lease
> - the project faces high financial hurdles for approval
> - the project must have access to the management and organisational expertise necessary to carry it out
> - there must be an exit strategy available, in case the project does not meet expectations.
>
> Thus, before a project is approved, a great deal of work has taken place to minimise the chance of failure.
>
> When a project is approved within Lend Lease, the operating schedules and financial outcomes that form part of that approval are expected to be achieved. They are not simply guidelines or hoped-for outcomes. And someone is responsible for those outcomes. Knowing how seriously these plans are regarded, that person will move heaven and earth to ensure that the project meets its planned outcome.
>
> During the life of the project, Lend Lease conducts weekly project review meetings. Everyone with a responsibility for the project must be there but equally, no-one must be present at the meeting who does not have a role—there are no passengers! Everyone must contribute to the meeting and everyone must perform to the weekly plan.
>
> Finally, Lend Lease systems are tremendously detailed and are being continually improved. They are backed up with strong links to key performance indicators (KPIs) and big incentives for achieving outcomes.

From a logistics perspective, it is interesting to reflect on how smoothly Qantas handled the tumultuous period between 2000 and 2006. This included:

▶ the domestic airfare war begun in mid 2000

The First XI

- Qantas' acquisition of Impulse Airlines as a result
- the September 11, 2001 terrorist crisis (when planes were not allowed to take off or land in the US for several days)
- the maintenance groundings of Ansett at Christmas 2000 and Easter 2001
- Ansett's cessation of flying in September 2001 and again finally in February 2002
- the SARS crisis in early 2003, resulting in many cancelled flights and employee unwillingness to fly to risky locations
- the Bali bombings in 2002 and 2005, and the Asian tsunami in December 2004, resulting in the need to change flight plans for thousands of Australians (cancelling trips and returning unexpectedly)
- rapid escalation of the price of oil, resulting in the need to hedge oil prices and impose oil surcharges on passengers.

Qantas' ability to handle the rapid increases in customer enquiries and significant changes in passenger numbers and aircraft movements in these very short time periods was remarkable for the lack of disruption that occurred within the industry. Of course, Qantas had some practice at this with its experience of the 1989 pilots' strike and the 1991 and 1992 collapses of Compass and Compass Mark 2 low-cost domestic competitors.

Rigorously measuring performance

Winning organisations measure their performance in two ways — using rigorous application of their systems and processes, and developing a small number of key performance indicators.

Rigorous application

In using systems and processes to get results, what makes winning organisations different from their competitors? It is not that they have unique systems or procedures. It is not that their IT systems or capabilities are superior. Indeed, our winning organisations in general were rather dismissive of the value of their IT efforts, even when outside organisations believed they had a competitive advantage in this area.

The difference is the rigour and discipline that they use to make the systems work. One Macquarie executive said:

> We make sure the conflict (i.e. differences between executives and business areas) happens. Most mistakes in companies are a result of not voicing concerns early enough. You have to bring this conflict to the surface.

Rio Tinto conducts three separate evaluations of risk before approving a project—a technical, financial and business case analysis. Each analysis is done by independent groups and is completed before the project goes to Rio Tinto's investment committee. Interestingly, its close competitor BHP Billiton, stung by a string of poor major project outcomes during the 1990s, announced in April 2002 that it would be instituting a similar system.

Rio Tinto also undergoes a rigorous planning, rather than budgeting, process. It considers what is happening in the industry, how the product is positioned within the industry and what the goal is for positioning the particular Rio Tinto product within the industry. As we have shown in illustration 2.1, Rio Tinto has a great history of bringing in major projects on time and on budget.

Woolworths developed a system of 'everyday low prices' in its Big W stores, which it subsequently rolled out into its supermarkets and other businesses. This system is based on market-leading Wal-Mart's similar system in the US. It took 12 years to develop, because it is a complete logistics system involving the cooperation of suppliers, not a short-term discounting price initiative.

Key performance indicators

Using a control system to measure performance requires that some target measures exist. Key performance indicators (KPIs) provide the final link in the chain of performance measurement. The development of KPIs, however, is a relatively recent managerial phenomenon. This project did not find that KPIs were regarded as critical to success, relative to some of the other issues discussed here. We suspect that best practice has not yet evolved in this area.

Woolworths is developing a system of no more than four KPIs for its top managers, gradually cascading these down to lower levels in the organisation. At least one of those KPIs has to be qualitative. NAB is another that limits the number of KPIs—in this case to not more than five areas and not more than three measures each—all quantifiable and all objective. These are reviewed on a three monthly basis. Organisations such as Brambles and Macquarie have very few KPIs, primarily centred on growth, profits and return on investment. One interviewee commented on the Brambles approach:

> There's a heavy emphasis on financials forecasting. Brambles is tough on the numbers but it is OK to change the forecast beforehand if times are tough. But to not meet the target without having changed the forecast is considered bad management. If you don't ask for help, you better get it right.

Handling mistakes positively

Winning organisations are not error-free in their execution. What do they do when they make an error? Four elements consistently arose in our discussions (see figure 2.3). They were:

▶ People who make a mistake need to admit it early.

▶ Something must be done to fix the mistake as best as possible.

▶ The organisation needs to learn from a mistake and do so quickly.

▶ Making the same mistake twice, or three mistakes in total, is grounds for dismissal.

Again, how different is this from most organisations, where often people don't admit errors, errors are hidden until the last possible moment, the organisation doesn't learn from errors and mistakes are often repeated.

Figure 2.3: handling mistakes

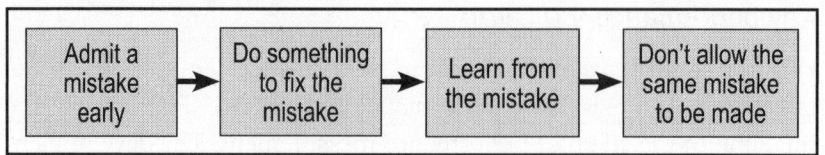

Admit a mistake early → Do something to fix the mistake → Learn from the mistake → Don't allow the same mistake to be made

Admit a mistake early on

This equates to the well-known 'no surprises' rule. Managers don't like to be surprised, at least not with bad news. People who are aware of errors made or problems looming in their own areas need to admit or own up to the mistake early so that action can be taken to correct it, minimise its effects, or prepare for the widespread recognition of that error, particularly publicly. Said one executive:

> One of the only ways to get fired from this organisation is to keep a problem hidden in the bottom drawer and not let anyone know about

it. If we know about it, we can do something about it. The earlier we know, the more chance there is we can do something and the smaller the total cost is likely to be.

Brambles put it slightly more clearly:

> Above all, staff are advised to adhere to the doctrine of 'no surprises'—in traditional Brambles language, the 'primary arse covering rule'; own up immediately if something has gone wrong and you will be helped, not crucified. Fail to draw attention to the error or stupidity and there is a strong likelihood of crucifixion. (Carew, 2000, pp. 237–38)

The difficulty for the person—and the reason why people are so reluctant to admit to mistakes—is that their career is likely to be affected in the short term. Consequently, there is a significant personal incentive in most organisations—and even in some of the winning organisations—to hope the mistake is not discovered, that it fixes itself, or that the individual has changed roles before it is discovered and blame can be sheeted home. So the culture has to support admitting a mistake without it being career limiting.

Fix the mistake as best as possible

Winning organisations don't make mistakes very often, but when they do, they fix them quickly. When Qantas had a plane slide off the runway at Bangkok airport in heavy rain in September 1999, its safety record—and reputation—was threatened. Qantas worked feverishly to repair the plane and fly it out. As a result of this event, Qantas significantly reviewed its maintenance and safety procedures to minimise the chance of a recurrence.

Macquarie fixed a 'mistake' that wasn't really a mistake! When it won the bid for Sydney Airport, it was perceived to have paid around $600 million too much. Commentators criticised the organisation roundly, even though the amount was allegedly only 10 per cent more than the second-highest bidder. A senior Macquarie executive then criticised one of the commentator's ability to assess this decision, so the nationally influential commentator attacked the organisation in the media. Though Macquarie felt it was correct analytically, it did not want to make the mistake of making an enemy of such a powerful media influence. They apologised to him and rode out the tide of criticism. When their forecasts were proved to be correct, they did not chastise the commentators. Indeed, few remembered the 'mistake' had even been made.

Learn from the mistake

After minimising the costs of a mistake, a winning organisation learns from it, in order not only that the mistake will not happen again, but that any changes that might need to occur to systems are made. Winning organisations enquire into their mistakes early and quickly. They see mistakes as opportunities to improve. Macquarie said that, once it had addressed a mistake, it undertook an investigation, with a full written report being prepared within four to six weeks.

At Brambles and Lend Lease, provided the person responsible for the error could learn from it, it can actually be seen as a positive experience in the longer term for a person to have survived a mistake and prospered subsequently. To have demonstrated the ability to fight back after adversity or to demonstrate success after a mistake is not uncommon. One example of surviving adversity was Malcolm Gibb at Brambles (see illustration 2.3).

> **Illustration 2.3: from 'Death Row' to CEO (almost)**
>
> Malcolm Gibb was in charge of a major Brambles Industrial Services job in Sydney that went badly wrong. He was sent to what Brambles called 'Death Row'—level 14 administration in Brambles' head office. Eventually CEO Oliver Richter asked Gibb to 'do something with industrial waste in Melbourne', not exactly regarded as a plum job within the organisation. He took Gary Pemberton, who later became a CEO at Brambles and Chair of Qantas, with him. Cleanaway Waste Management, which became one of Brambles' major international divisions and greatest successes, was born under Gibb's leadership. When Richter retired, Gibb and Pemberton were both considered as his replacement.

In this respect, it was interesting and disappointing to see NAB's delayed and long time scale in 2002 for coming to terms with its failed acquisition of US business HomeSide. This failure to adequately deal with the situation was subsequently reflected in the eventual sacking of much of the board and top management team after both the Korean fraud in 2003 and the Melbourne forex scandal in 2004. This is an example of how failing to deal with a mistake causes that mistake to be repeated, with much worse consequences.

Three strikes and you're out

This baseball phrase was popularised by US politicians in regard to the requirement that lawbreakers go to jail on their third conviction for an offence, regardless of the circumstances. Several of the winning organisations use variations of this 'rule'. The idea is that, while it is okay—even good—to make one mistake and learn from it, three mistakes of any significant type would be enough to have you removed from the company. Even making the same mistake twice would have the same result.

Winning organisations take positive action to get rid of people who do not meet their standards. Unlike regular organisations, they do not simply move the person sideways or to another division or position. They do not leave the person to carry on. They do not promote the person in order to move them on! This sends clear signals to the organisation: performance matters. Mistakes affect performance. Don't make too many of them. We care, we are monitoring performance and we will take action.

Interestingly, winning organisations—which might appear 'hard' and 'tough' from this discussion—do not in practice seem to fire many people. They do not have a 'hire and fire' culture. People who underperform (as opposed to making big mistakes) are dealt with, but perhaps not as quickly as they should be. Even some of the winning organisations considered themselves too 'soft' on their weaker people, but they do manage them out of the organisation, rather than fail to address the problem at all. The database we are developing on 'normal' Australian organisations indicates that, of all the issues we identify in this book, this is the one that is *least* well handled.

No cross-subsidisation

A final factor emerged as being different for winning organisations in executing to effectively deliver results. Not only is there a concern across the whole organisation about delivering results, this is also expected to occur at each unit. We call this the 'no cross-subsidisation' approach. Essentially, the poor performance of a business unit will not be allowed to drag down the overall performance of the organisation (or at least not for very long). Every business unit needs to meet the standards. No organisation wants to carry underperforming businesses.

In contrast, many large organisations have at least one unit that is not performing well. A typical managerial response if this issue is raised is that the organisation can 'carry' the unit while it finds its feet/ improves/turns around/waits out an industry slump. This is the classic diversification argument. By averaging out performance across units, diversification reduces risk (volatility) for the whole portfolio. What is not explained by this 'risk reduction' argument is that the cost of this is a lower overall portfolio performance than would be obtained if the loss-maker was sold off or did not exist.

Such non-performing units within organisations are not well regarded within the organisation, even if some internal logic exists to explain the 'value' of the unit. Being manager of such a unit is not much fun. Peers tend to give little weight to that manager's arguments, feeling that such managers have to constantly justify their existence using all manner of arguments.

In winning organisations, this game is played differently. At diversified corporations like the old Brambles and Lend Lease, it is well established that each unit has to pay its own way. At Brambles, the criteria were strictly financial. Meet your own profitability and ROE targets and everything was fine. At Lend Lease, the criteria are not simply financial, but they do include strict financials. Units are begun or closed, based on their ability to support themselves.

'No cross-subsidisation' also holds true at what are regarded as conventionally integrated organisations:

▶ At the Salvation Army, if a particular church or social service unit cannot support itself, it will be closed. (Similarly, new churches or social service units are opened if it is expected that there will be enough of a base to support it.)

▶ Harvey Norman, through its franchise system, treats every store as an independent entity. Franchisees who do not meet targets are replaced and turnover is very high, as it is difficult to find franchisees who can suddenly run their own small business to the level desired by Harvey Norman.

▶ Qantas expands and contracts routes all the time, based on route profitability. For instance, when the 1998 Asian financial crisis hit Korea, Qantas withdrew from Korea in 48 hours, based on assessments of expected future losses.

This concept of 'no cross-subsidisation' has received support from Jack Welch, former CEO of General Electric, the most highly rated diversified conglomerate and one of the only companies in both the *In Search of Excellence* and *Built to Last* high-performing company samples. In his memoirs, Welch (2001) said:

> My 'big' message...was intended to describe the winners of the future...The managements...that hang on to losers for whatever reason—tradition, sentiment, their own management weaknesses—won't be around in 1990. (p. 106)

This led to his initial corporate strategy for GE of being number one or number two in the industry: 'fix, sell or close' each business in the corporation. He also said:

> Making tough-minded decisions about people and plants is a prerequisite to earning the right to talk about soft values, like 'excellence' or 'the learning organisation'. Soft stuff won't work if it doesn't follow demonstrated toughness. It works only in a performance-based culture. (pp. 124–25)

In talking about how ideas are spread through the businesses, he notes that plants are rated against each other. As 'no-one wants to be last', everyone rushes off to find out what the best-performing plants are doing, so that their practices can be replicated in lower performing plants. This is also done in the knowledge that, if performance does not reach acceptable standards, the business or unit will be closed or sold.

Acting as small businesses within a large organisation

This 'no cross-subsidisation' principle leads unit managers to care deeply about the results of their own unit—and to act as a small business within a larger organisation. This helps to explain why unit managers are so motivated to get the results that are in their forecasts. If they don't, and that outcome persists for any time, it is likely that the organisation will close the unit, leaving the manager without a clear position. By contrast, in most organisations losses or low performance are tolerated, and there is no motivation for the unit leader to fix the problems! The unit becomes an accepted drag on organisational performance.

Macquarie believes that one of the foundations of its success is this idea: the creation of a small business entrepreneurial environment. It views itself as an organisation of numerous businesses, in which the operating decisions are made by those closest to the clients, markets or business problems. This entrepreneurial environment—coupled with rigorous project evaluation by the centre—encourages rigorous execution of projects and acceptance of individual responsibility in delivering results.

Throughout its history, until it merged with GKN and developed a global strategy, Brambles attracted the type of people who are drawn to operating their own business. Speaking of the Brambles system of small businesses, one interviewee said:

> Managers see the businesses as their own businesses, as independent business units. It is up to you to grow them. Growth

> is expected—not so much incremental growth as growth through new deals.

This system was established in the early stages of the growth of Brambles. Warwick Holcroft, who became CEO in 1962 was:

> Not content to entrust key positions to people who were merely good managers or good accountants—each had to possess an aptitude for the skills of the other... 'We try to make all our managers as close to being proprietors as possible, but one thing we can't do is substitute proprietor's capital'... That's one of the reasons we introduced stock options. (Carew, 2000, p. 26)

Qantas is another example of this approach. While appearing to be a single integrated business, the developments of Australian Airlines, Qantaslink, Jetstar and Jetstar Asia have led to 'Qantas' people identifying with individual brands. Also, Qantas has been putting many operating units up for competitive tender, allowing both outside organisations and the current management and staff to compete to provide the service. The result for Qantas has been that some units have been outsourced while in others, although the current staff have won the tender, substantial changes in work practices and cost savings have occurred. This has both improved the efficiencies of the business units and also aligned the behaviour and interests of those in the units with that of Qantas as a corporation.

Similarly, Harvey Norman franchisees identify first with their own franchise and second with Harvey Norman as a corporation. At Telstra people identify with being in Telstra Country Wide, Business and Government, Consumer and Marketing, Sensis, Telstra Foundation and so on, rather than simply with 'Telstra' the corporation.

Summary and key messages for leaders

To summarise, the ability to execute effectively, to do what you say, to deliver results on time and on budget is a critical differentiator between winning organisations and others. In this chapter we focused on the set of internal processes that facilitate execution. Having clear processes starts the process off. Being efficient in operations and in the technical systems used will assist in getting outcomes. Having people who take responsibility for the outcomes of the work they do helps to ensure that the systems achieve what they are able to do. Having good control systems and measuring performance rigorously round

Effective execution

out the processes needed, if all goes well. When mistakes are made, winning organisations see them as opportunities to learn, not to blame. Finally, structuring around small units to encourage and allow personal responsibility to flourish, and to prevent cross-subsidisation of business units, forces effective execution across the whole organisation.

The messages for leaders from this chapter are:

- ▶ Focus on execution to deliver results. Do what you say. Get the job done, on time and on budget.
- ▶ The keys to delivering results are to:
    - ▷ Have clear processes that are accepted.
    - ▷ Be operationally and technically efficient.
    - ▷ Ensure people take personal responsibility for their work.
    - ▷ Have good management control systems.
    - ▷ Rigorously measure performance.
    - ▷ When mistakes are made:
        - Encourage people to admit a mistake early on.
        - Fix the mistake as best as possible.
        - Learn from the mistake, after minimising its effects.
        - Be prepared to take tough action on those who make more than one significant mistake.
- ▶ Don't cross-subsidise businesses or even units.
- ▶ Develop a small business atmosphere within the framework and advantages that the large organisation possesses.

3 Perfect alignment

Align everything
Consistency

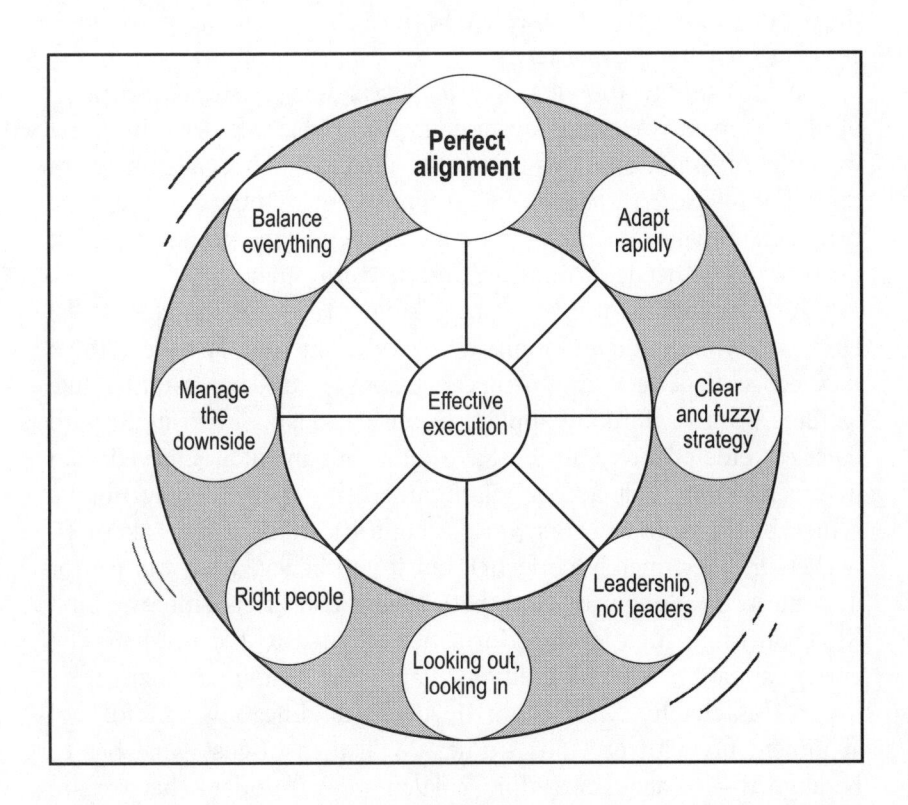

Diagram: Perfect alignment wheel with central "Effective execution" surrounded by: Perfect alignment, Adapt rapidly, Clear and fuzzy strategy, Leadership, not leaders, Looking out, looking in, Right people, Manage the downside, Balance everything

During the course of our research, we found our thinking drawn to the fact that each organisation we analysed was so consistent in what it did. Consistency comes out in many ways—consistency of leadership, of strategy, of process, of balance and so on. Our interviews confirmed this, with consistency being mentioned by most interviewees in some shape or form. As a result, we came to the view that consistency had value by itself, regardless of the specifics of exactly what it was that was consistent.

As we refined our view over time, we realised that it was not static consistency that we were observing. After all, each of the organisations has changed radically over its lifetime. It was consistency *for the situation*. But the term 'consistency' has a static feel to it. People think that it means the same thing over and over.

The reason the organisations are consistent is that their parts and activities—the organisation's functions, business units, information technology, financial, human resources, marketing, ordering systems and so on—are closely aligned with each other. We also found that this alignment developed over time. As an element of the organisation changed (for example, external conditions, its strategy, its leadership), the organisation was able to realign itself to the new situation, so that it could again achieve consistency.

So we came to the view that *alignment* was a better description of the element we were observing. And what we saw in these winning organisations was not just alignment, but alignment of everything—*perfect alignment*. Aligning everything to achieve consistency makes for the operational efficiency and commonality of purpose that is needed to execute and deliver results.

'Perfect' alignment seems impossible of course, and so it is! However, winning organisations don't see it like this, or believe it, so they act as if perfect alignment can be achieved. This is rather like extreme positive thinking applied to business. Not surprisingly, with these extreme positive attitudes, a lot more alignment is achieved than in organisations that accept misalignment. So 'perfect' may not be achievable (was Brian Lara's world-record 400 runs or Jim Laker's 19 wickets in a test match 'perfect'?), but if you believe it is, and try for it, you can go a long way! And that's what it takes to get into the First XI—consistent high-level performance, aligned to the needs of the current situation, and the ability to adapt when conditions change.

In this chapter, we'll begin by understanding how our idea of alignment fits with previous studies. We'll then discuss what has to be aligned—what is 'everything'? Then we'll consider what we are aligning everything to—what starts this process? Finally we'll consider how realignment occurs over time.

The history of 'alignment'

Alignment is not a new idea. Peters and Waterman (1982) developed the famous '7S' model. In this model, all the Ss—strategy, systems, style, staff, skills, structure and shared values—are connected by double-headed arrows to demonstrate that each one affects all of the others. Thus, in order to deliver results, the concept behind the model is to line up—or align—all the Ss in the same direction, so they are consistent with each other, supporting each other.

It turns out in practice that 'lining up the Ss'—achieving alignment across the organisation—is incredibly difficult. This is one of the reasons why implementing strategy is so difficult and why delivering results distinguishes winning organisations from others. But it is surprising how little attention is given to this issue in the practice of managing organisations well.

Collins and Porras (1994) addressed the issue of alignment through the idea of 'cult-like cultures', which they described as:

> A series of practices that create an almost cult-like environment around the core ideology in highly visionary companies. These practices tend to vigorously screen out those who do not fit with the ideology (either before hiring or early in their careers). They also instill an intense sense of loyalty and influence the behaviour of those remaining inside the company to be congruent with the core ideology, consistent over time, and carried out zealously. (p. 123)

Although again not specifically referring to alignment, Collins and Porras refer to 'tightness of fit' as being a key characteristic of these 'cult-like cultures', enabling them to develop the 'congruence' that is observed.

In Australia, Hubbard (2000) developed and adapted the 7S model further (see figure 3.1 overleaf). The 7S model focuses on the internals of the organisation—but internal consistency is not enough. To create value for customers, the organisation must deliver what is wanted externally by customers. Hubbard's model effectively integrates three separate sets of ideas:

▶ The 'Environment—Strategy—Capability' (E-S-C) strategic analysis model, which seeks both external consistency and internal alignment.

▶ The 7S internal implementation model. This model better reflects what each 'S' was actually intended to convey:

  ▷ 'capabilities' replaces 'skills'

The First XI

- ▷ 'people' replaces 'staff'
- ▷ 'culture' replaces 'shared values'
- ▷ 'leadership' replaces 'style'.

▶ Two new elements—perception and communication—are included. These are key elements that influence whether or not an organisation can actually deliver the results it wishes. Will people see the issues that the organisation faces (perception), so that they are able to address them? Will people understand what the organisation is trying to do (communication) in order that they can carry it out?

This work expands the number of elements that are identified as needing to be aligned.

Figure 3.1: Hubbard's model of strategic implementation

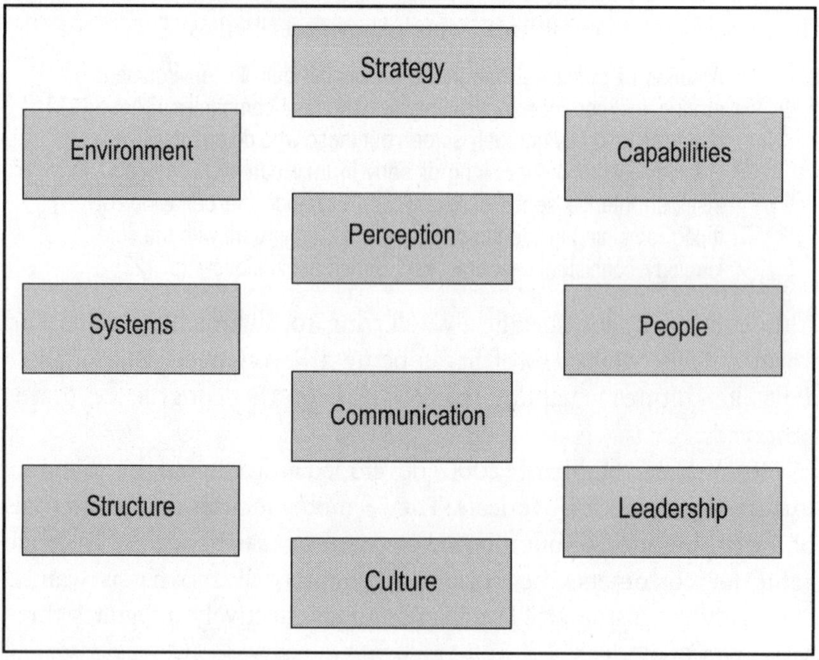

Environment	Strategy	Capabilities
Systems	Perception	People
Structure	Communication	Leadership
	Culture	

From these models, we can see that alignment and consistency are not new ideas. But they are ideas that are difficult to implement and ideas that are undervalued in the continual quest for the new and the different.

Many people find the concept of consistency boring. Yet consistency is critical, particularly for organisations like Telstra or Woolworths that depend on a very large number of sales of very small units. One of the biggest problems that these types of organisations face is how to deliver consistency of service to go with consistency of product. We all know how difficult it is to deliver service consistency in large organisations.

Similarly, alignment is also much less exciting as a management initiative than new product development or innovation or change. Yet our study finds that—in fact—alignment is more important than these ideas. The ability to line up all the activities within the organisation so that they are internally and externally consistent is a daunting task! No wonder so few organisations are able to do this and those that do are winning organisations.

What is 'everything'?

It is easy to say 'align everything' to achieve perfect alignment, but how can we get a handle on 'everything'? How can we focus on the key elements of 'everything', yet retain the idea that it is 'everything' that should be aligned? The models that we introduced at the start of the chapter—the 7S model and Hubbard's implementation model—cover the key elements that must be addressed. They are external environment, strategy, capabilities, culture, systems, people, leadership, structure, communications and perception (see figure 3.2). We'll comment on each one, though not all were seen to be equally important to winning organisations from the research.

Figure 3.2: aligning everything—what is 'everything'?

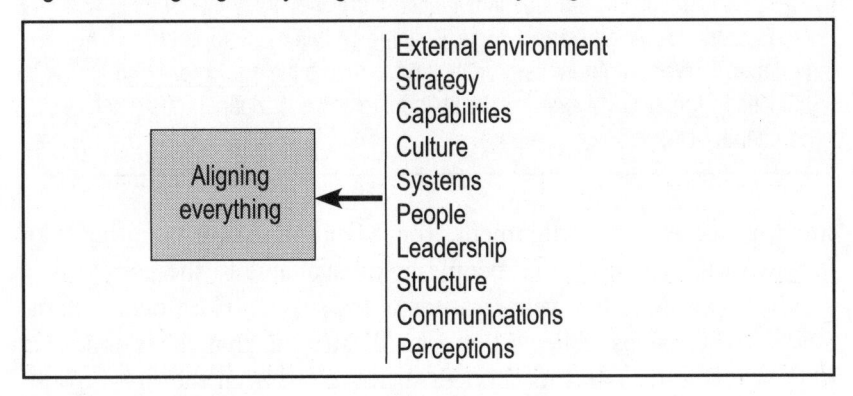

| Aligning everything | ← | External environment
Strategy
Capabilities
Culture
Systems
People
Leadership
Structure
Communications
Perceptions |

External alignment

One point that was clear from our research is reflected in our winning framework: winning organisations are externally focused as well as trying to align everything internally. We cover the issue of external focus in detail in chapter 7. From an alignment perspective, winning organisations are focused externally on customers and their needs. Qantas, Telstra, Woolworths and NAB all face mass consumer markets. For them, market research into the ever-changing needs of customers is very important and they spend a lot of time and money on it. Of these organisations, Woolworths relies most on customer feedback to its people, while the others have focused on more formal market research mechanisms. Since Woolworths regards itself as the buying agent for customers—rather than a retailer selling to customers—it is likely to be much more responsive to customer needs than other retailers. Another example of external alignment is given in illustration 3.1, which shows how NAB aligned its home mortgage product to what customers wanted.

> **Illustration 3.1: developing products that customers actually want**
>
> NAB achieved a significant advantage from its Tailored Home Loan package (which became known as 'Aussie mortgage loans' in the industry) for retail customers. Beginning in the late 1980s, NAB developed the first customer-based information file, followed shortly afterwards by its Customer and Management Service System (CAMS) in 1989. However, it was not until the early 1990s that the Tailored Home Loan was developed. This product relied on a choice-modelling technique that was built into the software to price different choices. It enabled NAB customers to make their mortgage home loans much more flexible than those of competitor products, meeting the specific needs of particular individuals. It took several years before competitors offered similar products. Building on this market research, NAB began to actively segment its organisation to match the customer segments identified from its CRM systems, enabling it to serve its defined customer segments better than competitors.

In terms of external alignment, the Salvation Army is rather like Woolworths. It relies on its people being available to the community and being aware of the welfare needs of the society. The slogan 'Thank God for the Salvos' reflects the grateful attitude that the public has to the organisation and its services. It has often been the first or only organisation to tackle difficult problems in society, such as providing family welfare, crisis counselling, court services, detoxification services and safe housing for victims of violence and survivors of suicide. Over time, the range and size of services offered by the Salvation Army has expanded dramatically to reflect increasing and broadening community needs. Its ability to get the job done has meant that it is well supported by governments and by corporate sponsors, raising over $350 million in 2005.

External alignment is more than just about customers, though. For instance, both Qantas (for most of its life) and Telstra (which still does) have had government owners who have determined or influenced the strategy for the organisation, regardless of what customers might have wanted. Rio Tinto's strategy is very much constrained by what local communities want in locations where it wishes to mine.

This external orientation—and the ability of the internal organisation to deliver the products and services that are wanted, rather than those the organisation can produce—is a critical part of alignment that is not reflected in the original 7S model, but that is vital for winning organisations.

We turn now to the internal elements that need to be aligned—strategy, culture, systems, people, leadership, structure, communication and perception.

Aligning strategy

As with external focus, strategy is an important element of the winning framework for our winning organisations and we discuss its importance in detail in chapter 5. Strategy setting must take account of the external environment, of the capabilities of the organisation, of its people resources and of the culture, systems and structures that exist. It is no good proposing a wonderful strategy if the organisation cannot deliver it!

For instance, the Salvation Army is very short of resources to meet its strategy to help alleviate suffering. But the government is outsourcing many of its welfare functions in the belief that other organisations can perform them more efficiently. The Salvation Army is a prime outsourcing candidate and receives over half of its funds from various governments to undertake a variety of welfare initiatives. However, it still has to say 'no' to a number of initiatives that it would like to pursue but for which it does not have the funds.

Qantas always had a strategy based on high-quality customer service. Yet there are significant signs that low-cost airlines have a winning formula that is gradually emerging in this industry. Qantas has responded in several ways. First, it re-established the Australian Airlines brand to act as a low-cost—but not low-service—airline to fly to international destinations that Qantas could not afford to service with its own high-cost structure. Second, it acquired and absorbed low-cost domestic competitor Impulse Airlines under the Qantaslink brand, redirecting its services to low demand routes. Third, it started Jetstar Asia as a Singapore-based, low-cost international airline as a joint venture with a Singapore government subsidiary. Fourth, it started Jetstar to compete as a low-cost domestic airline with Virgin Blue. Fifth, it closed Australian Airlines as it decided to have Jetstar fly internationally, having proved its business case domestically. This has enabled Qantas to 'bend' its strategy to align it better with emerging market needs.

Aligning culture

Culture is the most difficult aspect to change in an organisation. Hence, aligning it—or more likely realigning it—is the most difficult area to address. All the winning organisations in our research spoke of the importance of their culture. It is not a *particular* culture that is required, though. There is no 'best' culture. It is having a culture that is aligned to what the organisation wants to achieve. But how does an organisation align it in the first place? What would an organisation have to address if it wished to align the culture?

First, the organisation needs to have a clear view of where it wants to go and what it wants to achieve. For instance, the Salvation Army wishes to alleviate human suffering and distress by supporting needy and disadvantaged people, while preaching the gospel of Jesus Christ.

Second, this strategy needs to be communicated widely to people throughout the organisation by the leadership (not just the CEO). This communication needs to be continuous and through many channels and people. It needs to be consistent throughout. Most of the CEOs and senior managers we talked to said that a key part of their role is to communicate, communicate and communicate what the organisation is trying to do, why it is trying to do that and how people fit into that picture.

Third, there is the issue of understanding what the culture currently is. What do we want to keep? What do we want to change? For instance, for the Salvation Army, the uniform is a key part of their culture. It is readily identifiable. It immediately recalls the history and good image of the organisation. It is consistent with the 'army' style of the organisation, as are the titles that its people use (Colonel, Lieutenant Colonel, Major, Captain and so on). The Salvation Army continually reviews the style and use of the uniform to try to ensure that is is up to date. However, in the 2000s, the idea of dress discipline,

Perfect alignment

suits and uniforms is seen as old-fashioned, a turn-off for young people in particular. Should the Salvation Army keep its uniform, which has been a key element of its culture, or should it change to reflect modern society?

Almost at the other end of the cultural spectrum, Macquarie has a very clear view of its culture and what it seeks from its people culturally. Like the Salvation Army, this has largely remained unchanged since Macquarie was set up. Macquarie sees its entrepreneurial energy, innovative approaches and its focus on seeking inspired solutions to difficult problems as key cultural advantages compared to its international competitors. Macquarie's management philosophy involves:

- loose/tight management structure (referred to in 2006 as 'freedom within boundaries')
- full service in Australia, New Zealand and Asia and a focused service elsewhere
- commitment to growth
- focus on great people
- formula-based profit-sharing remuneration system
- small business entrepreneurial environment.

It believes this represents the cultural keys to its success. However, originally it focused on a small number of niche markets in Australia—and provided no international service—so its culture is actually changing, slowly, over time.

Values statements

Increasingly, organisations are turning to values statements as ways of making the foundations of their culture explicit and enabling the organisation and individuals to understand what the organisation stands for. In winning organisations, these sets of values are not just rhetoric, but values that their people are expected to 'live'. Illustration 3.2 (overleaf) shows the values of some of the winning organisations from their 2006 values statements. We noticed several things from analysing them. First, look carefully for the 'different' words, rather than the 'normal' words to see what makes these statements different. Second, the statements include a lot of the same words and ideas that are expressed in this book—perhaps partly reflecting the influence of this work. Third, there is a lot of commonality among the words and ideas. Fourth, the differences in ideas reflect the specifics of the situation that each organisation finds itself in. Fifth, each organisation expresses itself individually rather than by a formula—the statements and their presentation are carefully, and differently, thought through. Finally, the focus is on actions and behaviour, not charts on the wall (as seen in some organisations).

Illustration 3.2: some examples of values from public values statements

Brambles:
- All things begin with the customer.
- We believe in people and teamwork.
- We have a passion for success.
- Always acting with integrity and respect for the community and the environment.

Lend Lease:
- Respect.
- Integrity.
- Innovation.
- Collaboration.
- Excellence.

Macquarie Bank:
- Integrity.
- Client commitment.
- Strive for profitability.
- Fulfillment for our people.
- Teamwork.
- Highest standards.

National Australia Bank:
- We will be open and honest.
- We take ownership and hold ourselves accountable (for all our actions).
- We expect teamwork and collaboration across our organisation for the benefit of our stakeholders.

Perfect alignment

> - We treat everyone with fairness and respect.
> - We value speed, simplicity and efficient execution of our promises.
> - And we do not have room for people who do not live these principles.
>
> **The Salvation Army:**
> - To assist all people in need without regard to nationality, race, belief, sexuality, ability, or judgement of behaviour... 'Do unto others as you would have others do unto you'.
> - To encourage people to spiritual wholeness through the teachings of Jesus.
>
> **Telstra:**
> - People. Power.
> - Customer. First.
> - Done. Now.
> - We get it. Together.
> - Compete. Win.
> - Anything. Possible.
>
> **Woolworths:**
> - Integrity.
> - Retail Passion.
> - Open communication.
> - TEAM (Together Everyone Achieves More).
> - CARE (Customers Are Really Everything).
> - Change.
> - Walk the Talk.

One of the biggest challenges faced by Australian organisations is that, as they go overseas as part of their strategic cycle—particularly by acquiring other organisations—their need to incorporate or allow for the differing cultures and values of the employees they may acquire or hire is often overlooked at the managerial level. The managers tend to remain mostly Australian (unless a foreign organisation is acquired), yet the organisation seeks to be international/global. As we see winning organisations becoming increasingly international/global, their cultures and underlying values will need to change to reflect this at the highest level. Illustration 3.3 shows how Lend Lease introduced international directors to align its board with its international, and eventually its global, strategy in the 1990s.

> **Illustration 3.3: Lend Lease aligns its board to its strategy**
>
> In the 1990s Lend Lease appointed several international board members, increasing in number slowly over time, reflecting its international strategy. These included:
>
> - Yong Hau Chua—appointed in 1994 from Singapore
> - Diane Grady—appointed in 1994 from the US
> - Rudi Mueller—appointed in 1996 from Switzerland
> - Albert Aiello—appointed in 1998 from the US
> - Jill Ker Conway—appointed in 1992 from the US (though she is an Australian national).
>
> Thus, of a board of 12, almost half were international by 2000 when the organisation committed to a global strategy. In addition, a number of others had worked for other organisations overseas.
>
> Is your board of directors aligned in experience for your future needs?

Aligning systems

Systems are a key factor in perfect alignment. Systems are pervasive. Consequently, unless they support the other elements, there is little chance of the ideas and wishes of the people and leaders in the organisation actually occurring.

There are many different ideas about what 'systems' means. Is it IT systems? Financial systems? Processes? We think of systems in terms of four different types, all of which are interrelated and interact, ideally to give perfect alignment (see figure 3.3):

▶ operating systems
▶ management information systems
▶ decision-making systems
▶ reward systems.

Perfect alignment

Figure 3.3: a framework of interacting internal systems that need to be aligned

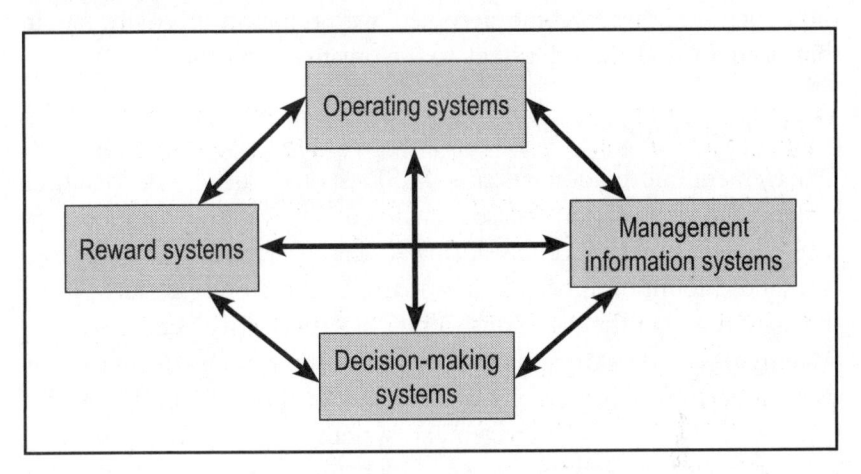

```
            Operating systems
           ↗       ↕        ↘
  Reward systems ←——→ Management
           ↘       ↕        ↗  information systems
            Decision-making
                systems
```

Operating systems

In chapter 2 we discussed the importance of operational efficiency in delivering results. This efficiency comes from having good operating systems in place. All the organisations had good operating systems. For instance:

▶ Brambles—management systems to control CHEP pallets

▶ Harvey Norman—franchising system and product ordering systems

▶ Lend Lease—project management system

▶ Macquarie Bank—ability to integrate its different business units to develop creative project solutions

▶ NAB—cost control and risk management systems (prior to the fraud and forex scandals in the early 2000s)

▶ Qantas—reservations management and safety systems

▶ Rio Tinto—mine production systems

▶ The Salvation Army—emergency systems

▶ Telstra—customer information systems

▶ Westfield—shopping centre redevelopment and management systems

▶ Woolworths—supply chain management systems.

Operating systems are often the key to an organisation's sustainable competitive advantage and they are generally built over long periods of time, such that they become 'accepted' within the organisation, rather than seen, or understood, as key to the organisation's success.

Management information systems

Management Information Systems (MIS) rest on the quality of operating systems. No organisation claimed that its success was due to its superior MIS, at least in terms of any formal IT-based systems. Nevertheless, from the amount of information available in these organisations, from the way in which they are consistently externally involved, their MIS systems are clearly of high quality. However, the winning organisations were in general rather critical of the value of their IT-based systems. Qantas, with its yield management systems, was an exception. In general, however, technology per se does not seem to be a route to being a winning organisation.

Decision-making systems

'Decision-making systems' refers to the process of how decisions are made as well as the structure of decision making in the organisation. Decision making involves the use of the information from the formal MIS, but it also requires the subjective analysis of, and judgement about, qualitative factors external—and internal—to the organisation, which do not appear in any formal MIS (see figure 3.4).

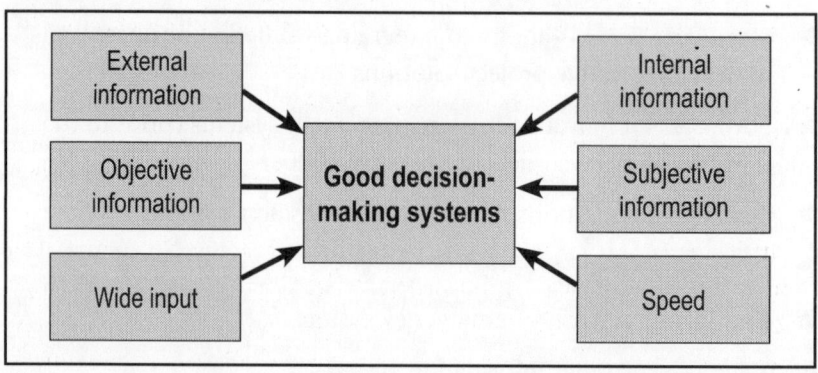

Figure 3.4: what makes good decision-making systems?

```
┌─────────────┐                              ┌─────────────┐
│  External   │ ──→                     ←──  │  Internal   │
│ information │                              │ information │
└─────────────┘      ┌───────────────┐       └─────────────┘
┌─────────────┐      │ Good decision-│       ┌─────────────┐
│  Objective  │ ──→  │ making systems│  ←──  │ Subjective  │
│ information │      │               │       │ information │
└─────────────┘      └───────────────┘       └─────────────┘
┌─────────────┐ ──→                     ←──  ┌─────────────┐
│ Wide input  │                              │   Speed     │
└─────────────┘                              └─────────────┘
```

We have noted that the winning organisations are very externally oriented. This helps them include a lot of external information from the industry and elsewhere when forming decisions. For instance, unlike its major domestic competitors, NAB has ownership of major banks in other countries. This gives NAB a better handle on events and issues in the international financial services industry, which it can then reflect back into decision making in the Australian setting.

Good decision making needs both objective and subjective views. Rio Tinto exemplifies the best of objective approaches in its mine development decisions. Using three separate analyses—a technical, a financial and a business case analysis—each of which is independent, maximises its chances of making the right decision. Macquarie similarly has its centralised risk management function assess any major investment proposal, in addition to considering the proposal from the sponsor division, thus providing at least two opinions on the proposal.

Nevertheless, despite attempts to obtain objective information, in the end decision making is subjective. The value of having different perspectives, of being externally focused, of being concerned with rapid adaptation and of having clear strategy and the right people all help to make the final subjective decisions right much more often than wrong. Woolworths highly values the subjective information that its checkout staff gather directly from customers. Brambles highly values the customer relationships it forms from personalised interactions with its customers, which provide opportunities to build new services for customers. Qantas gathers subjective information in a variety of ways—counter-booking staff, on-board flight attendants, and phone enquiries and complaints.

A third aspect of decision making is speed. Quickest is not necessarily best in decision making, but opportunities do pass by slow decision makers. Having bureaucratic processes and layers of decision making are two ways to slow decision making. Brambles, Lend Lease, Westfield and Macquarie all minimise the layers and the bureaucracy, while maximising the personal responsibility of the proposal's proponents to improve speed and trying to ensure that only good proposals come forward. Illustration 3.4 (overleaf) shows how Westfield typically moves quickly in its decision making.

In its quest to become more commercially oriented, Qantas has rapidly improved its ability to make quick decisions. After the terrorist attacks on September 11, 2001, American Airlines cancelled its order for new Boeing 737-800s to completely replace all its 737-400s. Qantas had been planning to replace a large part of its fleet in the next couple of years. It saw an opportunity to take advantage of Boeing's sudden shortage of customers. Within three weeks, the $1.5 billion decision to replace the fleet had been made and within three months the first planes began to arrive.

> **Ilustration 3.4: Westfield—quick is better than slow**
>
> Westfield believes in commitment, not committees—entrepreneurial and active rather than institutional and passive. Frank Lowy once said he would rather have a quick 'no' than a slow 'yes'. The company's decision making is highly centralised, but the centre is well aware that it needs to regularly go into the field and keep in touch with the business at the grassroots level. The keys to decisions are the thoughts and ideas of individuals, shared within the group and refined over time, using a 'toe in the water' approach to pilot new ideas.
>
> Steven Lowy, now joint managing director of Westfield, says, 'We are a company that focuses on change. We have adapted physically and, more importantly and more subtly, we adapt on a daily basis' (Harley, 2003).

Reward systems

'Reward systems' is an area of systems that is of significant importance for winning organisations. Since the late 1980s, there has been a major shift in attitudes towards remuneration in Australia (and overseas). Some of the main causes of this have been:

- *The introduction of the Enterprise Bargaining Award system in 1987.* This encouraged and enabled individual organisations to bargain directly with their own people, rather than be limited to the existing framework of arbitrated industry-wide awards, where all organisations, whether efficient or not, flexible or not, skilled or not, well-managed or not, paid the same rate for the same work classification.
- *The Silicon Valley dotcom-inspired fashion for options.* While share options have been available for many years to a limited number of senior managers in listed companies, the IT/dotcom/IPO explosion during the 1990s made options a very rewarding way of being paid. They provided very high returns for those prepared to take high risk and became available for a lot of people who would not previously have been able to receive them.
- *The privatisation fashion.* The privatisation of many government and mutual organisations also led many people working in organisations to change their views (positively and negatively) about the commercial value of their work. The wide boost in share ownership that followed these privatisations (Commonwealth Bank, Qantas, Telstra, AMP, NRMA, Colonial

Mutual, Commonwealth Serum Laboratories and GIO in particular) also changed attitudes towards pay and expectations of organisational performance. Many employees became share owners and the differences between the interests of these two groups was significantly decreased.

▶ *The 1990s booming stock market.* Though the Australian stock market did not increase as much as its overseas counterparts, it rose rapidly. This encouraged the options concept and the share-owning concept to spill over into all types of organisations.

▶ *The willingness of employees to share risk and responsibility and the expectation that they will do so.* As a result of the previous points, people have become educated about the rewards for taking risk and many have decided to accept more risk. Reward systems have become more aligned with the value systems of the organisation. Profit sharing and bonuses have become widespread elements of rewards. Australia has become the country with the largest percentage of shareholders per capita in the world. Compulsory superannuation, which was introduced in 1986 and rose to 9 per cent of salary in 2002, coupled with the view that retirees have a responsibility to look after themselves rather than rely on a government pension, has also been a key factor.

▶ *The development of the 'contractor' market.* As many organisations, particularly public ones, have focused on more commercial outcomes, a great deal of work has been outsourced. Some of this has gone to individual contractors, often previous employees who become 'businesses' contracting back to their old employer. Contractors working for themselves are more highly motivated to perform than are employees working for a fixed salary and many have also taken this role for the freedom that comes with it.

▶ *The lowering of tax rates on income and capital gains.* In recent years, the federal government has substantially changed the tax rates, reducing the top rates and applying them at much higher levels of income. In addition, capital gains are, in general, taxed at half marginal-income tax rates. Both of these moves significantly encourage people to seek profits or higher income without feeling excessively penalised by the tax rates.

▶ *The introduction of Australian Workplace Agreements.* This requires organisations to offer individuals the opportunity to contract individually, rather than collectively through a union, to determine individual pay and conditions. Introduced in 2006, this is likely to have substantial positive benefits for high-performing people who are prepared to take risks.

One outcome of these changes has been a huge increase in remuneration at the top end of most industries and a change in the structure of remuneration. Part of this is due to performance differentials, part is due to share price increases from share options, part is due to the recognition of increased risk in work and part to the fact that people who have a clear financial reward are often motivated to produce a lot more.

Another outcome is that there has been a big swing towards 'variable remuneration'—that is, where only part of the remuneration is conventional fixed salary, part is pay for personal performance and part is pay for sharemarket performance (see figure 3.5).

Figure 3.5: reward systems—then and now

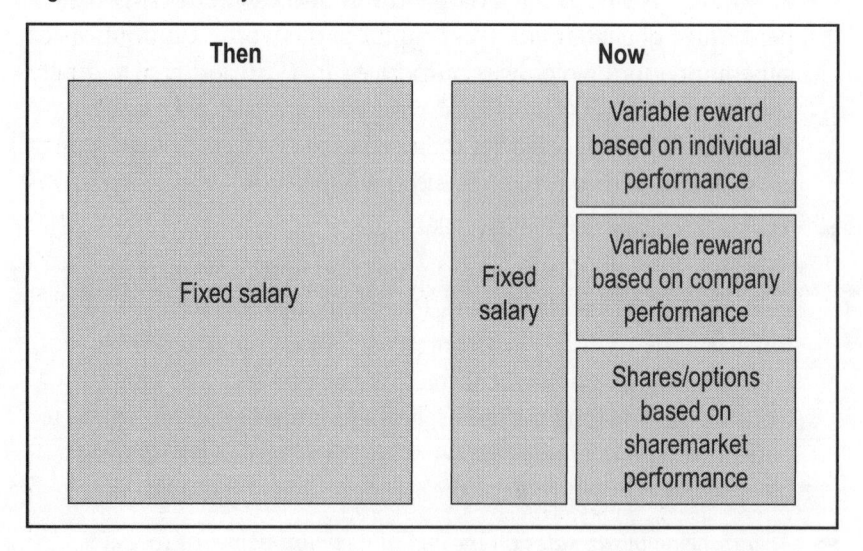

Then	Now
Fixed salary	Fixed salary
	Variable reward based on individual performance
	Variable reward based on company performance
	Shares/options based on sharemarket performance

However, a key finding from our research is that, while we found that all the winning organisations (except the Salvation Army) have embraced this concept, we were surprised to find that neither high pay nor high financial rewards were universally perceived to be critical to success. Interestingly, at all organisations, staff turnover was relatively low for the particular industry, regardless of their remuneration attitude.

What really matters is aligning reward systems to the strategy and culture of the organisations. Some organisations clearly pay and reward well. Rio Tinto and Westfield are renowned as high payers. Macquarie pays relatively highly, but the millionaire remunerations developed there are due to high incentive payments, not the high fixed salaries. Brambles, Lend Lease and Harvey Norman provide high incentives, but base remuneration is not high. At Woolworths, Qantas, Telstra and NAB, opportunities for promotion based on hard work and satisfaction from being involved in a cause in a good organisation have been regarded as part of the remuneration. The Salvation Army, however, pays very poorly, due to the values of its religious background. It seems un-Christian for Salvation Army people to be paid well when those they are helping are in dire need, especially when the money for those salaries comes directly out of donations. The Salvation Army expects its people to receive personal satisfaction from the 'cause' they serve and many non-officers accept lower paid roles with the organisation as their way of contributing to society.

The concept of 'reward', then, seems to be much broader than simply either fixed salary or even total remuneration (see figure 3.6). The remuneration formula varies. Personal satisfaction—which is not paid for by the organisation—is a part of the total 'reward'. There are personal costs too. For instance, large dollar rewards are usually associated with extremely long hours, large amounts of travel away from home, high stress levels and increased insecurity. Organisations that can show that they have a good cause, that are good organisations to work for and/or that are doing well, are always likely to attract and retain people. Clearly though, an organisation like Macquarie would not get the people it wanted by offering the Salvation Army pay levels. But neither would the reverse be true!

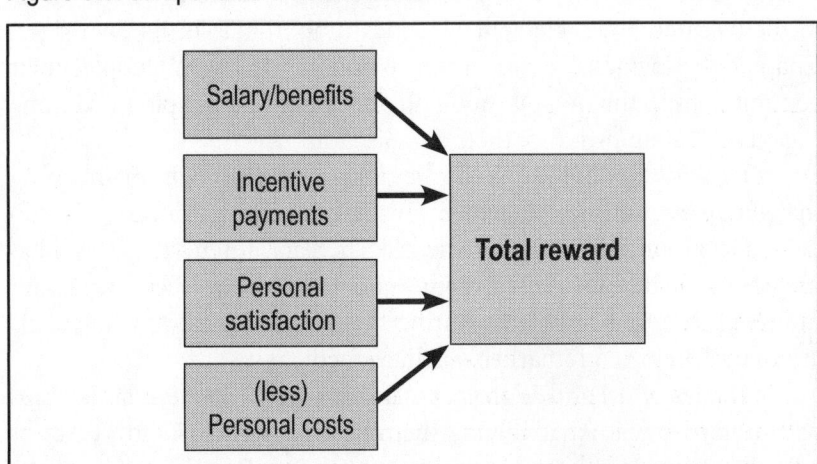

Figure 3.6: components of total reward

In summary, systems are important and aligning systems is essential for high and efficient performance. Operating systems are often the basis of the sustainable competitive advantage of the organisation, built up over long periods and taken for granted. Management information systems build on the operating systems. Decision-making systems are based on objective information where possible, but subjective information is also valuable. They take into account a variety of perspectives—both internal and external—and decisions are made quickly. Reward systems define 'reward' widely to include non-financial elements, align employee interests with the organisation's interests and have a large variable component. The package, not the level of pay, is the critical element.

Aligning people

We use the term 'people' deliberately, rather than the more common 'workforce', 'workers', 'employees' or 'staff', in order to try to focus on the whole person rather than focusing on that part of the person who works, or highlighting any classification differences between types of people employed at a particular organisation. 'People' also includes 'managers', unless we wish to distinguish 'leadership' as a guiding group. This was the terminology used by executives in interviews and it reflects a subtle, but significant, difference in attitudes. In these organisations, people really are important. This is not just lip service. We were also impressed by the lack of 'them' and 'us' that exists in winning organisations. Managers see themselves as responsible for the wellbeing of their people.

Like external focus, strategy and leadership, 'people' was highlighted in the research as an element of critical importance in its own right. Chapter 8 provides a detailed discussion of the 'right' people, their commitment to the organisation and about the way people in winning organisations are proud of their organisation.

In terms of aligning people, the key issue is developing or maintaining that alignment in times of change. Telstra has shrunk from over 90 000 people to around 40 000 over the last 15 years. Interestingly, in what has been a highly unionised environment, there have been no major industrial relations problems during this very large downsizing. This 'non-news' item is a remarkable achievement.

Brambles and Lend Lease have also had remarkable relationships with unions by either involving them in the process (Lend Lease) or talking directly, openly and honestly to them. One Brambles publication stated:

> Brambles was instrumental with Bill Kelty [then Federal Secretary of the ACTU] in totally restructuring the award system for the transport industry... Pemberton [then Brambles CEO] was pushing co-operation. He believed in keeping relations with the unions open and strong... Pat Geraghty [then Secretary of the Transport Workers Union] was blown away by Pemberton's sharing of information and Brambles is probably alone in having such solid relations with the maritime unions. Pemberton's approach of being so open and determined meant that he overcame all the obstacles. (Carew, 2000, p. 154)

On the other hand, to overcome disastrous industrial relations and continued disruption at its mine sites in Australia over many years, CRA took the complete reverse tack. Through the use of the principles of 'time span of discretion' of Elliott Jaques (1989), it defined the role of a manager at various levels. It also tried to define clear roles and responsibilities consistently for each level of a consistent structure. From this Rio Tinto introduced a system of individual contracts into a number of its operations to replace the industry awards—the precursor to the national introduction in 2006 of Australian Workplace Agreements. This has had the effect of directly linking managers and their people at each unit—leading to improved working relationships and increased productivity. Where collective agreements have been maintained, as in the coal operations, they have been revised to promote maximum operational flexibility.

Another way to align people is to make them shareholders. Over 30 000 of Woolworths' 170 000 people are shareholders, over 80 per cent of Qantas' 38 000 people are shareholders (holding around 2.5 per cent of the total number of shares) and Lend Lease employees hold 10 per cent of their organisation's shares. Shareholder employees thus receive shareholder benefits when the organisation performs well, over and above what they receive as employees. Macquarie pays a fixed percentage of its pre-bonus profit to its people for the same reason—it aligns stakeholder interest groups.

Corporate-wide change programs (see chapter 13) are an emerging way of aligning people. This is particularly so in organisations that have lost focus, where there is a need to change to meet a new strategy, or where international/global organisations are being developed. These programs seem to be an emerging way of clearly and explicitly communicating the expectations of the corporation to the individuals working there. Qantas' 'Sustainable Future', Rio Tinto's 'Improving Performance Together' and Telstra's 'The Transformation' are examples of such named programs.

What these examples show is that there is no one right 'formula'. The commonality here is the willingness to talk with and negotiate with people directly—which is generally regarded as the best way—or with unions, seeking win/win situations, even when overall job losses are a clearly necessary outcome. Unions or people were blamed for problems only once in all our interviews—by a long-retired executive.

Other issues with aligning people—hiring, training, promoting, rewarding and supporting them—are covered in detail in chapter 8.

Aligning leadership

As with people, leadership is highlighted in the research as another element of critical importance in its own right. Leadership is much more than the CEO or even the top management team. Leadership is discussed in detail in chapter 6.

While leadership is, and must be, involved in doing the 'aligning', it is important that the leadership team itself is aligned. John Saunders and Frank Lowy provide a perfect example at Westfield. As joint CEOs, they had separate offices with a meeting room in between. They were closely involved with all phases of the work, so they were not remote to people or the technicalities of the decisions. Decisions were always made jointly. It was only when Lowy's three sons entered the business and Frank Lowy had expanded his capabilities and horizons beyond those of Saunders, who remained an instinctive manager, that the partnership ceased to work satisfactorily.

This ability to discuss ideas is critical in organisations. At Westfield, when decisions have to be made, all those involved in the decision are invited to a formal meeting. A wide-ranging discussion is held, where every view is expected to be offered and every view is listened to. A decision is then made by the leadership if consensus has not been reached. Using this approach, the outcomes are then 'owned' by the team.

At Telstra, Frank Blount spent a great deal of time aligning his own leadership team, recognising that without a cohesive, focused leadership team, his chances of pushing major change through the organisation were significantly reduced. In 2006, Sol Trujillo followed a similar approach, after Telstra had experienced a quite different style of leadership under Ziggy Switkowski (see chapter 6). John Stewart at NAB was also following this approach in turning around NAB in the period 2004–07.

At Lend Lease, before a proposal is put up for approval, it is expected that the proposer will have consulted with everyone in the organisation

Perfect alignment

who has experience in any aspect of the project's activities, so that all previous available knowledge is brought to bear on the proposal. Not to consult widely is considered an organisational sin. A similar view is taken at Brambles.

We noted during our interviews that there were significant differences in the views held by the current leadership at some of our winning organisations. This is not really surprising. Not every CEO and top management team at every winning organisation throughout its history has been happy or agreed! Indeed, the histories we read of Woolworths and Brambles indicated violent and significant disagreements at board and top management team levels. For instance, in summarising the role of Woolworths' co-founder Percy Christmas as CEO, Murray commented:

> Woolworths was never a one-man band, rather a team operation comprising tough-minded individuals whose board meetings were still remembered more than 50 years later...as being of table-pounding, door-slamming intensity. Yet the tensions were ultimately creative. (Murray, 1999, p. 14)

No organisation progresses evenly throughout time. There are spurts and setbacks for all organisations. What sets the winning organisations apart is their ability to overcome such differences and move forward. For instance:

▶ Woolworths was almost out of business on several occasions in its history and was proposed for takeover by Coles by co founder and CEO Percy Christmas to the board in 1936. This proposal was thwarted by the board.

▶ Rio Tinto survived extremely lean years throughout the 1980s, believing that the resources cycle would turn upwards again shortly, before eventually coming to focus directly on the commercial aspects of its operations during the 1990s.

▶ Westfield lost millions from 1986 to 1989 when it diversified by buying a controlling shareholding in the Channel Ten television network and starting a listed cashbox investment company.

▶ Qantas and Australian Airlines were competitors when they were merged by their common parent (Qantas was allied with Ansett at the time, so Australian Airlines was very much the opposition). The merger was extremely acrimonious, described by one of our interviewees as the 'red and blue wars' (reflecting the different colour schemes of the two organisations).

▶ Lend Lease was unable to implement its well-rationalised global strategy of real estate development and funds management in the period 2001–02, resulting in the resignation of the CEO and wholesale change in the top management team and the board.

▶ Brambles' centralised global strategy also went wrong when it merged two operating divisions under an external new CEO.

▶ NAB lost $3 billion on HomeSide and then experienced a Korean fraud attack and an Australian forex fraud, resulting, like Lend Lease, in a CEO resignation and wholesale change in the board and top management team.

▶ Telstra has struggled since its second public share sale as its majority owner, the federal government, has been hopelessly conflicted in seeking high cash and share price returns at the same time as subsidised country investment, low prices for customers and easy access for competitors.

But it is also true that it is much more enjoyable to be on a winning team, to have a unified leadership and a leadership that is aligned to the rest of the organisation rather than the reverse!

Aligning structure

The dominant finding about structure from the research is that structure is not an important element for winning organisations. Structures are constantly being changed and realigned in most of the winning organisations (the Salvation Army is the notable exception and Rio Tinto has a structured view of the roles of particular job levels—see chapter 4). Only one organisation, Macquarie, shows its organisation structure in its annual report and it is a series of concentric circles—hardly traditional!

These organisations see structure as supporting the activities —aligning to them—rather than having the idea that there is any one 'ideal' structure. For instance, Macquarie develops a new division or a new group as new ideas come to the surface. As groups or divisions feel that a new structure would work better, it is introduced. Consequently, Macquarie is constantly changing its structures to fit the perceived needs of the people. One Macquarie executive said:

> Structure is determined by what each group wants. The restructure that formed my division occurred because two divisions had merged under joint heads and it didn't work. So they asked Big Al[Ian Moss]

Perfect alignment

to fix it and he said, 'What do you want me to do?' So one group said they'd be happy to come in with us and I agreed, so that's what we did.

Another said, 'We are not very tolerant of time wasting, of committees, or of bureaucracy around here'.

One ex-Lend Lease executive said, 'They're always changing, restructuring. It's a part of life. They are very quick to adapt'.

Woolworths, NAB, the Salvation Army and Harvey Norman mainly tend to evolve new business units with similar operations to their existing ones, so that new structure mainly emerges to manage the increasing number of (similar) units. Qantas and Telstra have been changing their structures rapidly, reflecting the changing orientations of their organisations since privatisation and the rapid changes in each of their markets. Having been global for over 11 years now, Rio Tinto is developing a fixed structure around global product lines. The other international/global organisations (Brambles and Westfield) are also developing more permanent structures. Brambles is based on products and Westfield on geographical areas.

In summary, the above variety of approaches suggests that no particular structure or pattern of structures is key to success. As we reported in chapter 1, structure is essentially a non-factor in terms of differentiating the practice of winning organisations. Structures evolve to align to changing needs, such as changing strategy. Most organisations spend far too much time worrying about structure. Focusing on people would be much more valuable.

Using communication to align the organisation

Most CEOs (and senior managers) say one of their main tasks is to communicate, communicate, communicate. Executives at all the winning organisations mentioned the importance of communication with each other and with their people in terms of aligning organisational activity and behaviour. Most felt more needed to be done. But they also felt that the amount of communication was never sufficient. Getting the senior leadership out among the people is seen as critical to facilitate the opportunities for communication.

Several have formal methods of doing this. For instance, Macquarie has its CEO present at every management development program and runs lunches and discussion groups throughout the year to promote two-way communication. When trying to develop the new culture at the newly merged Australian Airlines and Qantas, James Strong indicated in a letter to all the people how important he saw communication:

> There is one essential ingredient of management... and that is the best possible communications within the group... success stories have the common ingredient of investing a lot of time and resources in people, communicating both ways, training, involving and encouraging individuals to meet their maximum potential... (*The Australian Way*, December 1993)

Rio Tinto uses its own managers to 'teach' management development programs, rather than bringing in outside experts. It also has regular video or telephone conferences to overcome the tyranny of distance between the London head office and its global operations. And the CEO normally visits several sites when he is in Australia (and similarly elsewhere in the world).

Woolworths CEO Roger Corbett was famous for his unannounced visits to stores, a process that enabled him personally to keep in touch with the essence of the business and also to give direct information to people throughout the organisation. Dick Dusseldorp at Lend Lease was another who was famous for this type of direct communication, which is highly valued by those receiving it.

In summary, winning organisations see communication as important. They undertake a lot of activity to support that belief. But there are no specific or unique practices here that are widely practised.

Aligning perceptions

During our interviews, we noticed that all the interviewees presented virtually the same picture of the causes of success for the organisation and its history, despite their different backgrounds and work histories. In one or two cases, there was less than complete agreement. As pointed out earlier, this is as we would expect. Organisations do not do equally well all the time and views about them vary. Drawing on our experience of other organisations—where differences in perception are the norm rather than the exception—we felt confident when we heard similar perceptions from our interviewees (and held similar ones ourselves!).

Sharing a common understanding of the situation is essential if correct analysis and decision making is to follow. Having an external focus, bringing in external views, sharing these views and communicating frequently help to develop common perceptions. So

Perfect alignment

do hiring practices, providing training and management development experiences and the consistency of the actions that the organisation undertakes.

Alignment to what?

Having found that in winning organisations everything is aligned, what is it that they are all aligned to? What is it that drives alignment? Three possible contenders emerge (see figure 3.7):

▶ alignment to strategy
▶ alignment to culture
▶ alignment to leadership.

Figure 3.7: alignment to what?

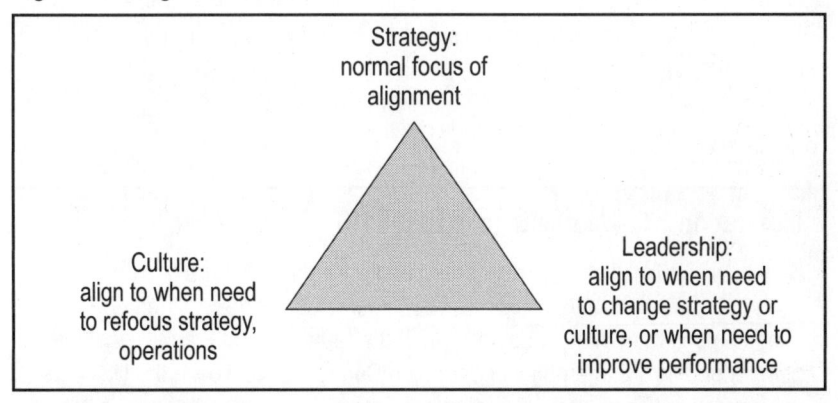

```
                    Strategy:
                    normal focus of
                    alignment

   Culture:                              Leadership:
   align to when need                    align to when need
   to refocus strategy,                  to change strategy or
   operations                            culture, or when need to
                                         improve performance
```

Each winning organisation is in a different position in its strategic cycle and its industry. Consequently, what specifically drives alignment at a particular time will vary for each organisation and circumstance. Emphasis on one aspect will, at least for the time, reduce the emphasis on the other two. However, since we seek to align everything, the issue of what we are aligning to is about timing differences, not conceptual differences. Everything needs to be aligned to achieve 'perfect alignment'!

Aligning to strategy?

Standard research suggests that alignment should normally be to the strategy of the organisation. We note from the original 7S model that the development of strategy is itself affected by the other Ss, so that the internal alignment of the Ss may determine or, at minimum, constrain strategy options and development.

What we find in the winning organisations is a consistency of strategy over time and, where there is change, an incremental change (see chapter 4). The strategy will change over time, for a variety of reasons:

▶ changes in external pressures and opportunities
▶ changes in leadership
▶ changes in the capabilities that the organisation develops
▶ changes in the values and culture that the organisation possesses
▶ changes in the people, systems, processes and structures of the organisation.

As the strategy changes over time, there is a need to realign the activities of the organisation if it is to deliver the new strategy. Illustration 3.5 shows how Westfield changed its strategy over time, requiring realignment. This idea of incrementally changing strategy is also captured in the strategic cycle. In this sense, alignment normally follows strategy.

Illustration 3.5: Westfield goes to the US

By the 1970s Westfield was concerned about the limited future growth potential of Australia. Westfield had been interested in entering the US shopping centre market for some time. John Saunders and Frank Lowy had been attending the International Shopping Centre Convention in the US since the late 1950s. They were interested in entering the US market, using a 'toe in the water' strategy.

In 1972, the Australian Government began to reduce currency regulations and restrictions, facilitating the development of international business from Australia. In 1976 Westfield bought Trumbull Shopping Park in Connecticut for $US21 million, beginning its development in the US. To support this development it established Westfield America Trust as a separate company to hold all the US assets and to gain funding in the US specifically for US assets. By 2006 it had increased from one to 59 shopping centres and was the biggest player in the US industry.

Aligning to culture?

Another possibility is that everything should be aligned to the culture of the organisation. This is essentially Collins and Porras'

Perfect alignment

argument — preserve the core ideology and stimulate progress in every other area of the organisation's activities. A former Lend Lease executive said:

> [Lend Lease] has a unique entrepreneurial culture that embraces challenge and innovation, that empowers people. The culture is the core of the company. It is the competitive advantage of the company.

The difficulty with this is that, periodically, the values of the organisation and the associated culture need to change. The obvious examples in the winning organisations are the originally government-owned organisations of Telstra and Qantas (see illustration 3.6 for some detail about Telstra's cultural change).

Illustration 3.6: cultural change at Telstra

Telstra's original strategy was very consistent for over 70 years — provide a phone for every home in Australia. But by around 1990, this strategy had been achieved. Coupled with this was the emerging deregulation of the industry and the proposed privatisation of the organisation.

What should Telstra have done? The high-quality engineering and technical standards that had been built up around providing phone connections were no longer of such high value.

The values and culture had to change from that of a government-owned monopoly, where people worked for life, to that of a commercially oriented, publicly listed organisation in one of the fastest-growing, newly deregulated, industries in the world. This explosive growth was also based on a dramatic change in product mix — from local fixed-line phone calls to global mobile communications.

In 2006, Telstra was again facing major cultural change. The arrival of a new external CEO, the rapid rise of internet penetration and application, the rapid development of digital technology in many areas of communications, the development of wireless technology, the high penetration of mobile phones and their increasing replacement of fixed-line phones threatened to obsolete the two bases on which Telstra had built its sustainable competitive advantage — its fixed-phone monopoly and its national cable network.

How well would your organisation have fared or be faring faced with these tremendous change in the fundamentals of the organisation and the environment it faced? How would you have approached the cultural change required?

So aligning everything to existing values and culture is problematic in changing environments. As values and culture are the hardest elements of an organisation to actually change, they will limit the change that is possible and certainly limit the speed of change. And inability to change speedily could consign an organisation to its deathbed if its industry faced some fundamental upheaval.

Aligning to leadership?

A third possibility, coming from the 'one great leader' theory of organisations, is that as CEOs change, strategy changes, so alignment should be to the CEO—the one great leader. Clearly, in practice, a new CEO can affect or change the organisation incrementally or dramatically, requiring significant changes to achieve realignment. John Stewart at NAB and Sol Trujillo at Telstra both seek to initiate major cultural changes to develop, in their views, higher performing organisations.

But organisations survive CEOs, and often the direction of the organisation is actually little changed by different CEOs, even when they appear to be proposing major change. And of course CEOs are themselves reacting to external changes, as well as following their own perceptions, preferences, values and styles.

We have already noted that one thing winning organisations are not about is the one great charismatic leader. Consequently, while many of the CEOs—and their leadership teams—over the long histories of these organisations have influenced their direction, very few have made such radical changes that the organisation is little recognised from what it was before. For instance, Qantas has had four CEOs over the last 20 years. Their main contributions have been:

- John Menadue—aligning the head office with operations; increasing the focus on Asian routes
- John Ward—presiding over the integration of Qantas (international only) and Australian Airlines (domestic only), which were in competing networks prior to the merger
- James Strong—making the integration work; developing common high service standards and a sense of commercial reality as Qantas became a listed company
- Geoff Dixon—focusing on commercial performance while preserving (relatively) high service standards; surviving a domestic airfare war; managing the consequences of September 11, 2001 and the collapse of Ansett; developing a low-cost airline business model in the face of horrendous global industry losses.

None of them actually changed the fundamental direction of the organisation substantially. Yet all faced significant challenges during their periods in office. Therefore, we do not think that it is really about aligning everything to the leadership. We see leadership as a catalyst and an influencer in the alignment process, but not the focus of the alignment.

To sum up, the underlying process is normally to align 'everything' to the strategy, recognising that the strategy will itself change over time. Being dynamic, however, alignment is constantly changing. Attempting to align everything to achieve perfect alignment is a formidable task. That so few organisations come close to achieving it suggests the size of this task is very great. Alignment—and the consistency that follows from it—needs more attention in management practice.

Alignment over time

So far we have been considering alignment of activities to the current or desired (short-term or medium-term) future position of the organisation. That is, we know what we are trying to do. What do we have to align to make it happen in the near future?

As we have seen, the winning organisations have grown and developed a long way from their original business. For people working in these organisations, the changes have indeed been significant. Growth and expansion have brought opportunities, but most of the organisations have also sold and/or closed businesses (and hence people have been transferred into other organisations, or lost their jobs). Some organisations have been involved in continual job reductions, in the pursuit of increased operational efficiency.

How is alignment managed over time and over a changing range of businesses and business situations? Our study shows that:

▶ Winning organisations are oriented to the external world. Consequently, they are more aware of the opportunities—and the threats—that exist. This enables them to prepare earlier and more carefully for contingencies. A focus on managing risk also helps.

▶ Adapting rapidly is one of the keys for winning organisations. Their ability to adapt rapidly to planned and unplanned changes is a key of their success.

▶ The ability to change—appropriately—over time is influenced by the choice of the CEO and the leadership team. Most of the organisations felt that the line of their CEO had been 'right for the time', even though the thrust of each CEO was actually different. This is consistent with the strategic cycle of development. Different stages in the cycle require different capabilities and different visions for the future, and new CEOs develop new strategies to meet those different visions.

▶ As winning organisations proceed overseas as part of their strategic cycle, the type of people they require in terms of capabilities, attitudes and often nationality is different. As winning organisations diversify their businesses, or focus them, the type of people and leaders needed also changes. Winning organisations are always developing their people, communicating with them about where the organisation is going and what will be needed, and providing them with opportunities for personal growth.

▶ Communication — formal and informal, written and oral — is vital. Managers often underestimate the intelligence and understanding of their people. People generally have a very good idea of the state of the business and what changes are being considered.

▶ Managers apply the 'no surprises' rule to their people, too. They try to keep their people as informed as possible, to give them the opportunity to change work practices if this is important, to adapt to a new environment if this is important. And if they must close down or sell businesses, they try to ensure that their ex-employees are well treated.

Winning organisations do not have magic formulas for realigning over time. There are many elements to be addressed. They are oriented early to external information, rapidly adjust, choose their leadership well, choose and manage their people well, and communicate widely and frequently.

Summary and key messages for leaders

Perfect alignment is a difficult concept to get your head around or your hands on, especially when 'everything' needs to be aligned. But alignment is necessary to 'execute to deliver results' efficiently and effectively. Perfect alignment is the ultimate achievement. It may not be

- p27 [28 ~~at the end of ch. the Sal. Army & Woolwich~~] makes the link between the business model, the culture & effective execution. What could this look like at WM?
  (& or does)

- p43 - Quote by Jack Welch; CEO of General Electric.
  "   " - What would this mean to Wesley mission?

Ch 3 - Perfect alignment
. The concept of perfect alignment is impossible - but strived for goal. What would pursuit of this goal mean to your area?

- p59 - Systems (operating, managerial, decision making and reward) are developed over time to become "accepted". Culturally, how are we developing our systems.

p79 - Summary - discuss!

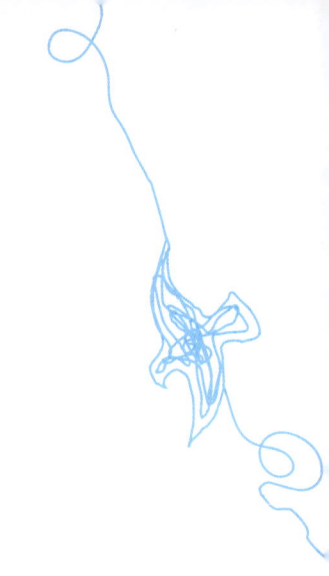

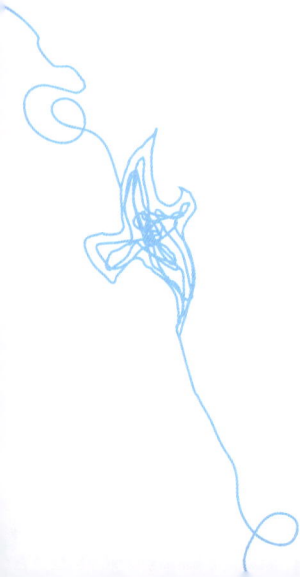

possible, but if you believe it is possible, you will get a lot further than if you accept the misalignments that your organisation has.

The key elements to align are strategy, culture, systems, people, leadership, structure, communications and perception. Alignment must be external as well as internal. Alignment should normally be to strategy, but the roles of culture and leadership are important at different times in driving alignment. Perfect alignment outcomes change over time, as changes occur in the external and internal environment.

The key messages from this chapter are:

▶ Everything must be aligned.

▶ Alignment must be to external forces as well as internal factors.

▶ Strategy should normally be the driver of alignment, but culture, values and leadership may be valid drivers themselves at times.

▶ Culture is the most difficult area to align, if change is required. Understanding the real culture is the starting point.

▶ Systems are crucial foundations. Decision-making systems and reward systems are underestimated in achieving perfect alignment.

▶ Aligning people is essential for delivering results.

▶ Leadership must be a major driver of the alignment process.

▶ No particular structural solution is best. Structure should be flexible enough to meet specific short-term needs. Much time is wasted on restructuring.

▶ Communication of messages throughout the organisation by leaders is an essential element of success.

▶ The role of aligning perceptions is often overlooked in alignment — not everyone sees things the same way and this must be addressed in aligning everything.

▶ In times of change, everything must be realigned to the new situation.

4 Adapt rapidly

Continuous improvement
Speedy innovation

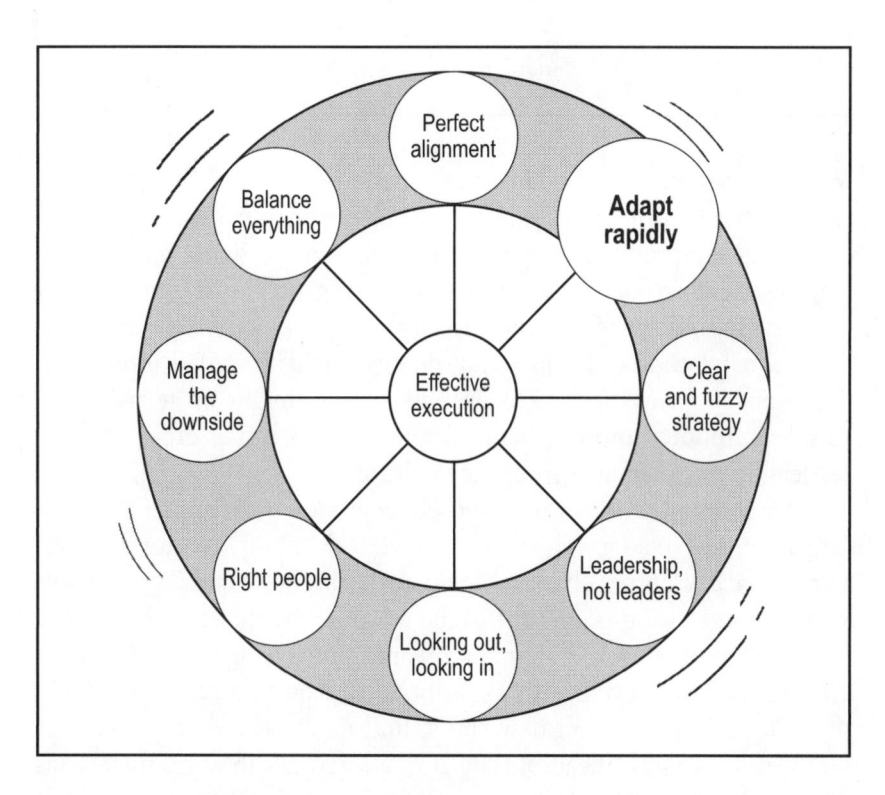

Closely related to 'perfect alignment' is our finding that winning organisations adapt rapidly. As mentioned in chapter 3, not only do they need to be aligned to be consistent, but they also have to be able to adapt over time — and then realign to become consistent again! But even more important than having this ability to adapt is being able to adapt *rapidly*, and at the same time maintain control over the organisation. Many organisations struggle with the ability to adapt, but that is exactly what these winning organisations are able to do — change quickly to meet new situations (see figure 4.1).

Figure 4.1: the process of adapting rapidly

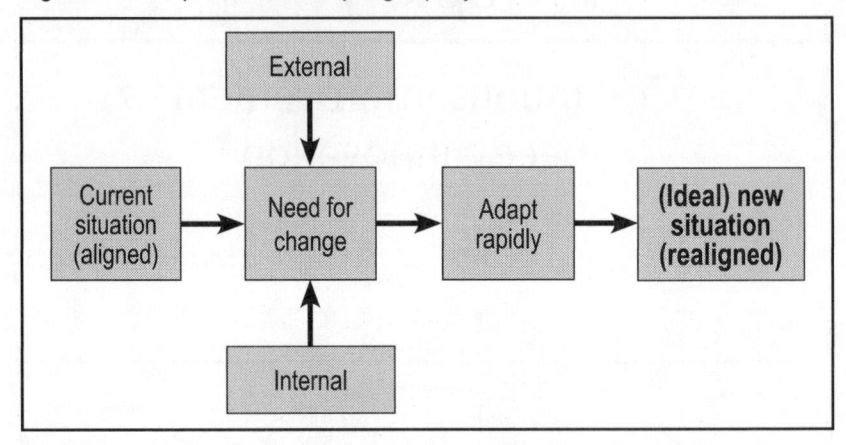

```
                    ┌──────────┐
                    │ External │
                    └────┬─────┘
                         ▼
┌──────────┐      ┌──────────┐      ┌─────────┐      ┌──────────────┐
│ Current  │      │ Need for │      │ Adapt   │      │ (Ideal) new  │
│ situation│ ───► │ change   │ ───► │ rapidly │ ───► │ situation    │
│ (aligned)│      │          │      │         │      │ (realigned)  │
└──────────┘      └────▲─────┘      └─────────┘      └──────────────┘
                       │
                    ┌──┴───────┐
                    │ Internal │
                    └──────────┘
```

What causes this rapid adaptation, or the need for it? Two concepts related to adapting rapidly kept coming up in our discussions and analysis — continuous improvement and innovation. Continuous improvement is related to changing existing processes, products or services. Innovation is perceived to be about developing new products, services or processes. Of course, any change might be termed 'innovative' while any improvement, whatever its source, might be termed part of a 'continuous improvement'. Both require people, creativity and leadership to create an appropriate culture.

We concluded that these two concepts were components of the larger concept of adapting rapidly. We view the ability to rapidly adapt to external or internal change, big or small, as a key capability for these winning organisations and one of the reasons why they are able to stay ahead of competitors. Rather than waiting for change to occur, First XI organisations develop the concepts that require other competitors to change. They develop new shots, find new ways to score, seek to be different, to stay ahead of the game. Sometimes they get their ideas from within and sometimes from observation of others overseas. But First XI organisations are always seeking to improve, to innovate, to be better, to lead the way.

In this chapter, we'll first focus on the idea of 'rapid'—what it is that enables winning organisations to be quick in changing. Then we'll look at what constitutes 'adapting'—the ways in which adapting takes place and what it is that enables or encourages winning organisations to rapidly adapt, and adapt, and adapt (see figure 4.2).

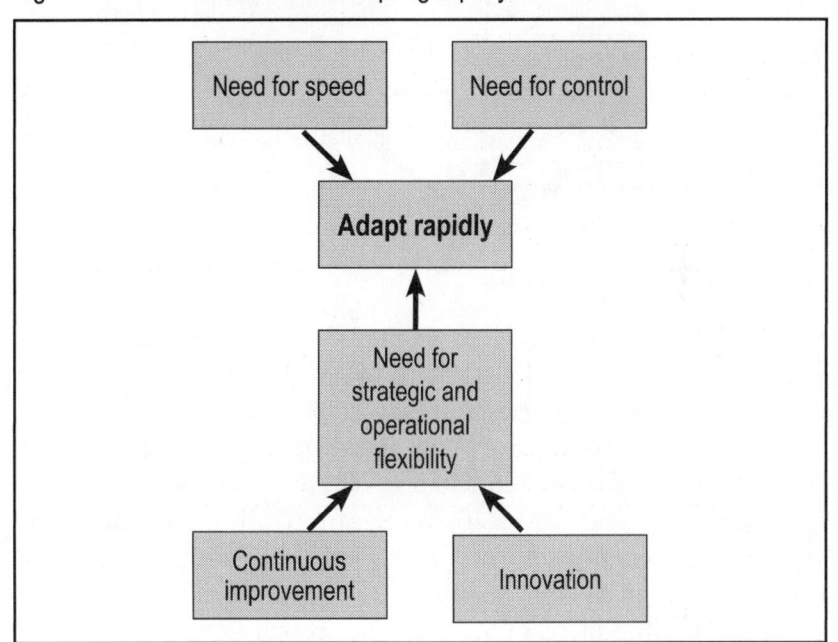

Figure 4.2: the factors behind adapting rapidly

```
   Need for speed        Need for control
              ↘         ↙
              Adapt rapidly
                   ↑
              Need for
              strategic and
              operational
              flexibility
              ↗         ↖
   Continuous            Innovation
   improvement
```

What is 'rapid'?

What does 'rapid' mean? We have said that a key aspect of the ability of winning organisations to adapt is the speed at which they can do it. Winning organisations have a sense of urgency in everything they do. Part of this is attitudinal—they simply *expect* that things can be done more quickly than in other organisations. Part of it is that they have a clear idea of what the organisation wants to do, both strategically and operationally. Part of it is organisational—they set themselves up to be able to do things quickly by having good systems, good people and good structures. Part of it is having the resources to be able to carry out what they want to do (see figure 4.3 overleaf). There's a lot to get right to be able to adapt rapidly!

Figure 4.3: factors enabling speed in adapting

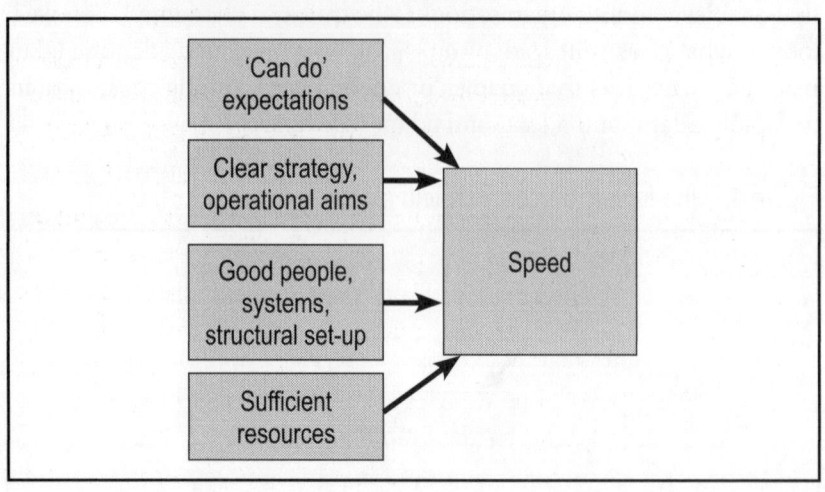

- 'Can do' expectations
- Clear strategy, operational aims
- Good people, systems, structural set-up
- Sufficient resources

→ Speed

Westfield provides an excellent example of speed. Its emphasis on speed comes from the founders of Westfield, John Saunders and Frank Lowy, who were described as 'hyperactive and in a hurry'. They expected to do things quickly and they had clear views of what they wanted to achieve. For instance, on their first trip to the US to investigate shopping centres, they would typically record the layout with both a camera and a notebook—and they even did the same thing with the motels they stayed in! (One of Westfield's first projects was the Shore Inn motel in Sydney.) They sought both to understand what existed and why, and also how the layout could be improved. In the evenings, Frank and John would discuss their findings and work out how they would improve the layout if they were in charge. Frank Lowy described his own attitude to speed:

> I have this force within that constantly drives me to improve, not necessarily for financial gain but for being able to do more...I can't sit around and do nothing. My mind just doesn't rest, whether it's five o'clock in the morning or midnight, I still give all I have to everything I do. (Margo, 2000, pp. 185–86)

> I drive myself and spare no effort. It is sheer slog that allows for no laziness of mind or body. I allow myself no latitude and give up all comforts, day and night, until I achieve the goal. (Margo, 2000, p. 254)

This approach pervades Westfield management. Commenting on the roles of his three sons, who became joint managing directors during the 1990s, Frank Lowy said:

> We eat, sleep and talk business. This is not an eight-hour-a-day commitment. We are at it 24 hours, on the weekend too. The business hovers over us constantly. (Margo, 2000, p. 264)

This constant involvement means that many more decisions can be made in the same chronological time period than in a normal organisation that only works eight to 10 hours a day, five days a week. Some of the non-executive directors commented on their experience of the results of this speed at Westfield:

> Each time we have a meeting there is a new deal on the table... These deals... are concrete, formidably researched and entirely reality-based. It's impressive. Carla Zampatti (*The Detailed Westfield Story*, p. 131)

> When I think of Westfield, I think of great activity. Rob Ferguson (*The Detailed Westfield Story*, p. 130)

> During my board membership there has never been a dull moment... Most of the centres have been upgraded or are in the process of doing so, and at the same time all options of further expansion are on the table. I sometimes have the feeling that we are playing soccer with more than one ball. Directors asked management many times if they could cope with this... management proved to be completely in control. Herman Huizinga (*The Detailed Westfield Story*, p. 139)

This intensity of activity leads to speed of decision making. The fact that Westfield does everything possible in-house also assists the speed of the total process. Illustration 4.1 (overleaf) provides an example of how this works for a major project.

Speed and control

Many organisations can do things quickly. They rush about in a state of chaos, and somehow the job gets done, but it is exhausting, costly, inefficient and often out of control. In winning organisations, speed comes with control too. For instance, Westfield used the critical path method to plan the development of its first shopping centre in 1966, and has been using this technique ever since to minimise development and redevelopment time. When Westfield is redeveloping its centres, it tries to minimise disruption to the trading time. Therefore, the construction shift starts at the end of the trading day. It continues throughout the night, clearing up before the start of the next trading day.

> **Illustration 4.1: how Westfield speeds up the development process**
>
> When Westfield buys a shopping centre, it does not begin to think about how improvements can be made. It has already worked out how it will improve the centre in great detail and embarks upon that improvement process as soon as possible after the centre is acquired. For instance, when it purchased the Garden State Plaza in New Jersey in 1986, it immediately embarked on a plan to increase mall space and attract upscale retailers to improve the quality of the centre. This was all done by its in-house development, design and construction team, enabling much quicker implementation than if outside contractors had been involved.
>
> A typical innovation was the conversion of a former truck tunnel under the property into a basement shopping level, resulting in 140 000 square feet of new space with 50 new specialist retailers.
>
> Upscale clothing retailer Nordstrom was targeted as an anchor tenant. Nordstrom had no locations in the north-east of the US at the time. Through intense personal lobbying and selling of the benefits to Nordstrom's owners, Nordstrom was encouraged to make a quick decision to take up the opportunity. The addition of Nordstrom provided the attraction for other upscale stores, including clothing company Neiman Marcus, and many other subsequent changes and expansions.
>
> By the end of the process (the plans were completed in 1989 but the improvement process continued until 1997) Garden State Plaza had become the dominant shopping centre in its area.

This focus on speed without losing control of operational detail is seen in other winning organisations. When Woolworths planned to open its first shopping complex in Newcastle in 1964, senior management feared a disaster due to lack of an anchor magnet store (Murray, 1999). These fears surfaced at a planning meeting only four months before opening. Following discussions after the meeting about what to do, a proposal to rectify the problem was on CEO Theo Kelly's desk by the following morning. By midday, Kelly indicated preliminary approval. A meeting was held the next day and the proposal—to develop Woolworth's own 'magnet' store—was approved. What should it be called? 'Big W' was suggested, based on a US idea called Big E. Kelly approved the name over the weekend and the centre opened on schedule—Big W was born.

Emergency relief services in Australia cater to unexpected and significant events that cannot be planned for. Speed and control are essential to meet each emergency. The Salvation Army is one of the best-placed organisations in the community to respond. It has a clear command structure that readily translates into an efficient field operation during an emergency and it is readily identified as an organisation that helps in times of need. The Salvation Army sees this capability as one of its services and plans for emergencies of all types.

Telstra and Qantas also have excellent reputations for assisting in emergencies. When community emergencies occur, despite no longer being the sole provider of telecommunications services in Australia, Telstra is still expected to be able to restore communications in minimum time. The fact that it is able to do this is due to the attitudes of its people—they feel a responsibility to the country to do whatever it takes to solve the emergency. One Telstra executive said:

> Telstra people rise to the needs of the community. There is a real empathy between Telstra workers and the community. There is an expectation that the 'mail will get through'. Telstra workers work really hard to overcome crises, but those stories never appear in the newspaper.

Qantas people have a similar view. Qantas has detailed contingency plans at all times to cope with unexpected maintenance needs, weather problems and missed connections, as well as with industry disasters. Margaret Jackson, chair of Qantas, commented on the calamitous industry events of September 2001:

> On Sunday September 9, Qantas was invited to buy Ansett for $1... On Tuesday, September 11 the terrorist attack on the US took place. The next day, Wednesday September 12, an administrator was appointed to Ansett. On Friday September 14, Ansett was grounded...
>
> Qantas embarked on a huge logistical exercise... We transferred 2600 anxious passengers to and from the US. We transferred 115 000 Ansett domestic passengers free or at a steep discount. We operated an additional 196 regional flights. We arranged for services to 22 regional destinations previously served only by Ansett...
>
> We managed well because we were managing well before. We had programs in place...
>
> But when the crisis hit we no longer had the luxury of long lead times for making decisions. Decisions that we might once have agonised over were made in two days. If they proved wrong, we made new ones.

> It was vital to keep staff and the community informed...Even with such intense communication...we had to let go and rely on each other...We had to trust our senior executives. (Jackson, 2002, p. 5)

Since 2001, Qantas has had several further needs to use this speed of adapting. The Bali bombings, rapid changes to international security processes, particularly in key US and UK markets, and cyclones are just a few of the events it has had to contend with since then. Illustration 4.2 is an excellent example, outlining how Qantas rapidly developed Jetstar to become the first low-cost airline successfully operated by a full-service traditional airline.

Illustration 4.2: Qantas goes low cost!

By 2003 the Australian airline industry had settled down after the 2001 collapse of Ansett. Qantas and Virgin Blue were developing a new two-airline competition, but this time Virgin Blue had 35 per cent lower costs than Qantas and was beginning to set pricing as it gained market share. Deciding it could not 'do nothing' and that its own cost structure could not match Virgin Blue's, it set up a task force to establish a low-cost airline.

Qantas had several firm principles, learnt from errors by other full-service airlines that had tried this approach:

- It had to have the lowest cost in every area of operations.
- It had to be as independent of Qantas as possible.
- The airline had to be 'complementary' to Qantas — that is, it should not compete with Qantas on routes.
- Pricing and routes would be determined at Group level, arbitrated by the CEO if necessary.

In less than 12 months, Jetstar was established, with costs lower than Virgin Blue. Though less profitable than Qantas, Jetstar has added to the Qantas Group's overall profitability by segmenting the market. It has replaced Qantas on a number of routes with low numbers of business travellers. It has increased the total market size and, in 2006, it had begun to expand internationally, testimony to its success. Not bad when no successful model existed in the world!

Flexibility: the ability to adapt

In order to adapt, an organisation must be prepared to change. How is it able to change? The winning organisations are committed to their strategy but show considerable flexibility within their aims. That is, they do not see flexibility as a virtue by itself, but as a capability to be used to achieve a particular end goal or position that is carefully thought out, or to take advantage of an opportunity that fits with the values of the organisation.

Flexibility within winning organisations is a consequence of both customer demands and internal expectations that the organisation will be able to meet those demands. Therefore, they force themselves to be flexible to achieve this. But what is 'flexibility'? How are winning organisations flexible? We see two types of flexibility—strategic and operational (see figure 4.4).

Figure 4.4: types of flexibility

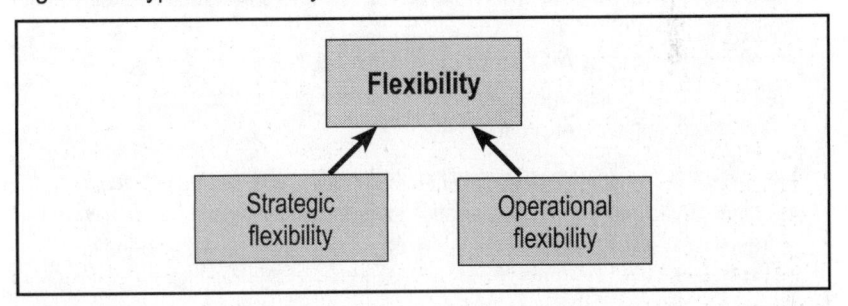

```
                    Flexibility
                   ↗         ↖
         Strategic          Operational
         flexibility         flexibility
```

Strategic flexibility

Of the two types, strategic flexibility is the more challenging issue. How can you be 'strategically flexible' when you have a clear strategy? The answer is 'over time'. Woolworths provides a good example (see illustration 4.3 overleaf).

For Macquarie, flexibility is a key element in the development of its strategy. The choice of products and services that Macquarie offers depends not on top-down planning of the senior management team, but on bottom-up, entrepreneurial efforts of Macquarie people. Before establishing Macquarie, co-founders Mark Johnson and David Clarke had worked for other merchant banks and had learnt what they did not like in the processes of merchant banking organisations. Their concept for overcoming these deficiencies—to hire bright people, empower them to use their ideas, reward them using a profit-sharing formula agreed to by shareholders, yet to be cheaper than international competitors, and maintain a very high ethical reputation and control risk centrally—did not specify any particular products or services. Hill Samuel (the original name of what is now Macquarie) searched for niches in Australian banking to begin its growth. Over time, it has covered so many niches that it now regards itself as a full-line investment bank in Australia, as well as in New Zealand and Asia, but it still regards itself as a niche player in the rest of the world, for the time being.

> **Illustration 4.3: never say never**
>
> During the early part of Woolworths' life, CEO Percy Christmas stated vehemently that the company would never enter food retailing as it knew nothing about food. Despite this statement, Woolworths did in fact sell very minor amounts of food in its variety stores.
>
> Then, in 1957, an 'egg war' broke out in Sydney as Woolworths imported cheaper eggs from Victoria into New South Wales. Despite bans put in place by the Transport Workers Union and the NSW Egg Board, Woolworths reached a compromise agreement that allowed it to sell cheap eggs, so long as it was with some other product!
>
> A Woolworths executive had recently visited the US and had recommended entry into supermarkets. The success in lowering egg prices substantially and the resulting publicity, coupled with this report, encouraged Woolworths to set up its first food supermarket in Sydney that year. The acquisition shortly after of 32 Brisbane Cash and Carry food stores from under the nose of arch-rival Coles signalled Woolworths' substantial entry into food. Woolworths came to dominate food retailing in Queensland and is now the dominant food retailer in Australia. In 2000, 85 per cent of its total sales came from food, a percentage that has continued to 2006!

One example of how this process of generating ideas works is shown in figure 4.5, a diagram of the way Macquarie moved from gold futures to agricultural commodities. One product Macquarie already offered was gold futures. Arbitraging of this product by Macquarie staff led to actual physical trading of gold becoming another business. This brought the company into contact with gold-producing companies. Macquarie discovered that these businesses wanted to sell gold forward over longer periods than were currently available, and so gold mine assessment and the financing of gold mines (against future production) became part of its activities. This led to the development of the derivatives business. This led to Macquarie thinking it could apply this model to other precious metals, such as silver. This led to Macquarie applying it to base metals as well, which resulted in the company conducting international business in these metals. This then led to a similar business in agricultural commodities. None of this was planned by the centre or the CEO, though each stage was approved centrally to control risk.

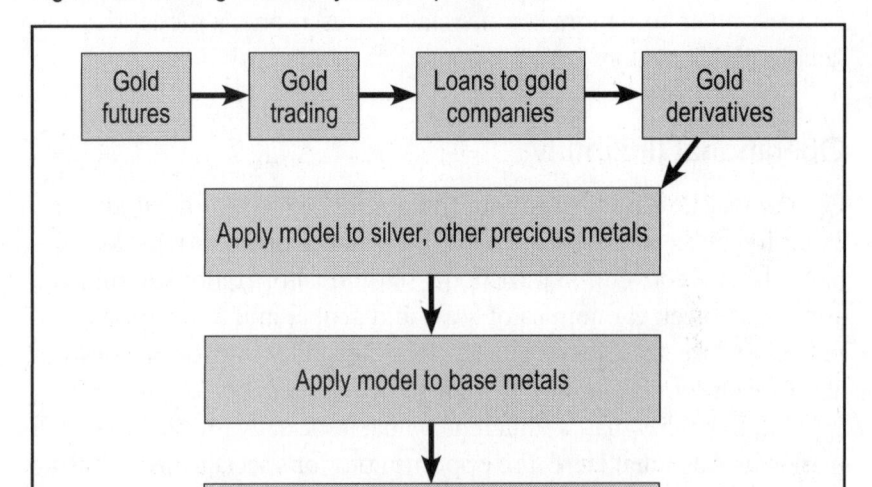

Figure 4.5: strategic flexibility at Macquarie Bank

```
Gold futures → Gold trading → Loans to gold companies → Gold derivatives
                                                              ↓
              Apply model to silver, other precious metals
                                  ↓
                    Apply model to base metals
                                  ↓
                Apply model to agricultural commodities
```

Macquarie is not limited to Australia in terms of its strategic flexibility. For instance, it entered the Korean market in 1996 as a coadviser to a Korean client in a cross-border leasing transaction—hardly a key area of its activities! Soon afterward, Macquarie began to establish joint ventures and alliances with top Korean financial institutions such as Shinhan Financial Group, Kookmin Bank and Woori Bank. In late 2002 Macquarie launched Korea's first private infrastructure fund, the Korea Road Infrastructure Fund, which was listed in March 2006 and renamed the Macquarie Korea Infrastructure Fund. In 2004 Macquarie Property Advisors Korea became the first asset manager wholly owned by a foreign investor to list a corporate restructuring REIT (CR-REIT) on the Korea Exchange. By 2006, after such a small start, Macquarie had developed a very broad range of business activities in Korea.

There are many other examples. Harvey Norman was long opposed to entry into computer retailing. Yet it changed its mind and now it has over 40 per cent of the personal computer retail market. Lend Lease decided funds management would be the key plank of its portfolio of businesses, using MLC as its vehicle. Yet, in 2000, Lend Lease changed its strategy to become a global real estate player. It sold MLC, which was focused on Australian general investment and accounted for around 50 per cent of its total profits, to NAB because it no longer fitted its new global strategy. The Salvation Army moved heavily into aged-care accommodation, but in 2005 it sold 15 of its 19 facilities (to a Macquarie investment fund) as it found the industry model was changing from a compassionate to a more commercially focused one, a model that did not suit the Salvation Army's strategic aims and capabilities.

Operational flexibility

Operational flexibility is a more traditional concept of flexibility and easier to appreciate. Yet its practice by winning organisations also flies in the face of conventional wisdom. Traditional operations-dominated approaches seek economies of scale and scope, and focus on a small product range to achieve efficiencies. Flexibility, however, does not allow maximum economies of scale to be pursued.

But flexibility has a different value, especially in such a small market as Australia. Here, the opportunities for specialising and using long runs or large volumes to take advantage of economies of scale are limited, so the very good organisations often developed through being able to do a lot of things well.

Lend Lease and Brambles both try to provide operational flexibility by customising their products and services to particular customer needs. Lend Lease also shares any savings that it makes on planned construction costs with its clients. This provides a significant incentive for both parties to look for different and innovative solutions to getting the job done.

Qantas continues to improve its operational flexibility, which has helped it come to dominate the local market over the last five to 10 years. With the merger of Qantas and Australian Airlines in 1993, Qantas—traditionally a long-haul international airline—began to operate short-haul domestic flights. The merged entity had a wide variety of different flight patterns, types of plane and types of people (both in terms of skills and desires). While this flies in the face of the concepts of focus and specialisation, it gave Qantas a very interesting—and highly valuable—degree of operating flexibility. When demand is very high on domestic routes, some capacity may be diverted from international routes and/or different plane types may be used so that, for the same landing slot, more passengers can be handled. For start-up international routes with low demand, some smaller planes from the short-haul operation can be used to test out commercial viability. The wider range of routes—and wider range of staff—also improves opportunities to progress for those who perform well. One of the reasons Qantas was able to handle the almost simultaneous domestic collapse of rival Ansett, and the collapse of international travel following the World Trade Center attacks in 2001, was its ability to rapidly divert capacity from international routes to meet the unexpected domestic demand.

Qantas was able to further increase its operational flexibility more recently through the acquisition of low-cost airline Impulse and the development of Jetstar, allowing it to alter its capacity mix as consumer demand for different types of flying changes over time.

The constant restructuring of organisations is another indicator of flexibility that we observed in the winning organisations. Restructuring is not seen by winning organisations as a strategic solution but as a short-term tactical response, taken in stride, to improve efficiency by being flexible. Telstra is constantly changing its divisional structure to reflect changes in the market as well as changes in its strategy and operational efficiencies (see table 4.1)

Table 4.1: Telstra's changing structure

	2001	2002	2003	2005
Divisions	• Domestic Retail • Applications and Content • Wholesale • International	• Domestic Retail • Networks and Technology • Wholesale • International • Country Wide • Mobile	• Consumer and Marketing • Business and Government • Infrastructure Services • International • Country Wide • Broadband and Media • Technology	• Consumer and Marketing • Wholesale • Infrastructure Services • Telstra Asia • Country Wide • Telstra Media • Technology • Sensis • Bigpond

Adapting by continuous improvement

Let's move from the 'rapid' to the 'adapting'. Adapting can be achieved by either continuous improvement or by innovation (see figure 4.6 overleaf). We see 'continuous improvement' as consisting of the vast array of small and continuous changes that an organisation makes to improve its performance. We see 'innovation' as significant new ideas introduced to the organisation. Let's look first at the role of continuous improvement in adaptation, as this is the less well-understood approach to creating value and delivering results.

Figure 4.6: continuous improvement and innovation give 'adapting'

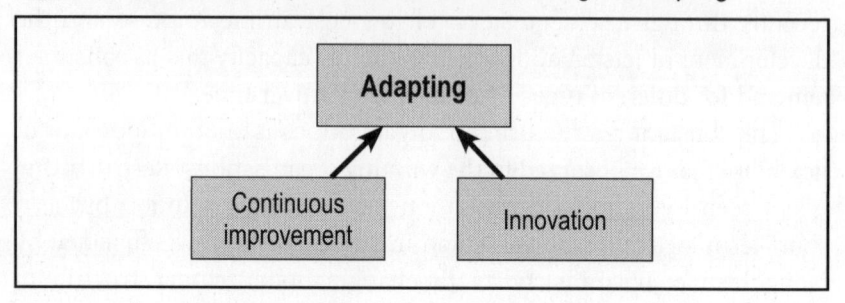

The history of continuous improvement

At one level, continuous improvement is simply a mantra. Of course, every organisation wants to 'improve' and do so constantly. Who can disagree with this statement of desire?

The origins of the term are mainly associated with the quality movement and its plan-do-check-act cycle (see figure 4.7). This technique of continuous improvement encourages organisations to consider that better results can be achieved by:

▶ 'Planning' before doing the event. What do we want to achieve? How are we going to do it?

▶ 'Doing' and getting some outcomes.

▶ After doing, 'checking' back against the plan. Was the outcome satisfactory? What do we need to do now to improve our performance?

▶ 'Acting', making any corrections considered necessary to achieve the expected results and to embed the new ways.

In this way, if action is unsatisfactory—that is, it does not meet targets or benchmarks—it can be reviewed before being repeated, with the aim of improving the outcome each time. When the target or benchmark is reached, it can then be raised to a higher level to continue the improvement process.

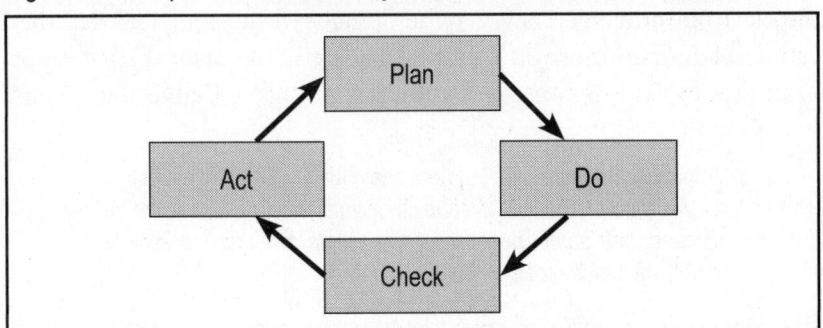

Figure 4.7: the plan-do-check-act cycle of continuous improvement

```
         Plan
    ↗         ↘
  Act           Do
    ↖         ↙
         Check
```

But in practice this cycle rarely happens in most organisations. While there is a lot of 'doing' and some 'planning', our experience is that there is not a lot of 'checking' done—there is little post implementation review and summarising of lessons learnt before doing it next time—and even more rarely are changes made before the next 'do' occurs.

Collins and Porras supported the importance of this concept when they identified 'good enough never is' as one of their elements for success. They said:

> Our research findings clearly support the concept of continuous improvement... it is an institutionalized habit—a disciplined way of life—ingrained into the fabric of the organization and reinforced by tangible mechanisms that create discontent with the status quo... visionary companies apply the concept of self-improvement in a much broader sense than just process improvement... it means doing *everything* possible to make the company stronger tomorrow than it is today. (p. 186)

Continuous improvement in winning organisations

Practice in winning organisations is different. All the phases of the plan-do-check-act cycle are important and they are executed. But there are some surprises. For instance, our research showed that winning organisations spend little time benchmarking against local direct competitors. They are too busy running their own races. When we raised the issue of competitors in our original interviews, we were surprised that interviewees had little to say and seemed relatively unaware of the details of their close competitors. What they were passionate about was their own performance and position against their own targets, goals and strategies.

Despite this lack of direct external comparison, they were quite critical of themselves. Winning organisations don't praise themselves greatly. They set quite demanding targets. That's one of the reasons why they keep improving! They may be doing well but they feel that they can do better and must do better if they are to maintain their position or improve it. This is consistent with the findings of Collins and Porras, who said:

> Visionary companies, we learned, attain their extraordinary position not so much because of superior insight or special 'secrets' of success, *but largely because of the simple fact that they are so terribly demanding of themselves.* (p. 186)

In many ways, winning organisations are concerned with creating their own future, not benchmarking against laggards. We did find more evidence of benchmarking in our recent research, but the focus is on best practice within the organisation, on international competitors or on best practice for a process from outside the industry. For instance, Rio Tinto's 'Improving Performance Together' program is designed to take best practice from within the group globally and apply it across all units. Brambles has a similar focus within each of its CHEP and Recall businesses. Qantas and Woolworths consider external global best practice in the industry. Illustration 4.4 shows how Woolworths used this approach for its 'Project Refresh'.

Illustration 4.4: achieving alignment with Project Refresh

In 2000, headed by Mike Luscombe (who was subsequently appointed CEO), Woolworths began Project Refresh, a play on its 'fresh food people' campaign of the late 1980s. The aim was to look at every activity the supermarket business performed and to consider how to 'refresh' it to get the best outcomes possible.

Project Refresh had four stages. At the first stage Woolworths reorganised from a state to a national structure, thus aligning its structure, strategy and operations. At the second stage it considered how to make the business lean and efficient internally. This required myriad incremental changes to be made, all of which contributed to an almost 10 per cent saving in the cost of doing business in three years.

At the third stage Woolworths looked outside its store operations and considered its whole supply chain. It reorganised into a small number of large distribution centres (reducing the number of centres from 30 to nine—two national distribution centres for slow-moving products and seven regional centres for fast-moving products). Each distribution centre cost $150 million to $250 million to build and the 3000 people who worked in them had their jobs moved, but only three people were retrenched. This required changes

> to suppliers (from local to national) and their practices (many suppliers had delivered direct to stores but were now required to deliver—more frequently and in different packing configurations—to distribution centres), as well as changes to Woolworths own distribution practices. This stage was completed in 2006.
>
> At the fourth stage, it developed world-class information technology to support both the changes in supply chain management and also in internal store operations. Targeting Wal-Mart and Tesco as world best in retail information technology, Woolworths found that both used Inform technology, which is based on a very old technology platform. It took new I2 technology, which had not been successfully run before, and customised it in-house. Woolworths had up to 500 people working on developing this technology and in 2006 had around 70 operating projects under way. Woolworths believes this project has developed significant intellectual property for the organisation and also that it is a world leader in this area.
>
> Since 1999, Woolworths has reduced its cost of doing business from 24.4 per cent of sales to 20.5 per cent of sales in 2006, achieving cumulative cost savings from the project of $5 billion! It now plans to apply the technology to the other parts of the business and expects to achieve cumulative savings of $8 billion from the project. Not bad for a project that began with the aim of saving $100 million!
>
> Asked in 2006 what the 'magic' of Project Refresh was, CEO Roger Corbett said, 'It's not magic. It's a mindset'.

The focus of winning organisations is on their future and the future of their industry, and how they can maintain or improve their position in it. They are ahead of the game. They define the rules of the game. By being leaders, and maintaining focus on real continuous improvement, these organisations are hard to catch.

How do winning organisations continuously improve?

So how do these organisations continuously improve to meet and exceed the changing expectations of customers? Figure 4.8 (overleaf) outlines the key internal factors that our study found. They are:

- ▶ having a culture of change
- ▶ focusing on the customer
- ▶ being dissatisfied with their own performance
- ▶ having growth as a driver

The First XI

- having a clear view of a desirable future position
- having good people
- having good systems
- having a cost focus
- planning for continual upgrading.

Figure 4.8: internal drivers of continuous improvement

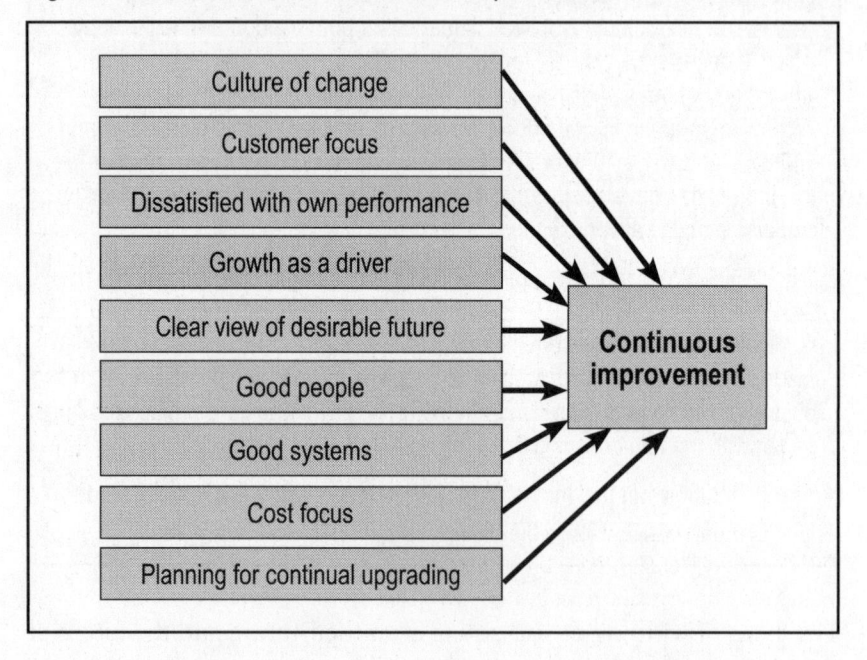

[Diagram: boxes labelled "Culture of change", "Customer focus", "Dissatisfied with own performance", "Growth as a driver", "Clear view of desirable future", "Good people", "Good systems", "Cost focus", "Planning for continual upgrading" all pointing with arrows to "Continuous improvement"]

At its best, continuous improvement is a significant element of the organisation's culture. In such a culture—a culture of change and dissatisfaction with the current situation, however good it may seem to outsiders—people continue to seek new ways of operating. New opportunities are continually spotted in such a culture. No sooner is one idea implemented than another is underway (in practice there are many ideas in various stages of implementation simultaneously).

Westfield created a new area in the centre court of its shopping centre at Tuggerah, ACT, when it introduced a 'lifestyle' section instead of a 'fashion' area. It was so successful that Westfield took it to the Marion centre in Adelaide and extended it so that it became the best in the country. The concept was next taken to Southland in Melbourne where, with more improvements, it was called 'The Street'. After further refinements it was taken to Carousel in Perth, then Burwood, Sydney. Said one executive, 'We watch, we monitor and we anticipate where change is coming from. From this and from constantly talking to retailers, we keep our competitive edge'.

Others confirmed this Westfield approach and the need to focus on the changing needs of customers. One said:

> Retailers have to adapt or die. It's that simple. And the mall industry is like that too ... 20 years ago there were no sporting shoe shops, no junk jewellery shows, no phone shops, no food courts, no cinemas, no restaurants, no pubs in malls. The pace of change might seem gradual, but it is really rapid. Trading hours are changing. The mall is becoming a quasi-community centre. You have to listen to the market and the community.

Having growth as a driver also creates the need for continuous improvement. For instance, in 1984 Brambles held a planning workshop in Manly. After two days of discussion, little had been achieved. After dinner that night, one executive said that if they were any good as a management team and an organisation, they should be able to add $100 million profit in five years. At that time, profit was $30 million. The challenge was taken up by those at the table and the 'Manly Manifesto', as it became known, was drawn up on paper napkins, identifying intentions, capabilities, financial objectives and possible acquisitions. Next day the plan was hammered into shape with clear details. CEO Gary Pemberton said:

> It doesn't sound like a big deal but it has a very dramatic effect on people to go to the end and work back. It changes the perception of what is possible, it forces people to think about big things, not about the little things. (Carew, 2000, p. 146)

The plan was achieved by 1989, as per the challenge.

Having a clear view of the desired future is similar to having growth as a driver. Qantas' 'Sustainable Future' program focuses its people's views on the need for constant change and improvement if Qantas is to survive in an industry that has collectively failed to make economic returns for many years, a situation that is itself not sustainable.

Good people and good systems are other key components of continuous improvement. Macquarie, which has growth as a driver, hires good people and heavily incentivises them to seek that growth. Interestingly, in both Macquarie and Brambles, the growth target is largely a consolidation of bottom-up business level plans rather than a centrally determined target. This suggests again how powerful the combination of good people and good systems can be.

Another way to continuously improve is to focus on cost control. This is quite a different emphasis but it can be equally effective. Being tight with costs can force organisations to look for new ways to decrease their costs or improve their productivity. Woolworths, for example, is a technology leader in its industry and seeks to achieve cost efficiencies by using the latest technology in the key areas of its business. In the 1920s, it was the first store in the world to acquire receipt-printing machines. In the 1950s, it had the largest punched-card stock control operation in the world. In the 1960s, it was one of the first in Australia to adopt computers and one of the first to adapt them to its broader needs rather than simply mechanising the accounting system. In the 1980s, it was a leader in the use of scanning technology. In the 1990s and 2000s, it has become a leader in cost control through its Project Refresh focus on supply chain management efficiencies.

NAB became the national cost leader in its industry through the use of technology (with the slogan 'simplify, standardise, automate'), large amounts of training and rigorous measurement. Operational improvements made in one area of its business are moved to another business. Its lack of investment in these systems in the early 2000s meant that NAB lost this advantage—something it is now redressing under its new management team.

Qantas has spent much of the last 10 years focusing on cost control, to improve its commercial returns. In the early 1990s, Qantas set up 20 continuous improvement teams to establish world-best practice in engineering and maintenance. Yield improvements, working with Boeing to achieve 'industry leader' status in engineering and maintenance, improving scheduling techniques and developing Jetstar as a low-cost airline are some of the means it has used.

Planning for continual upgrading is another valuable way to continuously improve. Westfield never rests in regard to improving its shopping centres, with around 20 per cent under redevelopment at any one time. It believes that each centre has a life of only seven to 10 years before needing upgrading.

Adapting by innovation

Adapting is not just continually improving what already exists. The second approach to achieving successful adaptation is via innovation. Winning organisations are innovative. However, in Australia this innovation is not generally big bang/big idea innovation. This finding is consistent with earlier research findings about innovation in Australian business by Carnegie et al. (1993), who undertook a major study of leading innovators in Australia and another recent study by the Business Council of Australia (2006). Illustration 4.5 summarises their findings on innovation and compares them with ours.

> **Illustration 4.5: innovation in Australia**
>
> Carnegie et al. (1993) defined innovation very broadly as 'something that is new or improved done by an enterprise to create significantly added value either directly for the enterprise or indirectly for its customers' (p. 3). In our study, this would cover both continuous improvement and innovation.
>
> The work was based on a largely qualitative study of 120 businesses of leading innovators. They classified innovation into the following types:
> - creating better processes
> - providing new and improved products and services
> - combined process and product innovation
> - technological breakthroughs
> - market-driven continuous product and service improvement
> - across the board improvement.
>
> The key findings were:
> - 90 per cent of innovation is the result of incremental improvement
> - five major themes are important for innovation:
>   - focusing on customers
>   - building a competitive supply system
>   - sustaining innovative leadership
>   - building a systematic approach to innovation
>   - committing scarce resources to competition.
>
> Good leadership, good management and good employee relations need to be in place to have an innovative culture. Our research did not find much in the way of 'technological breakthroughs' and we treat the last two categories as 'continuous improvement' rather than 'innovation'.
>
> The Business Council of Australia (2006) studied 19 cases from its member companies. Its major conclusions were:
> - there are widely different views of what organisations consider to be 'innovation'
> - innovative activity extends across all parts of a business and is not limited to conventional research and development

> **Illustration 4.5 *(cont'd)*: innovation in Australia**
>
> - the drive for customer value determines the need for and nature of innovation for an organisation
> - in many cases, innovation is more to do with human capital and organisational processes than with technology or invention
> - cultivating a supportive innovative culture is a key to generating and exploiting innovative ideas.

We categorise innovation in winning organisations into the following types (see figure 4.9):

▶ borrowing ideas from overseas

▶ process innovations

▶ product and service innovations.

Figure 4.9: sources of innovation for winning organisations

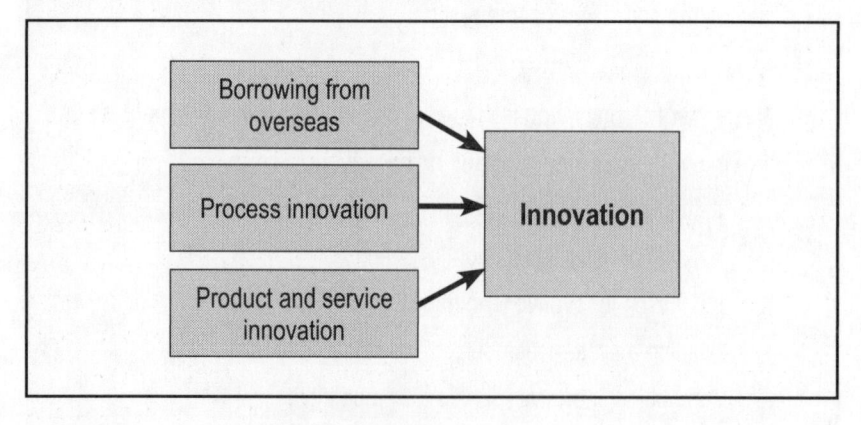

```
Borrowing from overseas ─┐
Process innovation ──────┼──▶ Innovation
Product and service      │
innovation ──────────────┘
```

Borrowing ideas from overseas

A classic approach to 'innovation' in Australia is to find an idea overseas, to copy it and to offer it in Australia. Several of the winning organisations used this approach to get started. The original ideas that started Woolworths (cheap variety stores) and Westfield (mall shopping centres) as corporations came from overseas. The Salvation Army (church and welfare), Rio Tinto (mining) and Macquarie (investment banking) all began as subsidiaries of overseas organisations. Dick Dusseldorp came to Australia as a representative of a Dutch construction firm looking for opportunities. He found construction opportunities, stayed and Lend Lease began.

The first Woolworths shop in Sydney was based on Cash and Carry, a business run by three of the founders (Ernest Williams, Percy Hall and Charles Humble) in Adelaide. But Hall had worked for FW Woolworth in the US and the UK. Woolworth was a 'five and ten cents' store—a discount variety store—which had 1000 stores in the US by 1919. In searching for a name, they found that Woolworths was not registered in New South Wales so, since that best represented the type of business they sought to offer, they registered it and began business.

Most organisations continue to look at developments overseas, particularly, it seems, in the US. For instance the 'wheelie bins' now in common use for rubbish collection in Australia were discovered by Gary Pemberton in the US in the early 1970s (Carew, 2000). Pemberton was impressed by the one-person trucks that operated the system so he bought three and shipped them to Australia. The bins were first introduced into industrial waste collections, as Brambles foresaw industrial relations problems if they were used in domestic waste first.

Another example is Woolworths, which modelled Big W on Wal-Mart (its rivals have competing Kmart and Target stores, which are also modelled on their US originators!), spending some 12 years to perfect the 'everyday low price' logistical and merchandising system in Australia. Woolworths' entry into petrol retailing was also copied from European supermarket chain practice, though it appears 'innovative' in Australia. Qantas' Jetstar development is based on several years of low-cost airline practice in both the US and Europe. Harvey Norman's discount retailing of computers is similarly based on US examples.

Why is borrowing from overseas so important as a source of innovation? While our study did not address this issue, we speculate that the small market size of Australia, the fragmented nature of the state-based market, the consequent lack of local research and development activity, and the derivative and import-based nature of the society and business (Australia has been heavily dependent on its links with first the UK, then the US, then Japan and now China) are key drivers of this approach to 'innovation'. While there are many great Australian innovations, few organisations seem to develop in Australia by commercialising those innovations, which are often sold or licensed to overseas organisations to become commercially successful.

Process innovations

Several important innovations for winning organisations came through process, rather than the more conventionally understood and expected area of products and services. Process innovation was addressed by Carnegie et al. and the Business Council of Australia as one of the major sources of Australian innovation, so our findings are consistent with those.

The co-founders of Harvey Norman—Gerry Harvey and Ian Norman—had previously owned and run Norman Ross—a precursor discount retail chain—from 1961 to 1982. This had been enormously successful in New South Wales and Queensland until it was acquired by Waltons Bond, a subsidiary of the diversified conglomerate Bond Corporation, and both Harvey and Norman were sacked. As no non-compete clause had been inserted in the takeover documentation, they established Harvey Norman in the same year to compete in the same line of business.

However, they made one crucial change to the formula. They believed that the future of 'big ticket' retailing lay in smaller owner-operated stores, where the owner's expertise and dedication to personal service would be backed up by the financial muscle, buying power and management services ability of a larger organisation. The system they established has several unique features:

▶ franchisees are personally chosen

▶ each franchisee is limited to owning only one franchise

▶ people are not charged a franchise fee to join the franchise

▶ as part of the franchise agreement, franchisees provide information to the franchisor, enabling Harvey Norman to centrally monitor individual and total franchise performance, including sales, cash, profit, sales mix and stock levels, thus enabling Harvey Norman to reduce the chance that franchisees get into financial difficulties

▶ Harvey Norman retains the right to withdraw franchises should they not comply with the franchise agreement requirements

▶ Harvey Norman can reallocate a franchisee from one franchise to another at its discretion.

Harvey Norman has come to dominate its field and its innovative system has not yet been replicated! In 1982, it opened the first complex in

Sydney with seven franchises—hardware, furniture, bedding, electrical appliances, kitchen and bathroom renovations, and carpets. By 1988, when it listed, Harvey Norman had 12 complexes, and in 2006 had over 200 stores. Further, it had diversified by acquisition into other areas of retailing, such as sports stores, where it was applying similar principles.

Lend Lease and Macquarie similarly apply the principle of financial incentives to get people to see themselves as running little businesses within a large company framework, but they do not use the franchising concept. Lend Lease provides very high levels of welfare support for its high-quality people and has high-quality and customised large-scale construction projects. It sees itself as developing a 'community of interest' of stakeholders (see illustration 4.6).

Illustration 4.6: process innovation—Lend Lease's 'community of interest'

From its beginnings, Lend Lease has had a philosophy of a 'community of interests'—balancing the interests of its people, clients, suppliers, shareholders and the community. This is quite a different perspective to that of a financially oriented organisation.

In terms of looking after its people, some of the examples of Lend Lease's original innovative practices were that it:

- hired the best people

- offered shares to employees so that by 1981 employees were the largest shareholding group with 17 per cent of total shares

- initiated a Building Trades productivity agreement in 1958, updated it in 1973 and established the ACTU/Lend Lease Foundation to develop training skills in 1983

- introduced profit sharing in 1973, raising this to 5 per cent of pre-tax profit in 1981

- introduced a company-paid employee health plan for all Australian employees and their families in 1980

- introduced disability insurance cover for subcontractors in 1982.

Rio Tinto works in a commodity business. As such, it has very limited opportunities to develop new products or services. So its focus on innovation is also process-oriented. Rio Tinto's approach to management systems is unique (see illustration 4.7), though it is being applied at Telstra and some other major Australian organisations.

> **Illustration 4.7: process innovation—formalising the roles and responsibilities of management**
>
> Frustrated with high levels of industrial disputation, in the early 1980s, CRA/Rio Tinto's Tom Barlow recommended the work of Canadian academic Elliott Jaques to CEO Rod Carnegie, who was concerned about improving the financial performance of the organisation.
>
> Jaques believed that the work of managers is to get their people to deliver the goals of the organisation. To do this, Jaques believes that getting the roles, accountabilities and structures right is critical. An effective structure makes clear who the manager is, what the manager is accountable for and who judges performance.
>
> According to Jaques there are seven levels of work, each with a different time span of discretion—that is, the time before a decision can be determined to be correct or not. The longer the time span of discretion, the more important the job. Job levels should be determined by time span of discretion. A person at one job level should manage people at lower levels. Each manager should judge the performance of their subordinates and, in turn, be judged by their manager.
>
> CRA introduced this radical process of rigidly defining and practising the roles and responsibilities of management at the Woodlawn mine in 1984. When this pilot experiment was successful, the process was moved to other mines on a unit-by-unit basis, managed by the head office Organisation Development Unit, and accompanied by heavy amounts of staff training and development. At one location, the levels of management were reduced from 14 to five.
>
> As a result of the rigorous application of the Jaques organisation development process throughout the group, substantial improvements in efficiency, quality of work and people relationships were made. While the principles sound relatively simple, applying the principles to work roles is difficult and tends to upset existing embedded organisation processes that have simply grown up over the years.

Rio Tinto has many other process innovations to its credit. Indeed, process innovation at its first mine at Broken Hill in 1905 enabled the company to commercially produce zinc when existing processes did not work. Currently it is working on three major innovations. They are:

- ▶ the Mine of 2020, which is intended to be an environmentally sustainable mine

- the HIsmelt iron ore smelting process, which was in development for over 20 years and which reached commercial plant status in 2005
- block caving, a relatively new process for developing the deep underground mines that are expected to become increasingly important in the mining industry's future.

These projects indicate the commitment necessary for research and development in this industry, which operates on extremely long time scales from discovery to mine development to full production. How many other Australian organisations would even be prepared to invest in this type of research with such long time scales?

Product and service innovation

The third area of innovation—products and services—is the most traditional perception of what innovation is. But the examples of winning organisations are of incremental innovation rather than fundamental innovation, consistent with the findings of Carnegie et al. and the BCA. Brambles has been the most successful of the winning organisations in using product and service innovations (see illustration 4.8 overleaf).

Lend Lease was the first company to turn the financing of its real estate assets into a property trust financial product. The innovation here was that the risk in construction and the risk in managing an existing asset are quite different. Capital can be raised more cheaply for the lower risk management of existing assets.

By separating the assets—creating General Property Trust (GPT) as a vehicle for managing property and selling the assets into GPT when they were constructed—Lend Lease was able to develop two related businesses with different costs of capital. Westfield followed this example a little later with the formation of Westfield Property Trust and then Westfield America Trust for its US assets. However, in 2004, Westfield reversed this decision and integrated all the activities into one Westfield Group company. It argued that this was necessary to gain economies of scope for financing the increasingly large-scale developments it sought.

Westfield provides another interesting example of incremental product and service innovation. While the original idea of modern shopping malls came from the US, Westfield has been constantly experimenting with the 'product' in Australia and has exported the concept of 'branding' the centre back to the US! In Australia, going to 'Westfield' has become synonymous with going shopping for retail customers. Using common signage, cross-marketing in newspaper, television and radio advertisements, clustering of centres in areas, making centres more social than competitor centres and using the continual-improvement process to transfer learning from one centre to another rapidly have enabled Westfield to build its brand in the US, where it now has more centres than it does in Australia.

> **Illustration 4.8: product and service innovation at Brambles**
>
> Brambles' international developments and extensions of the CHEP pallet system, Cleanaway waste management and Recall records management all represent products that, though they existed, have been taken to extraordinary levels by Brambles.
>
> The humble CHEP pallet—a wooden pallet used to enable goods to be lifted and transported more easily—was introduced to Australia by US ships in 1943 when forklift trucks and pallets started to be used to unload ships instead of manual labour. The Australian Government developed a pool of pallets and forklift trucks during the war to speed up ship movements. In 1946 the committee was renamed the Commonwealth Handling Equipment Pool (CHEP) and became a trading organisation. In 1958 the government decided to sell CHEP and Brambles was part of the successful consortium, buying out its partners' interests shortly after. Brambles' development of a national pool of pallets, its control and guarantee of supply of the pallets, its development of a variety of pallets for different product types and its market expansion of this pallet system throughout Europe, North America and now parts of Asia all represent product and service innovation to particular markets.
>
> Brambles saw waste management as an extension of materials handling and transportation. In 1970 Brambles bought Purle Waste Disposals for $120 000. Purle was part of the UK Purle group, which was the recognised world leader in waste management. The Brambles self-styled 'garbos' group, which became Cleanaway, had begun. Brambles' development of a wide variety of binning systems and collection systems, and its application of these ideas to different markets, are further examples of product and service innovation. Future CEOs Gary Pemberton and John Fletcher both came to prominence through this group.
>
> Finally, when Brambles acquired Grace Bros Removals in 1983, it included box storage facilities. In 1991 Brambles bought the Vault Company in the US and several subsequent US acquisitions led to the development of Brambles' third major business—Recall records management—where a similar approach is being followed for both hard copy and electronic storage of records.

The Salvation Army is a good example of an organisation that sees the problem the customer faces and comes up with innovative solutions. For instance, its 'Employment 2000' initiative was piloted in Perth in 1983! Research showed that employers of unqualified and low-skilled labour were primarily looking for people with positive work attitudes, while the long-term unemployed felt worthless, powerless and lacking in self-confidence. Employment 2000 trained disadvantaged people and aimed to place them in full-time employment. It had very high placement and success ratios. In 2003, it became Employment Plus and a major part of the new, outsourced, government unemployment arrangements (Employment Plus is the number one national provider in the industry) and a major business for the Salvation Army.

Similarly, in 2004, as part of the South Australian Bridge Program, the Salvation Army developed a Problem Gambling Unit, recognising a new problem area that had arisen from the widespread development of and easy access to gambling activities.

Woolworths has primarily innovated by expanding its product and service range incrementally, with innovation of new products and services being more evident since the late 1990s. The most dramatic event that occurred was when Woolworths was doing quite poorly in the mid 1980s. It decided to focus on fresh food as a point of differentiation from arch-rival Coles. Since adopting the slogan, 'The Fresh Food People' in 1987, Woolworths has grown rapidly in a mature industry. Innovations for Woolworths have included:

▶ expansions into petrol retailing
▶ a banking alliance with the Commonwealth Bank (replaced with ANZ in 2005)
▶ an entry into wholesaling to independent competitor supermarkets and convenience store chains
▶ expansion into national liquor retailing
▶ expansion of Dick Smith Electronics into superstore formats
▶ development of the Crazy Prices discount chain (since sold)
▶ development of Metro small-shop format shopping centres.

Each of these organisation examples represents incremental product or service innovation, but the application of that product or service to areas/services/industries well beyond its initial scope has made these innovations of great significance to each organisation. Importantly, little of this is the result of fundamental research, or highly detailed market research or research and development programs. It is primarily based on an interesting formula:

- motivated, capable people, with the right attitude for the organisation's values and with credible expectations about future rewards
- seeing a problem from the customer's perspective
- applying some creative thinking
- large amounts of determination and effort
- a supportive, but not munificent, organisation (rewards are based on outcomes)
- leveraging a concept into other geographies and industries.

Of these requirements, the only one in short supply in the community is likely to be the supportive organisation. All the others are widely available but rarely combined to get the results that winning organisations achieve.

Summary and key messages for leaders

Winning organisations adapt rapidly and continuously over time. The 'rapid' part is based on attitudes, clear strategy, good organisational systems, people and structures. Speed with control is required. The 'adapting' part is based on the flexibility to respond. Both strategic and operational flexibility are needed to allow and encourage continuous improvement and innovation.

The key messages for leaders from this chapter are:

- Seek to change and adapt to new circumstances.
- Seek to adapt rapidly and continuously.
- Provide the supporting mechanisms of clear aims, good people, systems and resources to enable adapting to happen quickly.
- Speedy actions and responses must come with control.
- Some flexibility of strategy is required over time.
- Develop a culture of continuous improvement.

① Balanced scorecard → 4 financial performance.

② 3 of 14 coys were eliminated. Following in-depth discussion. Perception ≠ reality. Where does WM sit? (eg, reverse)?

③ P10, what are the challenges to building a long term winning org?

④ What do you think about the 8 myths - or p 10-14
   (detail each)

⑤ Of the 9 elements of a winning organization why (do you think) that effective execution is at the centre eg, over strategy, alignment, etc

⑥ In what ways does WM demonstrate these principles?

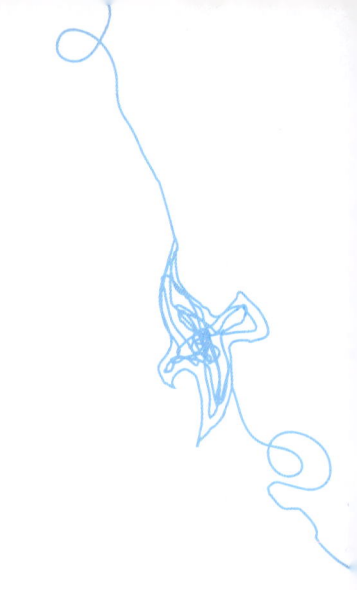

- ▶ Seek innovation in process as well as in products and services.
- ▶ Seek innovations from overseas sources, as well as through local research and development.

5 Clear and fuzzy strategy

Consistent articulation over time
Flexible at the margin

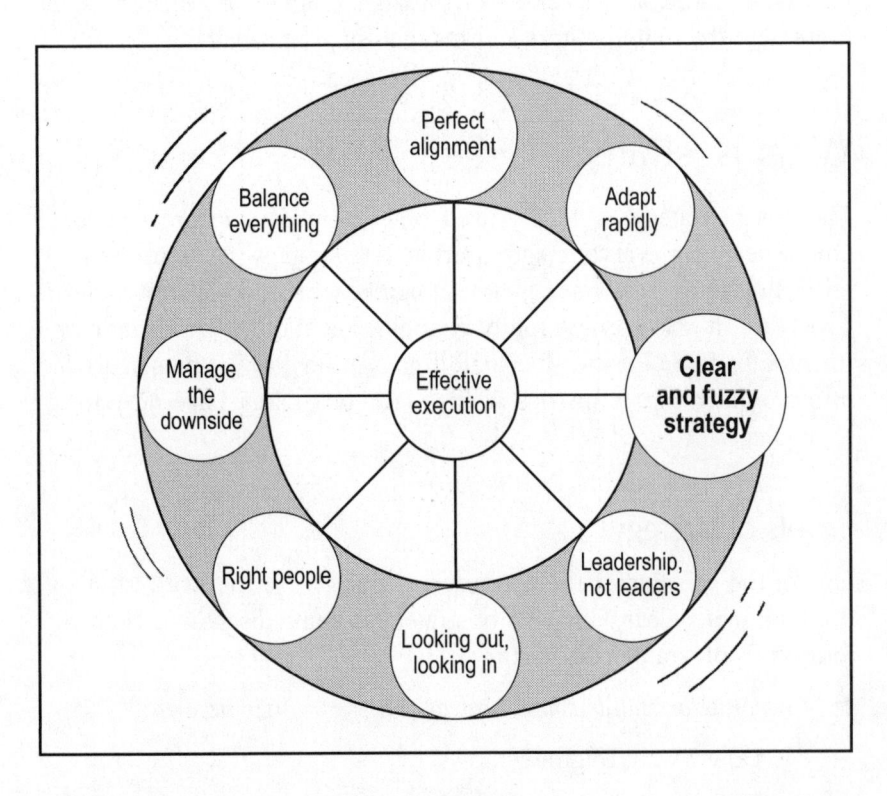

Everyone knows that strategy is important, so what's different for winning organisations? Unfortunately, while many people think that 'strategy' is important—and it is—the concept of 'strategy' is not well understood. So the first issue we need to understand is just what 'strategy' is. Then we will look at how strategy for winning organisations is clear. Strategy is a driver of direction and action for the organisation. We measure execution and results against the strategy. But, as the winning wheel framework demonstrates, strategy is not the only driver and it's also influenced by the other elements in the framework.

We'll consider the link between values and strategy and see how values support the strategy. We'll then consider how a clear strategy can also be 'fuzzy' and when and how this 'fuzziness' is not only sensible, but desirable. We also cover the development of a 'cause' for the organisation—an emotional reason for coming to work, rather than simply a cold, objective strategy that sits as a statement in a plan. The cause, which amplifies and supports the strategy, is key for winning organisations.

Members of the First XI team know what they are trying to achieve. They believe in what they are doing or striving for. This helps them to get that extraordinary level of performance that enables them to score more than their competitors and make it into the top team.

What is 'strategy'?

The word 'strategy' is widely used—and abused—in organisations. One aspect that everyone agrees on is that 'strategy' is about the long term. But 'long term' itself is not an agreed-on concept, varying from two years in an internet/rapidly changing technology-based industry, to three to five years for 'normal' organisations, to 10-plus years for mining and other industries where decisions taken have very long-term effects.

Levels of strategy

One of the reasons for the confusion is that use of the word 'strategy' does not make clear what *level* of strategy is being discussed. There are four levels of strategy (see figure 5.1):

▶ *Corporate or multibusiness strategy*. The key issues here are:
  ▷ Do we want to grow?
  ▷ What businesses should we have in our portfolio? What is our 'vision'—our view of what the portfolio of businesses

should be—of how we might describe them (and describe what is not in the portfolio)?
- How is value created by having these several businesses collected together?
- How do we want to position the corporation? (For example, GE's famous 'number one or two in every industry we are in', News Corporation's 'a leading global media company')?

▶ *Business strategy.* The key issues here are:
- Do we want to grow?
- What products and services do we want to offer?
- What customers and markets do we want to serve?
- What generic strategy do we want to use to achieve this?
- What position do we want to hold in our industry?

▶ *Business unit or functional strategy.* The key issue here is:
- How do we best carry out our unit or function activities to deliver the business strategy of the organisation?

▶ *Personal strategy.* This is not part of 'strategy' for an organisation, but of course it is very important for the people who work in the organisation. Their behaviour and aims can significantly affect whether or not the organisation is able to achieve its own strategy.

Figure 5.1: four levels of strategy

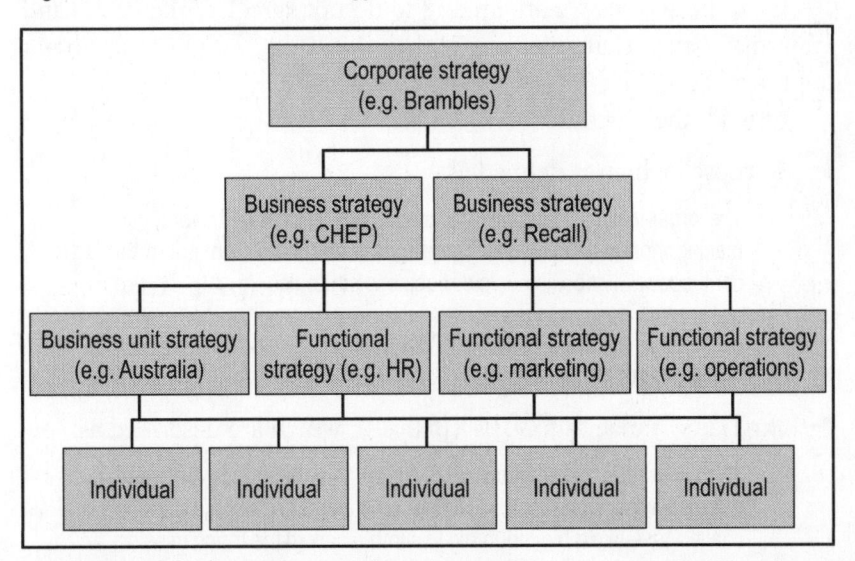

```
                    Corporate strategy
                     (e.g. Brambles)
                    /               \
          Business strategy      Business strategy
           (e.g. CHEP)            (e.g. Recall)
          /      |         |            |
Business unit  Functional  Functional  Functional
 strategy      strategy    strategy    strategy
(e.g. Australia) (e.g. HR) (e.g. marketing) (e.g. operations)
    |            |          |          |          |
Individual  Individual  Individual  Individual  Individual
```

Confusion over 'strategy'

These different levels of strategy are one reason why the term 'strategy' might be confusing. Discussion about 'strategy' can be associated with quite different levels of organisational thinking and action.

While we have outlined a clear view of the different levels of strategy, unfortunately this is not clearly understood—or accepted—in general organisational practice. There are also many terms that are used to convey strategic concepts. For instance, apart from the terms used above for the different levels of strategy, the following terms are also used widely in practice to convey strategic ideas:

- goals
- objectives
- aims
- vision
- mission
- purpose
- strategic intent.

While one organisation may use one or more of these terms consistently over time, there is simply no consistent agreement in practice—or in theory—about which are the 'right' terms to use for describing the essential features of what the organisation is trying to achieve, in the long term.

Even the studies we are linking to do not agree! While Peters and Waterman have 'strategy' as one of their 7Ss, Collins and Porras do not use the word!

Instead, they include:

- 'Purpose', which is defined as:

    The organization's fundamental reasons for existence beyond just making money—a perpetual guiding star on the horizon; not to be confused with specific goals or business strategies. (p. 73).

In our view, this is clearly a major part of what corporate or business 'strategy' is about.

- 'Big Hairy Audacious Goals' (BHAGs), which are described as:

    All companies have goals. But there is a difference between merely having a goal and becoming committed to a huge, daunting challenge—like a big mountain to climb. Think of the moon mission

> in the 1960s...a true BHAG is clear and compelling and serves as a unifying focal point of effort—often creating immense team spirit. It has a clear finish line...people like to shoot for finish lines. (p. 94)

This could also be the essence of corporate or business strategy, but to Collins and Porras it represents only a part of the totality of what an organisation might be pursuing in the long run.

So even the experts are confused! Is it any wonder 'strategy' is so poorly understood!

Normally, the main focus of strategic thinking is on the competitive positioning of the business in its industry—that is, business-level strategy. However, most of the winning organisations are collections of several different businesses, so for them, corporate strategy is the area to focus on. How do these organisations think about their corporate strategies? For the rest of the chapter, we will use the term 'strategy' to cover both corporate and business levels of strategy. We should not do this and would not if we were referring to a single organisation! However, as the winning organisations cover both businesses and corporations, we will combine them here to avoid confusion.

Strategy is clear

Our research found that, even though organisations often didn't have a specific statement of their strategy, such as a vision or mission statement, they were quite clear about the direction in which they were headed. Table 5.1 (overleaf) indicates the essence of the strategy followed by the organisations over the 20-year period we analysed in detail, and also how that strategy was conveyed to people outside the organisation. Table 5.2 (on page 119) shows the essence of the strategy for each organisation in 2006, together with the name of any statement used to convey it. Together, these two tables show two things. Firstly, that we are able to get at the essence of the strategy for a long period with very few words! In this sense, strategy is both clear and quite stable. Secondly, they show the variety of mechanisms used to communicate the essence of that strategy and the difference in what 'strategy' looks like.

For instance, Westfield's strategy has always been about the development of regional shopping centres. It has always been highly vertically integrated in designing, constructing and managing them, with ownership separately held by associated property trusts (Westfield

Property Trust for the Australian, NZ and UK centres, and Westfield America Trust and Westfield America Inc. for the American centres) until 2004, when the three organisations were merged into one.

Table 5.1: how strategy was publicly conveyed between 1980 and 2000

Organisation	Essence of strategy, 1980–2000	How strategy was conveyed
Brambles	Specialised industrial services	CEO reports
Harvey Norman	Specialist discount retailing	CEO reports
Lend Lease	Property construction, development and funds management	Chair and CEO reports
Macquarie Bank	Niche-based financial services	CEO reports
National Australia Bank	Retail financial services	Some use of vision statement
Qantas	Australia's international airline	Earlier use of mission statement
Rio Tinto	Finding, mining and processing resources	Untitled statement at front of annual report
The Salvation Army	Preaching the gospel and alleviating hardship	Some use of mission statements
Telstra	Full range telecommunications	Variety of mechanisms used
Westfield	Shopping centre development and management	CEO reports
Woolworths	Food and general retailing	Variety—objectives, CEO reports, Chair reports

Table 5.2: how strategy was publicly conveyed in 2006

Organisation	Essence of strategy in 2006	How strategy was conveyed
Brambles	World's leading provider of innovative business solutions in support services	Mission statement
Harvey Norman	Franchisor of discount retail home products	Inferred
Lend Lease	International retail and residential property group, integrated with strong investment management and construction management businesses	Annual report
Macquarie Bank	Pre-eminent provider of investment banking and financial services in Australasia ... International focus on select markets where special value can be provided	Annual report
National Australia Bank	International financial services organisation that provides a comprehensive and integrated range of financial products and services	Annual report
Qantas	Airlines	Inferred
Rio Tinto	Finding, mining and processing resources ... via large, long-life and efficient operations	Annual report
The Salvation Army	Global evangelical movement with extensive social services	Website
Telstra	Leading telecommunications and information services company	Profile; separate vision and mission statements
Westfield	Vertically integrated shopping centre owner, manager and developer	Profile
Woolworths	Deliver customers a better shopping experience—each and every time	Mission statement

Woolworths has always been a retailer. Since the 1950s it has specialised in food retailing. In 1993, when it was relisted, Woolworths said:

> Woolworths is Australia's largest food retailer and, with its general merchandise and specialty retail groups, is the second largest retailer [in Australia]. (1993 annual report).

This statement was backed up by a set of objectives, a statement of culture and an operating philosophy. This is typical of the idiosyncratic nature of strategy statements. They are all individual in construction.

In 2006, Woolworths said:

> Our mission is to deliver our customers a better shopping experience—each and every time...

> We're a great Australian retail company made up of a number of businesses all providing our customers with quality, range, value and everyday low prices. We're built on a passion for retail, attention to detail, working hard, ensuring the safety of our customers and staff and having fun. We're continuously refreshing and improving our business and our people. (2006 annual report)

While the words have changed — and they changed in most years — the intent and direction is clear and consistent — growth in retailing. Close analysis will note the dropping of 'food', 'general merchandise' and of 'Australia' from the 1993 statement. Woolworths has expanded its product and service range during the period to include petrol, liquor, banking services and shopping centre developments. During the period, CEO Reg Clairs saw Woolworths as a 'significant global supplier of food' by 2020. Roger Corbett institutionalised the 'refresh' idea from Project Refresh. So we can see the consistency, but we also note the subtle changes that typically occur through development over time.

The Salvation Army has had several experiments with mission statements over the period we analysed, all with slight variations. However, the key elements have always been the same. In 1983 it said:

> Primary aim [is] to preach the gospel of Jesus Christ to men and women untouched by ordinary religious efforts... From this service to God flows service to man... The Army has always sought to make practical and spiritual responses appropriate to individual and community needs.

In 2006, the mission statement said:

> The Salvation Army, an international movement, is an evangelical branch of the universal Christian Church. Its message is based on

> the Bible. Its ministry is motivated by the love of God. Its mission is to preach the gospel of Jesus Christ and to meet human needs in His name without discrimination.

This shows that it sees itself primarily as a church, but a church having a practical side, serving people who are in need.

Macquarie Bank, which is quite a young organisation, has never had a mission or vision statement. However, it has developed its own statement—called 'What we stand for', which states:

> Macquarie Bank aspires to be a pre-eminent provider of financial services over the long haul. We recognise that, however our achievements to date are judged, the quest for improvement is never ending. The Macquarie culture is represented by the way in which we act and work together. The values to which we aspire can be summarised in six principles ... integrity ... client commitment ... strive for profitability ... fulfilment for our people ... teamwork ... highest standards ... Our commitment to the six principles is vital for our continued growth and prosperity.

Here the first sentence clearly describes the strategy, while the rest of the statement describes how that strategy will be achieved from a process perspective. It is interesting to see the specific mention of continuous improvement, of culture and also of growth, all of which are common recurring themes in winning organisations, wherever they may be expressed or discussed. This statement, developed during the 1990s, was exactly the same in 2006.

How do vision and mission statements fit into 'strategy'?

Vision and mission statements are often proposed as the way to provide the essence of its strategic direction for an organisation. Many organisations have spent a great deal of effort and expense developing vision and/or mission statements to try to articulate the direction in which their organisation is heading—how do they fit into this picture?

Surprisingly, our research found that vision and mission statements are rarely used to illuminate strategy in winning organisations. *None of the winning organisations consistently used either or both a mission or vision statement over the 20-year period we studied.*

Table 5.3 (overleaf) indicates whether each organisation used a vision, mission or values statement in 2006. As you can see, only four of them had either or both in 2006. While some organisations used one or both during part of the period, vision and mission statements per se are not seen to be of great importance. Having a vision or mission statement, then, is not a key to being a winning organisation. Time and money spent developing vision and/or mission statements may well be wasted.

Table 5.3: vision and mission statement use in the winning organisations in 2006

Organisation	Vision statement	Mission statement
Brambles	No	Yes
Harvey Norman	No	No
Lend Lease	No	No
Macquarie Bank	No	No
National Australia Bank	No	No
Qantas	No	No
Rio Tinto	No	No
The Salvation Army	No	Yes
Telstra	Yes	Yes
Westfield	No	No
Woolworths	No	Yes
Total	1	4

These winning organisations *did* have a clear view of their strategy and strategy is important, as interviewees in the winning organisations confirmed. The examples in tables 5.1 and 5.2 are clear statements of strategy, but they rarely involve vision or mission statements, as you can see from tables 5.2 and 5.3. While mission and vision statements can be useful methods of defining and communicating clear strategic views, there are no mechanical or consistent ways that winning organisations use to communicate strategy.

Growth as a driver of strategy

One of the key findings about the winning organisations is that growth is a key driver of the organisation. This growth—of profits, not just sales—comes from the strategy (and the leadership that makes the strategy work). This is a key difference for winning organisations.

Where other organisations are happy to accept lower rates of growth, or focus on sales growth, winning organisations are driving hard for high-profit growth rates, which they manage to achieve without overstraining the organisation. For instance, Westfield, Woolworths, Lend Lease, Brambles and Macquarie have all had very long periods of profit increases before a reduction occurred. Macquarie has a specific stated 'growth strategy'—'to expand selectively, seeking only to enter markets where we perceive there is an opportunity to add real value'.

Linking strategy and values

The studies of Collins and Porras and Peters and Waterman both emphasise the importance of values and of them being aligned with the strategy or core purpose. 'Shared values' is one of the Peters and Waterman 7Ss. Collins and Porras see 'core values' as part of the 'core ideology' of the organisation, along with 'purpose'.

Our research found that the strategy and the values of the organisation were closely linked and aligned. Strategy development is constrained by the current set of values and, for strategy to be implemented, values must be consistent with the strategy (see figure 5.2).

Figure 5.2: the relationship between strategy and values

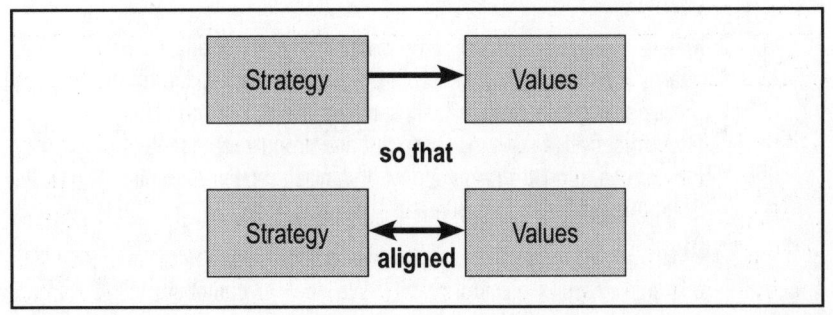

```
    Strategy  ———▶  Values
             so that
    Strategy  ◀——▶  Values
             aligned
```

All of the winning organisations have strong and clear values, whether explicit or implicit. In 2006, nine of the organisations had specific statements of values. The Macquarie statement given earlier includes its values. The Salvation Army has a separate list of values (along with its mission) printed on cards for widespread distribution. The values are:

▶ human dignity
▶ justice

The First XI

- hope
- compassion
- community.

Some winning organisations don't have specifically named values statements, but their implied values are heavily supportive of their strategy. Rio Tinto implies its values from the strategy statement—called 'The way we work' (see illustration 5.1).

Illustration 5.1: Rio Tinto's implied values—'The way we work'

Rio Tinto publishes 'The way we work' on its website. It contains a clear view of the values, albeit implied, that Rio Tinto has. It includes the following statement:

> Rio Tinto is a leader in finding, mining and processing the earth's mineral resources. The Group's worldwide operations supply essential minerals and metals that help to meet global needs and contribute to improvements in living standards.
>
> In order to deliver superior returns to shareholders over time, Rio Tinto takes a long term and responsible approach to the Group's business. We concentrate on the development of first class orebodies into large, long life and efficient operations, capable of sustaining competitive advantage through business cycles.
>
> Major products include aluminium, copper, diamonds, energy products (coal and uranium), gold, industrial minerals (borates, titanium dioxide, salt and talc), and iron ore. The Group's activities span the world but are strongly represented in Australia and North America with significant businesses in South America, Asia, Europe and southern Africa.
>
> Wherever Rio Tinto operates, the health and safety of our employees is our first priority. We seek to contribute to sustainable development. We work as closely as possible with our host countries and communities, respecting their laws and customs. We minimise adverse effects and strive to improve every aspect of our performance. We employ local people at all levels and ensure fair and equitable transfer of benefits and enhancement of opportunities.

This is a rather long statement—certainly much longer than could be remembered by anyone! This long statement is supported by several pages more, covering transparency, business integrity, corporate governance, internal controls and reporting procedures, a variety of policies, and board committee terms of reference. But a careful analysis shows clearly both what the organisation plans to do, how it wants to position itself and what its values are. The values implied are:

- having a responsible approach to development
- having large, efficient operations
- helping to improve humanity's wellbeing
- making lasting contributions to the economies where it mines
- having respect and sensitivity for the laws, customs and way of life of host countries
- minimising adverse environmental and community impacts
- being a good neighbour
- being a good partner
- having the highest quality health and safety for employees.

Another example is Lend Lease, which has always had a 'community of interest' approach to its businesses. In 1997, Lend Lease published a statement called 'Our beliefs', which brought together some of the main values that have been running through the organisation since its inception (see illustration 5.2 overleaf).

Lend Lease said about these beliefs:

> If our beliefs are genuinely held and practised throughout the group, we will attract the best people to work for us, the quality of work will attract the attention of customers, demand for our services will grow and our global family will prosper — all of which contributes to delivering superior value for shareholders.

Relationship between strategy and values when change occurs

We concluded that, when strategy underwent significant change, such as a move from government to private ownership, when organisations developed overseas or when they realigned from multidomestic to global operations, values changed to adapt to the new strategic perspective. We also concluded that values should be aligned to strategy, rather than the other way around.

The First XI

Illustration 5.2: Lend Lease's beliefs

Belief	Observations
Sound corporate governance policy	We believe there is a strong link between good governance and performance.
Community of interest between shareholders and employees	We wish all employees to be shareholders, and they collectively own over 13 per cent of the issued capital. We aim for all to share annually in the profits.
Being a leading employer	A reputation that we have enjoyed domestically needs to be created globally.
A pillow stock, or no nasty surprises	We aim to increase earnings and earnings per share every year, irrespective of the economic climate.
Enhance the environment	We are conscious of the impact Lend Lease can have on environment. We aim for it always to be positive.
Relationships	We cannot do it all ourselves. We need a number of special relationships that enhance our capabilities.
Collaboration	No individual has a monopoly on good ideas.
Let the community be the judge	We will only prosper with the support of the communities with which we interact.
Ethics and standards	We should not do anything that would diminish the pride our parents have in us.
Dare to be different	The theme of this report and the enemy of mediocrity.

When Telstra began its change process in the 1980s from being a government-owned public sector utility to a commercial—and eventually a publicly listed—organisation, it developed a Vision 2000 program with three explicit—and quite new—values:

▶ customers come first
▶ we make it possible
▶ business success builds our future.

For an engineering-oriented organisation at that time, the idea of 'customers come first' was a radical change. The idea that 'we make it possible' overturned the existing view that the bureaucracy had rules for everything that could not be changed. The idea of 'business success builds our future' conflicted with the previous idea that 'the government gives us the money we need to build the system we propose'. These represented radical changes in values, but they were consistent with the new strategic direction. Variations on these ideas have continued since that time.

In summary, winning organisations have clear strategies but they are expressed in a wide variety of ways. Vision and mission statements, one of the standard recommended tools of strategy development and communication, are rarely used. Strategies vary over time, changing on an incremental basis. All winning organisations have strong and clear values, most of which are now expressed in values statements. Strategies are linked closely to values. Sometimes values need to be realigned as strategies change.

Strategy is fuzzy

While we have used many examples to demonstrate 'clear' strategy, you may feel that even these are open to interpretation. So it will almost certainly be obvious to you that the examples we have *not* included here are likely to be 'fuzzy'!

There is a degree of fuzziness about the strategy of each winning organisation. Indeed, absolute clarity was not sought in most cases, primarily because of the perceived need to be open to relevant opportunities and not be completely locked in. This is consistent with the ideas of adapting rapidly, continuous improvement and innovation (see chapter 4), and being externally focused (see chapter 7).

The lack of a clear statement, such as a vision, mission or some other named statement, means that the issue of what the strategy of the organisation is remains open to interpretation, both within and outside the organisation. If there are inconsistent sets of words in the many statements issued by the organisation, it is likely that the organisation is not fixed, or clear, about its strategy.

So what is 'fuzzy' strategy and how can it be desirable for winning organisations? There are at least three reasons why strategy might be 'fuzzy' (see figure 5.3 overleaf):

- ▶ a desire to take advantage of opportunities that come up
- ▶ a desire to be flexible and adaptable at the highest level (see chapter 4)
- ▶ the possibility that the organisation's strategy is not clear, or not known.

Figure 5.3: reasons for 'fuzzy' strategy

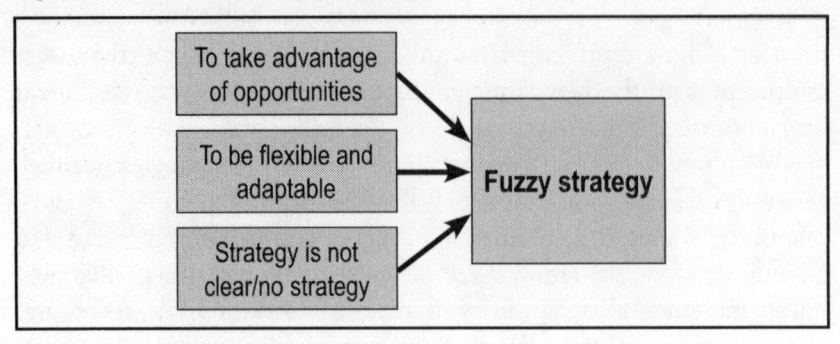

[Figure: Three boxes labeled "To take advantage of opportunities", "To be flexible and adaptable", and "Strategy is not clear/no strategy" all pointing to a box labeled "Fuzzy strategy"]

In most organisations, our experience is that the last reason is quite common. But in the case of winning organisations, it is for the first two reasons, not for the third.

Desirable 'fuzzy' strategy: to take advantage of incremental opportunities

The first reason why organisations might want to have a fuzzy strategy is to be able to take advantage of future opportunities. These opportunities may not be predictable and being too fixed—not flexible enough—may lead organisations to pass opportunities by. However, these 'opportunities' must be closely linked to the main activities of the organisation if the 'fuzziness' has a chance of working. In practical terms, this means the organisation must have large areas of overlap in capabilities between its existing operations and the new activity.

Until it became a global organisation, Brambles was a good example of a winning organisation that did not want to be too clear about its strategy, so that it could take advantage of opportunities. CEO Gary Pemberton banned the word 'strategic' in the organisation. Successor CEO John Fletcher boasted of never having conducted a press conference, which reduced his risk of having to publicly define and narrow down his stated strategy.

The fundamental driver at Brambles was growth of profits, though its set of products and services was described in its earlier days as 'dig, lift, load and haul' industrial services. Noticeably, what is now one of its major global businesses, Recall records management, does not fit into this, but Recall came into Brambles via a 'haul' operation (Grace Bros Removals) and the managers in charge saw an opportunity to turn it into a separate industrial service business.

The same is true for each of the major businesses that Brambles has or had—they were all perceived as opportunities that were in some way linked to existing operations but which were new. CHEP was seen as a diversification of materials-handling techniques. Cleanaway was a diversification of industrial services. Groupe CAIB was seen as a geographic stepping stone into Europe (though Brambles had no railcars in its operations at the time).

Macquarie makes it clear that it depends on the entrepreneurial talents of its people to take advantage of opportunities, rather than having a fixed view of products and services. In its 1986 annual report, it said:

> Macquarie Bank is a market maker... in the sense of developing new products and introducing innovations to existing markets. Macquarie Bank is regarded as one of the most creative financial institutions in Australia.

And in 1989 it said:

> The Bank's aim is to maintain and diversify business activities while continuing to develop as a strong, reliable financial institution. The people at Macquarie are among the best in their respective fields. They share an ability to bring imagination and flair to their work, yet their entrepreneurial talents are guided by prudence and integrity.

And in 2006 it said:

> This approach offers two important advantages:
> - The flexibility to enter new markets as opportunities arise
> - The freedom to respond to the special requirements of individual markets in the region and around the world
>
> Entrepreneurial spirit drives success.

These statements show the emphasis on innovation, imagination and flair as drivers of future business growth—not a top-down strategy but rather a focus on the development and creation of opportunities.

Desirable 'fuzzy' strategy: for flexibility and adaptability

In some cases, fuzzy strategy is not due to the desire for opportunism but to the desire to be flexible. In chapter 4 we noted the value of strategic flexibility in allowing winning organisations to rapidly adapt.

Harvey Norman and Woolworths define themselves simply as retailers, even though they are each focused on particular aspects and formats of retailing—in fact, they hardly touch each other in terms of products and services. This general description of 'retailing' allows them to be flexible and adaptable if new products or formats arise. Woolworths has used this flexibility to enter petrol retailing. The original idea was to use its own carparks to set up petrol retailing, and thus get a return from what is a non-producing asset! For Harvey Norman, the Loughran Group and the Joyce Mayne Group, acquired in 1998, have become the Domayne chain—an upmarket chain with similar types of goods as Harvey Norman stores. (It has subsequently relaunched the Joyce Mayne brand as a regional chain.) In 2001 it bought Rebel Sport, a sports products retailer, and a new product range for Harvey Norman. In 2005, it developed Harvey Norman Renovations, a design and installation service for people buying kitchen, bathroom, laundry or home theatre products from its stores. These have been incremental strategic developments—flexibility to expand at the margin—rather than opportunism.

The Salvation Army makes it clear that it will care for people, but the specific services it offers vary from period to period. It enters areas perceived to be of increasing need and sometimes withdraws when others, particularly governments, come along to take over or to do a better job. For instance, it has developed drug rehabilitation, homeless youth and problem gambling services, reflecting developing increased needs for those services. The Salvation Army also entered the government contracted unemployment job placement service, through Employment Plus, as the government withdrew from that area. It has become the leading provider in this industry in the country. On the other hand, it has largely withdrawn from aged-care centres, as that industry is consolidating and others can serve the need better. (Interestingly, it sold its aged-care centres to Macquarie, which acquired others in 2005 and 2006 to become the third-largest competitor in that market, virtually overnight.)

Lack of strategy?

A third interpretation of the lack of a clear strategy is that perhaps winning organisations don't actually have a strategy. This raises a crucial issue: can an organisation be successful without a strategy? Are we just seeking strategy—and forcing ourselves to find something—even where there is actually none? Certainly, many small organisations manage to operate quite well with little idea of 'strategy', simply because they are good operators — effective execution at work.

However, from both our own analysis and the interviews we conducted, we formed two conclusions. First, we concluded that all winning organisations do have a strategy and that strategy is important in guiding them for the long term. Second, we found that, because the organisations were in different positions in the strategic life cycle, because they faced different individual contexts, and because the concept of strategy is neither mechanical (like accounting) nor agreed on by theorists, the 'look' and description of strategy varies by organisation over time.

Strategy for winning organisations is clear, but slightly fuzzy. It is communicated with a high degree of clarity and consistency, but in different ways and it develops and changes incrementally over time.

Clear *and* fuzzy strategy

So what does a clear *and* fuzzy strategy look like? Our research found that strategy needs to be clear enough to provide guidance to constrain the range of activities to those that already exist or can be easily and incrementally linked to current activities. (There are no cases of unrelated diversification in our winning organisations, suggesting this is not a likely strategy for success.)

It also needs to be fuzzy at the edges so that:

▶ opportunities that are related and/or incremental can be taken up

▶ innovation is encouraged

▶ the organisation is flexible enough to adapt to external changes (but not so flexible that anything goes as 'strategy')

▶ the organisation can change its strategy over time as it develops and grows.

How important is strategy?

Given the lack of clarity over what constitutes strategy, a major issue is how important strategy really is for organisational success. While winning organisations have clear (and fuzzy) strategies, many organisations also have clear strategies. Is 'good strategy' really a differentiator for winning organisations?

Contrary to our prior beliefs and expectations, we concluded that the ability to execute effectively is more important than having a great strategy. Organisations need effective execution to get started and be successful. Without this, there is no organisation of any substance! But to grow, strategy is useful and for long-term growth, it is critical. That's why effective execution is in the centre of our winning wheel framework and why we started the book with the chapter on effective execution. Good strategy is a driver of success, but good strategy alone is not enough to guarantee success. Organisations need the other elements to achieve effective execution. Good strategy does, however, help alignment (see chapter 3), encourage consistency and focus execution. And winning organisations need them all!

Who sets the strategy?

The theory is that the direction for the organisation—the strategy—is set at the top of the organisation, ideally via a vision or mission statement or at least a clear communication from the CEO or top management team. The lower levels of the organisation then 'fit' into this espoused strategy.

In our original research, we found that the direction of the company was set in a variety of ways (see table 5.4). In several cases—Brambles, Lend Lease and Macquarie—it was set by the actions of divisional managers and their divisions. The role of the top management was to encourage and reward people for entrepreneurial behaviour, set some general boundaries and manage risk.

In other cases—Harvey Norman, Qantas, Telstra, Woolworths, NAB and Westfield—strategy was tightly controlled at the top, as suggested by conventional theory. In yet other cases—the Salvation Army and Rio Tinto—strategy had mixed controllers. In these cases, the central head office tightly controlled major decisions and policies, but individual units had considerable flexibility to meet local needs and conditions.

By 2006, Brambles, Lend Lease and Rio Tinto—all organisations that had a global strategy or that had experimented with a global strategy—had become organisations where strategy was set at the top. This suggests that, as organisations become global in their orientation, more control is likely to be needed to achieve the standardisation, control and efficiencies necessary to make that type of strategy work.

Table 5.4: alternative approaches to setting strategy

	Conventional strategy	Oportunistic strategy	Mixed strategy
Locus of control	Top management team	Divisions	Top and division
Role of top management team	Set direction Take control	Set general boundaries Encourage divisions Manage risk	Set general strategy Facilitate idea transfers Monitor for control
Role of divisions	Follow and implement direction	Determine what opportunities to pursue	Follow general strategy Customise to local opportunity Specialise in an area of competence

From strategy to 'cause'

Time and again we were surprised in interviews by the passion that emerged about the reasons why the organisation existed and why that was so important. The reason for their passion was the existence of what we term a 'cause' for the organisation. The Telstra archetype research in the early 1990s showed that Australian employees needed to believe in what their organisation was doing—that is, in the 'cause' of the organisation. Illustration 5.3 (overleaf) shows the 'causes' of the winning organisations from the original research. These are not 'statements', like visions or mission statements, rather they are the implicit drivers that inspire people to work for these organisations.

This is consistent with Collins and Porras' finding about the importance of what they called 'core purpose':

> The organization's fundamental reasons for existence beyond just making money—a perpetual guiding star on the horizon; not to be confused with specific goals or business strategies. (p. 73).

The 'cause' of an organisation is more powerful than even the strategy itself, yet it underlies and supports the strategy of the organisation.

Illustration 5.3: the 'causes' of winning organisations

Organisation	Cause
Brambles	We undertake boring services that no-one else wants to do better than anyone else and we do it very profitably and have very satisfied customers
Harvey Norman	The chance for individual small businesspeople to share in a national chain with a better range at cheaper prices
Lend Lease	Highest quality, innovative, large-scale construction
Macquarie Bank	Unique solutions to large-scale customer financial service needs
National Australia Bank	Lower costs and better risk assessment
Qantas	Highest quality, most-reliable flying; representing Australia on the world stage
Rio Tinto	Lowest cost, highest quality, environmentally sound mining developments that benefit all stakeholders
The Salvation Army	Save souls, grow saints and serve suffering humanity
Telstra	Building a high-quality communications system for Australia
Westfield	Building and redeveloping the best shopping centres
Woolworths	Getting lower prices for customers

The Salvation Army is the clearest example. Salvation Army officers do not work at the Army for the money or the conditions! (Note, however, that regular employees are paid the relevant award wage.) Indeed, before you can become an officer there is a long training program to undergo and the word 'work' is not used — officers 'belong' to the Army. They are drawn to the cause from all walks of life. Some believe they have been chosen for this calling. Salvationists combine work and personal life into an intermingled holistic single way of life. People have to be passionate and determined to stay in the Army and to succeed to leadership. And leaders demonstrate passion for the cause.

Strategy development over time

Organisations develop and grow. As a consequence, and often as the reason behind the changes, the strategy will also develop over time and change. We have developed the concept of the strategic cycle to explain this variation in types of strategy over time. 'Winning' looks different at different stages of the cycle. We explain this in detail in chapter 12. In that chapter we also cover strategic mistakes, which appear to occur even in winning organisations as they change over time, branching out into new and different activities.

Summary and key messages for leaders

Strategy is an important element of the winning wheel framework, but—contrary to the belief of strategists—it is not the most important. Strategy is a driver of effective execution, but the other elements are also needed if effective execution is to occur. An organisation's strategy must be aligned with its values, and growth—of profits, not just sales—must be a key element in it.

Strategy in winning organisations is clear, but it is also fuzzy at the margin to allow for opportunities, innovation and the need for future flexibility. Despite their popularity in general organisational life, vision, mission and other such statements are not used greatly; however, clear and consistent strategies do exist for long periods of time. Values are important and are increasingly explicit. Values are aligned to strategy and may need to change as strategy changes over time.

Underlying strategy in winning organisations is a sense of 'cause'—an emotional driver of the intrinsic value of the work—that makes working for the organisation more than just a job, more than just following a stated strategy.

The key messages for leaders from this chapter are:

▶ Have a clear strategy, but don't worry about what it is called.

▶ Allow for some flexibility in the strategy at the margin to adapt to opportunities and allow for future related development.

▶ Ensure that this strategy is clearly understood throughout the organisation.

▶ Develop a clear set of values and ensure that the strategy and values are aligned.

The First XI

- Emphasise profitable growth, not growth by itself.
- Consider what the 'cause' of the organisation is or might be.
- Recognise that strategy will change over time as the organisation develops.

6 Leadership, not leaders

Captain-coach leadership Teams

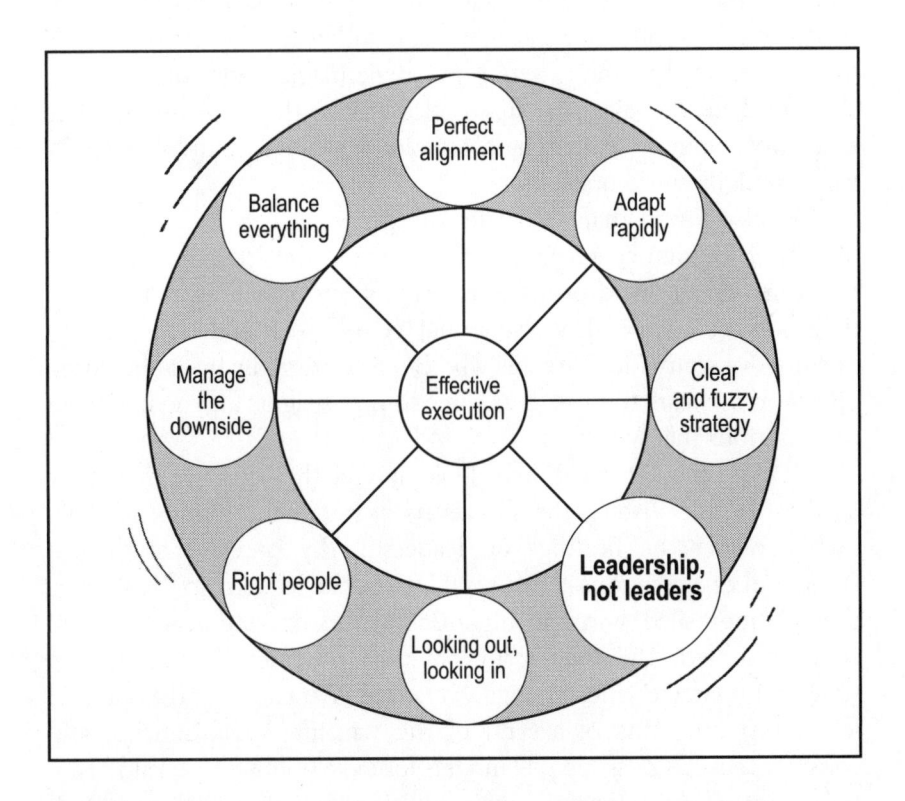

In organisation after organisation as we analysed our findings, we came up with the elements in our framework, except for leadership. So we asked ourselves, 'How is it possible for these results to come about? Where did the strategy come from? Who hired those right people? How was the organisation externally focused?' Is it possible for a First XI organisation to have no captain and no coach to lead and guide the team?

We realised that leadership must be an important factor, since it is often the driver of the other factors. The question was, 'Is it the individual CEO "leaders" themselves who are the cause of the success of the organisations, or is it "leadership" as a whole?' We found that there were many good CEOs—which is the conventional view of 'leader'—in all the organisations. We wondered whether the success of the organisation might be due to the catalytic or visionary influence of perhaps a single one of these CEOs in each organisation.

What we found was an emphasis on team leadership, not individual leaders, and not just a single visionary leader. So we call this element 'leadership, not leaders' to focus on the characteristics of leadership, not on a single leader. Indeed, each leader and leadership team in the winning organisations faced quite different circumstances from their predecessors—and successors. We concluded that leadership needs to be 'right for the time'. There is no single magic leadership formula. We found no one size that fitted all. Perhaps this explains why the search for common leader characteristics across past individual CEOs was singularly unsuccessful.

We also found that the leadership styles needed in Australia are different. 'Captain-coach leadership'—where the leaders are part of the team, on the field of play, yet leading and coaching at the same time—is the style of leadership that people seek and that winning organisations provide. Captains who can lead from the front and coach others on the team to raise their game to new heights are the leaders of organisations that win.

In this chapter we'll first look at exactly what we mean by 'leadership' and discuss the four levels of leadership that exist. We'll then consider the findings on leadership by previous studies of successful organisations. Then we'll look at the leadership capabilities that distinguished winning organisations in our study. As we are concerned with the long term, we also consider how leadership style and characteristics change over time. We examine the internal leadership programs of several of the winning organisations, and consider these as possible role models for developing future leadership from within. We'll conclude by considering whether—despite all of the above—there really is or has been one dominant leader for each organisation. We reject this conclusion, but think the debate is worth having, as we know many people think this is what good organisations are about!

Who or what is 'leadership'?

The term 'leadership' is used frequently and often its use is confused, much as use of the term 'strategy' is confused. We see 'leadership' as 'behaviour of the key group of people in the organisation that positions the organisation for its future'. We distinguish this from 'management', which we see as 'behaviour that enables the organisation to carry out its current activities most efficiently'. Leadership is about the future. Management is about the present. While both are necessary, the future of the organisation depends on its ability to move forward, not just to undertake its current tasks efficiently.

This does not define any particular organisational position as 'the' or 'a' leader. You do not have to be CEO to be a leader, but you do have to be acting in such a way that it helps the organisation position itself for the future. Indeed, our definition specifically suggests that it is a group of people, not just a single position, that constitutes the leadership of the organisation.

Levels of leadership

We see four levels of 'leadership' (see figure 6.1 overleaf):

▶ *The CEO.* This is the conventional, and media-based, view of leadership. The CEO-as-leader view personalises the organisation. Whatever the organisation does is seen to be the responsibility of, and caused by, the CEO. At one level (that of ultimate organisational responsibility), this is true. At another level it is ludicrous, but it makes good media copy. Rupert Murdoch is News Corporation. Bill Gates is Microsoft. Frank Lowy is Westfield. Gerry Harvey is Harvey Norman. While we agree that the role of CEO is the most influential and is one of the keys to how an organisation will behave, we reject this view that leadership is just the CEO. Moreover, since the first edition of this book was published, it's a view of leadership that has increasingly been rejected by other research evidence too. Superstar CEOs are not the way to organisational success. (And by the way, none of the four examples above are even the CEOs of their organisations any more, though you'd never guess this from the media coverage they generate!)

▶ *The top management team.* A more realistic view of leadership is that the top management team around the CEO (and including the CEO) is responsible for the organisation's performance. The 'team' generally consists of those who report to the CEO, but sometimes it can include others and sometimes not all of those.

▶ *All business unit leaders.* What good organisations seek now is for all business unit leaders to pursue leader behaviour. Those who are able to do so are likely to rise up the management ranks to the top management team. In winning organisations, many of the business unit managers do exhibit leader behaviour—that's one of the key reasons why they are able to execute and deliver results! But it's too hard for the media, or others outside the organisation, to focus on such a large group or identify the high-flyers with potential, so most of these names are unknown in the public discussion of leadership.

▶ *The board of directors.* Another group that has received limited attention until recently has been the board. The board is often viewed as just a rubber stamp unless the executives are doing poorly. A more modern view is that the quality of the board and its relationship with the top management team is an important part of business success. Until recently, very little attention has been focused on boards in terms of their actual contribution to good organisational performance. However, as board decisions are collective, good and bad directors can be painted with the same brush.

So 'leadership' is much more than just the CEO leader. Within each organisation, the 'leadership' will be a different group of individuals, at different levels, coming from the four levels identified here. Who is the 'leadership' group in your organisation?

Figure 6.1: four levels of leadership

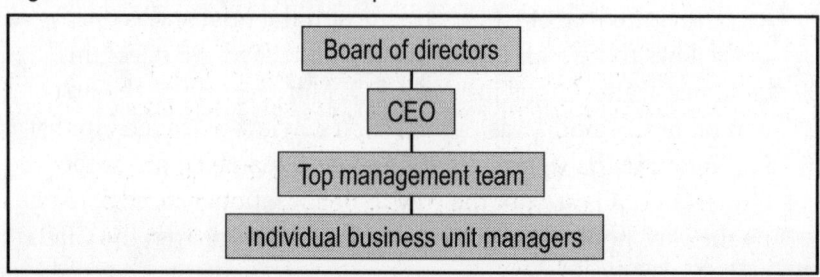

```
┌─────────────────────────────────────────┐
│         Board of directors              │
│                 │                       │
│               CEO                       │
│                 │                       │
│       Top management team               │
│                 │                       │
│   Individual business unit managers     │
└─────────────────────────────────────────┘
```

Leadership is a team-based capability

Why do we focus on a group of leaders? The executives in all the winning organisations talked about their leadership teams rather than individuals, both in external reporting and in interviews. Reflecting on his years as CEO of Macquarie, and on the role of CEO, Allan Moss said, 'Our success has been very much a team effort...' (Moss, 2001).

Reflecting on what a fortune-teller would have told him in 1977 when he joined the organisation about his role as CEO in 2001, he said that his role as CEO did not seem as important as might be expected:

> She would have replied: 'From what I see, you don't do a lot. You read a fair bit, you spend some time staring at what appears to be a small television screen. A lot of your day involves meeting with people but you usually do much more listening than talking. You have a lot of lunches with people but they cannot be important because you don't get to drink much alcohol. However, there is one productive activity—you do quite a lot of typing.'

Reflecting, just prior to retirement, on his time as CEO at Woolworths, Roger Corbett said:

> You need a really top team around you, and you need to have clear parameters for managing the business, and responsibility and accountability so people feel free to act and lead within their business areas. (*AFR BOSS*, September 2006)

At Westfield, while Frank Lowy is acknowledged as the driver of the business since the original partnership with John Saunders ended in the mid 1980s, the style of decision making shows that it is not simply Lowy's ideas that are accepted. Large meetings are called to discuss key issues. Everyone is expected to contribute and Lowy is widely acknowledged as a good listener, keen to learn. The resulting decisions are likely to benefit from the wide input and few bad decisions have been made. In fact, since 2000 Peter and Steven Lowy, two of Frank's three sons, have been joint managing directors of Westfield, ironically replicating the joint managing director roles that Frank had with John Saunders for many years in setting up Westfield. Commenting on Frank Lowy's influence in 2006, Steven said:

> Whilst my father is a strong individual and of course has a view, the company is not run in a manner where maybe he and John Saunders made every decision and instructed the executives what to do. That's a long time gone in our organisation. My father is obviously the leading member of a large team of people [but] I can't recall a board decision where we've had to take a vote or my father has said 'We're going to do this', because it doesn't work like that. (*AFR BOSS*, July 2006)

The role of boards in leadership teams

How do boards fit into the leadership of winning organisations? Though only some of the winning organisations talked about the value of their boards, we found that several board members were represented on more than one of the winning organisation boards over time (see table 6.1). We think this is no coincidence. Winning organisations are likely to value good people from other winning organisations. For instance, Gary Pemberton went from being CEO of Brambles to being Chair of Qantas. James Strong went from being CEO of Qantas to being Chair of Woolworths. Don Argus went from being CEO of NAB to being Chair of Brambles. Roger Corbett was Chair of the Salvation Army board while also CEO of Woolworths. Those who are on the boards of winning organisations would also be sought after by other organisations seeking to learn from their experiences of those winning organisations.

Table 6.1: some common board members in winning organisations

Person	Boards
2000	
Margaret Jackson	Telstra, Qantas
James Strong	Qantas, Woolworths
Gary Pemberton	Brambles, Qantas
John Ralph	CRA, Telstra
John Morshel	Lend Lease, Rio Tinto
Diane Grady	Lend Lease, Woolworths
2006	
Stephen Johns	Brambles, Westfield
Catherine Livingstone	Telstra, Macquarie

Previous findings on leadership

Both Peters and Waterman and Collins and Porras included leadership as a key element in their models of successful organisations. Leadership is one of the elements of the 7Ss under the term 'style' and Peters and Waterman see leadership as the driver of the eight elements they identify in their 'excellent' organisations.

Collins and Porras include 'clock building, not time telling' in their model. They say:

> Having a great idea or being a charismatic visionary leader is 'time telling'; building a company that can prosper far beyond the presence of any single leader... is 'clock building'.
>
> ...
>
> Instead of concentrating on acquiring the individual personality traits of visionary leadership, they take an architectural approach and concentrate on building the organizational traits of visionary companies.
>
> ...
>
> We found that creating and building a visionary company absolutely does not require either a great idea or a great and charismatic leader. (p. 23)

In commenting on 'home-grown management'—another factor in their model—they say:

> In short, it is not the quality of leadership that most separates the visionary companies from the comparison companies. It is the continuity of quality leadership that matters... (p. 173).

In his more recent work, Collins (2001) focused on leadership as the key variable, arguing that it was key executives who transformed their organisations and turned them from 'good' to 'great'. He developed a concept called 'Level 5 leadership'—'a paradoxical combination of personal humility and professional will'. He argued that there are five levels of leadership:

▶ *Level 1*: highly capable individual with talent, skills and hard work.

▶ *Level 2*: team manager who contributes to group objectives.

▶ *Level 3*: competent manager pursuing effective and efficient predetermined objectives.

▶ *Level 4*: effective leader who generates commitment to and pursuit of a clear and compelling vision, developing higher standards of performance.

▶ *Level 5*: an executive who 'builds enduring greatness through a paradoxical blend of personal humility and professional will'.

However, Collins was referring here to an individual CEO, rather than a leadership team, as we have identified. So leadership was identified as an important factor in the earlier studies and the focus is also on building the organisation, rather than on the charisma of the individual.

Australian leadership team capabilities

The previous studies are all from the US. What are the capabilities that leadership teams of winning organisations in Australia emphasise? From our research we found the following factors were the important capabilities (see figure 6.2). Leadership teams in winning organisations:

▶ have captain-coach leaders

▶ build the business, not their own careers

▶ are grown from within and have long internal experience

▶ walk the talk

▶ are passionate for the cause

▶ are decisive

▶ have a long-term view

▶ communicate

▶ are consistent

▶ have few trappings.

Figure 6.2: key capabilities of leadership teams of winning organisations

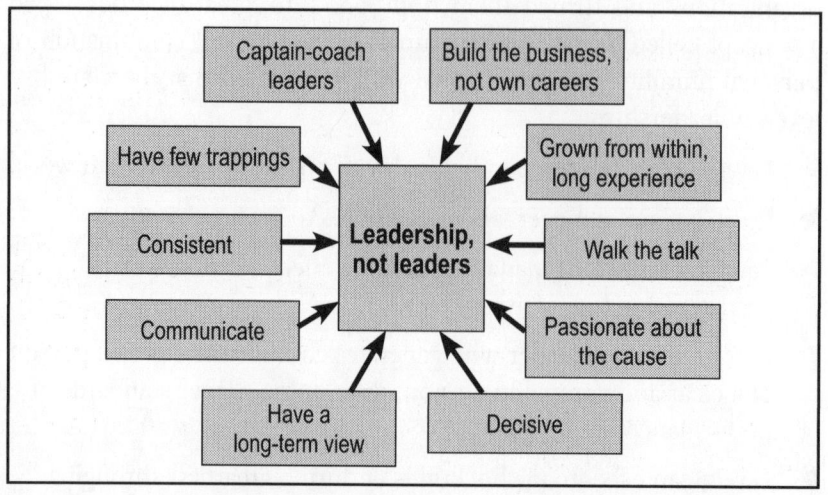

Of course, there are many other characteristics that 'leaders' have. For instance, this list doesn't mention competence, responsibility, or ability to influence! But these are the ones that our research found make the difference from leaders and leadership teams in normal organisations. We'll explore each of these ideas below.

Captain-coach leadership

A key difference in the leadership capabilities emerges between US studies and our study relating to the style of leadership. The Telstra archetype study was conducted in the early 1990s to see what the differences were between Australian expectations of leadership and those of other countries (see illustration 6.1 overleaf).

The study showed that Australians want their organisational leaders to be coaches—people who exhort them and encourage them to improve performance—rather than generals providing a vision and telling them what to do. They also want their leaders to be players on the ground during the game, showing captaincy skills in the field, supporting them during the play and sharing the work involved, not generals who are removed from the battle. It is a very egalitarian view of leadership, consistent with the historical value of mateship in the Australian culture. This view applied to leadership in general, not just to the CEO or to the top management team.

The study also found that, unlike Americans, Australians view change negatively, not positively. Australians view change as a cause of insecurity, instability and chaos, rather than as an opportunity or a challenge, as Americans do.

As a result, Australians want change to evolve and build on an existing situation, within a structured framework. Leaders are expected to provide support and nurturing during times of change, with acknowledgement and reinforcement of who their people are, in order to develop their sense of worth. Leadership that creates instability, communicates crisis, apportions blame and is authoritarian is not what they seek. Australians want a relationship with their leaders and a 'cause' to follow.

Our findings were consistent with this research. We found that leaders were surprisingly low key. They were not particularly charismatic and did not seem very egotistical. Leaders constantly referred to their 'teams' and to 'we', rather than to 'I', when discussing achievements.

Macquarie provides an example of captain-coach leadership. One Macquarie executive said:

> The role of leadership here is to create an environment that is supportive of entrepreneurs. This is a collegiate environment, not an individual one and it is definitely not an environment of command and control.

Illustration 6.1: the Telstra archetype study—desired leadership style in Australia

Telstra contracted for some research to be performed during the early 1990s to explore the 'mental highways' that were shared by its people, compared with those in other countries, and to gain a greater understanding of how Australia's unique cultural characteristics should shape its approach to business effectiveness. The study was based on a similar study done for AT&T during the 1980s.

What Telstra staff wanted from their leadership was:

- a 'cause' that had social and/or moral implications for why the organisation was moving in a particular direction
- acknowledgement of who they were
- clear guidelines about their direction
- constructive feedback on what they were engaged in.

Telstra termed this 'captain-coach' leadership—a leader who creates stability by:

- explaining reality
- defusing crises
- creating a goal or cause to strive for
- providing clear instructions
- providing a sharp focus on how to achieve results
- providing support and nurturing through difficult times
- acknowledging and reinforcing who its people are
- adding, growing and helping to develop their sense of self-worth.

What they did not want was a leader who:

- communicated crisis
- created instability
- focused on results
- provided unclear instructions
- apportioned blame
- provided no or negative feedback
- was authoritarian.

Another said:

> [The leadership team] doesn't really like to tell you what to do. The idea is to let each business operate like a small business. Each business can control its own costs.

One of the founders of the firm confirmed this:

> There is a collegial decision-making process. It is consensual, not decided by the CEO... There are very little top-down imposed decisions... If you're in the 'brains for rent' business, a dictator style of leadership does not work.

Finally, the view of the CEO at the time of writing was, 'We started out as a professional partnership doing M&A [mergers and acquisitions] and we have retained that philosophy'.

CRA (now Rio Tinto) provides us with another example. In 1986, it had already formed the public view that the role of 'manager' was to be a leader and also a coach. In 1993, CRA said in its annual report:

> An important part of our management process philosophy is to encourage a commonality of interest among all the people who work in our businesses. We are promoting managerial behaviour that breaks down the distinctions between different classes of employees: we want coaches, not bosses.

A Rio Tinto executive confirmed this view:

> Leaders are expected to lead. They have a lot of discretion. But other things are more important than [individual] leaders. For instance, the ability to listen, teamwork, operations, being well-rounded people... our ability to critique the work and to improve it... This is due to self-empowered managers trained in the principles of management, which is mostly to do with working with people, i.e. teams and relationships with others downwards, sideways and upwards.

Building a sustainable business, not their own careers

The first factor given for success in *Built to Last* is 'clock building, not time telling'—that is, leaders are focusing on building the organisation (the clock), not simply reporting on where the organisation is up to (time telling). We also found this. The leadership team focuses on building a sustainable business, rather than egotistically promoting their own careers.

James Strong provides a good example. When he was trying to integrate Australian Airlines and Qantas in 1994, he published his views in *The Australian Way*, then the in-flight magazine for both airlines. Strong was speaking to employees as much as to customers, though. In the August 1994 edition, he said:

> It is always a delight to observe a group of people displaying true teamwork... One of the greatest shortcomings of any large organisational structure is the extent to which it will tolerate people who do not really care about their jobs or have regard for the impact of their uncaring behaviour on other people... It is up to leadership to be aware of and counteract the negatives, and build the positive benefit by a committed program of activities over a period of time, creating the right atmosphere.

In September 1994, he commented on the changes that he had introduced in his first year as CEO:

> The initial steps late in 1993... were designed to bring about a different style of managing, with a flatter organisational structure and more specialised management functions... this focus on the detail of our passenger products and services... represents the most comprehensive overhaul since the early 1970s.

Brambles executives were known as never being afraid to 'get dirty' to build the business. The 'dig, lift, load and haul' philosophy of the early days, the 'garbo' mentality and the lean head office demonstrated the focus on building the business rather than enjoying the spoils of being CEO or of being in the top management team.

Home grown and stable

We found that the vast majority of leaders came from within the organisation, had been with the organisation for long periods and remained as CEO for long periods. Looking at CEOs as indicative of the leadership team, of the 40 CEOs over the 20 years in all 11 organisations, 37 (93 per cent) came from inside the organisation. For the additional period 2001–06 we found:

- ▶ five organisations had no change of CEO
- ▶ five organisations had one change of CEO
- ▶ one organisation (the Salvation Army) had two changes, consistent with its three-year rotation policy
- ▶ of the seven new CEOs, two were from outside the organisation (one of whom was brought in to address a major organisational mistake).

In total, then, over the 25 years, 42 of the 47 CEOs came from inside—89 per cent—a remarkable percentage.

This focus on promotion from within means that the organisation's strategic direction is likely to change incrementally, rather than dramatically. Of course, since the organisation is doing well and is externally focused, it only needs to change incrementally. Promotion from within also means that the organisation 'understands' the new CEO and vice versa—there are not likely to be many management changes at the top in this kind of incremental promotion, so the role of the specific individual CEO matters less.

When managers are brought in from outside, it is usually because the organisation is not performing well or it wants or needs to change significantly. Telstra, Qantas, Lend Lease, Brambles and NAB have been in that position at some point during the 25-year period (which is not surprising, given the length of time!), resulting in some introduction of external people into the top of the organisation. However, Frank Blount and Sol Trujillo at Telstra, John Menadue at Qantas and Greg Clarke at Lend Lease remain the only complete outsiders. James Strong at Qantas had been on the Qantas board and been CEO of Australian Airlines, which became part of Qantas. David Turner had been CFO at Brambles following the merger with GKN. John Stewart had been hired by Frank Cicutto to run NAB's UK businesses. Blount and Trujillo brought a number of outsiders into the top management team once they were appointed (as did Stewart at NAB and Switkowski at Telstra when promoted from inside).

These findings are consistent with Collins and Porras' work. They said:

> Visionary companies develop, promote, and carefully select managerial talent grown from inside the company to a greater degree than the comparison companies... Of 113 chief executives... only 3.5 per cent came directly from outside the company, versus 22.1 per cent of 140 CEOs at the comparison companies. (p. 173)

Similarly, Collins found only two of 42 CEOs (5 per cent) were from outside the company compared with 31 per cent from the direct comparison companies.

It is interesting to compare our winning organisations with their competitors where they have close competitors. Table 6.2 (overleaf) shows that competitor organisations were much more likely to bring in CEOs from outside. Again, this is consistent with the findings from *Built to Last* and *Good to Great*.

Table 6.2: some winning organisations and competitors—where do their CEOs come from?

Winning organisation	CEOs, 2000–06	Inside/ outside	Competitors	Recent CEOs	Inside/ outside
Woolworths	Luscombe/ Corbett	Inside/ Inside	Coles Myer	Fletcher/ Eck/ Bartels	Outside/ Outside/ Outside
National Australia Bank	Stewart/ Cicutto	Inside/ Inside	ANZ Westpac C'wealth	McFarlane Morgan Norris/ Murray	Outside Outside Outside/ Inside
Rio Tinto	Clifford	Inside	BHP Billiton	Goodyear/ Anderson/ Gilbertson	Inside/ Outside/ Inside
Qantas	Dixon	Inside	Air NZ	Norris/ Toomey/ Eddington	Outside/ Outside/ Outside

Most leaders have been with the organisation for a long period. Turnover in the winning organisations is lower than industry average. Much of what turnover there is occurs very early, as people who don't like the culture or who can't make it in the culture leave quickly.

CEOs at winning organisations lasted longer. Table 6.3 shows the range of numbers of CEOs over the last 25 years is two to six (excluding the Salvation Army, which has a policy of rotating CEOs) and the average CEO tenure is 10.5 years. This compares with the general average of around four to five years for public listed companies (at the time of writing). The advantages of leadership 'staying longer' include having more experience to make quicker decisions, avoid mistakes, develop teams, develop cover for individuals and to carry out long-term decisions.

Table 6.3: CEO tenure at winning organisations

Organisation	Number of CEOs appointed 1980–2006	Average tenure (years)
Brambles	4	9.5
Harvey Norman	3	21.0
Lend Lease	3	7.7

Organisation	Number of CEOs appointed 1980–2006	Average tenure (years)
Macquarie Bank	2	13.5
National Australia Bank	4	6.5
Qantas	4	6.5
Rio Tinto	3	10.7
The Salvation Army	9	3.0
Telstra	5	6.0
Westfield	3	24.7
Woolworths	6	6.2

Walk the talk

Another noticeable feature of these leadership teams is their links to the people in their organisation, not just to the management team, and their ability to 'get dirty', as Brambles would say. The best example of 'walking the talk' is clearly the Salvation Army. Not only do the Salvation Army people receive low pay, which gives them a common viewpoint with their clients about the materialistic economy in which we live, but Army people are also expected to live their lives according to the values the organisation is promoting. The role of the family is paramount—with couples being required to both accept the role before one member can be promoted. Alcohol is banned. The uniform makes leader behaviour very conspicuous and easy to monitor in a doubting world.

When Woolworths was undergoing a turnaround in the mid 1980s, newly appointed Executive Chairman Paul Simons discovered that Woolworths had lost its price competitiveness and its closeness to the customer. He felt that Woolworths was no longer being run by merchants and traders but by people who analysed computer printouts. Managing Director Harry Watts, future CEO Reg Clairs and other senior executives went back to working in the stores. Clairs recalled:

> We got in at five in the morning. We unloaded trucks. We stacked the delicatessen. We stacked the fruit and vegetables. We made mince in the butcher's shop. We served customers on the check out. We did all the basics. (Murray, 1999, p. 215)

Simon cut out the 'silver service, three-course lunch culture' that had evolved at head office. He cut out first-class travel, five-star hotels, insisted all company cars be Holdens and reduced the size of head office as he got the head office culture to align with the values of the stores.

In 2001, CEO Roger Corbett carried on this theme:

> I'm just a shopkeeper, not a great strategist ... Every Saturday, I drive my car out the driveway and visit stores to see them as customers see them and to meet and speak with the staff. If I know how the store runs, then everyone will need to know about it.

Gerry Harvey part-owns one store in the Harvey Norman network. This enables him to keep a direct handle on what is happening in stores, gives him direct access to customers and forces him to think and act like a franchisee. For some time he was the 'face' of Harvey Norman through doing most of the television advertising himself for the chain. While this is consistent with the idea of reducing costs and being efficient, it also had high risk for both Harvey and the organisation. If the advertising did not work, Harvey himself was right in the firing line, especially in a mass market consumer industry such as discount retailing. It would have been a lot easier to sit back and let a professional agency do all the work.

Lend Lease has an interesting approach to 'walking the talk'. Its Code of Conduct says:

> We say to our employees that if you are in doubt as to whether anything you are contemplating might breach the Code, apply the following test: 'Would I be willing to see what I'm doing or about to do described in detail on the front page of a national newspaper to be read by family and friends?' <www.lendlease.com.au>

In addressing the problems he faced when he arrived from outside Lend Lease as the new CEO, Greg Clarke noted the importance of being available:

> In a situation like that there is a deep, abiding suspicion among the management that you're here to break it all up, sell it all off and run away giggling with a sack full of money. The only way you get over that is in the long term: you stay, you commit to the organisation, you work with the people, and you prove that you're there for the long term. You build trust over time. (*AFR BOSS*, July 2006)

Be passionate for the cause

We found that the leaders were passionate about their organisations. As we noted in chapter 5, we were surprised by the passion that emerged for the reasons the organisation existed—the 'cause'. One CEO we spoke to was quite clear about the importance of passion to the success of his organisation. He said:

> You have to be passionate about the business you are in. You have to live and walk the talk. You can't just sit in the office analysing the numbers, mouthing the words. You have to really love the business if you want to inspire people to work with you.

But can you really be passionate about digging up resources, working at a bank or a telecommunications company, selling discounted goods, storing records or collecting rubbish? Yes you can! To leaders in winning organisations (and to other people in the organisation too), it is not just a job. There is a cause. This is the real reason for existence—the bigger picture altruism and raison d'etre—a cause about which the leaders (and the people) are passionate. Without that passion, a job is just a job and that isn't very motivating for most people. People want more than just a job from an organisation.

One executive, commenting on this, said, 'Normal, rational, straightforward people don't build billion-dollar businesses. It takes someone with passion, heart and emotion to do it'.

Be decisive

Leaders are expected to make decisions. Of course, through being close to their people, being open to external influences and having good information systems, they are well placed to make good decisions, and make them quickly (adapt rapidly).

A good example is when Westfield was shown a potential development site in its early days in the US:

> When David and Frank Lowy first saw the Westside Pavilion site in Los Angeles in 1980, they took two seconds to visualise its potential and told Richard Green to go ahead and see if the redevelopment they envisaged could be done. (*The Detailed Westfield Story*, p. 90)

Stunned by the speed of their decision making, Green went ahead, got the approvals and then watched as Westfield produced the necessary $8 million to pay for the land.

We have cited other examples of this speed elsewhere in the book—for example, Woolworths' change of decision over its first shopping centre tenancy, Qantas' decision to replace its fleet and Westfield's decisions on redevelopment when it purchases existing shopping centres (see chapter 4).

Have a long-term view

Being decisive is not simply about speed. It is also about commitment. Leaders in winning organisations are not simply short-term oriented, even when things are not going well. They have long-term views and this provides stability and encourages the pursuit of a clear long-term purpose. Chapter 5, on clear strategy, is about the long term and has several examples.

Rio Tinto toughed out the 1980s in the belief that its long-term view about the value of its resource deposits was correct. It was only after almost 10 years of dogged persistence that it changed its view to a more commercial perspective, when it realised that the industry paradigm had changed fundamentally. The HIsmelt revolutionary iron ore smelting procedure is another example. It was under development for 25 years, only beginning production in 2006, providing another demonstration of the organisation's ability to take a long-term view. The 30 years Rio Tinto spent developing relationships in China (and 40 years in Japan) are further testimony to this long-term perspective.

Harvey Norman has just begun to develop its portfolio of international businesses (just out of the international experiment stage of the strategic cycle) with 21 stores in New Zealand, 13 in Singapore, two in Ireland and one each in Malaysia and Slovenia. The organisation entered Ireland in 2003 and sees it as a 10-year investment. However, it expects to break even in 2007.

Brambles knew the difficulties of expanding CHEP and its other businesses into other countries, especially where it had not been operating before. Yet it announced what it was planning to do, how long it would take and did it. In 2006, CHEP was in 42 countries. Westfield has been operating shopping centre developments in the US for almost 25 years and in the 2000s has grown to become number one in the industry. It entered the UK market in 2000 with the same concept and sees the UK as a beachhead for Europe eventually.

Communicate, communicate, communicate

Since leaders are captain-coaches on the field and walk the talk, and since the organisations are externally focused, have clear strategies and adapt rapidly, the role of communicating might be assumed. But the ability to communicate and the need for communication is underestimated, while the effectiveness of communications is usually overestimated in most organisations.

What do winning organisations do differently here? Formally, leaders go to great lengths to find different channels in which to communicate frequently. At Macquarie, the CEO has a series of lunches with newly promoted leaders to explain what the role of leadership is. The CEO also attends every 'Camp Macquarie' orientation program for new employees, to present the essence of the Macquarie history, its culture and expectations. Lend Lease uses its annual planning conference to make the leadership team available to a large number of its people and propagate the views of the leadership team. Harvey Norman's conferences for its franchisees are legendary for the passion and commitment generated. At Woolworths, Roger Corbett met monthly with the 2700 staff in head office and met with a group of 50 young leaders monthly. Weekly videoconferences were held with managers across the country to rapidly disseminate the messages.

Internal newsletters are an easily available, and frequently used, tool for communicating widely. At Woolworths, which now has over 145 000 employees, the internal newsletter is used as a vehicle to extol both the position of the whole organisation and the virtues of individual successes that have made it possible — role models for others to applaud. Telstra had a daily newspaper for similar purposes. One Telstra executive said:

> Some of our people carry out extraordinary acts that don't get into the public news. But they are appreciated internally. They'll be mentioned in our daily newspaper and they'll often get a personal email from the CEO. That type of reward and recognition means more to them than... being highlighted in an external publication.

These days, the internet, intranets, video clips, road shows and videoconferences are commonly used to quickly make information available to those who want to know, due to the rapid expansion of broadband capability across organisations and the world. For instance, Rio Tinto ran a session on its corporate program, Improving Performance Together, which was webcast to cater for widely dispersed locations and stakeholders, and was broadcast live simultaneously in Australia and the UK. These types of communications will revolutionise communication in the future.

Informal communication is undoubtedly more important, however. Walking the talk, being available ('visible management'), decreasing internal structural levels, encouraging open (and two-way) communication, social activities, celebrations and casual recognition for a job well done are some of the methods used. We found, however, that while winning organisations understand the importance of communication, there were no consistent individual or unique techniques being used. They just communicated as often, as widely and in as many ways as they could.

Be consistent

Leadership needs to be consistent in its actions and its communications. Walking the talk is a clear way to achieve this. Having leaders who are home grown and having a stable leadership team are key ingredients.

We discussed consistency in some detail in chapter 3. Consistency implies incremental changes rather than revolutionary changes. So it is not surprising that when there are major changes for an organisation (such as commercialisation and public listing for Qantas and Telstra), or the organisation makes radical changes as a result of its interpretation of its environment (such as NAB, Brambles, Rio Tinto and Lend Lease), such changes are difficult to introduce, even for a winning organisation.

The concept of adapting rapidly, which we discussed in chapter 4, appears to be opposed to consistency, but if the organisation understands the need for speedy change, and the reasons for the change are communicated and understood and the culture is accepting of this, adapting rapidly can be accommodated into a consistency model.

Have few trappings

We were surprised by the relatively modest offices that most of the senior executives we visited had, considering how well their organisations had been performing for such a long time. It must be tempting for winning organisations to stop to 'smell the roses', reward themselves or relax and enjoy their success. But few, if any, seem to have this view.

In many cases, the trappings (or lack of them) reflect the strategic position that the organisation is trying to achieve. For instance, Harvey Norman, Woolworths and Brambles desperately seek to keep head office costs down for fear of the impact any blow out may have on their ability to compete and because they simply hate waste and extravagance.

The organisations attack the issue of trappings in different ways. Because Macquarie is run as a series of small businesses, each of the business leaders is anxious to keep its costs down. Parts of the 'millionaires club' look more like a computer-based sweat shop, which

Leadership, not leaders

suggests there is little correlation between success and office size, space or furniture.

There were some anomalies here though. One or two of the winning organisations had surprisingly well-appointed head offices that seemed perceptually inconsistent with their stated strategies of low-cost operations. However, each was either changing to a more aligned structure—that is, lowering the costs of head office—or had a different model of operation—that is, high quality leads to high productivity—that meant the perceived 'expensive' offices were not in fact expensive relative to the model.

Woolworths' history shows that, when it went off the rails in the early 1980s, the top management had become less focused on the business and more focused on themselves. As we mentioned in the 'Walk the talk' section, when Paul Simons came in as Executive Chair in 1987, one of the first things he did was to get rid of the silver service dining room in the executive office. Interestingly, when John Fletcher left down-to-earth Brambles to go to discount retailer Coles Myer in 2001, one of the first changes he made was to dismantle the luxurious floor of the head office building where the senior management team were and put in offices for 90 where there had been five people located previously. The trappings message was clear!

Since the first edition of this book, Woolworths, NAB and Lend Lease have all moved into new head offices, while Macquarie has announced its intention to do the same, and Rio Tinto has moved buildings. The Woolworths new office is a spectacular building, but its focus is on creating a sense of community within and of encouraging efficiency, rather than simply being glamorous. Using the stairs and walking are encouraged; lunch is to be had in open spaces, not offices; and meetings with visitors are conducted in meeting rooms rather than offices. But the overall cost of the office, which is located in the outskirts of Sydney, is said to be no more than the costs of the small head offices of each of the businesses that were scattered around the Sydney CBD.

Why do we raise this issue of few trappings? Often people are impressed by the luxury of the offices, fittings or accompanying facilities that an organisation possesses. Leaders in many organisations are notorious for the trappings they encourage or support and 'justify'. Our findings suggest that the quality of trappings is a very poor way to judge how well an organisation is likely to perform. Focus on aspects such as the people, the leadership, the strategy and the ability to execute, not the trappings. Trappings cost money. Someone (customers) has to pay for it! Do they really add value to the product?

In summary, we found a distinctive set of characteristics marked the leadership teams of winning organisations. Leaders are captain-coach leaders, building the business and grown from within. They are passionate, they walk the talk, are decisive but have a long-term view, they communicate widely—formally and informally, are consistent in behaviour and actions, and don't focus on the trappings of office. These are not the characteristics that we see in our experience of normal Australian organisations, but they should be. Thankfully, over recent years in Australia, we seem to be seeing less ostentatious behaviour from major corporations and their leaders.

Leadership right for the time

Consistent with the strategic cycle concept, we found that leadership styles varied according to the particular needs of the time for each organisation. Leaders—and leadership—focus on the issues that the organisation faces at that time. We term this 'leadership right for the time'.

However, the capabilities we have identified here for leadership in winning organisations do not vary across time periods. Only the specific nature of the issues for the particular organisation and the consequent decisions it must make vary. Being decisive, walking the talk, communicating and having a long-term view, for instance, are important regardless of the industry or the time, but the actual decisions made will depend on the specific context.

Illustration 6.2 shows how leadership issues have varied for Rio Tinto over time. Each leader was faced with quite different issues that were successfully managed at the time. In other words, Maurice Mawby's approaches for CRA, which were 'right' in 1962–74, would clearly have been inappropriate for Leon Davis in 1994–2000. Does this mean Mawby did not succeed? Or that Mawby in some way led the organisation inappropriately or incorrectly? No.

We would speculate that any 'Mawby-capable' person would be able to adjust to the needs of the organisation at the time. Indeed, the ability of the leadership and the organisation to adjust rapidly to changing needs is one key characteristic of success. But it does mean that leadership must be 'right for the time'. The issues, skills and needs change.

Leadership, not leaders

Illustration 6.2: leadership issues at Rio Tinto over time

Years	CEO	Key issues
1962–1974	Maurice Mawby	Develop CRA into a strong Australian mining house by discovering and exploiting large, high-grade deposits in Australia. Focus on technical and operational skills.
1974–1986	Rod Carnegie	Become more commercial, more analytical in considering the competitive position and customer needs. Change the nature of the working relationship between management and their people. Diversify into different industries where CRA might be able to grow more quickly and use its capabilities. Create an Australian company competing on the world stage.
1986–1994	John Ralph	Improve profitability. Implement ideas. Make it work.
1994–2000	Leon Davis	Integrate CRA with RTZ into a reunited Rio Tinto. Create a single, profit-oriented global company. Create global product businesses.
2000–	Leigh Clifford	Grow a profitable set of global businesses.

Another case is Telstra. Prior to commercialisation, Telstra CEOs were public servants who were part of government departments, and their role was to carry out the government policy of getting a phone in every home in Australia. At the time when commercialisation was introduced to Telstra (and other public sector organisations), Mel Ward's role was to develop the commercial skills of the organisation so it could change from a public sector orientation to the idea that activities had to make profits and a return on investment.

As partial privatisation approached, Frank Blount was brought in from outside to focus on improving the quality of customer service and on increasing the commercial focus. In this he succeeded admirably. However, he was fortunate, because during this time the domestic telecommunications environment was rapidly expanding. The industry—and Telstra—grew rapidly, almost regardless of what Blount and his team did!

His successor, Ziggy Switkowski, faced an industry environment where double-digit growth no longer existed but investor expectations for growth had not changed! Switkowski therefore had to seek new avenues of growth, and to increase margins to maintain profit growth. His international expansion into Hong Kong and New Zealand, his attempts to diversify revenue streams and to make substantial cost savings via reducing head count and capital expenditure were rational responses to a different set of issues.

Dissatisfied with Switkowski's results, the board hired Sol Trujillo in 2005. Trujillo faces different issues—the decline in revenue from Telstra's main fixed-line business, the need to replace the network, alternative communications technologies and the ability of the government to sell its controlling shareholding in Telstra since it gained control of Parliament in 2005. However, Trujillo 'sees' it differently as well. He is focused on the business drivers rather than managing the financial outcomes. He has been extremely aggressive in his public statements towards government, competitors and the media, demonstrating this different view as well as a completely different style.

Indeed, the ability of the leadership and the organisation to adjust rapidly to changing needs is one key characteristic of success. But it does mean that leadership must be 'right for the time'. The issues, skills and needs change.

How is 'right' leadership selected?

In each case, we see that leadership and strategy have been adjusted to meet the particular issues and needs for the time. How does this adjustment occur? How are the 'right' leaders selected?

Our research suggests two factors are responsible (see figure 6.3). First, in winning organisations, new leaders are generally selected from within. Successful organisations have good teams of leaders. They are not dependent on one single leader. As winning organisations are also externally focused and rapid to adapt, they are able to perceive the capabilities needed for the future leaders, understand that these needs are different from those of the current leaders and have a group of good leaders to choose a new CEO from.

Second, the choice of CEO, and sometimes of the other top management, is made by the board. We have noted that there is some commonality across the boards of these winning organisations. We do not think this is coincidence. Good organisations often have good boards. Good board members are desirable. Good companies seek good board members—which they find on the boards of other good organisations! So there is overlap between boards of winning organisations. They recognise each other's competence, even if they are in different industries. Interestingly, quite a number of executives we interviewed commented that 'x' company ought to be in the group of winning organisations—and it was (however, this was not revealed to them at the time)!

Figure 6.3: selecting leadership right for the time

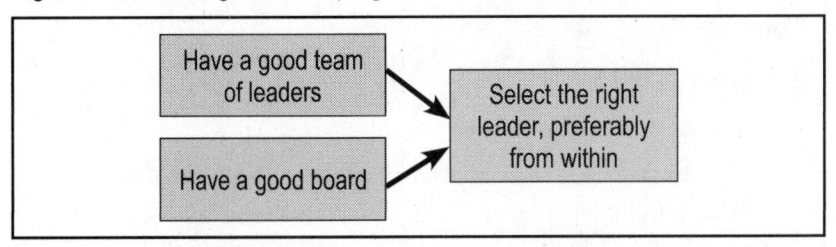

```
┌─────────────────────────────────────────────────────┐
│    ┌──────────────────┐                             │
│    │  Have a good team│──┐                          │
│    │    of leaders    │  │   ┌──────────────────┐   │
│    └──────────────────┘  └──▶│ Select the right │   │
│                              │ leader, preferably│  │
│    ┌──────────────────┐  ┌──▶│   from within    │   │
│    │ Have a good board│──┘   └──────────────────┘   │
│    └──────────────────┘                             │
└─────────────────────────────────────────────────────┘
```

NAB's recent experience also demonstrates the importance of the board, particularly when the organisation is not performing well. The forex scandal that resulted in wholesale top management team changes not only split the board but resulted in a new chair and several new board members. The board was seen as partly responsible for the scandal through failing to address the cultural and performance issues early enough. A change of board was seen as an important part of changing the culture. Indeed, a new area of business activity related to the role of the board has emerged globally. Measuring and assessing board performance is seen now as an important organisation function, as is having qualified and competent board members.

Leadership programs in winning organisations

Recognising the importance of good leadership, most of the winning organisations have formal internal leadership programs and/or models to develop the type of leadership capabilities that they wish to encourage. Illustration 6.3 (overleaf) highlights models of some of them, together with our comments. It is important to note that these leadership models do change over time (see 'Leadership right for the time'). So these models are more indicative of how the organisations see their future leadership needs than what they may have sought in the past. The variety in these models suggests the different needs of the organisations, the complexities of leadership and the difficulty of developing agreement about what are the specific sets of characteristics and capabilities required. An important aim, however, is to develop home-grown and consistent leadership and values.

> **Illustration 6.3: leadership models from some of the winning organisations**
>
> **Macquarie Bank:**
> - loose/tight management
> - sense of identification with team
> - take responsibility for results, even where support areas are also responsible
> - achieve good levels of profitability and growth
> - enhance the productivity, work satisfaction and personal development of other team members
> - protect and enhance the bank's reputation and brand name
> - enhance the quality of client relationships
> - maintain harmonious relations with competitors
> - observe limits of authority
> - cooperate with other teams
> - be agents of change to improve and develop the bank
> - communicate and promote the goals and values of the bank.
>
> Comment: this model highlights the roles of team, of balance, of entrepreneurship/growth, of managing risk, of external focus, of change and of communication.
>
> **The Salvation Army:**
> - live the mission
> - establish pastoral relationships
> - demonstrate spiritual knowledge
> - Christian discipleship
> - build the community

- develop others
- lead with firmness and compassion
- think strategically
- be personally motivated
- be adaptable
- have self-confidence
- implement plans
- be tenacious, innovative and have initiative
- understand the organisation
- work cooperatively with others
- have respect for others
- develop cooperation
- build networks
- have professional expertise.

Comment: this model covers a wide range of factors including self-management, relationships with others, building and developing networks, adaptability, walking the talk and personal competence.

Lend Lease:

- empowerment
- delegation
- autonomy, responsibility and authority
- feedback, coaching and mentoring
- strategic interdependencies—inside and outside
- collaboration.

Comment: this model is focused on structural issues, supporting mechanisms and external networking.

Illustration 6.4 (overleaf) covers another contemporary view of desired leadership styles and needs in Australia. It shows the tremendous variety of perspectives that exist in the leadership area. However, it also provides more evidence for the cause-based, egalitarian model for Australia we mentioned earlier in this chapter. It is also interesting to compare this with Collins' (2001) 'Level 5 leadership', which is related to his work in *Good to Great*. The findings are consistent with his conclusion that powerful leaders possess a 'paradoxical mixture of professional will and personal humility'.

> **Illustration 6.4: contemporary views of desirable leadership styles for Australia**
>
> A 62-nation Global Leadership and Organisational Behaviour Effectiveness (GLOBE) program was conducted by 170 researchers over 10 years in 62 cultures (see <www.thunderbird.edu/wwwfiles/ms/globe/>). It developed six culturally different leadership profile indicators:
> - values-based leadership that inspires and motivates ('values based')
> - leadership that emphasises team building ('team oriented')
> - leadership that involves others in decision making ('participative')
> - supportive and considerate leadership ('humane')
> - independent and individualistic leadership ('autonomous')
> - leadership that focuses on the safety and security of the leader ('self-protective').
>
> The table below indicates the scores for some of the different cultures of most relevance to Australian operations (Australia is in the 'Anglo' group; scoring is on a seven-point scale).
>
> | Culture | Values based | Team oriented | Participative | Humane | Autonomous | Self-protective |
> |---|---|---|---|---|---|---|
> | Anglo | 6.05 | 5.74 | 5.73 | 5.08 | 3.82 | 3.08 |
> | Germanic Europe | 5.93 | 5.62 | 5.86 | 4.71 | 4.16 | 3.03 |
> | Southern Asia | 5.97 | 5.86 | 5.06 | 5.38 | 3.99 | 3.83 |
> | Confucian Asia | 5.63 | 5.61 | 4.99 | 5.04 | 4.04 | 3.72 |
>
> Universal facilitators of leadership effectiveness were found to be (Javidan, Dorfman, de Luque and House, 2006):
> - Being trustworthy, just and honest.
> - Having foresight and planning ahead.
> - Being positive, dynamic, encouraging, motivating and building confidence.

- Being communicative, informed, coordinator and a team integrator.

Universal impediments to leadership effectiveness were found to be:
- Being a loner and asocial.
- Being non-cooperative and irritable.
- Being dictatorial.

Ashkanasy and Trevor-Roberts (2002) participated in the GLOBE program. Their key findings for Australia were:
- Values-based leadership provides vision and inspires people if done tactfully, diplomatically, but in a decisive manner.
- Leadership must be unselfish and collaborative with friends and workmates—generous, compassionate, group-oriented, i.e. egalitarian. The leader should be honest, sincere and modest while building a collaborative team.
- Leadership should not be individualistic or self-centred.
- Leadership should not be bureaucratic i.e. formal and needing to follow routines and patterns.

Young (1996) surveyed practising Australian managers looking for the most common descriptors of excellent managers they had seen. He produced the following list. Good managers:
- listen first
- acknowledge result and effort
- continuously encourage
- empower people
- celebrate even small achievements
- model appropriate behaviours
- continuously look to challenge current practices
- share the vision
- spend real time in planning
- learn from everything
- enjoy their work.

Overall, these detailed themes are also represented in our findings and are completely consistent with them.

A dominant leader?

Throughout this chapter we have argued that it is a leadership team, not an individual or charismatic leader, that is needed for success. We have also argued that the issues change over time, so that winning organisations need the 'leadership right for the time'. But the nagging doubt will remain with many readers—wasn't there one single leader who had such an influence on the organisation that that person determined its future fate? This is a very popular view.

Table 6.4 summarises our views of some of the leaders for the winning organisations in terms of this concept of a single dominant leader. It shows that, apart from the possible exception of Gerry Harvey at Harvey Norman, no one leader can be singled out as the person having the dominant effect on the organisation.

Table 6.4: a dominant leader as the driver of winning organisations?

Organisation	Possible dominant leader(s)	Comment
Brambles	Oliver Richter	While he was the 'father' of CHEP, Brambles is much more than CHEP.
Harvey Norman	Gerry Harvey	The original establishment of Norman Ross was a partnership, but Harvey has been the dominant figure in Harvey Norman to date. His wife, Katie Page, has been CEO for eight years and is well regarded in her own right, but keeps a low profile.
Lend Lease	Dick Dusseldorp	Certainly established the concepts and ideas behind Lend Lease, but the acquisition of MLC and the later development of a global real estate strategy have been just as significant in Lend Lease's development.
National Australia Bank	Nobby Clark/ Don Argus	Clark was responsible for starting the program of acquisitions that took NAB offshore and Argus carried this on. But the core of NAB had been in existence for many years prior to this and the retreat from the US in 2001 suggests that Clark and Argus have not fundamentally changed NAB.

Table 6.4 *(cont'd)*: a dominant leader as driver of winning organisations?

Organisation	Possible dominant leader(s)	Comment
Westfield	John Saunders	His role in the establishment of Westfield and its operators and welfare was critical.
	Frank Lowy	He first learnt from, then partnered with, Saunders. Then he led Westfield into overseas markets and played a dominant role in its international development. His sons have been joint MDs since 2000.
Woolworths	Percy Christmas	One of the founders and CEO for the first 21 years, when the essence of Woolworths was established.
	Theo Kelly	CEO for 26 years after Christmas and chair for 17 years till 1980.
	Paul Simons	Credited with the recovery of Woolworths from 1987 to 1995.
	Roger Corbett	With Simons as his role model, his development of Project Refresh, petrol retailing and liquor, along with his open, 'hands-on' style, have led Woolworths to great heights. Each played key roles, but none could claim to be behind the key elements of Woolworths, which has always been a team-based organisation.

Summary and key messages for leaders

In summary, leadership, not individual leaders, is important in winning organisations. Leadership is team-based behaviour, not about individuals. We found a distinctive set of characteristics marked the leadership teams of winning organisations in Australia. Leaders are captain-coach leaders, building the business and grown from within. They are passionate and they walk the talk. They are decisive but have a long-term view. They communicate, are consistent in behaviour and actions and don't focus on the trappings of office. These are not the characteristics that we see in our experience of normal Australian organisations.

Leadership is right for the time. Winning organisations often have internal leadership models and leadership programs, recognising the importance to them of developing appropriate leadership behaviour. The idea that a winning organisation might be entirely due to a single dominant leader is not substantiated.

The key messages for leaders from this chapter are:

▶ Develop a leadership team.

▶ Treat the board as part of the team.

▶ Focus leadership behaviour on building the business.

▶ Develop captain-coach leader behaviour.

▶ Ensure that the leadership team is passionate about the business.

▶ Develop and grow leaders within the business.

▶ Have a long-term view.

▶ Make decisive, consistent decisions.

▶ Communicate widely, formally and informally.

▶ Recognise that future leadership will face different circumstances and need different skills from those currently used, and select leaders from within who have those skills.

7 Looking out, looking in

Externally focused Future orientation

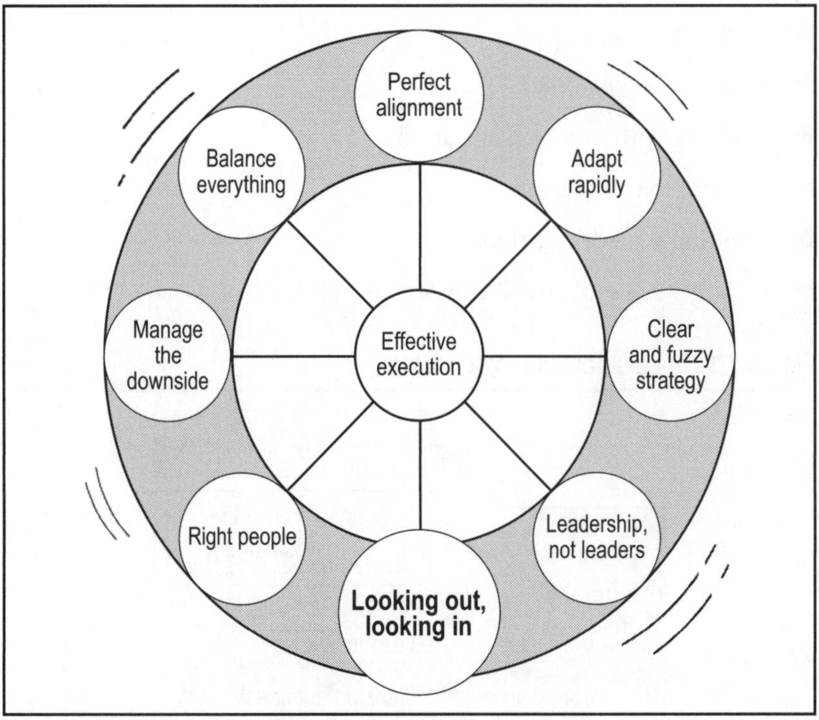

Perfect alignment
Adapt rapidly
Clear and fuzzy strategy
Leadership, not leaders
Looking out, looking in
Right people
Manage the downside
Balance everything
Effective execution

So far, our research has suggested that the essence of winning is internal focus—having a strategy, good leadership, aligning and adapting, in order to execute. Does this mean that winning is simply about extremely good internal focus and execution? Can we ignore what is happening outside the organisation?

Our research found that, while the winning organisations were concerned with aligning all their internal activities, they were also externally focused. They were not simply looking within their own organisations and their own physical environments. They were actively engaged in looking out—exploring what customers wanted, what other organisations were doing, what the community wanted, both in Australia and overseas, now and in the future.

It's not enough for those wanting to be in the First XI to concentrate on just playing the game. These days winning players have to be role models off the field. They have to represent their countries diplomatically, give time and money to charities, perhaps even start their own charities, and be able to speak well and often to the media. There are many aspects of 'looking out' for winning organisations!

Our research found that this element of looking out, being externally focused while also looking in as we have already shown, demonstrated itself in several specific ways (see figure 7.1), which we'll look at in this chapter:

▶ focusing on customers
▶ working with other organisations
▶ focusing on the future
▶ thinking outside Australia
▶ having a sense of community responsibility.

Figure 7.1: key elements of external focus

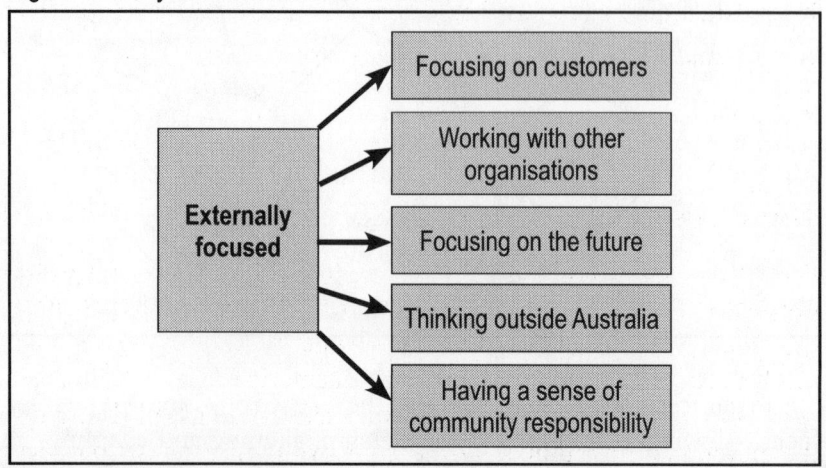

What about shareholders? Aren't they a key part of 'looking out'? We have not included focus on shareholders as a part of external focus. Good results for shareholders, or key stakeholders in the case of non-profit organisations, are a prerequisite for considering an organisation to be successful. All organisations understand that solid shareholder or key stakeholder returns are required.

But shareholder or key stakeholder returns are an outcome, not a cause of success. We are concerned in this research with the causes of success for winning organisations, from which the outcomes—including shareholder returns—follow. Winning organisations do not think of focusing on shareholders or key stakeholders as a *means* of winning, but as *measures* of winning. The concept of 'effective execution' as an outcome includes the results for shareholders. Shareholders, then, are not forgotten or omitted by any means! But they are not a key area winning organisations are externally focused on.

Focusing on customers

It should be no surprise that winning organisations focus on customers. After all, unless customers strongly support the organisation's products and services, how will it succeed? Indeed, over the last five years, the pressure on organisations to be responsive to customers has increased dramatically; however, many still fail to deliver what customers want.

But what is it that winning organisations do to make 'focusing on customers' work? Our research found four factors that winning organisations used (see figure 7.2 overleaf). They:

▶ think 'customer'
▶ conduct intensive market research
▶ develop customised products and services
▶ manage customer relationships.

Think 'customer'

Perhaps the most important aspect is 'think customer'. Each of the organisations is clear that its very existence is dependent on satisfying customers. By thinking from the customer's perspective, the organisation can better meet the real needs that customers have.

The Salvation Army provides a very clear example of this. Since the Salvation Army, unlike all the other winning organisations, is a not-for-profit organisation, it has no real reason for existence if its 'customers' (it does not use this word) do not value its services. But there are lots of welfare organisations with which the Salvation Army competes. Most of its services are also provided by other welfare or government organisations.

Figure 7.2: focusing on customers

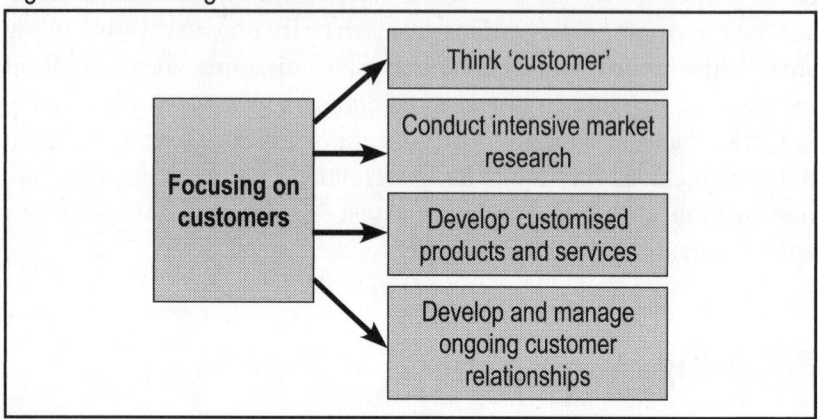

```
Focusing on customers → Think 'customer'
                     → Conduct intensive market research
                     → Develop customised products and services
                     → Develop and manage ongoing customer relationships
```

Why is it, then, that the Salvation Army is so well trusted and supported? One reason it is trusted is that it really understands the problems its clients face and produces practical solutions that have as an underlying philosophy the value of the family unit. The services are delivered not by do-gooders, not by government bureaucrats, but by people who are themselves not very well off, are committed and non-judgemental and who can therefore empathise with the issues faced by clients.

Moreover, research indicates that it is consistently named as the charity that people would most like to donate to. Its public slogan 'Thank God for the Salvos' has 98 per cent public recognition. The Red Shield logo is widely recognised and its uniform gives it a visible presence, even though its uniformed officers make up only around 10 per cent of its staff <www.superbrands.com.au>.

'Thank God for the Salvos' is not just a marketing slogan; it is based on the real experience of the Salvation Army as an organisation that faces the issues when sometimes no other organisation does. 'Put your hands together for Sally. She's the only one who cares'—a line from a popular song by Sade—captures this idea. How many organisations are so well loved and respected that they have songs written about them?

Winning 'for-profit' organisations also 'think "customer"'. Westfield Shoppingtown developed its 'Ten commandments for customer relations' (see illustration 7.1) to remind staff of this. In addition, it developed a Westfield Shoppingtown promise:

> We promise to keep you smiling each and every time you visit. Our friendly Westfield people are always here for you, with directions, gift suggestions and of course, a friendly smile. If there's anything you need, just let us know. Service with a smile.

Illustration 7.1: Westfield's 'Ten commandments for customer relations'

1. The customer is never an interruption to your work.
2. Greet every customer with a friendly smile.
3. Call customers by name.
4. Remember, you are the company!
5. Never argue with a customer.
6. Never say 'I don't know'.
7. Remember the customer pays your wages.
8. State things in a positive way.
9. Brighten every customer's day!
10. Always go the extra mile!

It also developed door decals ('Welcome to our town'; 'You are now leaving our town') that reinforced the same message of friendliness and community. All of this has the same, consistent message—and yet it is the specific retailers, not Westfield, that these customers are visiting!

Woolworths thinks of itself as a buying agent for the customer, committed to the idea of passing on cost savings in the form of lower prices. The dramatic reductions in milk and egg prices to customers in 2001, achieved by negotiating nationally for lower supply prices, are examples of delivering that result.

Conduct intensive market research

Another way to focus on customers is to undertake extensive market research. This is particularly appropriate in mass markets, where customised products and services may be less feasible. Telstra undertakes continuing major market research studies through its

Telecom Customer Attitudes to Service (TELCATS) operation, which it began in 1987. TELCATS enables it to understand customer attitudes and preferences, and hence design products to suit those needs. Since it was partially privatised, the number of products and services offered by Telstra has dramatically expanded to reflect the needs of particular customer segments, often identified through the market research.

Qantas is another that invests heavily in market research, for similar reasons. A selection of passengers is surveyed and passenger comments are encouraged as a stimulus to improving service levels. In 2001, Qantas involved 65 000 customers in 14 countries in its market research activity.

Woolworths does not focus so much on formal research, though it does use a lot of focus groups, but feels it gets a lot of customer feedback through its checkout operators, who are encouraged to gather and summarise it. Its attention to detail keeps managers close to customers, enabling them to sense changes in the market very quickly. Woolworths also has installed a small supermarket in its head office complex, which it uses to trial new products or new processes on its own staff first.

There are many other examples. For instance, the Salvation Army carries out extensive market research before deciding to embark on offering a new welfare service. Brambles extensively researches the market before entering a new country with its products and services. Woolworths seeks input from its customers whenever possible and Westfield conducts extensive end-customer surveys to ensure that changes meet customer needs.

Develop customised products and services

A closely related aspect to 'think "customer"' and conducting market research is designing products and services for particular customers or for particular customer niches. This ensures that the products and services meet the real needs of those particular customers, not customers in general. For Brambles and Lend Lease, this is apparent in the development of unique products and their long-lasting relationships with customers over time. Brambles developed a variety of CHEP pallets to suit different markets and industries. Cleanaway developed a variety of waste containers to suit different types of waste, again based on the needs of particular customers and industries.

Lend Lease sits down with its customers and develops cost-saving sharing plans so that, if certain savings are made, they are shared with customers. This process builds trust and commitment, especially when the savings are actually delivered. It also aligns customer and organisational goals. But it is not easy, or common! Most organisations are concerned about how to charge more to customers and simultaneously give less! And then they don't deliver!

Macquarie seeks out niches where customers are either poorly served or not served at all. It developed the first cash management trust in 1980 for retail investors seeking access to the then-high wholesale investment rates available for their surplus short-term cash balances. In the 1990s, it pioneered the development of private infrastructure financing and investing through the use of specialised listed trusts to provide opportunities for retail investors. Subsequently, it has used this same process to develop specialised trusts for a wide range of asset types such as tourism, telcos and utilities.

The Salvation Army, in conjunction with several government departments and academic bodies, developed Youthworx in 2004—a multimedia radio broadcasting and media arts project to help homeless and disadvantaged youth. Broadcasting of Youthworx is undertaken through SYN-FM, a youth radio station launched in Victoria in 2003. The aim is for the young people involved to gain skills and confidence from their participation.

Harvey Norman has developed Renovations as an add-on for those customers ordering more than $18 000 of kitchen, bathroom or laundry products from its stores. Renovations provides a design service that is integrated with the store products, and solves the frequent problem of aligning the designer or builder and the desired product range through the provision of a full project management service.

Developing and managing ongoing customer relationships

Another way to focus on customers is to develop ongoing customer relationships. Customer relationship management (CRM) is a developing field of marketing, designed to focus on the whole customer over a period of time, not just on a particular transaction. Because of this relative newness, our research did not find many examples of the use of formal CRM systems. However, developing and managing customer relationships on an ongoing basis is recognised as important by winning organisations.

NAB's Customer Account Management System (CAMS) began in 1988 and was one of the first attempts by a bank to understand and manage customers. It enabled the bank to understand the customer's whole position with the bank, instead of focusing on the results of individual bank products, as was common elsewhere in the industry. As a result, bank staff are able to approach customers with a full picture of their current and past history and use this information to anticipate and meet customers' ongoing, and changing needs. This proactive approach compares favourably with the usual tactic of waiting to react to a customer enquiry.

Qantas' frequent flyer scheme is another example of developing and managing ongoing customer relationships. Qantas is also a member of the global Oneworld alliance, which treats top-tier frequent flyers of one airline in the alliance as frequent flyers of all partners. Though its scheme, introduced in 1990, was not significantly different from that of its close competitor Ansett or other international airline schemes, it gave Qantas a terrific advantage when Ansett collapsed. This was due to the inability of the competing Star Alliance to offer a viable product in Australia following Ansett's collapse and the lack of interest in offering a frequent flyer scheme by low-cost competitor Virgin Blue. It was not until 2005 that Virgin Blue introduced a frequent flyer scheme—a key to encouraging the business market to travel with it.

Other organisations have less formal ways of managing customer relationships. In industrial businesses, relationships with customers are often critical. Lend Lease described the way its relationships with international customers have evolved over time, as follows:

> What is emerging is a series of clients who require a spectrum of services, often starting with consulting and advisory and progressing through to development, project management, finance and structuring. With this range of services come long-term relationships and alliances, and greater security and predictability of revenue and profit. (Lend Lease 2000 annual report)

One example of a long ongoing customer relationship exists between Westfield and Coles Myer. In 1960, Coles wanted to expand into New South Wales, which it did by takeover initially. Westfield approached Coles to persuade it to take space in one of its centres. During the negotiations, Coles mentioned that it was looking for other sites. Westfield staff drove Coles staff around Sydney looking for sites. Coles nominated the sites and Westfield then obtained them:

> Westfield quickly understood exactly what Coles required and deployed scouts to locate sites. In the early 1960s, in a matter of three years, it had built seventeen supermarkets for Coles. (*The Detailed Westfield Story*, p. 33)

It was a mutually beneficial partnership. Westfield played a major role in getting Coles established in New South Wales and Coles contributed to getting Westfield launched in Australia.

Westfield provides a range of extra services to its retailers, including retailing education seminars, skills development, consulting advice and retail study tours in Australia and overseas. In this sense, many of Westfield's customers see it not as a 'landlord' but as a 'business partner', even though it is renowned for being quite hard in its negotiations of rentals with retailers. Its vacancy rate of less than 1 per cent in its shopping malls is testimony to the desire of its retailers to remain with Westfield. One retailer said:

> I regard Westfield as a business partner, not a landlord. A landlord is only interested in the rent and sues you when you can't pay. Westfield is different. It cares about your business succeeding. If you are in trouble, it will send in consultants to help. On many occasions I have used this assistance. (*The Detailed Westfield Story*, p. 129)

Working with other organisations

Focusing on customers is just one way of thinking about 'looking out'. Working with joint venture partners, suppliers and governments are some other ways in which winning organisations think about being externally focused (see figure 7.3). Winning organisations see other organisations as extensions of their own business. They see the cooperation and coordination with other organisations as essential to their own success, so they manage these relationships!

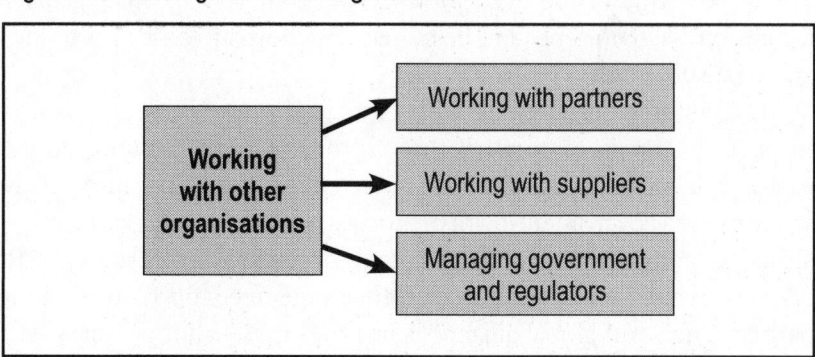

Figure 7.3: working with other organisations

- Working with other organisations
  - Working with partners
  - Working with suppliers
  - Managing government and regulators

These relationships have several themes in common:

▶ An ability to reduce an organisation's capital commitment. By working with other organisations, their capital can be used as part of the organisation's own expansion.

▶ An ability to reduce the risk involved in any activity. Joint venture arrangements not only reduce capital costs but lock in either guaranteed suppliers or customers, reducing the risk of the activity failing.

▶ An ability to achieve the idea through the resources, capabilities and skills of the other organisation. Other organisations bring their own sets of capabilities, increasing the combined capabilities well beyond those of the organisation itself. Some also share the rewards as the counter to sharing the risk.

▶ An ability to undertake projects that would not otherwise be feasible. Combining capabilities and capital enables the organisation to undertake projects it would be unable to do by itself.

Working with partners

Our research found that most of the winning organisations are deeply involved in a range of long-term joint venture relationships, particularly as they spread out into new locations and markets. These joint ventures are a clearly chosen style of operation, rather than a set of opportunistically chosen, short-term activities. Working with joint venture partners enables organisations to expand their operations more quickly and access the capabilities of other organisations. However, the loss of control and the need for effective joint venture management means joint activities need to be closely monitored if these approaches are to be successful.

In Qantas' case, working with partner airlines is essential if it is to offer the range of services that customers want. Because airline routes are negotiated between governments, and because many airlines are government-owned, the ability to work with other airlines—competitors in many cases—is essential if Qantas is to offer its desired route structure. Qantas' membership of the multi-partner Oneworld global alliance is one way in which it operates very closely with partner airlines. Codesharing is another, which it also uses extensively. Achieving common standards and levels of customer service is a key issue for both customers and for partner airlines, to deliver what customers want and expect from such an alliance.

Brambles began its partnership with Guest Keen Nettlefold plc (GKN) in 1972, when it convinced GKN that its (Brambles') idea for introducing CHEP into the UK was economically viable, even though none of the GKN businesses was similar to CHEP. Success in the UK led to GKN partnering Brambles' expansion with CHEP into Europe, and then into North America. The merging of operations of the two organisations in 2001 was the final cementing of the partnership arrangement, resulting in a single organisation.

Lend Lease has maintained important relationships with a wide variety of partners. For instance:

- Lend Lease worked with MLC as a major investor in its buildings beginning in 1958. In 1982, Lend Lease acquired 50 per cent of MLC and in 1985 it moved to 100 per cent ownership.
- In 1981, it partnered with the ACTU to develop skills training.
- In 1994, it partnered with IBM to establish Integrated Systems Solutions Corporation Australia (ISSC), a technology outsourcing organisation.
- It has also partnered with:
  - BP to provide all its service stations globally
  - Brambles to enter the airport privatisation market
  - John Lewis and Mirvac in building and construction
  - Prudential in investment
  - Vanguard and Maple-Brown Abbott in funds management.

On any particular project, Lend Lease is also very good at managing partners and suppliers. It is very disciplined up-front in terms of briefs, scoping the project, undertaking all appropriate pre-planning activities and getting the best people from all over the world to work on the project.

Macquarie Bank also uses partnerships extensively. Recent partnerships include:

- 2001—joint venture with Industrial Bank of Japan; alliance with Shinhan Bank in Korea
- 2004—alliance with Nedbank in South Africa

- 2005—joint venture with Thai Military Bank; joint venture with Macquarie Pacific Star in Singapore
- 2006—joint venture with First South Financial Services in South Africa.

Over the same period, the Salvation Army has worked with the Australian Bureau of Statistics, RMIT University, Guest Furniture, Victorian Relief, Baxter Healthcare and St Vincent de Paul on a variety of projects. Woolworths' joint venture with Caltex has been key to dominating the petrol retailing market.

Working with suppliers

In contrast to our findings about working with other organisations and focusing on customers, we were surprised to find that supplier relationships were not regarded as nearly as important to winning organisations as a key for success. The only 'supplier' that was clearly important to all organisations was people—those who worked for the organisation (see chapter 8).

However, there are examples of how suppliers are important. Lend Lease and Brambles both have as a philosophy that they wish to work with the best organisations they can find. This is on the basis that the best organisations will be leaders in their fields, pacesetters in industry standards and are likely to have good and professional relationships and practices. Each finds that it works with the same organisations—as supplier, partner or customer—over and over again. This also reduces the degree of marketing needed to 'find' customers for the future and the administrative costs of purchasing in seeking suppliers.

Woolworths is another that sees suppliers as important. In its annual report in 1995, it said:

> We intend to work closely with our suppliers to improve the supply management chain as part of our commitment to support major branded products. Our suppliers have recognised us as being fair, open and responsive in our dealings and our promotion and development of their own branded products has resulted in the strong growth of product category sales and brand management in our stores...

Telstra partners with its major technology suppliers—Alcatel, Ericsson and Cisco systems—to gain access to the huge global research and development budgets that they have.

Westfield and Lend Lease both recognise the importance of suppliers of capital as suppliers. Lend Lease set up General Property

Trust—and Westfield followed with Westfield Property Trust—as a source of funds to support the growth of their large-scale property developments.

Nevertheless, in our original research, these examples were not seen by the winning organisations in general as key factors in their success. This may well be an area where even winning organisations can develop in the future. The development of supply chain management as a discipline of equal importance to managing operations internally has grown rapidly in recent years. Woolworths' Project Refresh began concentrating on supply chain management once it became efficient internally.

Managing government and regulators

Many Australian organisations believe it would be better if the government and regulators simply left them alone to get on with business. However, regardless of the accuracy of this sentiment, it is not going to happen! Therefore, managing government involvement in the industry, or in business in general, is necessary if organisations are to either reduce government interference or receive government assistance for better business outcomes. In some industries, managing government agreements or rules is critical for organisational success. Hence, managing governments and their regulation processes can be a critical element for success or failure. This element is often overlooked by organisations that focus only on internal operations, or even on their competitors. Lobbying and public relations skills can be very important, if under-publicised, for obvious reasons! Macquarie has hired a large number of ex-politicians or public servants to provide them with access, information and thinking about the ways governments and regulators make decisions.

Most of the winning organisations are intimately affected by government rules and regulations. Telstra is perhaps the most affected, since the federal government still owned 51 per cent of the telco in 2006, while it simultaneously controls industry regulation. Telstra's ability to manage the regulatory process, and 'manage down' its 100 per cent pre-deregulation market share to levels that allow sustainable competitors to emerge, has been a major component of its success since its partial privatisation. After almost 15 years of this deregulations process, only Optus and Vodafone have emerged as sustainable competitors, and then only in defined segments of Telstra's total market.

The federal government has had a major conflict of interest. It received half of Telstra's annual dividends and has received all of the sale proceeds from the three share sales to date. Yet, through its regulatory arm—the Australian Competition and Consumer Commission—it has been trying to develop a competitive industry, which requires Telstra to 'lose' market share and customers! While its competitors have complained bitterly, the regulators have been unable to enforce quick changes to the industry as Telstra has successfully used the court appeal system to slow the process of change and thus slow the loss of its customers and market share—and profits—which benefit the government! The sale in November 2006 of most of the government's shares in Telstra has significantally reduced this conflict of interest.

For Qantas, also coming from a government-ownership background, managing government and regulators has been similarly important. While there are almost 40 airlines that fly into Australia, some who have sought to enter the international into-Australia market have been denied permission. These denials of new entrants often suited Qantas' wishes—as well as its government owner! Of course, governments in other countries have similarly denied Qantas' own requests to expand its routes—in particular the US and Hong Kong. Now, as a completely privately owned airline, Qantas in some ways competes at a disadvantage in country-to-country negotiations where many other airlines are still government-owned. Nevertheless, Singapore Airlines and other non-US airlines have consistently been denied access to the Australia-US market by the government, a decision that would seem to favour Qantas more than customers.

Rio Tinto deals with a variety of governments (national, regional and local) that approve lease exploration or mining, so good government relationships are very important. CRA took the extreme tack of becoming 'Australianised' under Foreign Investment Review Board (FIRB) legislation in 1978, so that it could be treated as an Australian company, even though it was majority-owned by UK miner RTZ. CRA committed to work towards majority Australian ownership within a specified time limit and had achieved that by 1986. Its highly nationalistic CEO of the time, Rod Carnegie, was convinced of the importance of Australia developing its own international mining companies. He saw the Australianisation process as a way for CRA to succeed at this. It gave CRA greater freedom to pursue projects with more flexibility than if it had been bound by the restrictive provisions of the foreign investment policies of successive federal governments. This step of becoming Australianised shows how CRA was prepared to manage the government relationship to its advantage.

In the Salvation Army's case, government is the biggest source of welfare funds. Coupled with the increasing desire of governments to get out of the actual provisioning of many welfare services, the Salvation Army's ability to work with government—as partner in terms of achieving the objectives of the funding—is critical to its ability to receive funds for its desired and required services.

Westfield is another organisation whose management of government relationships—mostly local government in its case—is critical to its success. Westfield's ability to get rapid planning permission for its sites has been outstanding. This ability has been important for getting developments and redevelopments started earlier than competitors would dream imaginable. Occasionally Westfield has been involved in controversy over its practices but, when challenged, it has always made it clear and open what those practices have been.

The 'battle for Eastgardens' provides an interesting glimpse. In the early 1980s, General Motors-Holden closed its Sydney plant and WD & HO Wills signalled it was about to do the same with a nearby site. Reluctant to lose more jobs, the NSW Government brought Wills and Westfield together and, after the government added a piece of Crown land to the package, Wills agreed to stay and expand while Westfield agreed to build a shopping centre—Eastgardens. Protests from all sides came regarding the use of Crown land and sweetheart deals for mates from other retailers who were affected by the new shopping centre. In July 1982, the appeal on the rezoning was heard in the NSW Land and Environment Court and the future of the development looked shaky. However, the NSW Government intervened and passed an Act of Parliament that ended the proceedings and precluded any appeal.

Steven Lowy commented on Westfield's fierce defence of its planning rulings:

> We...often...fight against re-zonings, particularly from industrial to retail sites...We have of course over the years put hundreds of millions into a site, sometimes billions of dollars into a site, based on certain planning laws, and we will go to great lengths to make sure that those planning laws that are set down by government, and decisions that we are making based off those planning rules, are adhered to...We see it as protecting our shareholders' interests; we see it as protecting the interests of the hundreds of retailers that are in our malls. (*AFR BOSS*, July 2006)

There are many ways in which relationships with governments and regulators may need to be managed. Winning organisations see this as an important part of their activities for achieving success. The specific issues and approaches will vary from one organisation and industry to another, but government relationships cannot be ignored. They must be managed.

Focusing on the future

So far in this chapter we have shown that winning organisations do focus externally, not just internally. The implication has been that they focus externally on the present. However, we found that winning organisations also focus on the future, not just the present. They are concerned with how their industries and organisations will develop and what the implications of these developments will be. Consequently, they are frequently ahead of their time, or ahead of their industry, in making changes to the way they are run, where they compete and what product and service set they compete with. They are leaders, not followers, in industry and organisational change.

There are two ways in which they focus on the future (see figure 7.4):

▶ taking a whole-of-industry view of the future

▶ focusing on the future of the organisation.

Figure 7.4: focusing on the future

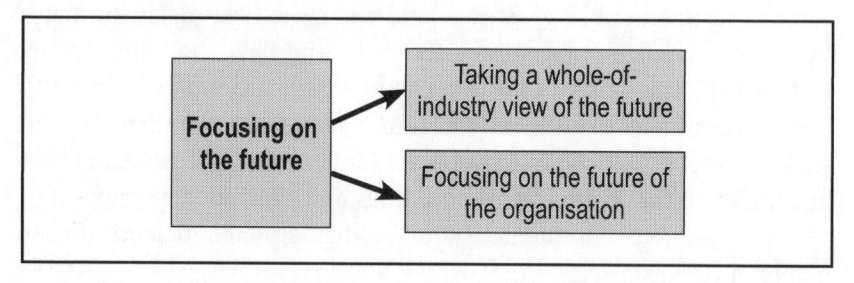

Taking a whole-of-industry view of the future

We frequently observed that winning organisations had a clear view about the nature of their industry and its future development, not just their own organisation. When Brambles decided to go global during the mid 1990s, it was to a large extent a repudiation of its past ways of operation as a series of independent small business units focused on local opportunities. Commenting on this, CEO John Fletcher said:

> This is not in any way to say that the old ways were not right... They were fine, but the world has changed... we were always out in front of our competitors, who were by and large 'little guys', and our people were on average better than them. But our competition is no longer the 'little guy' over whom Brambles has an advantage. (Carew, 2000, p. 233)

Qantas is another that has always had a whole-of-industry view. Qantas has always been aggressive about proactively pursuing its view of the future rather than reacting to industry pressure. For instance, it:

- ▶ pursued its goal of becoming a round-the-world airline in 1958
- ▶ tried to acquire Air New Zealand when it was privatised in 1988, and then tried to form a variety of strategic alliances with it in the 2000s
- ▶ sought $6 billion from the government for plane fleet expansion in 1989 to ride the wave of tourism growth
- ▶ cut costs and improved profitability as low-cost airlines became common throughout the world during the late 1990s
- ▶ developed Jetstar Asia in 2004 as a joint venture to be a low-cost Asian airline flying out of Singapore
- ▶ developed Jetstar as a domestic low-cost airline in 2004, competing directly with the Qantas brand
- ▶ seeks to be one of the world's major airlines in what it sees as the coming industry consolidation in the 2000s.

In quite different industries, for different reasons, Rio Tinto and NAB both saw the commoditisation of their basic products and services, resulting in them being unable to sustain existing cost levels. Both focused on cost control well before their competitors. For Rio Tinto this meant trying to change the nature of workforce management in the mining industry by moving to negotiated individual contracts, rather than accepting industry-wide union-negotiated agreements that reduced opportunities for flexibility, initiative and cost reduction.

For NAB it meant the early recognition that, in a more open regulatory environment, costs were far too high in the industry and low-cost operation would be an industry-leading position with competitive advantage. NAB's successful focus on cost control in the 1990s forced its competitors to address their own cost levels explicitly, rather than simply continue with existing industry practices.

Westfield is always concerned with industry developments. When the Chadstone shopping centre was developed in Melbourne in 1960—and set the standard for shopping centres in Australia—John Saunders and Frank Lowy were not invited to its opening. Undeterred, Saunders flew to Melbourne, crawled under the protective wire and gatecrashed the opening. He spent most of his time observing in great detail the specifics of the layout of the centre in order to improve his own thinking about the latest developments first-hand, rather than enjoying the celebrations.

Focusing on the future of the organisation

Another approach to considering the future is the narrower way of simply thinking about where the organisation itself is going and what its future is likely to be, regardless of industry developments.

Lend Lease constantly referred to its views of the future in its annual reports until it ran into global strategy implementation problems in 2000 (see illustration 7.2). From its early days Lend Lease held conferences considering external views that might have an impact on the future of the organisation. For instance, in 1981 Lend Lease held its 'Viewpoint 81' conference for 20 of its own leaders and 20 invited distinguished representatives from labour, business and government, to consider the theme of resolution of the conflict between capital and labour. This topic was relevant to how Lend Lease might compete in the future and was highly advanced thinking compared with other industry competitors at the time. It was not for another six years that the Industrial Relations Commission formally allowed enterprise bargaining to begin and thus allowed management and unions to sit down with only the particular enterprise's future, and the future of its particular people, to be taken into account.

Rio Tinto also looks into the future. As part of its Improving Performance Together program, Rio Tinto embarked on a major future scenario planning exercise for its iron ore business (see illustration 7.3 on page 190). Rio Tinto is also developing the 'Mine of 2020' concept—the idea of a completely ecologically sustainable mine. It sees ecological sustainability as a future trend and wishes to be ahead of that trend, rather than have the concepts forced on it.

Qantas' corporate-change program, 'Sustainable Future', is clearly aimed to position the airline for a future where much lower cost levels will be necessary for efficient—and sustainable—flying.

In summary, winning organisations consider their own future and also that of the industry from an external perspective. They are proactive, not reactive, and are leaders in thinking about—and acting on—how they see the future developing.

Leadership, not leaders

Organisation	Possible dominant leader(s)	Comment
Macquarie Bank	David Clarke/ Mark Johnson	Established the key elements of the Macquarie 'system', but both acknowledge that Macquarie has developed in businesses and locations that they in no way envisaged.
Qantas	James Strong	Oversaw fundamental changes in Qantas in terms of commercialisation and integration of the domestic airline, but Qantas was a high-service, high-reliability airline for many years before his term in office.
Rio Tinto	Maurice Mawby	In charge when the fundamental large-scale discoveries for CRA where made.
	Rod Carnegie	Changed CRA from an excellent Australian miner to a commercial international organisation, but this was an important 'add on' rather than a fundamental change—CRA could not have been successful without its earlier mining excellence.
The Salvation Army	William Booth	Established the Salvation Army in the UK, and provided initial support, but had nothing in particular to do with the success of the Australian church.
	John Gore/ Edward Saunders	Started the Australian church. No particular Australian leaders are credited with determining the future of the Australian organisation's welfare activities.
Telstra	Frank Blount	While he changed the customer service and commerical orientation of the organisation, this work had been in progress for five to 10 years previously. Like Qantas, Telstra had a high technical competence that had been in existence for many years.

Illustration 7.2: Lend Lease forecasts its future

1981

Its future lies in the further development of the group's business in Australia and further expansion in the USA, Asia and the Pacific region.

1983

The successful companies of tomorrow will be those that... become international in outlook. Increasingly, companies compete on a multinational basis... The next five years will be devoted to a consolidation in the USA and Asia... Lend Lease sees the trend from an industrial base to one of services and information.

1987

Objective is to identify and act on trends at least five years before they become evident in the market...

1988

Some years ago we identified financial services as a growth business... We have embarked on providing basic financial services with the ultimate aim of also closing that loop so as to be able to provide all financial services to individuals under one contract throughout their life...

1991

Globalisation also means we can no longer gauge ourselves from a peculiarly rational perspective... A director has also been made responsible for researching and implementing the best environmental practices... An integral part of the change process involves the transformation of Lend Lease into a learning organisation...

1995

Lend Lease's markets will undergo rapid change in the next 10 years... Two major shifts... the emergence of South East Asia... and the impact of technology.

2000

We are now a global company, recently established and largely through acquisitions, but the objective is quite clear—to carry on Lend Lease's traditions and become the most respected real estate organisation in the world...

(Lend Lease annual reports)

> **Illustration 7.3: Rio Tinto looks to the future**
>
> In 2004, Rio Tinto Iron Ore (RTIO) was expanding by 120 per cent to meet Chinese demand. The RTIO executive group recognised that new capabilities would be required. The executive also knew that such growth periods are prone to cause sudden shifts in industry structure, so decided to conduct a comprehensive review of alternative futures for the business.
>
> Over six months, the top team was involved in 130 days of team workshops, plus numerous one-on-one meetings, and the next tier of management was involved in more than 200 days of structure workshops to test the findings and prepare for implementation.
>
> The whole process was designed and managed in-house, but some external support and independent experts were involved. The process involved:
>
> - development of external scenarios for the iron and steel value chain
> - definition of positioning and capability options, considering people, technology and value-chain management as key capabilities
> - development of six fundamentally different business models, thinking well beyond the status quo
> - evaluating the options, using financial, value variance, aspirational fit and probability of success perspectives
> - the executive team choosing the final business model
> - affirming the choice through public exposure to global companies displaying best practice components of the recommended model. (This proved to be critical in building implementation resolve.)
>
> The outcomes were not simply agreement on a future direction but deep understanding of the business model and buy into it, which was critical to enabling ownership of implementation processes.

Thinking outside 'Australia'

Most growing Australian organisations become 'international' at some point in their lives. As part of being externally focused, we found that winning organisations are very aware of what is going on in their industries outside Australia and are not just focused on the domestic market. We found there were four aspects to this (see figure 7.5):

1 going overseas early

2 bringing overseas ideas to Australia

3   taking Australian ideas overseas

4   recognising that they are competing in an international market.

This links to our comments on innovation (see chapter 4) that a great deal of innovation in winning organisations seems to be related to moving ideas across geographical boundaries, rather than developing fundamental 'big bang' new ideas.

Figure 7.5: thinking outside 'Australia'

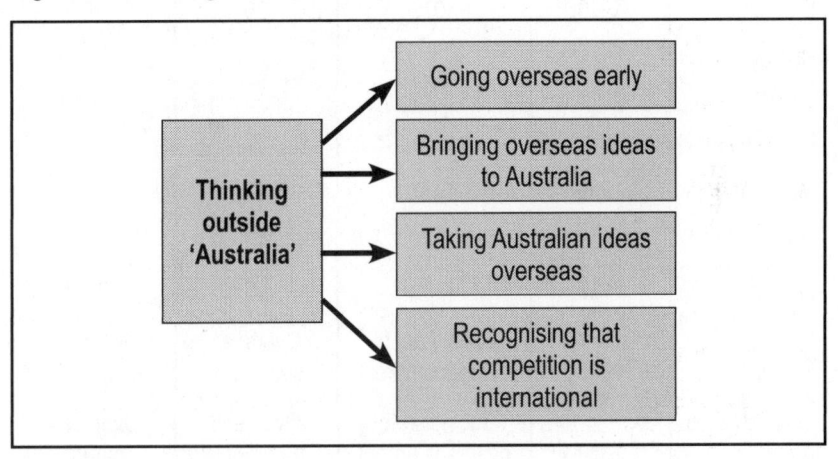

Thinking outside 'Australia'
- Going overseas early
- Bringing overseas ideas to Australia
- Taking Australian ideas overseas
- Recognising that competition is international

Going overseas early

Many of the winning organisations went overseas early in their lives (see table 7.1 overleaf). This move overseas was, generally, ahead of their competitors and was generally dictated by the strategy of the organisation rather than inspired by industry activity or forecasts. For instance, NAB pursued an opportunity to expand when other local banks did not have the capacity to do so. Westfield moved into the US—the heart of the global industry—by buying one centre at first. Qantas has been 'international' for most of its life. Lend Lease, Harvey Norman and Macquarie all ventured overseas to experiment with their particular form of business.

Because entering overseas markets is much more difficult than is often anticipated by organisations (see strategic cycle discussion in chapter 12), the first move is often very minor. But the clear strategic intention of moving into international markets is seen very early. Winning organisations are committed to that move, so they continue to work away at it, seeking sustainable success. Since relatively few Australian organisations have operated internationally until recently, this characteristic suggests another way in which winning organisations are different.

Table 7.1: winning organisations go overseas early

Organisation	Year established	First overseas activity	Years of international experience by 2000	Years of international experience by 2006
Brambles	1916	1971	30	36
Harvey Norman	1982	1999	2	8
Lend Lease	1951	1964	36	42
Macquarie	1969	1983	17	23
NAB	1858	1987	13	19
Qantas	1920	1935	65	71
Rio Tinto	1905	Subsidiary of overseas parent	Overseas subsidiary	Overseas subsidiary
The Salvation Army	1880	Subsidiary of overseas parent	Overseas parent	Overseas parent
Telstra	1901/1975	1985	15	21
Westfield	1956	1977	23	29
Woolworths	1924	1929 (but retreated in 1974)	45	51

Bringing overseas ideas to Australia

In chapter 4, we noted that bringing overseas ideas back to Australia is a major cause of innovation for winning organisations. Brambles found the bin for Cleanaway overseas. Qantas copied other international airlines in introducing its frequent flyer scheme and its low-cost airline, Jetstar. Rio Tinto imported Elliott Jaques' ideas on 'time span of discretion' from Canada and the UK. Telstra's approved products are mainly from overseas manufacturers. Woolworths' base idea of the discount emporium came from Woolworths overseas and it cooperates with Wal-Mart in the US to have access to Wal-Mart's latest research on product and process innovations. Woolworths' entry into the petrol retailing market is also copied from European operators. Westfield saw enclosed shopping centres (malls) from its early visits to the US.

These examples suggest the importance of this route for 'new ideas' or 'innovation' for Australian organisations. The winning organisations find inspiration for many of the keys to their success by exposing themselves to international ideas and adapting them to the local market. As winning organisations begin to operate overseas, this further exposes them to overseas practices and possible innovations, which they can also 'import' back to their Australian operations.

Taking Australian ideas overseas

The reverse aspect to the practice of importing ideas has been the exporting of some ideas developed locally and the use of them on the international stage. And some of these ideas are improvements of ideas originally brought in from overseas!

While the idea of the CHEP pallet was actually introduced to Australia by US shipping practices during World War II, the Australian government developed the idea of pooling pallets centrally to conserve resources while providing an innovative service. Then Brambles bought the pool, took the idea and developed it into a control and tracking system. It exported the system to the UK, then through Europe, then North America and is spreading the system through Asia. It has also done this with the Cleanaway system and with Recall records management.

Westfield has re-exported the mall shopping centre idea to its home—the US! In particular though, Westfield developed skills in redeveloping shopping centres, branding them, clustering them, and providing professional asset management and separate asset ownership of the centres through the development of property trusts. Now it is taking these ideas to the UK.

Macquarie's development of listed infrastructure trusts has been a leading global innovation and it has taken this concept to a wide range of overseas markets with a range of specific specialised trusts.

Recognising that the competition is international

During the course of our research, it was clear that, for some organisations, an important aspect of success is the recognition that they are competing internationally, not domestically. Regardless of conditions in Australia, particularly on the supply side, these organisations realise they must be internationally competitive, especially regarding customers. These days, competing internationally or competing against international competition domestically is 'normal', but the winning organisations understood this early on.

Rio Tinto is an obvious example, since the scale of its Australian operations is such that most of its sales are made to overseas corporations, where prices are set regardless of where the product is sourced from. Way back in 1981, CRA noted in its annual report:

> CRA operates in world markets. We must pay constant attention to costs and operating efficiency... particular attention is being given to service functions and overhead costs... there have been 33 major tax policy changes in Australia over the last seven years... [compared with] none in Brazil... [Our] competitors are strengthening their position.

Macquarie has always viewed its main competitors as international players in investment banking. It realises that to compete, even locally, it must be better than these international players, since they have scale, experience and brand reputation beyond what Macquarie can aspire to. One Macquarie executive said:

> Being the only Australian investment bank but competing against the international/global players, everyone is bigger than us. We will never win on brand name. We must have a better idea or we will lose. We need to do more than just the job... Each time we lose, it is because we stuffed up, not because of luck or other external reasons.

Increasingly, in an internationalising world and, as organisations proceed through their strategic cycle, it becomes imperative that they understand international competitive forces rather than rely on their strong local position for success. The globalising moves of Brambles and Rio Tinto and the international experience of Lend Lease, Westfield, Qantas and NAB, together with the experience of Telstra in Hong Kong and New Zealand, Harvey Norman's experience in Singapore, New Zealand and Ireland and other similar developments by the winning organisations show that international competitive forces become more important for organisations over time.

Having a sense of community responsibility

A final aspect of external focus for winning organisations is that they have a sense of community responsibility, rather than a simple responsibility to maximise returns to shareholders, to provide maximum value to customers, or even to optimise returns to key stakeholders.

In 2000 we did not see this sense of community responsibility as being particularly consistent or different from best practice in this area. Increasingly, more and more organisations have such a sense. But, given the outstanding financial and market performances that these organisations exhibit, it may be considered surprising that they are also providing benefits to the general community and that they see this as a part of their role and responsibility. When we revisited the First XI we saw three areas in which this sense of community responsibility was evident (see figure 7.6):

▶ whole-of-organisation views about community responsibility
▶ the development of 'Foundations' for giving back to the community
▶ increased emphasis on environmental practices and reporting.

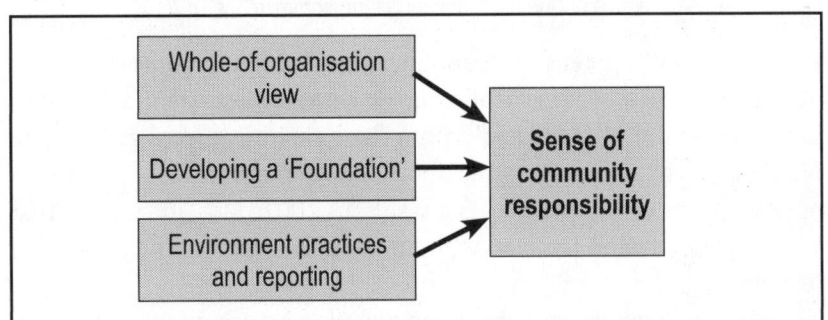

Figure 7.6: developing a sense of community responsibility

```
Whole-of-organisation view ──┐
Developing a 'Foundation' ───┼──▶ Sense of community responsibility
Environment practices and reporting ──┘
```

Whole-of-organisation views on community responsibility

One early example of a holistic approach is Lend Lease's community of interest. It is a deeply held value within Lend Lease that the best organisation performance occurs when all interests are actually aligned, and this includes the interests of the community. In 1996, Lend Lease introduced the idea of encouraging—and paying for—all its employees to undertake a day's work in the community. In its 1997 annual report, it said:

> On 21 November 1996 we requested employees from all Group companies in Australia and overseas to spend a full day working at a community or charitable organisation of their choice...The benefit to our employees as well as to those they worked for was very obvious.

The Salvation Army sees the 'community' as its effective 'customer'. While the Salvation Army helps to improve the lot of individuals and of particular families, it sees the ultimate beneficiary as the whole community. For the Salvation Army, 'sense of community' is what the whole of life is about. 'Community' is not some separate group.

Rio Tinto's exploration and mining activities often disturb the natural environment. This can create a great deal of local community resistance, even though large economic benefits follow this activity for the local community as well as for Rio Tinto. Rio Tinto has enshrined both its environmental policies, and its aim to benefit local communities and respect local community customs and practices, as much as possible, in its principles. Part of its statement 'The way we work' says:

> We strive to understand and interact constructively with local communities, governments and others ... we set out to build enduring relationships with our neighbours that are characterised by mutual respect, active partnership, and long term commitment. (p. 7)

This can cause potential economic costs to an organisation. For instance, Rio Tinto owns Jabiluka, the third-largest uranium deposit in the world. But it is located within the Kakadu National Park in the Northern Territory and local Aboriginal communities are strongly opposed to its development. As a result, in 2001, Rio Tinto stated that it would not develop Jabiluka without the full support of the traditional owners.

Westfield is another organisation that places community very highly in its thinking. Westfield has had its 'four objectives' since 1986:

1. to reward its shareholders with maximum benefits
2. to provide its employees with satisfying work opportunities in a progressive enterprise
3. to give its retailers the right environment to maximise sales in its shopping centres
4. to fully meet the expectation of society and the interests of the communities in which Westfield operates.

Westfield shopping centres are different because of the way in which they take account of the community and become community centres, not just shopping centres. They focus on the human side. They are more 'social'. Their initiatives appeal to the mass market, irrespective of social composition.

The development of 'Foundations' to deliver community responsibility

Over time, many of the winning organisations have developed 'Foundations' to formalise their processes of corporate social responsibility or corporate philanthropy—that is, handing out grants to community organisations that request them. Table 7.2 lists the key Foundations and their purposes. It demonstrates the wide and differing ranges of views about which activities to support. Note the number of recently established Foundations, though, indicating the growing importance of this trend.

Table 7.2: 'Foundations' for community benefit

Organisation	Foundation name (year established)	Purposes
Brambles	Brambles Community Reach (2003)	Charities nominated by employees who are actively engaged in community service work.
Lend Lease	ACTU/Lend Lease Foundation (1983)	Development and wellbeing of employees, their families, our communities and communities in which we live.
	Dick Dusseldorp Employees Foundation (1988)	Develop training skills for the construction industry.
	Stuart Hornery Institute (2000)	Relationships between communities and their environments; to make communities more effective and have less impact on the environment.
Macquarie Bank	Macquarie Bank Foundation (1984)	Long-term strategic partnerships with community organisations in six core areas—education, the arts, health research, health care, welfare and the environment. Looking for opportunities that are innovative, responsive to community needs and enable Macquarie to utilise its unique approach in a manner that will make a difference.
National Australia Bank	Has a wide range of community organisations	Covers a wide range of issues without specific themes.

Table 7.2 (*cont'd*): 'Foundations' for community benefit

Organisation	Foundation name (year established)	Purposes
Qantas	Sharing the Spirit	Six main areas—employees, arts, youth, environment, community and sport.
Rio Tinto	Has 22 trusts, funds and foundations	Cover a wide range of issues including health, education, community, social and economic development. Focused on the communities where Rio Tinto is mining.
The Salvation Army	Specific activities have program names	All activities designed to foster improved community outcomes, especially family-based ones.
Telstra	Telstra Foundation Community Fund and Telstra Kids Fund (2002)	Focuses on children and young people and their communities. Also sponsors sport, business, arts, health and community initiatives.
Woolworths	Woolworths Australian Communities Foundation (2004)	The wellness of children, rural and regional Australia, education and employment, grassroots giving.

Increased focus on environmental practices and reporting

Environmental practices and reporting has emerged as a new key issue, related to the increased focus on the development of community responsibility. As with the latter, winning organisations are increasingly becoming involved in this area. For instance:

▶ Brambles introduced environment reporting in 2001 and aims for the highest standards possible. It was included in the Dow Jones Sustainability Index in 2006.

▶ Lend Lease developed a sustainability vision, a sustainability covenant and its new head office, in 2005.

▶ Rio Tinto added environmental performance to its reward system in 2002, started over 2000 socioeconomic programs in 2004 and started reporting against the Global Reporting Initiative in 2005. It has been in the Dow Jones Sustainability Index for several years.

- ▶ Westfield began an energy and water usage, transport cost and waste management pilot scheme in 2006 at the Sydney Central Plaza.
- ▶ Woolworths started work on waste minimisation and recycling programs in 2002.

While these approaches are not unique, our experience is that, although the situation is changing rapidly, most organisations have not seen community responsibility as a necessary part of their business model. Many organisations have eschewed this role altogether, exemplified in the statement, 'Our role is to make money for shareholders'. Any charitable contributions or actions made by such organisations are idiosyncratic and discontinuous. They are often related to the whims or personal interests of particular individuals in the organisation, with no clear relationship to any defined 'community'.

Recent developments in winning organisation practice and the combination in 2006 of Australia-wide record droughts and record high temperatures, coupled with changes in attitude of key business leaders, such as Michael Clancy, Rupert Murdoch and Richard Branson, and the publication of the Stern Report in the UK suggest that taking a wider view of the role of the organisation and its relationship to its communities is necessary. It is another indicator of the importance of 'balance everything' for winning organisations (see chapter 10).

Summary and key messages for leaders

Winning organisations look out as well as look in. They are externally focused as well as internally focused. Our research found five ways in which this external focus showed out. Winning organisations are focused on customers. They work with other organisations to extend their own boundaries. They are focused on the future, not just the present. They think beyond 'Australia' and beyond their own organisation's situation. They have a real sense of community, social and environmental responsibility, and they have a responsibility to the many other stakeholders in the organisation.

The key messages for leaders from this chapter are:

- ▶ Think 'customer'.
- ▶ Develop customised products and services, using intensive market research.

- Develop and manage ongoing customer relationships.
- Work with other organisations on a partnership basis to expand resources and reduce risk.
- Manage governments and regulators as part of normal activity.
- Work with suppliers on an ongoing relationship basis.
- Focus on the future, from a whole-of-industry perspective.
- Think outside Australia.
- Go overseas early.
- Bring overseas ideas home.
- Have an active community, social and environmental responsibility program as part of the normal activity of the organisation.

8 Right people

Committed and proud
People for the cause

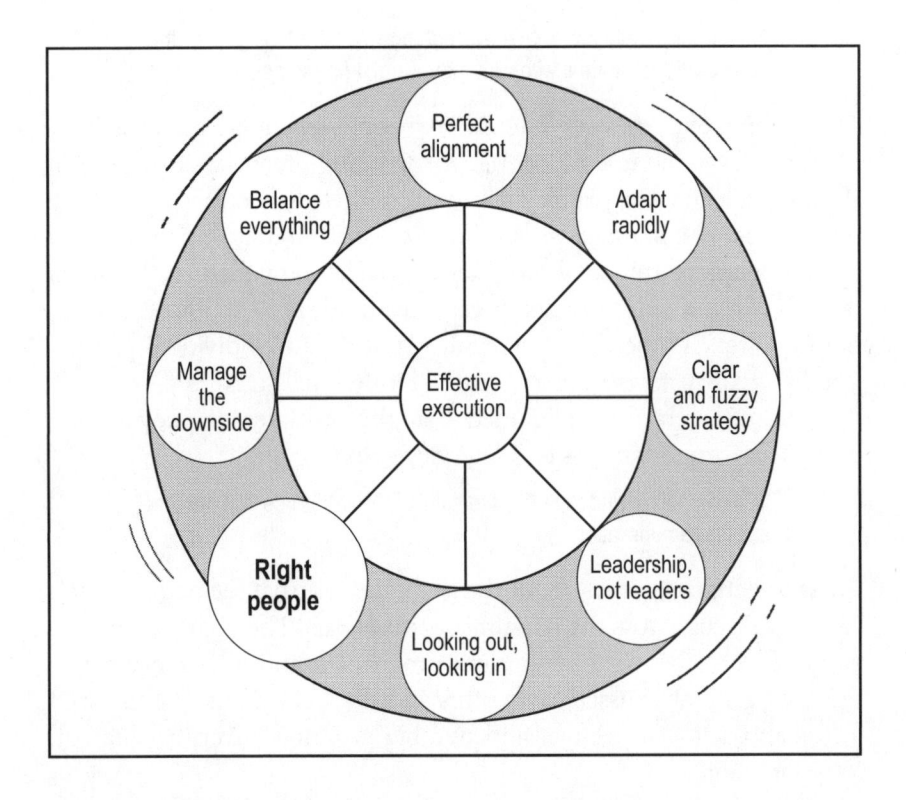

*Figure: wheel diagram with "Effective execution" at center, surrounded by eight segments labeled: Perfect alignment, Adapt rapidly, Clear and fuzzy strategy, Leadership, not leaders, Looking out, looking in, **Right people**, Manage the downside, Balance everything.*

When we were writing the first draft of this chapter, we asked our secretary to get a copy of a recent research study that suggested CEOs thought people and culture were more important than financial results.

She retorted, 'Everyone knows people are the key. If you get the right people, everything else follows'.

Unfortunately, not everyone does 'know' this. Indeed, this important idea of 'right people' is buried in most organisations.

Many organisations state somewhere in their public material, 'People are our greatest asset'. But every time we hear this statement, we cringe. Why? Because we know from experience that most of the organisations that espouse it simply don't really believe it and certainly don't deliver on it.

But this is not what we heard from the winning organisations. In fact, what we heard was quite the opposite. We heard:

> We create an environment of ownership. It's the environment that is more important than the people. It allows good people to shine.

> No, our people aren't better than our competitors. Our systems are.

> I think our people are above average now, when I look at the other organisations we deal with. But they weren't [in the past].

These statements are very different to 'people are our greatest asset'.

So what is the role of 'people' for winning organisations? As we'll show in this chapter, people are critical. But we found that it is having the *right* people, not necessarily the *best* people, that is important. And having people within a system, not people as individuals or as prima donnas. An individual wants to get into the First XI to join the team, but the First XI functions as a team, not as a set of individual players. The best team always beats the team of individual stars.

Our research also concluded that the attitudes of people were particularly important. As one interviewee put it:

> In a competitive industry, it is the spirit of the workforce that matters, not the remuneration.

There are characteristics about the 'right' people that seemed common to interviewees across the winning organisations. The 'right' people are committed to the organisation and proud of it and its achievements, but they get embarrassed saying this and don't want to make much of a fuss about it. It is a quiet and humble proudness. Very egalitarian. Very Australian.

In this chapter, we'll first explore what we mean by 'right' people and why these people are rarely the 'best people' that organisations so often talk about. We'll discuss the process of selecting these 'right' people and of investing in them, and discuss other supporting mechanisms that are necessary to ensure right people can produce the results the organisation needs and wants. Then we'll talk about what 'committed and proud' means and how it shows in an organisation (see figure 8.1).

Figure 8.1: right people

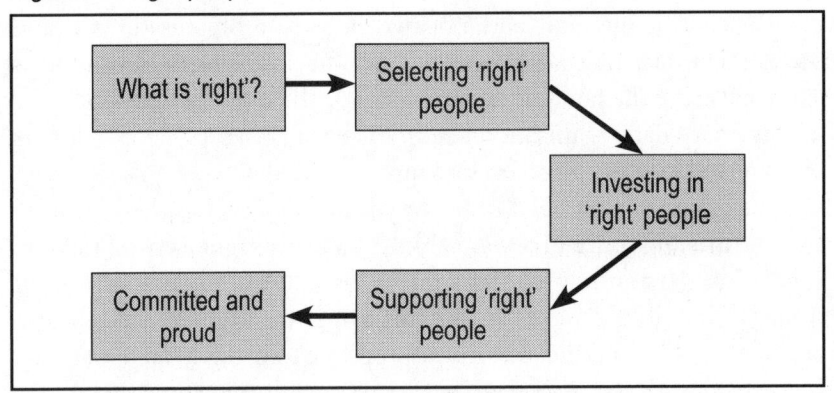

What is 'right'?

So what is it that determines whether or not we have the 'right' people in winning organisations? We found two determining features—people need to fit the culture and the strategy, and people need to have the right attitude (see figure 8.2).

Figure 8.2: what makes 'right' people?

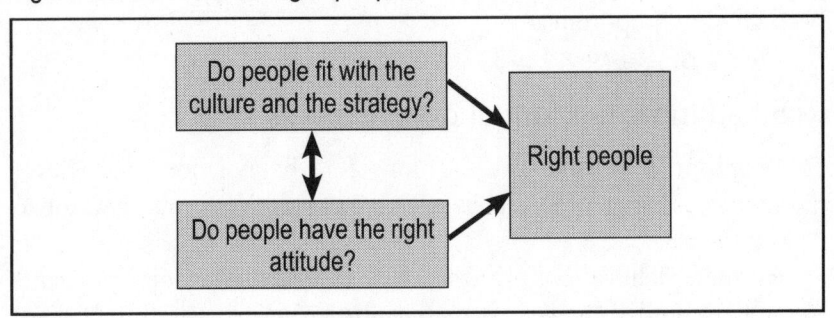

Fitting the culture and strategy

The essence of 'right' is alignment to the culture and strategy of the organisation. What this means is that the 'right' people for one organisation are the 'wrong' people for another, even in the same industry. Imagine that the right people from the Salvation Army took over running Macquarie Bank and vice versa. Would either organisation work well with its new set of people (assuming they had the operational skills to perform the tasks necessary)? We doubt it! We think neither organisation would be successful! There is no universal type of person who is ideally suited for every organisation. Different people will be attracted to—and attractive to—different types of organisations.

This is encouraging and positive news for organisations—and people! The fact that a person does not 'fit' into one organisation is likely not to be the fault of the individual or the organisation, but more simply that that organisation seeks different types of people for its strategy and culture. Keep on looking!

But organisations need to be very clear about what their strategy and culture are, so that they are able to seek the 'right' type of person. Lack of understanding of the strategy or culture, or lack of a clear strategy or culture, makes it difficult to get the right people. It also explains why it is not necessarily appropriate to bring in an apparently successful leader from a very different organisation and expect to achieve the same success. Illustration 8.1 shows the 'right' type of person that might be sought by some of the winning organisations at particular times in their history.

As the situation changes for organisations, the type of person sought would also change. For instance, over time technical skills have become less important at Rio Tinto and Qantas while commercial acumen has become increasingly important. At Brambles, financial and local entrepreneurship skills have become less valuable and having an international perspective and the ability to fit into a global system have become more important.

Right attitude, not formal qualifications

The appropriate formal qualifications for the position were never mentioned as being important in selecting people. What was mentioned was attitude.

Formal qualifications are essentially assumed. They get applicants to the line, but they never get them over the line. Right attitude does. Attitude is a differentiation that winning organisations seek. For instance, half of the top management team at Woolworths in 2002 did not have a degree, enough to disqualify them from even applying for a management position at many organisations. But all of them have the right attitude. It's the same for selecting checkout staff. Woolworths is looking for those with the desire to serve customers, not those with the right qualifications.

Illustration 8.1: 'right' types of people at some of the winning organisations

Brambles 'right people':
- are growth-oriented/opportunistic/have a nose for a deal
- are profit-driven
- thrive on challenge/able and willing to grow and learn
- are macho, egalitarian, grassroots, down to earth
- can develop good long-lasting customer relationships
- can find creative ways of doing a job efficiently
- are tight with cost control
- know how to 'crunch a quid'.

Qantas 'right people':
- provide great customer service
- epitomise the spirit of Australian people
- are concerned with doing things the right way
- can handle crises
- are able to change quickly/can find creative solutions.

Lend Lease 'right people':
- are entrepreneurial
- are innovative
- value highest quality
- work well with all types of people
- take responsibility
- deliver targeted outcomes
- are young.

The Salvation Army 'right people':
- are practising Christians
- like to help underprivileged people
- are prepared to follow the systems and structures
- get the job done
- are frugal
- are efficient.

Having the appropriate skills is also assumed, at least on entry to the organisation. (Winning organisations mostly develop new skills on the job or in-house as people rise through the organisation.) So skills and the ability to carry out the job for which people are being interviewed are also assumed to exist. Interviewees definitely need these, but they won't lead to success in the organisation. The right attitude will, however.

What is the 'right' attitude? This is really a subset of the 'right' people theme above. Each organisation has a view about the type of attitude it wishes to encourage, and that attitude varies from organisation to organisation. For instance, at Qantas, willingness to give great customer service is a critical element, as it is at Woolworths. Westfield looks for drive, a spark, confidence, but not arrogance, rather than simply skills developed in a particular industry. Increasingly, as it becomes more international, it looks to learn from people from other industries. At Brambles, being willing to get dirty through being involved in the operations or being able to 'crunch a quid' were key attitudes desired in its people prior to its move to global businesses. At NAB, values are changing from being conservative, liking hard work and being tough on cost control, to teamwork, speed, simplicity and efficient execution—quite a change to make!

Another way to look at 'right attitude' is to consider the values of the organisation. (We discussed values previously in chapter 5.) By making organisational values explicit, organisations can promote the 'right' type of behaviour they seek—behaviour should match expected values.

Best people or not?

While organisations like to argue that their people are the 'best', and that they want to hire only the 'best' people, this saying is just like 'people are our greatest asset'. Few organisations actually hire—or even try to hire—the 'best' people in practice.

Surely though, part of being a winning organisation must be that they hire the 'best' people? Isn't this implicit in 'right' people? The clear, but uncomfortable, answer is 'No'. Even winning organisations don't hire the best people, unless you take 'best' to mean the narrow view of best fit with the desired culture. Illustration 8.2 shows our analysis of the practices of winning organisations regarding hiring 'best' people and why they choose those practices.

Illustration 8.2: the 'best' or not the 'best'—who is hired?

Hire the 'best'	Why this practice?
Lend Lease	Culture is hire the best, hire young, empower them, support them and reward them, to get high-quality, innovative solutions.
Macquarie Bank	Need the very best people to come up with the innovative ideas needed to succeed against international competitors.
Rio Tinto	Philosophy is that the best people give better ideas, which gives better productivity, which gives low cost.

Don't hire the 'best'	Why this practice?
Brambles	Company has grown from low-skilled areas and relied on 'good blokes' who are financially astute, happy to get dirty and can see opportunities.
Harvey Norman	Main 'people' are franchisees, who see the opportunity to work for themselves through Harvey Norman as an opportunity to move from being a very good salesperson to joining a system and making gains they could not otherwise aspire to. As franchisees are limited to one franchise, Harvey Norman doesn't want brilliant people with ambitions beyond this level.
National Australia Bank	Has been a 'rise-through-the-ranks' (promotion on seniority) organisation. You have had to be a lender to be successful. Entry qualifications have not been high.
Qantas	Seeks people who are good at customer service, have a desire to succeed, are reliable, professional and have a unique Australian approach. They also need to like people and travel, and be flexible to cope with unusual hours of work.
The Salvation Army	People are 'called' to join, so the organisation does not specifically seek out 'best' people. Remuneration makes it difficult to attract the 'best' people. Trains to ensure attitude is correct.
Telstra	Government 'job for life' background and low skill requirement of many jobs has not encouraged high-flyers to apply until recently. Government influences still make it difficult to attract the best.

Illustration 8.2 (cont'd): the 'best' or not the 'best'—who is hired?	
Don't hire the 'best'	**Why this practice?**
Westfield	Seeks hard-working team players who can fit into a family-led autocracy.
Woolworths	Depends on part-time and casual workforce, largely unskilled jobs with a heavy emphasis on youth workers. Values reliability, trust, honesty and hard work.

Again, we see this as 'good news' for people and also for organisations. You don't have to be the 'best' in any formal academic sense, though you do of course have to have the requisite skills. There are many opportunities in all types of organisations in all types of industries. For personal success, over and above skills, what matters is whether you fit the culture the organisation has or wants and—importantly—whether your attitude matches what the organisation seeks. The right attitude can be a winner—for both individuals and the organisation.

Selecting the 'right' people

If we know what 'right' people are like, how do we go about finding them? Selection is obviously the way in which people come into the organisation, while development within the organisation is a way to improve the abilities of those who are hired.

Selection is not the key

In most human resource or management texts, a great fuss is made of selection. An error in selection can be costly, both in getting rid of the wrong hire and then in restarting the selection process, so winning organisations obviously must get their selection processes right. Right? Wrong!

Our research found that the winning organisations were not particularly good at selection. Not one organisation claimed to have a unique or even a better selection system than its competitors. No winning organisation claimed that its selection processes were a key to its success.

One organisation stated that it used scientific psychological testing procedures, which were said to work, but it had quite a high turnover rate soon after people joined. The same organisation offers 'spotter's fees' to its people to find new people who would fit into the organisation. The logic here is that people who work in the organisation are best able to know who might 'fit' with them and the organisation. This approach also puts a large degree of personal responsibility on current people in the hiring process—no-one wants to bring in someone who doesn't fit. This process also implies that people in general may be just as good at judging selection fit as placing ads or using recruitment consultants and psychological tests.

A common characteristic was that winning organisations experienced high turnover early on—that is, shortly after the selection period. However, they also reported that their overall turnover rate was lower than average for their industry. Figure 8.3 shows this pattern. It is very similar to those of organisations with the 'cult-like cultures' described as a success factor by Collins and Porras—the culture ejects those who don't fit very quickly. Those who do fit are absorbed into the culture, which is effectively reinforced by these hires. Interestingly, when Lend Lease developed its global strategy in the period 2000–02 through buying six large US-based companies, it had four US CEOs in five years (from 2000), a point subsequent CEO Greg Clarke noted as a key problem for implementing the organisation's strategy at that time.

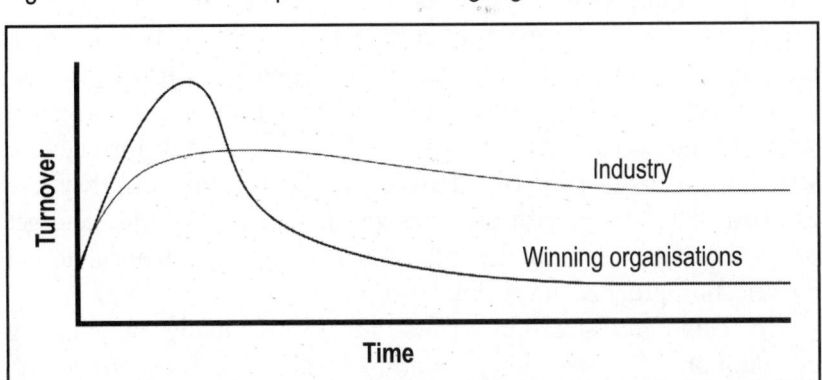

Figure 8.3: staff turnover patterns at winning organisations

So the overall hiring result for winning organisations is better than competitors, but they don't do particularly well at the start. This implies that, even though they are well aware of their cultures and what type of person they seek, they are not particularly good at selecting such a person.

Surprisingly, in our original research winning organisations did not seem particularly concerned about this. There are several reasons why this might be so:

▶ Their reputations as high-performing organisations means they have more and better people applying to join. A selection error may thus be easily overcome.

▶ Despite all the work on selection practice, there remains a qualitative component—a 'feel' about the final decision. No mechanical or quantitative process for selection has become accepted as definitively better than all the rest. Organisations are still searching for the most effective selection processes.

▶ The use of systems to provide good feedback and performance measurement and management of people in winning organisations means that selection errors are identified early and the problem is addressed.

▶ People who think they might fit but find they don't often take themselves out of these high-performance cultures.

Woolworths is an interesting example. It is besieged with applications from school and university students for part-time jobs, particularly in its 24-hour supermarket stores, where all kinds of people can work all kinds of different hours that suit them personally and also fit the needs of the organisation. Students fill out a standard application form. Woolworths interviews people, and most are offered a position. They attend some basic training and an introduction to Woolworths, then they begin to work part-time. Most drop out within a year or two, as their objectives and lifestyles change. A very small number—which Woolworths makes no attempt to identify beforehand or through the selection process—stay. They have particular aptitude and they like working there! They learn required specific skills on the job and get promoted. But promotion depends on on-the-job performance, not on the selection process, or qualifications.

In summary, selection errors are fixed rapidly at winning organisations. And while they would like better systems, there doesn't seem to be a perfect one, or one that is widely accepted as being most effective.

However, in our work for this edition, we found that winning organisations were starting to encounter the emerging problem of shortages of good people, a problem that did not exist for them five years ago. Lend Lease, Rio Tinto, Telstra and the Salvation Army all reported difficulty in attracting a sufficient number of good people to enable them to expand into the areas they wished to. Macquarie has always claimed that this has been a key constraint. Woolworths said it is not a problem for them, but it is for their suppliers, which affects their own ability to deliver. This is an Australia-wide economy issue, but, as these organisations are very attractive to people as employers, the fact that they are also encountering the issue suggests it is likely to constraint future growth for them (and for the country), particularly as this trend is expected to get worse in the future.

Investing in people

In contrast to the relative failure of their selection processes, winning organisations spend a lot of time investing in their people once they have joined. Several aspects of this investment were clearly followed by winning organisations. They were (see figure 8.4):

▶ commitment to training, learning and development

▶ focus on in-house customised training and development

▶ support for career development.

Figure 8.4: investing in people

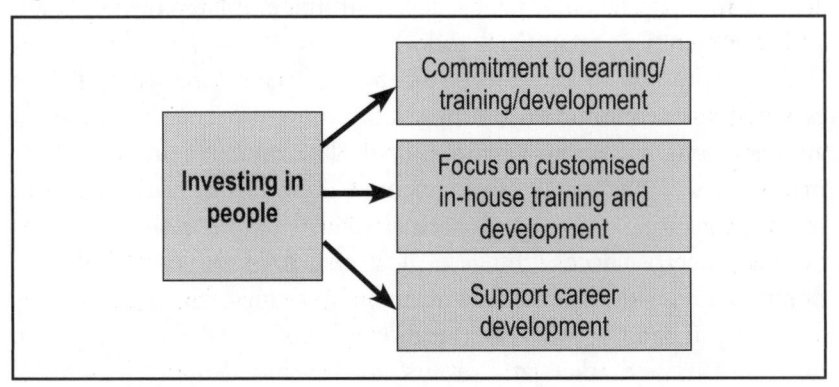

Commitment to training, learning and development

Most of the winning organisations have had a large variety of training programs for all levels of people in the organisation throughout their history. They have been consistently committed to training and development of their people.

In organisations with large volumes of small transactions, training to get details right is essential. So it is no surprise to find organisations like NAB, Qantas, Woolworths and Telstra consistently involved in heavy on-the-job training programs. For instance, when Qantas joined the Oneworld alliance in 1998, it became involved in a training program covering virtually all the 220 000 people involved in the original five partner airlines.

When organisations are involved in major cultural or strategic change programs, large amounts of training with some development is also essential, and we saw this across the winning organisations. For instance, as it prepared for the future through its Vision 2000 program in the late 1980s, Telstra trained more than 10 000 people each year to introduce more commercial skills and a different strategic vision into the organisation. Qantas undertook large amounts of customer service training in the early 1990s as it moved to merge Qantas and Australian Airlines, standardise service standards and also improve its customer service levels.

Of course, without such training, these initiatives have no chance of succeeding. This is exactly what does happen in many organisations! The concept of change in many organisations is often not supported with the training required and the change process fails. So, in this sense, what we see here is that winning organisations that undertake major changes do provide the training support necessary for the change agenda to succeed. This is consistent with the emphasis on execution and alignment (see chapters 2 and 3).

But winning organisations do much more than provide the essential basic or minimal training. CRA (now Rio Tinto) underwent an enormous proactive organisational development program over many years to change the fundamentals of working relationships in the organisation, unit by unit (see chapter 6 for details). There was no guarantee of success. Indeed, most external analysts would have doubted the chances of success of such a monumental effort. In 1982 it said that it had not reduced education and training despite the severe downturn in its markets and profits, another indication of its view of the importance of training and development. In 1990, CRA reported that it spent the equivalent of 7 per cent of payroll on training activities, much more than most organisations.

Rio Tinto continues to develop its people by encouraging the sharing of best practice. This is done by transferring middle managers around the group to expose them to a range of experiences, including best practices. This helps to develop the next generation of leaders.

In some cases, the winning organisations feel let down by the education system and have become large-scale trainers of apprentices themselves. For instance, Woolworths, now the largest employer of apprentices in New South Wales, recognised shortcomings and worked with the education system to adjust the focus of courses intended to fulfil the needs of large employers who needed skilled staff in non-traditional apprenticeship areas. Woolworths has over 4000 apprentices and trainees studying full-time.

Lend Lease has had a major relationship with the ACTU over almost 30 years, training over 21 000 apprentices and creating 50 000 new jobs. The ACTU–Lend Lease Foundation receives a share of the pre-tax profits of Lend Lease to be applied to help young people acquire skills. This program has been taken into other countries including Indonesia and the UK. In addition, the Dusseldorp Skills Forum developed training for retail and commerce programs as subjects for Year 11 and Year 12 high school students in New South Wales, subjects that are accredited as part of the students' normal study programs.

Other important aspects of training relate to personal development and self development. While no clear pattern emerged about any particular approach, or commonly agreed elements, most organisations encouraged or provided for a lot of this. For the Salvation Army, there is a five-year cadet-in-training program, including a two-year residential program, prior to being 'commissioned' into the Army. Organisations like NAB and Telstra encourage and support vast numbers of their people attending external degree and non-degree training and education courses. Rio Tinto engages all its employees in a variety of general and specific in-house programs, particularly focusing on developing teamwork through experiencing common training and development activities.

A focus on in-house customised training and development

An interesting discovery was that a number of the winning organisations had their own in-house training facilities. Woolworths, Qantas and the Salvation Army all have their own training colleges. This may partly be justified by the volume of training undertaken by these organisations. Partly it is explained by the desire to have control over premises, both in terms of programming schedules and confidentiality—running programs in company facilities rather than 'shared' venues reduces the risks of information leakage and information can be handled more freely in general conversation outside the formal training sessions.

A more interesting discovery was that a number of the winning organisations undertook the training and development activities using their own staff as teachers and facilitators. Most organisations outsource the majority of this work to specialist teachers and facilitators. However, some of the winning organisations view training as so important and so specialised for the organisation that it is best done by 'insiders'—managers responsible for day-to-day operations.

Managers in most organisations, if asked to lead a training activity, would reply that they do not have time and are not good at it. Organisations whose managers take on this role are sending out an important message: this is an important activity and you are best to learn from the people who understand the situation best.

The reason why so little is known of the CRA organisational development program, despite its size, duration and major effects, is that it was almost completely taught by in-house managers, using specially designed in-house materials. Few outside the organisation knew what was going on or took part in it.

Since some of the programs took managers out of the organisation for four to six weeks at a stretch, the investment in time as well as money was enormous. CRA spent around $50 million a year on training and development activities during this period.

However, what made this activity really different was that people were expected to deliver on the ideas, not just undergo the training. As one former executive said:

> You went away for training, ideas were implemented and those ideas would be seen in action. Everyone took part in training, implementation and running of systems...Management was committed to embedding it in the organisation. The ideas were connected to the job, not disconnected and they have a continuing life. They developed a common language and common principles.

In 2006, Telstra committed an extra $200 million in technical training and development. Its aim is to ensure that operating skill levels are up to date. This is a rebalancing away from the recent financial focus of the organisation to one of focus on the underlying capabilities needed.

Many other programs in winning organisations were developed in-house, used in-house materials and were taught by in-house people. Woolworths, Qantas and the Salvation Army, for example, developed their own materials or had customised programs undertaken in their own premises. Several of the winning organisations have developed leadership programs with universities for their top people. For instance:

- ▶ Lend Lease works with the London Business School and Columbia Business School.
- ▶ Macquarie works with INSEAD and the Melbourne Business School.
- ▶ Westfield works with the University of California, Los Angeles and the Australian Graduate School of Management.
- ▶ Woolworths works with the Macquarie Graduate School of Management.

In each case the programs are customised for the organisation. In 2006, Qantas, Brambles and Macquarie Bank, along with two recruitment consultants and two other blue-chip organisations, agreed to work with the Australian Graduate School of Management and the University of Sydney to develop an accelerated learning laboratory to create in-company simulations to fast-track management learning, spending over $5 million on the venture.

Macquarie's CEO attends every orientation program to explain Macquarie's history, its philosophy and, importantly, what it expects from its new people. Clearly laying out expectations right at the start makes it easy to set up consistent assessment procedures.

Lend Lease's orientation program is similar. Despite Lend Lease having a very supportive employee benefits package and strong mentoring systems, the orientation program was quite different. One former executive described it:

> They told you that two-thirds of you wouldn't be here in a year's time. It was very tough, even brutal. It was based on performance, but it got the best coming to the top. It was run internally by retired and semi-retired Lend Lease people who could bring real experiences to the program.

Many of the winning organisations are beginning to look at their training and development needs on an international or global basis. They are seeking the best international providers, benchmarking programs internationally and often undertaking programs internationally, even if the programs are provided by Australian suppliers. The Salvation Army has available to it two international leadership programs run in the UK for all the territories, to which it sends representatives on each occasion, seeing this as an opportunity for people in the same areas of operation to talk with others from around the world.

These experiences are quite different from the training activities of most organisations. Many operating managers are too busy to even speak to their subordinates who are attending programs, let alone attend the programs themselves or prepare and present them. Many organisations have turned training and development responsibility over to individual employees—'this is your responsibility'—yet are not prepared to properly support them, even if the people pay for it or undertake the work in their own time. Is it any wonder that employees of most organisations are less loyal, less committed and quicker to jump ship now?

Support for career development

In an increasingly uncertain organisational world, career development for the long term is being given less consideration in training and development activities. There is an emphasis on self-learning and the development of a culture of being individually responsible for your own personal learning. We found this was true on the whole for winning organisations too. Yet we found not only some excellent examples of career development activities during the period, but also a sense that career development was still important.

Perhaps the most famous example is the 'white room', which was set up at CRA under then chief executive John Ralph. On whiteboards in one room of the head office were arranged the current organisational structure of all the individual units of CRA, with the names of all the managers. Each year, when personal development reviews were done, the senior executives would meet in the white room to consider promotional opportunities and movements that might be made. The beauty of the room was that everyone's name was available for all to see and to discuss simultaneously. (Usually people who are a long way away are forgotten and not considered.) Another important difference is that appointments made were the responsibility of the whole executive team, not the particular manager to whom the appointee would report. Now that Rio Tinto has globalised, this practice is done for the top people globally, rather than from an Australian perspective.

Rio Tinto in Australia also uses a 'two levels down' process whereby managers do annual employee assessments not just of direct reports but also of those two levels down. This forces managers to have an 'eye' for talent and to seek good information on those who are not actually reporting to them. It also takes some of the subjectivity out of the assessment process between manager and direct subordinate, because other opinions are considered.

Lend Lease has a much more informal but equally important mentoring and coaching system. Each manager has a mentor, usually from another part of the organisation. This is part of the support network, essential when managers are given large responsibilities early on. It operates informally, which is consistent with Lend Lease's open communications style.

The Salvation Army rotates people through its territories, in traditional military fashion. One of the top two people in each territory comes from a different territory and leadership is changed every three years, facilitating the flow of new ideas across territories and developing its people through exposure to new challenges, often international ones.

In summary, winning organisations invest strongly in their people, while simultaneously encouraging them to take responsibility for investing in themselves. However, the specifics of each training, learning and development program depend on the particular organisation and its situation. No specific techniques or patterns were detected as common in our research, though it is clear in 2006 that an international approach to benchmarking and training is becoming the norm (consistent with 'looking out, looking in').

Supporting people

Investing in people is one thing. But what about the environment in which they work? Is it conducive to *using* the results of training and development? How well are people supported?

In each case, our research showed that the supporting environment was aligned and consistent with the people and the training they were receiving. This environment includes the elements of leadership, systems, culture, strategy and structure. Of course, as with other aspects of 'people', each supporting environment varied according to the culture and strategy being followed. But we did find some specific common supporting factors (see figure 8.5 overleaf). They are:

▶ having a team environment

▶ promotion from within

▶ measuring performance and providing honest feedback

▶ rewarding performance — financially

▶ rewarding performance — non-financially.

Figure 8.5: elements supporting the 'right' people

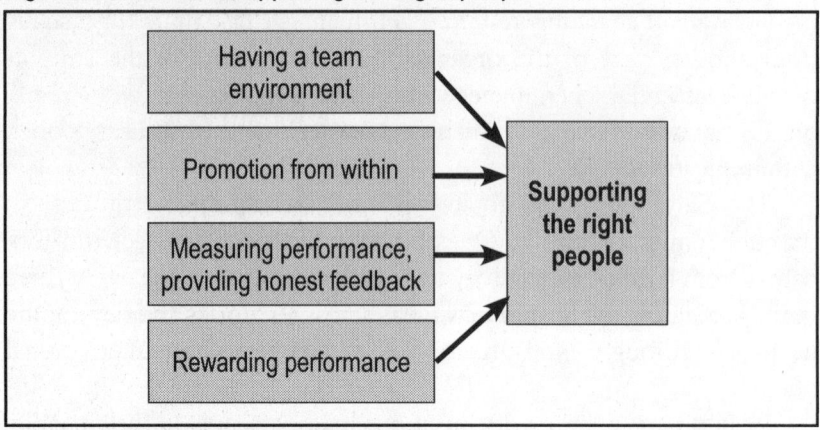

- Having a team environment
- Promotion from within
- Measuring performance, providing honest feedback
- Rewarding performance

→ Supporting the right people

Having a team environment

In chapter 6, we discussed the idea that leadership was about a team of people, not just an individual. We found this applied to people also. We found the word 'team' was used a lot, even where organisations were clearly wanting individuals to take responsibility. For instance, an executive at Rio Tinto said:

> We are very close, very collegiate. There is not fierce competition between the divisions. If it is a good project it will get funded. We are not competing for a given bucket of money.

Yet Rio Tinto heavily emphasises individual responsibility!

At Macquarie, getting into a team is important for individual success. People with ideas 'recruit' people to join the project team needed to make their idea work. Having the right skills—and particularly attitude—is important to be 'recruited' or 'chosen' to form part of one or more teams. At assessment time, cooperativeness and helpfulness are important attributes to be considered alongside individual profits generated, as Macquarie recognises that it takes teams to implement ideas.

Westfield and Woolworths are other organisations that are very team-oriented. Throughout the period of analysis, Westfield constantly referred to the role of 'team' in its success:

> The value of the 'Westfield Team' cannot be quantified ... [it is] even more important than the assets disclosed in the balance sheet. Fully recognising this value, Westfield actively pursues policies designed to maximise job satisfaction at all levels so that each team member is able to make a full, worthwhile contribution to the development of the company. (1986 annual report)

> Our ability to create and maintain such a busy schedule is only possible through the exceptional abilities and enterprise of our staff. (1989 annual report)
>
> [We have a] highly focused, dedicated and hard working team that is fully committed to the company's goals. (1995 annual report)
>
> Although [executive] left Westfield 10 years ago, like many other long-serving senior executives he often works as a consultant on special projects. [Executive] was an important member of the team that successfully took Westfield into the UK in 2000. (*The Detailed Westfield Story*, p. 100)

Westfield treats each centre as an 'asset' and has a centre management team, which includes leasing, design, development and mail merchandising, and has considerable autonomy within its own centre.

Woolworths says it believes in TEAM (together everyone achieves more):

> Our team is 145 000 strong. We've all got a part to play and a contribution to make...
>
> We're a team working towards a common goal, and learning from each other through coaching and listening. <www.woolworthslimited.com.au/aboutus/ourcompany/tww.asp>

Promotion from within

We have noted previously that leadership tends to be home-grown and stable. This also applies to the people as a whole. Each of the winning organisations experienced lower turnover than competitors in its industry and most had a clear expectation that promotions would come from within. Of course, if the people you hire are good, the organisation is doing well and growing, why *would* you hire from outside instead of promote from within? Westfield said that its management team in 2006 had an average age of 49 (very young) and had been with the organisation for an average of 13 years. Woolworths has around 1200 people with 25 years of service and the average length of a supermarket store manager is 16 years.

Promotion from within encourages those who join that there are future prospects for growth and development, not just for the organisation but for individuals. This provides an incentive for people to do well — and to stick around. If training is provided and development encouraged, these are further reasons for remaining and contributing.

The only cases where significant promotions came from outside were when organisations were changing culture, there were mergers and acquisitions, or when recovering from significant errors. Qantas and Telstra have had to emerge as more commercially oriented organisations from their public sector backgrounds, so significant changes in people have taken place at both. Brambles changed its top management team when it merged with GKN and also as it began to develop a global culture for its now truly global businesses, which has led it to bring in more people from outside than it had done previously. Lend Lease and NAB both incurred significant execution errors over the period 2001–06, resulting in considerable change at the top for both. Illustration 8.3 considers how NAB's promotion policy changed with its need to alter its culture, to correct poor performance.

> **Illustration 8.3: changing people to change culture**
>
> We noted in the first edition that NAB had sought to become less conservative, but few of those who had been hired in at the top levels had remained. We noted that this was a classic example of the cult-like culture ejecting those who did not fit. The problem in this case was that the culture had incrementally turned 'bad' during the 1990s, a point noted by several reports into the causes of the forex system control failure in 2004. To change the culture, in 2004 NAB brought in a relatively new executive as CEO, made significant changes to the board of directors and made almost a complete change to its top management team. It also introduced a new set of values (see chapter 4), including the explicit statement that people who did not conform to these values would not be welcome!

Measuring performance and providing honest feedback

What the winning organisations do very well is make it very clear what people need to achieve individually and in their teams, measure performance against those targets, provide honest feedback on that performance and reward based on the results (see figure 8.6).

Once again, there is nothing magical here, except that winning organisations actually do it (perfect alignment, effective execution, delivering results), they don't just talk about it—and that's a big difference.

For instance, NAB measures individual performance half yearly using a balanced scorecard approach and does it quantitatively. People have only a few key performance indicators that are set and agreed on beforehand. There are no more than five areas (for example, financial, customer, community, employees and process) with no more than three indicators in each. Each measure is weighted according to the specific role, and they are all quantifiable, all objective. The current scoreboard is seen as a powerful tool to align the organisation to the four key areas of organisational focus that it has recently developed—that is, restoring revenue growth, business efficiency, compliance and risk management and culture change. No bonuses are paid to senior management if compliance and behaviour measures are breached.

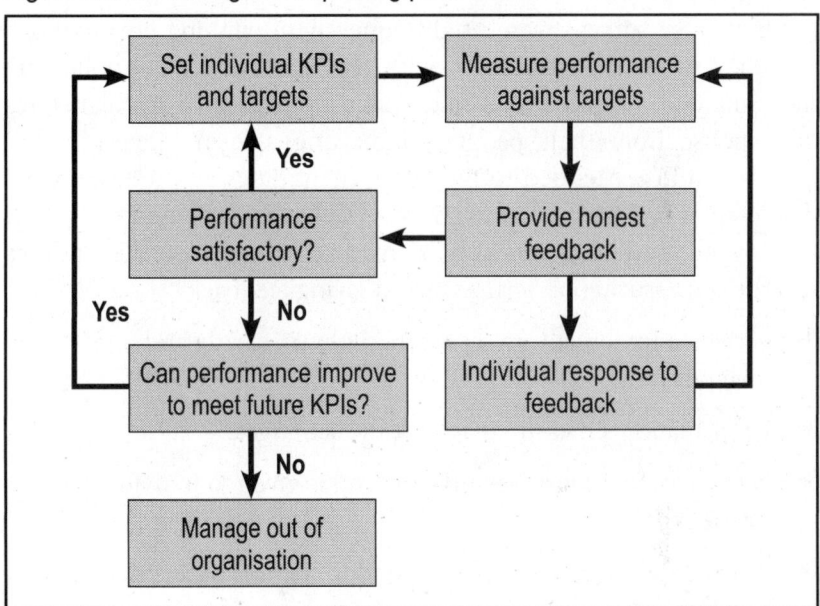

Figure 8.6: measuring and improving performance

```
┌─────────────────────┐     ┌─────────────────────┐
│ Set individual KPIs │ ──> │ Measure performance │
│     and targets     │     │   against targets   │
└─────────────────────┘     └─────────────────────┘
           ▲ Yes                       │
           │                           ▼
┌─────────────────────┐     ┌─────────────────────┐
│     Performance     │ <── │   Provide honest    │
│    satisfactory?    │     │      feedback       │
└─────────────────────┘     └─────────────────────┘
  Yes      │ No                        │
           ▼                           ▼
┌─────────────────────┐     ┌─────────────────────┐
│Can performance improve│   │ Individual response │
│  to meet future KPIs?│    │    to feedback      │
└─────────────────────┘     └─────────────────────┘
           │ No
           ▼
┌─────────────────────┐
│    Manage out of    │
│    organisation     │
└─────────────────────┘
```

At Lend Lease, the KPIs are very challenging, but there are very big incentives for achieving them. Lend Lease does not tolerate non-success. People will do everything they can to achieve the KPIs, which they have been involved in setting and which have been thoroughly considered in the pre-planning process. One former executive said:

> [My supervisor] didn't muck around. You knew where you stood. You got positive and negative feedback, but the negative was always framed positively.

Another said:

> They don't tolerate non-success. They would review performance, monitor you and coach you, but they will terminate you quickly if necessary.

Macquarie says that it does not have to fire people very often, as most people who are not performing know it very clearly, feel uncomfortable and leave of their own volition if they don't fit. At Macquarie, non-selection of an individual into new teams that are formed to develop new activities is taken into account in performance assessment, and is a good signal that an individual is not valued by peers.

Woolworths encourages its people to achieve their personal goals by taking advantage of the opportunities within the organisation. It measures managers performance partly on labour turnover and training delivery, and links the annual bonus payment to performance on these (and other) indicators.

Employee surveys were used frequently in winning organisations and they were taken seriously, with changes being made following their analysis. Organisations said that they received very high rates of response from their people—indicating a keen interest in the issues—and they tended to publicise the findings and indicate what would be or had been done to address the key issues raised.

Overall, several points can be made to summarise the findings regarding measuring performance and giving feedback:

▶ Performance targets are set for individuals, clearly and quantitatively.

▶ Performance is measured against the set targets.

▶ Feedback, both positive and negative, is given to individuals frequently.

▶ Individuals are expected to respond to the feedback, positive or negative.

▶ Organisations work with individuals to help improve their performance.

▶ If no performance improvement occurs, quick action is taken to manage the person out, instead of simply firing them straightaway.

Rewarding performance—financially

Apart from the Salvation Army, performance is rewarded financially by winning organisations, especially at the top. Table 8.1 summarises the financial rewards, and their make-up, for the top teams of each of the First XI in 2005.

Several aspects of financial rewards are significant:

▶ Rewards are highly correlated with individual and/or team performance.

Table 8.1: top management team total financial rewards—2005

Organisation	No. of people included in report	Salary ($m)	Performance-related reward ($m)	Other rewards ($m)	Equity ($m)	Total reward ($m)	Performance/ total (%)	(Performance + equity)/total (%)
Brambles	10	10.5	6.3	4.7	9.5	31.0	20.3	51.0
Harvey Norman	6	2.3	–	–	1.4	3.7	0.0	37.8
Lend Lease	11	6.6	12.2	2.6	0.1	21.5	56.7	57.2
Macquarie Bank	9	4.1	85.2	–	3.1	92.3	92.3	95.7
National Australia Bank	14	10.6	13.8	1.3	8.1	33.8	40.8	64.8
Qantas	8	6.9	3.8	5.1	3.2	19.0	20.0	36.8
Rio Tinto	9	6.7	5.8	4.7	11.8	29.0	20.0	60.7
The Salvation Army	10	1.2	–	–	–	1.2	0.0	0.0
Telstra	10	9.4	5.2	1.7	9.0	25.3	20.6	56.1
Westfield	7	8.2	10.1	1.4	3.4	23.2	43.5	58.2
Woolworths	8	6.2	8.4	1.6	0.9	17.1	49.1	54.4

Right people

- Individual rewards are highly variable.
- Financial rewards are not the only driver or reason for working at winning organisations — contributing to the 'cause', being in a winning organisation and other non-financial rewards were seen to be important.

In most of the winning organisations, there is a high degree of bonus or profit sharing or even share granting in the total remuneration package. As one Macquarie executive said, as we observed his team of people at rows of computers outside his glass-walled office:

> There are people out there earning a million dollars, but the person sitting next to them might be getting only a fraction of that. You wouldn't know from looking at them, or how they behave. It just reflects their relative performance. That's the system. They know it and they accept it.

The process is quite clear and transparent to everyone at Macquarie. A specified percentage of profit goes to the staff, as does a specified percentage of surplus earnings above a targeted ROE. All permanent staff receive profit share. The CEO cuts up the pool according to the dollar profit contribution of each division. Each division head then cuts it up on the same basis for groups, whose heads then cut it up for individuals. Each individual's performance is assessed, not only by individual profit created, but also for contributions to the team. Each individual's performance is reviewed and the bonus is linked to the review, which is very frank. Any individual who is not happy with their allocation is free to leave! Macquarie says it has not lost a senior person it wanted to keep in at least 15 years. One Macquarie executive commented on the system:

> We run the division like a business, judged entirely by the P&L statement. We know what our costs are [as a result]. The P&L is our greatest management tool, but others are copying it. We have total autonomy, but we are also totally responsible. There is no great money god in the sky.

Lend Lease has a much more complicated reward structure, primarily because it is more concerned with providing for individual welfare. Lend Lease was one of the first to introduce employee superannuation. It also introduced company-paid employee health plans in 1979 and introduced subcontractor disability insurance cover in 1980 — all far-sighted welfare moves. By 2002, it had introduced a 'cafeteria-style' employee benefits scheme where people could select their own package of desired benefits, confirming that it is still a leader in this area.

Like Macquarie, Lend Lease allocates a fixed percentage of profits for employees. This practice was introduced in 1973. However, Lend Lease uses it to buy shares in the company and they are allocated equally to all employees, regardless of position. The shares cannot be sold by the employee while they are employed but employees receive the dividends in cash each year. Employees own 10 per cent of Lend Lease, down from 17 per cent when MLC employees were also part of Lend Lease. In addition, senior staff can earn significant bonuses, based on individual performance.

At Harvey Norman, the franchisees are essentially highly incentivised employees. Their remuneration is determined by their sales, less their direct costs and controllable investments, less a fixed formula charge from the head office for its services in taking care of central decisions such as purchasing, advertising and financial control.

Rewarding performance — non-financially

But not all the 'rewards' from working at winning organisations are financial. People don't work at the Salvation Army in the expectation of receiving high salaries. A different type of person works there and receives rewards in quite a different way. The benefits include the satisfaction of helping a great world-renowned charity and, more importantly, of helping individuals in need.

Other organisations are not high payers or rewarders by their industry standards. For instance, those who work at Telstra and Qantas also get a great deal of their satisfaction out of the non-financial returns. At Telstra, it is the opportunity to work with new technology in a rapidly changing industry. Telstra is the only game in town of any size in its industry, so it is the only organisation able to undertake a whole raft of technology-related activities that make organisational life exciting for communications technologists. And being listed on the stock exchange adds more colour to working for an organisation that used to be government owned

At Qantas, the 'glamour' of international flying, Qantas' amazing safety record and reputation and the kudos from working at an iconic brand that is highly cherished by Australians, provide excitement, challenge and responsibility. People are proud to work for Qantas.

Non-financial rewards are valued in all the winning organisations. For instance, Lend Lease has its 'Chairman's Awards', Macquarie its 'Macquarie Awards' and Qantas has its 'Service Above And Beyond' awards to recognise people within the organisation who have done outstanding work that may not be recognised by the formal performance-measurement systems. These awards are peer-based and are often regarded as more valuable than any confidential monetary bonus that might be awarded.

Another non-financial reward from working for a winning organisation is simple but important — people like to work for successful organisations! It is a lot more fun and more enjoyable working for an organisation that succeeds than it is to work for an organisation that is struggling, or even failing.

Committed and proud

During our interviews, we continually found that the 'culture' of the organisation was a key to success. But, as with 'people', each culture was different, so there was no sense of one common culture that is the 'winning' culture. Each culture had many compelling and internally consistent characteristics, but they were not common across the organisations. Copying any one of these cultures could be achieved, but it might not be the appropriate culture for your organisation.

However, we found that the people we interviewed — and their comments about their colleagues — indicated that all were very committed to the 'cause' their organisation was pursuing. They were determined to succeed in achieving that cause or maintaining the success of that cause.

We also found that people were very proud of what their organisation had achieved and was achieving, but they in no sense wanted to brag about it or wave the flag in any patriotic way. In fact 'proudness' came out almost shyly. People were proud but embarrassed to say how proud they were of what their organisation had achieved. This is rather like family pride. People are often proud of their family but they often don't make a fuss of their family members outside the family and would be embarrassed if their family made a fuss of them.

So we came to the view that two common aspects of all the cultures were that the people were committed and proud. And as we reflected on our other organisational experiences, we realised that these are not attitudes most people have toward their organisations. Most people would like their organisation to succeed, but they don't feel committed to it, for a wide variety of reasons. Our experience is that most people would like to be proud of their organisations, but when they look at the practices and behaviour of their organisation or its leaders they have feelings ranging from neutral to anger (though they rarely express, or are given the opportunity to express, these negative feelings to their leadership).

Passion again!

As we have previously mentioned, we found interviewees were extremely passionate about their organisations. A number of interviewees wanted to give us the history of their organisation so we would understand why it had done what it had and why it was where it was. But it was a quiet passion we detected, not a table-thumping passion or a shout-out-loud passion.

'Committed and proud' is an outcome of getting the right people, investing in them, supporting them and making sure they are aligned with the rest of the organisation. There is no single formula for what makes people able to be, or want to be, committed and proud. It depends on the specifics of the organisation and its context. So we give here some examples of how 'committed and proud' came out for several of the winning organisations.

The Telstra experience

At Telstra, one interviewee's eyes lit up when he talked to us about the technological developments that had occurred and would continue to occur in the industry. He was eager to discuss how working at Telstra enabled technically minded people such as himself to be involved in the latest global technologies for the benefit of the whole country.

Another explained to us the egalitarianism that existed at Telstra, that Telstra had been able to develop and operate with a long-term view and that it was focused outwards, all of which made it an exciting organisation to be a part of and contribute to. People felt they could actually make a difference, not only to the organisation, but also to the nation, through the way Telstra operated and developed. He said:

> It's nice to know that what you do does actually make a difference to how the country operates.

Another interviewee noted how Telstra was valued by the community:

> Telstra people rise to the needs of the community. There's a great deal of empathy between Telstra workers and the community. The community expects Telstra to be there in emergencies and to help

the community in crises. We do it, we volunteer for it, but we don't get much recognition in the media for it.

The Brambles experience

Brambles is a difficult organisation to analyse because, for much of its time, it has been extremely unwilling to be open to the press or other external analysis. Carew said:

> Instead of corporate policy manuals Brambles operates with some rules for survival that include keeping away from politicians and avoiding being quoted in the press. Commenting to mainstream media or business press or to anyone connected, however vaguely, with the sharemarket is regarded as a serious offence. A Brambles staff person is well advised to remain discreet at dinner parties. Hiring of public relations consultants is discouraged... (Carew, 2000, p. 237)

But the degree of commitment at Brambles is clear. Gary Pemberton, chair in 1993, said:

> Brambles' corporate culture strips away a lot of the things people hide behind—a lot of the jargon, the reporting, the structure, a lot of the ceremonies and the committee meetings that go into traditional management. It is aggressively focused on return on investment and its employees are very aware that they are judged primarily on how they perform financially. You deliver or you don't. (Carew, 2000, p. 236)

An interviewee, when asked why Brambles was so unwilling to publicise its story, said:

> I really can't understand it. They have so much to be proud of. They are very hard working. They are humble and proud. It is okay to celebrate wins, but more important to know what we [Brambles] can learn or what we have learned from the experience.

The Lend Lease experience

When asked what it was like to work for Lend Lease, two interviewees who no longer worked there gazed into the distance and smiled in admiration as they remembered the experience. One said:

> It's a unique culture—promoting innovation and entrepreneurial behaviour, never standing still. It is very consistent. They treat people fairly and with integrity. They develop people... There is a strong level of personal and professional development... They leave it to you to develop... but you are thrown in, then picked up and supported... They have striking, good-quality leadership with the

ability to influence people to follow that vision... They don't tolerate non-success...

The other said:

> They have a culture of driving down responsibility. You took pride in your work and you'd do whatever it took to complete it. The leaders knew everything. They were smart, intuitive, good people judges, they digested detail rapidly. The company took care of its employees... As a young person, it was the company to join. You were able to be a decision-maker... It was about opportunities, not pay, about career development. Quality was never stated but the aim was always to 'be the best', to be a role model. They always picked the best option in terms of decisions, projects, people to do business with.

In the interviews we conducted for this edition, senior managers said (of the effect of the new leading edge sustainability building built for the head office):

> It makes people proud to work for the company when visitors come to this building and see it to know that we built it. It's an icon building. It's what we'll have to build in the future. It builds our reputation and brings us work, purely because we built it. We receive very high satisfaction scores for people working here, we have much lower absenteeism and people find it is a happy place to be and that all makes them proud to belong to the company.

The Qantas experience

Qantas is perhaps the easiest example to see how 'committed and proud' operates, as it is highly visible and has been an international success story for many years. Many individuals have experienced Qantas favourably as customers. One interviewee said:

> We have our own special pride in building a sense of history... Customers love the brand. They are very protective of the brand and its values. They see Qantas as synonymous with Australian success.

Another said:

> Staff are exceptionally proud to work for Qantas. Yes, some [technical staff] do complain, but technical staff are very opinionated and are sure 'their way' is the best... so they complain... but they still like Qantas and don't leave... The Qantas brand took a long time to build. It is built on the pioneering days, staff pride, the pride of Australia and an Australian international success story. Being an icon, it is emotional.

And another said:

> The people are personally committed to Qantas...We love the challenges, the diversity, the constant change. Volunteers are easy to get. There is a pride of working here for an Australian global company.

Humble: success is never assumed

In the comments quoted above, there is no real sense of shouting out loud about how good the organisations are. There is no sense of 'We are the best and we're going to let everyone know about it.' Perhaps that is why we haven't known in Australia which are the winning organisations. Or perhaps it reflects cynicism towards the all-too-frequent public relations statements that overhype an organisation.

We found none of this. Only one of the CEOs we interviewed could be described as extrovertedly proud and shouting about it. Yet when we interviewed him, he made it clear that his organisation had not been successful throughout its career. Indeed, he pointed out that, on at least two occasions in its history, it had almost 'gone under'. In his view, success had to be earned and could never be taken for granted.

> There are always competitors waiting to eat your lunch if you lose focus or intensity...I walk down the streets of the city now and think of all those good organisations that were there when I started that no longer exist.

Another senior manager was not even sure his organisation belonged in the sample! He felt his organisation was really four different businesses and was not sure its track record justified its inclusion, as it had so many problems and so many issues to address.

Managers from one of the organisations we interviewed for this edition described their organisation as a 'fallen blue-chip'. They (and other employees) were angry at what had happened in their organisation and were pleased that, in 2006, it was back on track, with a clear strategy, reinforced values and determined to become again the type of organisation it had been.

These are hardly the attitudes we might expect from proud and successful people in winning organisations. And these are not the attitudes found in lots of short-term high-flying organisations that burn brightly for a few years, then decline, collapse or are taken over and forgotten about. The cases of Enron and One.Tel are classic examples.

But they *are* typical attitudes of winning organisations. Collins (2001) calls this attitude 'Level 5 leadership'. He described this as 'the triumph of humility and resolve', noting that this style of leadership exists at all eleven of his 'good to great' US companies. This idea of humility and resolve is very similar to our findings of being committed and proud (but humble).

Are winning organisations patriotic?

There is a hint of patriotic nationalism in the winning organisations. As part of their external focus and wider view of the world, our winning organisations are proud of their 'Australianness' in their achievement. It is most obvious at the ex-government organisations—Telstra and Qantas—where each had a particular role for the nation for most of its life. But it also exists at other organisations. Table 8.2 considers how each of the winning organisations treats patriotism.

Table 8.2: how important is patriotism?

Organisation	Is patriotism important? How?
Brambles	Yes—showing the Europeans (and now the rest of the world) what Australians can do
Harvey Norman	No—not important
Lend Lease	No—not important
Macquarie	Yes—beating the global competitors and establishing a presence in their major markets
NAB	No—not important
Qantas	Yes—the only Australian international airline for most of its life
Rio Tinto	Yes—Australianising itself to develop the country for Australia and Australians (prior to globalisation)
The Salvation Army	No—not important
Telstra	Yes—responsible for developing and maintaining the Australian communications system for most of its life
Westfield	Yes—exporting mall developments back to the US—the home of malls
Woolworths	No—not important

From this evidence, we can't conclude that nationalism is important in its own right, but we do see that quite a number of the winning organisations are quietly proud of their success as an Australian organisation taking on the world. However, they clearly don't see this as something that is a reason for their success, nor part of their particular 'cause'. Being Australian is not the reason for their success in any way. We'll return to this theme of how important 'Australia' is in chapter 11.

Are winning organisations also 'best companies' to work for?

Surveys exist that assess which are the best companies to work for. However, winning organisations are balanced organisations, whereas the 'best company to work for' might be unbalanced—in favour of the people who work there! Nevertheless, as the 'right people' are important to the winning organisation formula, and looking after those right people is important, characteristics of organisations that are regarded as 'best to work for' should be closely related to our findings. Table 8.3 lists the findings of recent surveys of best practices for managing people in Australia and the US, and compares them with the winning wheel framework. Not surprisingly, there is close alignment. And several of the winning organisations have featured in various 'best company to work for' surveys. Nice to get some supporting evidence for our findings!

Table 8.3: comparing features of 'best companies to work' for with winning organisation practices

Best practices Australia 2006	Winning organisation practices
Employee engagement	Having a cause, having clear strategy, communicating, being available, perfect alignment and many other aspects
Inspirational leaders	Leaders having passion, walk the talk
Effective leadership	Effective execution, leadership not leaders
Employing the right people	Right people
Social responsibility	Having a sense of community responsibility

Best practices Australia 2006	Winning organisation practices
Open communication	Communicate, communicate, communicate
Living the values and walking the talk	Values, culture, walk the talk, do what you say, effective execution
Performance-oriented culture	Effective execution, rewarding people
Aligned and supportive people practices	Perfect alignment, right people, training and career development, promotion from within

Best practices US 2006	Winning organisation practices
Creating a sense of purpose	Clear strategy, cause
Caring about employees	Leadership not leaders, right people, perfect alignment
Creating socially responsible programs	Sense of community responsibility
Cohesive and trusting environment	Perfect alignment
Rewarding performance and commitment	Committed and proud, rewarding financially and non-financially

Sources: Adapted from *Australian Financial Review*, March 4–5, pp. 17–18 and *Fortune*, January 30, 2006

Summary and key messages for leaders

People are an important element of the framework for winning organisations, but it is getting the 'right' people, not getting the 'best' people, that is important. Selection is not as important as might be expected, as selection errors are fixed rapidly and winning organisations have more and better people to recruit from. Attitude is an extremely underrated component of selection.

Winning organisations invest heavily in all their people, focusing on in-house customised training and development. Coupled with a wide variety of supporting mechanisms—a team environment, a policy of promotion from within, strong measurement, feedback and reward systems—people know where they stand and are supported. An outcome of this is that people feel committed to and proud of their organisation and its achievements, regardless of the industry or context. And that's what we would all like to be able to say!

The key messages for leaders from this chapter are:

- Ensure people fit the culture and strategy.
- Select people whose attitudes fit.
- Invest in people through training and development.
- Focus on in-house, customised training programs that are properly supported by managers and management.
- Support people in their career development.
- Promote from within.
- Set individual and team targets and KPIs, measure performance, provide good feedback and reward performance based on outcomes.
- Reward in both financial and non-financial ways.
- Remain humble, even when successful.

9 Manage the downside

Managing risk
Being conservative

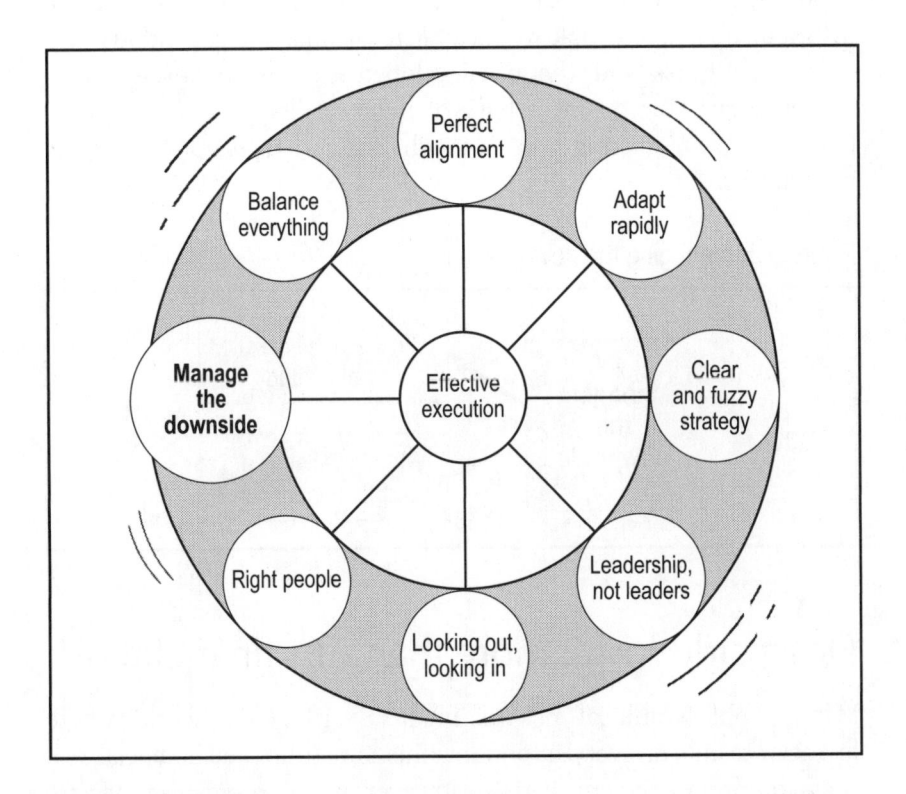

Although the winning organisations have been growing rapidly and entering new fields of activity, they described themselves to us as conservative! At first this surprised us. We did not see them as conservative at all! How could they describe themselves this way? In what ways were they 'conservative'?

Gradually, we came to see that winning organisations are not only conservative financially, but they are also conservative about risk. We came to the view, however, that this conservatism was not about avoiding risk but *managing* risk. Winning organisations are well aware of risk and realise that accepting risk is important if they are to progress, but they wish to manage the risks that they take as best they can. Players in the First XI play hard, but they don't take unnecessary risks, they keep their guard up, are watchful and alert at all times, aware that errors made will soon have them out of the team.

This awareness of risk and attention to managing the downside emerged as an important aspect of the success of winning organisations. But what is 'risk'? And how do winning organisations manage it? In this chapter we'll investigate the various types of downside risk that need to be managed and consider the range of techniques winning organisations use to manage risk (see figure 9.1). We also need to distinguish between what we mean *here* by 'managing the downside' or 'managing risk' and what has developed as a function for managing insurance risks in a business that is often now called 'risk management'. Our view of 'managing risk' is much wider than simply managing insurance risk.

Figure 9.1: managing the downside

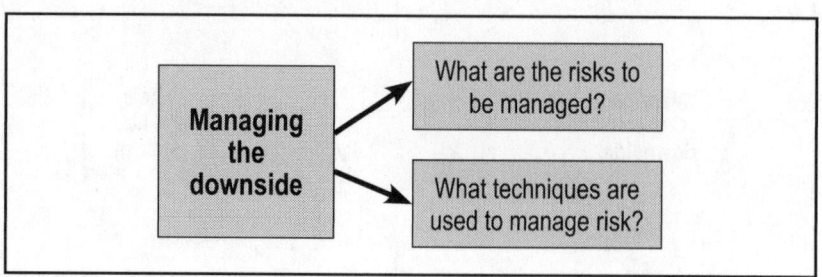

Managing the downside → What are the risks to be managed?
Managing the downside → What techniques are used to manage risk?

Downside 'risk': more than just financial risk

Many people think of risk as financial risk. In a world where financial results are very important, this is natural, and financial risk *is* an important element of risk. However, winning organisations are concerned with managing many different types of risk, and they describe the risks they see differently. Table 9.1 gives some examples

Manage the downside

of the classifications of risk that they have developed, together with a classification from a standard setting body in the area, Standards Australia.

Table 9.1: some classifications of risk

Brambles	Macquarie Bank	Rio Tinto	Standards Australia
Business risk	Market risk	Economic conditions	Commercial and legal relationships
Execution risk	Credit risk	Exchange rates	Organisation, country and international circumstances
Group-wide risk	Liquidity risk	Acquisitions	Management activities and controls
Health and safety	Operational risk	Exploration and new projects	Individual and group behaviour — internal and external
Environmental risk	Legal compliance	Reserve estimation	Natural and environmental events
	Documentation risk	Political	Political circumstances
		e-business	Technology and technical issues — internal and external
		Land tenure	
		Health, safety and environment	
		Mining operations	
		Rehabilitation	

There are other ways to more generally consider risk too. For instance, Brambles has a doctrine of 'no surprises'. This requires managers to notify the board of any issue or event likely to affect the company's share price as soon as they become aware of such an issue or event. People can be dismissed for failing to meet this obligation. At Macquarie, the CEO considers risk from the perspective of the potential impact on the company of a 40 per cent fall in the sharemarket in one day. A clearly unlikely scenario, but one that invites conservative thinking!

Similarly, Lend Lease has developed 'enterprise risk management' to consider the risk for the whole enterprise, which is based on a variety of risks of particular importance to it—for example, the housing market, exchange rates, oil prices, bird flu and so on. For each business it has developed value-driver trees to break the risk into components. By doing this, 'what if' scenarios can be conducted to establish the effects such events will have on the overall results of the corporation.

What you see from table 9.1 is that there is limited agreement about how to classify risk—though the detail in each classification suggests that managing the downside is considered very important and very complex. We have tried to standardise these classifications so you can apply them to your organisation. We have classified them as (see figure 9.2):

- strategic risk
- financial risk
- technical risk
- operating risk
- political risk
- legal risk
- reputation risk.

Identification of these types of risks, and the management of them, is a key to managing the downside. We emphasise that, for any particular organisation or situation, the risks listed here may or may not be linked and they may be more or less important. It will depend on the particular organisation, industry, location of operations, strategy, values and ways of operating. Let's consider each of these types of risk.

Strategic risk

Strategic risk is the most fundamental risk. When an organisation adds another activity to its business portfolio, even if it is simply expanding its existing business into another geography, it takes on a new risk. This type of risk is rarely given much attention by most organisations. It is simply assumed that the organisation will have the capabilities and resources to overcome any problems that emerge.

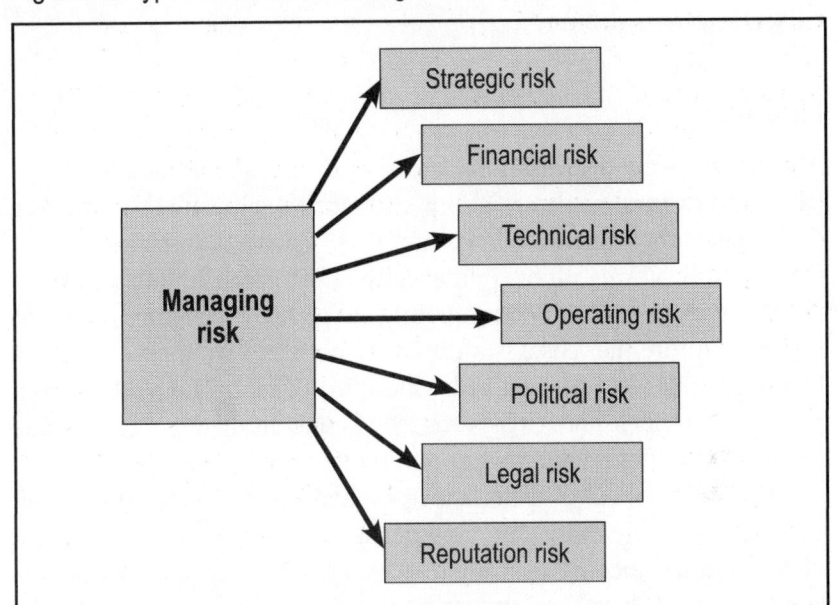

Figure 9.2: types of risk to be managed

```
Managing risk
  → Strategic risk
  → Financial risk
  → Technical risk
  → Operating risk
  → Political risk
  → Legal risk
  → Reputation risk
```

Even for winning organisations, we see the problem of strategic risk emerge when they go overseas or diversify. At this stage of their strategic cycle, they often struggle to continue to make the gains they have, partly because of taking on new strategic risk that they have not had to cope with before. For instance, Lend Lease took a huge gamble to become global, tripling its size with seven major acquisitions in one year. While it had spent considerable time analysing the desirability of becoming global, the short time in which it made the moves to globalise meant it simply did not have the capabilities to make it work, even though it was an excellent concept.

This new risk can't be avoided if the organisation wishes to grow its activities in either a product or market sense. But managing the risk is not about avoiding risk. It is about minimising risk for a particular outcome or optimising outcomes and risk. Qantas has taken a huge risk in attempting to operate both a high-quality, full-service airline (Qantas) while simultaneously developing no frills, low-cost airlines (Jetstar and Jetstar Asia)—a strategy that has not been successful anywhere else in the world!

Having a clear strategy is one of the best ways to minimise strategic risk. Having the ability to say 'no' to an opportunity that does not fit the existing strategy is one way of managing risk in this area. For instance, Woolworths sees itself as a high-volume, low-margin discount retailer. While analysts would like it to go overseas with its existing businesses, it continues to see enough growth opportunities in Australia within its current business definition.

Financial risk

All the winning organisations are concerned about financial risk, which they regard as the volatility of the financial results that are key outcomes of their operations. For instance, Qantas is concerned about the volatility of oil prices dramatically affecting its financial results, positively or negatively. Consequently, its policy of whether or not to hedge its future fuel costs is a critical part of its final financial result. Lend Lease has an aim that only one-third of its profits will be from building activities and two-thirds will come from ongoing revenue streams—building management and rental streams.

Macquarie and NAB focus heavily on financial risk, due to their high gearing ratios, which magnify any negative financial outcomes. Much of Macquarie's income is from management fees generated from its large number of listed and unlisted investment funds, which tend to be relatively stable despite sharemarket volatility. Brambles is another that focuses on financial risk because its organisational philosophy is heavily centred on profits and return on investment. So any misjudgement of financial risk will immediately affect its fundamental value.

Technical risk

An often overlooked element of risk relates to the technology choices made by organisations for their operations. Telstra's position has been heavily influenced not only by its original monopoly but also by the fact that, over time, it has been seen to make the right technology decisions for its (and the country's) telephone infrastructure. Throughout its life, Telstra has received little or no criticism of its technology choices. Had it got them wrong, it would not be able to hold its position so well in a deregulated environment. In 2006, it's choice of whether or not to build a fibre-to-the-node broadband digital network is clearly a critical choice for the organisation, especially in the face of emerging competitors who may build competing partial networks to cherry-pick customers, or alternative wireless technology that may bypass such a network.

Rio Tinto is another organisation for which technical risk is critical. It has rejected undertaking several major projects because of the perceived technical risk involved, such as the Wimmera industrial minerals deposit in Victoria.

Woolworths' development of Project Refresh involved significant technical risk. Using an IT platform that had not been used before, using in-house staff to develop and customise the platform, and considering the scale and importance of the task to the business required risk taking. However, the use of Project Mercury project management principles (see the section 'Project management') helped to manage the downside risk potential.

Major technical risks apply to most organisations. Qantas' choice of plane type and mix, Westfield's choice of mall shopping centre designs and Brambles' choice of business portfolios are some other examples that we tend not to hear about, because the decisions have been wisely made. Telstra's upcoming choice of 3G network system and its decision on the fibre-to-node-network will have a major impact on its future success.

Operating risk

Operating risk refers to the soundness of the systems for operating the technological system and the capability of the people to operate them. These are fundamental risks for any organisation—can we do what we say we can, when we say we can?

We should not take operating risk for granted, as it applies to the fundamentals of the business, and generally affects the whole business. One of the reasons the winning organisations have been chosen is because they do have these capabilities and are able to execute to deliver expected results. This is not true of all their competitors, and it is certainly not true for most organisations in our experience. Many organisations simply don't deliver what they offer or say they can. Telstra's failure to succeed internationally to date, NAB's withdrawal from the US and Irish markets, Brambles 'loss' of millions of CHEP pallets in Europe in the early 2000s and Westfield's and others' withdrawal from diversifications done during the 1980s illustrate that even winning organisations can be caught out occasionally. (Of course if they are caught out more than rarely, they would cease to be 'winning' organisations.)

A subset of operating risk is emerging—environmental risk. We have commented that sustainable development and sustainability reporting are emerging as new areas of organisation concern. The risks from environmental damage are also increasing, as they now receive more publicity and their effects are better understood.

Consequently, organisations are developing environmental risk policies to manage this new area of risk. For instance, Brambles developed an environmental policy in 2000, in which it aimed to achieve industry-best environmental practices for each business and to improve the efficiency of resource use and minimise waste generation. In 2004, it began extending the coverage of this policy to its major business partners.

In 2005, Rio Tinto said that environmental responsibility was integral to its planning and decision making. It saw that it had a clear responsibility to address the challenges of climate change, biodiversity and product stewardship across its own value chain and was working hard to ensure that all its businesses acted in accordance with these policies.

Political risk

Another underestimated risk is political risk. Political risk is the risk of failure or underperformance resulting from unfavourable political decisions being made. For some organisations, political risk is the crucial risk to manage. The ability to gain a licence or authority is necessary for many attempts to enter overseas markets (for example, Qantas for airline routes, Rio Tinto for rights to explore and mine, Telstra and NAB for government approval to operate). Inability to manage political risk can stop the organisation dead in its tracks. Yet very little attention is paid to political risk in normal strategic or operational management considerations. In Australia there are a number of key political issues that have an impact on the development of winning organisations and which they must manage successfully. These include:

- the four pillars banking policy
- digital television and media ownership policy
- land rights
- government-to-government airline route negotiations
- Australia's exclusion from ASEAN membership
- ACCC views about competition
- free trade
- environment policies
- tax rates.

Legal risk

Closely related to political risk, the law itself must also be managed. Lobbying activity by organisations can affect both political and legal decisions, with Telstra and Westfield being known for aggressively managing the legal system to their advantage. As well, there are of course fundamental legal issues, such as consumer and employee rights, contract law and insurance responsibilities and liabilities, that apply to all organisations. Legal outcomes in cases regarding issues such as smoking, public liability insurance and asbestos are typical of the sorts of decisions that are mostly out of the control of one organisation, but that can create havoc with their futures.

Being aware of these issues, lobbying to change (or not to change) laws and planning for changes in the law are necessary if an organisation is to successfully manage its legal risk.

Reputation risk

Related to political and legal risk is the risk to an organisation's reputation from the consequences of a particular event, where a risk is unforeseen, or where the outcome has much more dramatic consequences than are predicted. An organisation's reputation can even be damage by the behaviour of a single employee. That's what Brambles' 'no surprises' policy aims to address. For example, the damage caused to NAB's reputation by a small group of forex traders, or to the Salvation Army's reputation by a small group of individuals, in some cases for events that occurred 30 to 50 years ago, was significant.

Lend Lease suggests that, when making judgements about whether activities are appropriate or not, its people consider whether they would be happy if their activities were publicised in the national press. As part of its risk management function, Macquarie specifically considers what the risks to its reputation might be if it engages in particular events or enters a particular transaction. With the increasing public focus on corporate reputation and the beginnings of an industry to measure 'reputation', it seems likely that this risk will be seen as more important in the future.

Recognising this risk, Macquarie has created the position of integrity officer who reports to the executive chair, the managing director and the board corporate governance committee. The role is broad ranging. It covers the development and implementation of policies, education and advice for management and staff, procedures to ensure claims are properly investigated and development of an environment where people can voice genuine concerns.

In summary, there are many significant areas of risk that must be managed if an organisation is to be able to execute and deliver its results. Each individual risk can have a major impact on results, far beyond what would be considered the probable outcome, so each must be analysed and managed.

Techniques for managing risks

Winning organisations recognise that failure to allow for the various risks can completely overshadow the outcomes of their normal operations. Small omissions can have big consequences.

So how do winning organisations manage risks? Unlike most of the other elements and factors in our winning framework, there appears to be no clear set of techniques used by most of the winning organisations to address this important concept. This is probably because of the significant differences in the operations and industries of the winning organisations and the limited development of the concept of managing risk. So we cover here the range of techniques we observed, while noting that no one winning organisation used them all and no one technique was used by them all.

The techniques used are (see figure 9.3):

- up-front planning
- independent risk assessment
- laying off risks
- being conservative
- project management
- contingency planning
- good reporting and control systems
- quality of people, assets and systems
- being rigorous
- balance sheet management.

Macquarie has developed its risk management function more formally than most. Illustration 9.1 explains how Macquarie goes about managing risk.

Manage the downside

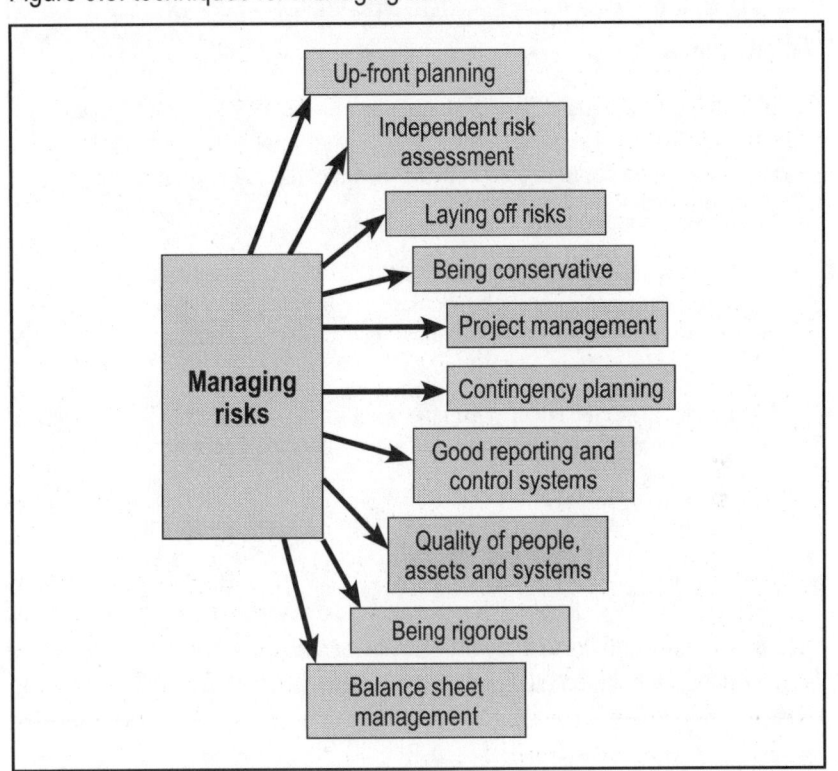

Figure 9.3: techniques for managing risks

Managing risks:
- Up-front planning
- Independent risk assessment
- Laying off risks
- Being conservative
- Project management
- Contingency planning
- Good reporting and control systems
- Quality of people, assets and systems
- Being rigorous
- Balance sheet management

Illustration 9.1: Macquarie Bank's approach to managing risk

Macquarie has a separate Risk Management Division that reports to the CEO and the board. It has responsibility for oversight of prudential management throughout the organisation.

This approach to risk management is part of Macquarie's 'loose/tight' management philosophy. Central management of risk is part of the 'tight' aspect, to be matched against the 'loose' management of entrepreneurial behaviour within each operating division.

At Macquarie, there is a risk management culture. The Risk Management Division's activity is not a policing function, as it often is in other organisations. The basic approach is that no new deals or businesses are entered into without a full understanding of all the risks involved.

The division considers risk in terms of credit risk, finance risk, market risk, operational risk and legal compliance. Limits are set in conjunction with the businesses and these are taken very seriously. Daily monitoring of credit limits allows for rapid intervention at an early stage on any problem.

> **Illustration 9.1 *(cont'd)*: Macquarie Bank's approach to managing risk**
>
> When problems arise and results do not meet expectations on a particular project, Macquarie goes back and works out what went wrong and what should have been done, usually within a month of discovering the problem.
>
> The director of the Risk Management Division said:
>
>> Most mistakes in companies are the result of not voicing concerns early enough. I look into the abyss and assume things won't go right. You have to bring this conflict to the surface...
>>
>> Risk management at Macquarie is not a stone wall or a hurdle. You have a right to respond. It's a deliberation between two parties.
>>
>> Risk remains with the business in the P&L and bonus pool. You need to keep faith with the cowboys. If we make a bad call, that's not our problem. It is the business' problem.
>
> Of course it is worth doing this well, because financial rewards are tied to performance. It helps focus on where the rewards will be.

Up-front planning

One of the best ways to manage risk is to conduct thorough planning before major activities are undertaken. Good up-front planning improves the chances of effective execution. Rio Tinto, Lend Lease and Westfield emphasise this, as they are very vulnerable to early errors on a project that will have an impact right down the line and may not be easily rectified. Rio Tinto's up-front planning includes undertaking several independent studies of the project before approval is given (see the next section, 'Independent risk assessment').

Lend Lease believes that the biggest risk to the viability of a project is in the bidding phase—the original cost estimates that form the basis for the price offered! In putting forward a project proposal at Lend Lease, the proposer is expected to have contacted everybody within Lend Lease who might have some knowledge or insight into the issue. The aim is to try to ensure that all issues have been considered and all the knowledge available is brought to bear on the project before the proposal is prepared. This approach forms the basis of the project management that follows.

Lend Lease makes it difficult to get a project approved through the planning process. Not only are internal rate of return (IRR) hurdle rates high, the project also needs to demonstrate that Lend Lease has the management and organisational expertise to run it. There also needs to be an exit strategy—what will Lend Lease do if the project goes wrong? This last feature is very unusual. One former executive described how this consideration of an exit strategy reduced the risk involved:

> Due to the policy of waiting until the development is pre-sold or tenants are pre-committed before construction begins, the worst thing that can happen is that the company may be forced to sell off the land which, as Lend Lease only buys prime property, is always in demand.

The Salvation Army is another organisation that does not begin a new project without having first undertaken a thorough investigation. A project could be establishing a new church community or setting up a new service. In each case, the Salvation Army is concerned about whether or not it has the resources to carry out the project, whether the project is really justified and whether other organisations can be brought in to share the resource input (for example, the government) and requires a business case to be prepared. Before beginning a new service, it carries out extensive market research to see what the real need is and to see how it might best be provided.

Independent risk assessment

A key problem for most organisations that carry out risk assessments prior to beginning a project is that the people carrying them out have a vested interest in whether the project goes ahead or not. Accounting and finance groups that often carry out this work have a vested interest in the project *not* going ahead, to show that they are not just 'rubber stamping' operational activities, and to preserve their conservatism principle and image.

Rio Tinto recognises this problem and requires three separate assessments:

▶ a case by those proposing the project

▶ a technical assessment of the project

▶ a financial assessment of the project.

Those who are proposing the project can't be involved as members of an evaluation unit and those in one unit cannot also be in another. As one interviewee said:

> This balances the enthusiasm of the project champions. The internal [evaluation] teams have also been operators so they are experienced in understanding the operations role.
>
> We have time to do this as it now takes about 18 months to undertake the environmental assessment, so that needs can be assessed and reassessed in that time period.

Lend Lease conducts peer reviews of project proposals. It gets a team from another project to review the proposal of the new project team. This provides independent assessment, the opportunity to improve the new proposal and learning for both the new team and also the peer reviewing team. As well, all specialist areas in the organisation—for example, tax, legal and finance—have to sign off, maximising their responsibility even though it is not their project.

NAB was the first of the major banks to introduce its own separate Credit Assessment Bureau, which provides an independent assessment of major credit proposals. NAB attributes its better bad loan performance through the 1989–92 recession to it having better credit assessment than its competitors. It was more prepared to say 'no', due to the existence of this independent bureau. Interestingly, it was this factor (lower loan losses) that enabled NAB to have the capital to bid for most of its overseas acquisitions at a time when competitors both here and overseas were strapped for cash.

Around 2000, NAB's conservative approach to lending got it into trouble. Fearing a downturn, NAB tightened its lending criteria. The downturn did not eventuate. Playing catch up, NAB loosened its conservative views and focused on short-term profits, which eventually led to major changes at the top of the organisation to try to get it back in balance.

Telstra also has its own risk management group. Its aim is to identify future industry and competitive issues and what Telstra's response should be. This allows Telstra to be proactive in trying to shape the industry for its own competitive advantage and to be better placed to react to problem issues when they emerge.

Laying off risks

One way to manage risk in a transaction, new project or new business development is to pass it off to other parties.

There are several ways in which this can be achieved (see figure 9.4):

▶ structuring the transaction

Manage the downside

- using networks to reduce risks
- sharing the risk with partners
- sharing the risk with customers
- sharing the risk with employees.

Figure 9.4: ways to lay off risk

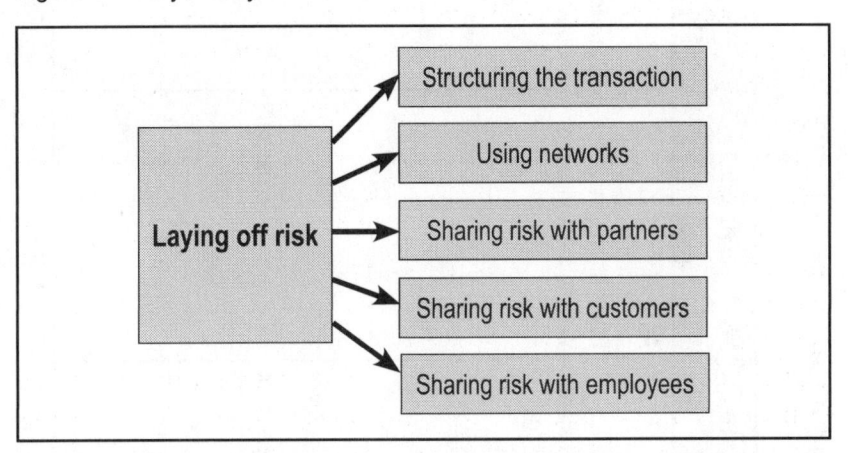

```
                    ┌──────────────────────────────┐
                    │  Structuring the transaction │
                    └──────────────────────────────┘
                    ┌──────────────────────────────┐
                    │       Using networks         │
┌────────────────┐  └──────────────────────────────┘
│                │  ┌──────────────────────────────┐
│ Laying off risk│→ │ Sharing risk with partners   │
│                │  └──────────────────────────────┘
└────────────────┘  ┌──────────────────────────────┐
                    │ Sharing risk with customers  │
                    └──────────────────────────────┘
                    ┌──────────────────────────────┐
                    │ Sharing risk with employees  │
                    └──────────────────────────────┘
```

Structuring the transaction is one technique for laying off risk. In building, a key issue is whether there are tenants who will take up the building when it is completed. Wherever possible, both Lend Lease and Westfield pre-tenant a building so that, as soon as it is completed, it is occupied and cash flows from sales or rentals begin. Pre-selling also gives early cash flows before development even starts.

Another way in which they reduce the risk to themselves is to sell the buildings to fund managers who specialise in property ownership. Until 2004, both had property trusts in which they had long-standing relationships and interests—General Property Trust for Lend Lease and Westfield Property Trust, Westfield America Trust and Westfield America Inc. for Westfield. This moved the asset out of their balance sheets as soon as it was completed, though they did retain a role in managing the building (which improves their financial balance sheet management).

Table 9.2 (overleaf) shows how the process worked for Westfield. It shows that Westfield accessed four different types of investors—the public in Australia and in the US, and institutions in both places—and splits its activities in three different ways—design and building, Australian ownership and US ownership. Although the apparently risky activities of development were in the holding company, given the

Table 9.2: an example of laying off risk in the building industry—Westfield in 1997

	Westfield Holdings	Westfield Property Trust	Westfield America Trust	Westfield America Inc.
Incorporated in	Australia	Australia	Australia	US
Activity	Designs, builds, leases and manages worldwide shopping centres. Manages public investment companies	Owns interests in Australia, New Zealand and Asian shopping centres	Owns shares in Westfield America Inc.	Owns interests in US shopping centres
Ownership (approx)				
Lowy family	35 per cent	—	—	—
Australian institutions	30 per cent	75 per cent	—	—
Australian public	35 per cent	25 per cent	75 per cent	—
US institutions	—	—	—	15 per cent
US public	—	—	—	20 per cent
Westfield Holdings	—	—	25 per cent	48 per cent
Westfield America Trust	—	—	—	17 per cent

Source: adapted from Westfield America case, Harvard Business School, August 1999.

Manage the downside

vertical connections the risks were substantially reduced, as a ready market exists for investing in shopping centres.

In 2004, Westfield merged its activities into one company, thus reversing the focus and specialisation that existed, while increasing the vertical integration. It did this so it could borrow larger amounts as its activity grew significantly during the period due to its international expansion. Lend Lease also tried to buy its partly owned property manager, General Property Trust, but it was unsuccessful and a divorce occurred, reducing Lend Lease's links with the property investment and managing industry and forcing Lend Lease to recreate the function within the organisation (called the investment management business).

The effect of Westfield's integration (and Lend Lease's recreation of investment management internally) was to reduce the risk of each corporation, but also to reduce the returns by including low-return investment management activities in the total corporation. In each case, this is consistent with the industry 'fashion' at the time, but inconsistent with the general practice of winning organisations of focusing on what they do best.

Laying off risk by *sharing it with a network* is another solution to risk management. For instance, Qantas codeshares routes with many other airlines and has formal relationships through the Oneworld alliance with several other major world airlines. Sharing networks enables Qantas to offer many other routes that appear to be its own but are actually run by partners or codesharers.

Macquarie does this with its managed funds. Macquarie generally conceives of the deal and then sells the assets bought into one or more of its funds, which attracts investors seeking specialised assets. Those funds then put several similar assets together (for example, several communications assets, several leisure assets) and seek to develop synergies between them to improve their performance compared with when they were purchased. Thus, Macquarie's risk is for a limited period, until it sells the asset to a fund, at which point it receives not only a return from the sale but also a stream of income from the profits and/or share price increases that may result from the asset being managed by the fund.

Sharing risk with partners is another approach to laying off risk. Joint ventures can be used to do this. Brambles used a joint venture with GKN to expand CHEP into Europe and then internationally. Initially this was 80–20 in favour of GKN, but over time it became 50–50. Rio Tinto often enters an exploration or mining activity on a joint venture basis and often with competitors. Westfield has had long partnerships with property investors General Shopping (Luxembourg), Credit Suisse (Switzerland) and Rodamco (Netherlands), and customer Coles Myer, which means it is far easier to raise funds and find anchor customers for its sites.

Brambles and Lend Lease lay off risk by agreeing to share gains with customers. While this sounds like giving up profits, what it actually means is that customers are as interested in cost savings as Brambles and Lend Lease. This alignment of motivations contrasts with the normal buyer/seller conflict and achieves better results for all, including more satisfied and loyal customers, thus reducing future risks of customer switching.

A final way to lay off risk is to *share it with employees*. Harvey Norman lays off some of its major risks—of buying the wrong products and of having too much stock—to its franchisees/employees. Stocks held are owned by the franchisee, not Harvey Norman. Salespeople are all employed by the franchisee. Therefore, it is up to the franchisee to deal with non-performers. Harvey Norman charges a fee for generic advertising and for the provision of central services. It also utilises the information from the sales floor, as franchisees and buyers together make better buying decisions than buyers alone—another way in which risk is reduced, with no negative effect on business activity. This system provides much higher motivation for franchisee employees to sell than a normal employment system. This is partly because the risk is with the franchisee and partly because franchisees may potentially receive much larger gains than might be available under a more conventional employee/employer remuneration agreement.

Macquarie is another where the employees receive a major part of the organisation's profits. This also means that, if profits turn down, so too do employee profit-sharing bonuses, so the profits do not turn down as much as might be expected. Most of the winning organisations have profit sharing or bonus schemes now, so they all use this method to some extent (with the exception of the Salvation Army).

Being conservative

Can entrepreneurial organisations be conservative? Yes, they can! A very interesting finding was that all the organisations see themselves as conservative in the decisions that they make. Yet they also see themselves as quick to adapt and entrepreneurial! We'll address this contrast in chapter 10. Suffice to say here that the organisations are indeed conservative. This conservatism showed in three ways. Winning organisations are:

- *Strategically conservative.* They stay with what they have been doing and do not move too far away from that (see chapter 5). For instance, for very different reasons, Westfield, Woolworths and Rio Tinto would be regarded as averse to strategic risk—unwilling to take on big risks by changing their strategies.

- *Operationally conservative.* If business leaders see their business activity as 'my business' they are much more conservative than if they see their funds as the money of a big corporation, so it doesn't really matter what happens to it or where it comes from. This concept is particularly strong at Macquarie and Brambles. Winning organisations are also averse to operational risk in that they desire to share risk, as we have demonstrated.

- *Financially conservative.* Winning organisations have a policy of low gearing ratios. Also, most winning organisations are very concerned about costs—for example, Woolworths, Telstra, Rio Tinto, the Salvation Army, NAB, Harvey Norman and Brambles. They do not wish to be exposed unnecessarily to financial risks.

Rio Tinto made an interesting comment in 2002 on being conservative. It said:

> We adopt a thorough assessment of investment decisions. This occasionally leads people to think of Rio as being conservative. This is not accurate as our philosophy is to adopt a risk aware approach to value creation. (Annual report)

Project management

Project management has traditionally been regarded as simply a collection of planning, monitoring and control tools that can be applied in project-based industries such as construction, engineering, aerospace and defence. But project management is emerging as a discipline in its own right—one that draws on an extensive range of management principles and techniques. Getting the job done on time, within cost and within quality dimensions of traditional project management have become increasingly important competitive factors in all industries. Winning organisations use project management as a powerful tool to implement change and effectively execute their strategies.

The project life cycle (project initiation, implementation and termination) is the most common framework (see figure 9.5 overleaf).

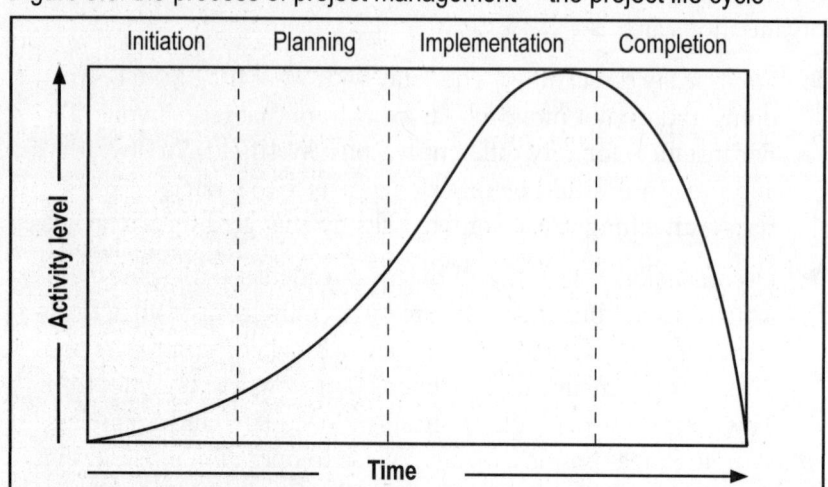

Figure 9.5: the process of project management—the project life cycle

Activity level vs Time, showing phases: Initiation, Planning, Implementation, Completion

Project managers define the end goals of the project, then work back to plan the project by breaking it into small, discrete activities. This creates a work breakdown structure of detailed activities. Each activity has its own set of deliverable outcomes, its own set of resources necessary for the activity and time required for completion. Identifying task dependencies (which activities come first, which can be done in parallel, which come later) is done using network diagrams. From this, a 'critical path' of activities can be plotted. This determines the minimum time in which the plan can be delivered. *A Guide to the Project Management Body of Knowledge*, published by the US Project Management Institute, covers nine functions that together comprise the modern approach to project management. These functions are time, cost, scope, quality, human resources, contract procurement, communications, risk and integration management.

Project management is useful both in up-front planning and also for ongoing control during the project. It has the highly desirable feature of predicting the date of the completion of the project, thus providing the basis for 'on time and on budget' effective execution outcomes.

This technique was first used in building construction and development in Australia by Lend Lease and replicated by Westfield shortly after. It is of great use in this industry, where there is a high risk of delays and failure to complete on time if activities are not coordinated. However, it is useful in many other industries. Rio Tinto is another winning organisation that applies it rigorously in the mining construction industry. It also provides a basis for ensuring effective execution occurs. Illustration 9.2 shows how Woolworths set up Project Mercury to manage its major projects.

Manage the downside

> **Illustration 9.2: Project Mercury manages Woolworths' projects**
>
> Project Mercury is Woolworths' project management control system and Woolworths believes it is an important part of their ability to complete projects successfully, on time and within budget. Project Mercury began in 2003 as part of Project Refresh.
>
> Each project has four stages. During the first stage the concept of the project is developed—what is it specifically that we are trying to achieve, how do we plan to do it and what, conceptually, do we think the benefits will be?
>
> If the project is approved, it enters the second stage—the feasibility study. Here real money is spent to quantify the benefits, work out how to get the benefits, cost them, develop the timing of the elements of the project and allocate resources to the project.
>
> At this point the project reaches the third stage—the active stage. Here the project is implemented with control focused on timing and budget. When the project is completed, it enters the fourth stage—the harvest stage—where the benefits are gained.
>
> The team running Project Mercury maintains a very detailed control system with each project listed on the left and each stage and substage of the project across the page. Stages are colour-coded for easy interpretation. Green means the project is on track. Amber or yellow means there are some concerns. Red indicates significant problems. While conceptually simple, most organisations simply don't do this for their projects. Does yours?

Contingency planning

Several organisations have very strong contingency planning processes to cope with short-term specifically unpredictable—but generally expected—changes.

Qantas faces daily schedule-matching problems, particularly for international flights where weather conditions across the world are quite different. But it can happen in Australia too, particularly if either Sydney or Melbourne airports are out of action, or running behind schedule for any reason. When planes are not on time, passengers miss connections, and crew, plane and maintenance schedules are thrown out. In addition, passengers are unreliable in turning up for flights, so Qantas (like other airlines) overbooks, risking the problem of not having enough seats if more than the forecasted number actually turn up. Qantas can't simply throw its hands up and say 'sorry' in these cases. So it mounts extensive contingency plans to ensure that such situations are effectively planned for as much as possible.

Apart from these daily problems, the handling of which rapidly affects—negatively or positively—the reputation of an airline, more major industry disasters can occur, such as the collapse of an airline, a major world political event such as the Gulf War, or even a plane crash at an airport. Through the last few years the collapses of Impulse, Ansett and its subsidiaries, the suspension of Ansett in peak Christmas 2001 and Easter 2002 periods, the SARS health epidemic in 2003, and the Bali bombings in 2002 and 2004 have all resulted in huge short-term fluctuations in the demands on Qantas' operating systems and people. Contingency planning greatly assisted in these cases, as did the determination and volunteerism of Qantas' people to help stranded passengers of all airlines complete their journeys.

Telstra is another organisation for which contingency planning is important. Like Qantas, Telstra must cope with daily emergencies—phone outages, partial network failures, extreme weather conditions—yet have a national (and international) system of millions of phones and computers working 24 hours a day, seven days a week. People and businesses have very little tolerance these days for communication system failures.

More than this though, in a deregulated system Telstra considers carefully what its competitors are likely to do—proactively and reactively—in the marketplace, and simulates what is likely to happen under various conditions. Using this game theory approach, Telstra is able to plan to effectively respond in the best way possible to predicted moves by competitors and to predict how competitors will likely respond to Telstra's own moves.

Our experience is that this type of gaming approach to competitors is rarely undertaken, though it is well known in theory. Telstra's experience suggests there is considerable value in this approach to forward planning for competitive moves.

The Salvation Army is another that relies on contingency planning. Much of the Salvation Army's work is difficult to plan for—how many emergencies will there be today or this year? Consequently, the Salvation Army has to be prepared to cope with these 'unexpected' emergencies. It copes through the extensive use of hierarchy and detailed and well-tried systems and procedures. Its military structure is highly valuable for these types of situations. For this reason, the Salvation Army is also very helpful in general civil emergencies, such as floods and bushfires, where it can apply the same skills and systems to get the job done.

Good reporting and control systems

When the project or operations are under way, the ability of an organisation to measure what is happening and to use that information to control or change operations is critically undervalued. We have already reported on this under 'effective execution' (see chapter 2). However, the same systems are valuable in managing risk as well as delivering positive outcomes.

Winning organisations specialise in having excellent reporting and control systems, though each system is necessarily specific to its own situation. Lend Lease was one of the first in Australia to develop exception reporting, enabling it to focus on the outliers rather than being swamped by 'normal' operating information. Harvey Norman receives information from its many individual store franchisees. This enables it to know how the whole range of franchisees are trading on a daily basis. It then provides information back to franchisees that could be used to help them run their businesses more profitably.

Qantas has excellent revenue management systems that enable it to conduct better analysis than its competitors, allowing it to better respond to market changes. Ironically, many of these systems were put in place under Gary Toomey, who left to become CEO of rival Air New Zealand/Ansett, where he found very poor information systems.

Qantas' cost, cash flow and treasury management systems deal with over 100 countries and thousands of agents on a system that is available in real time all the time. Sales need to be reconciled by passenger, by route and by agent. Qantas is sought out by banks and telcos for benchmarking costs, reliability and information quality from its systems. Qantas keeps all customer transaction data for three years and uses that to model its future business.

The Salvation Army is very strong on systems, consistent with its hierarchical structure. Systems cover everything from people management to expansion rules for congregations to training and selection to financial management to emergency planning. They enable it to keep close control of its activities. This is particularly important in an organisation with limited resources.

Quality of people, assets and systems

An interesting approach to reducing risk is to hire quality people, use quality assets and have quality systems for managing operations. The logic is that good people, assets and systems perform better than those of lower quality. Therefore, though the organisation pays more up-front for quality, it receives greater productivity, offsetting the up-front cost. Rio Tinto, Lend Lease and Macquarie use this approach.

However, it is largely untested as a general argument. Rio Tinto seeks low-cost outcomes from its mines, whereas Lend Lease and Macquarie seek more innovative, value-creating, high-quality solutions, for which they will be better paid. Each is happy with its outcomes. Interestingly, competitors have not sought to replicate the latter approach. This could be for several reasons. They could believe that this approach does not work, that it would not work for them, that they could not afford it, or that their own approach gives them a satisfactory position.

There does not appear to be any empirical evidence to support or oppose these approaches. Perhaps they are simply the result of the important process of aligning everything (see chapter 3) and effective execution (see chapter 2). Aligned systems, albeit starting from different points and with different organisational philosophies, are able to reach similar outcomes if appropriately managed.

Being rigorous

Of course, it is not just having the systems that gives good results, it is using them. Here again, the winning organisations distinguish themselves by their overall rigour in using what systems they have, particularly in the financial area, which is of fundamental importance for ensuring the survival and wellbeing of the organisation.

The difference from normal organisations is that, in winning organisations, budgets and targets are almost sacrosanct—you are expected to achieve them at a minimum, not a maximum. And significant individual rewards are based heavily on this, reinforcing the importance of the system.

Woolworths not only has rigorous reporting of quantitative and qualitative information, but it also has simple KPIs so that it is easy for individuals to focus. As one interviewee said:

> We are very focused. We have targets and budgets. This is a numbers game. You need to meet the budget…We assess and reward on a variable basis against last year—once you achieve 6 per cent over last year, rewards start and continue to increase.

Brambles is another that focuses on the numbers and is rigorous. Numbers are agreed with individuals who are responsible. They seek to make those numbers, knowing that is what is expected. Lend Lease, Macquarie, NAB and Harvey Norman are similar.

Balance sheet management

One aspect of managing risk that has received less attention than it might is that of balance sheet management. The focus in financials is usually on the profit and loss statement (now officially called the income statement). However, winning organisations have found that balance sheet management is an important tool for managing risks.

We are not suggesting that balance sheet management is a clear distinguishing feature of winning organisations. But there is certainly a suggestion that rigour and financial discipline is increasingly being applied to the balance sheet and not just the profit and loss statement.

For instance, until 2004 Westfield and Lend Lease sold the properties they built, often to vertically integrated property owners such as General Property Trust (Lend Lease) or Westfield Property Trust (Westfield). These were different organisations whose role was to hold or own the property and receive the rental streams. These cash flow streams were very stable, so returns were very predictable. As a result, investors in these companies were happy to accept lower returns (for lower risk) than investors in the construction organisations, where risk is perceived to be higher. Consequently, the balance sheets of the total operation was 'split' into component parts. This enabled the builders to borrow more cheaply and not have those borrowings on their balance sheet.

Another approach is to reduce the importance of the size of an investment in assets by generating income streams from services, rather than making profits from holding assets. Lend Lease, Westfield and Macquarie have all sought to achieve this. Woolworths is similarly unbundling its property assets to use the funds more in its core business of retailing. The use of joint ventures to share risks can also have the effect of valuable assets being held by others.

Table 9.3 (overleaf) gives some examples of how various techniques are used to match the particular risks we have identified in this chapter.

Standards Australia believes risk can be managed in a number of ways. This approach is more geared to operational risk than the larger area of business and organisation risk, but it certainly provides another interesting perspective. It covers the need for a good business case to have good contract conditions, the need for first-rate people and systems, for project management and includes the whole area of operational risk. Standards Australia's recommended categories for managing risk are:

- contract conditions
- formal review of requirements, specifications, design, engineering and operations
- inspection/testing and technical and process controls
- quality assurance, management and standards
- structured training
- supervision
- project management
- preventative maintenance
- audit and compliance programs
- investment and portfolio management.

Table 9.3: matching risk management techniques to risks

Risk	Useful techniques
Strategic	Up-front planning; independent risk assessment; laying off risks; quality of people, assets and systems; being conservative; contingency planning; being rigorous; balance sheet management
Financial	Being conservative; laying off risks; project management; reporting and control systems; rigour and financial discipline; contingency plans; being rigorous; balance sheet management
Technical	Up-front planning; independent risk assessment; project management; contingency planning; quality of people, assets and systems; being rigorous
Operating	Laying off risks; project management; quality of people, assets and systems; reporting and control systems; being rigorous
Political	Up-front planning; contingency plans; laying off risks; balance sheet management
Legal	Up-front planning; contingency plans; being conservative; laying off risks
Reputation	Up-front planning; laying off risks; contingency planning; being conservative; quality of people, assets and systems

Summary and key messages for leaders

Being conservative in managing downside risk is important for winning organisations. As well as seeking growth and progress, they also seek to reduce the risks involved in those activities. There are a wide variety of downside risks to be managed: strategic, financial, technical, operating, political, legal and reputation risk. A single omission or action by an individual can be devastating to the normal operating results if risks are not well managed.

There are a variety of techniques used by winning organisations to manage risks. There is less consistency here than in most other chapters, though, because of the differences in each industry's operations and situation. The lack of focus in the past on managing risks means that best practices have not yet developed here.

The key messages for leaders from this chapter are:

▶ Understand the variety of risks that can critically affect the long-term results of the organisation.

▶ Use techniques to manage those risks.

▶ Use up-front planning.

▶ Allow for independent risk assessment of major projects.

▶ Lay off risks to others involved in the activity.

▶ Be conservative in thinking and action.

▶ Use project management techniques.

▶ Allow for contingencies in planning.

▶ Develop and use excellent control and reporting systems.

▶ Use good-quality people, assets and systems.

▶ Be rigorous in operations and analysis.

▶ Manage the balance sheet.

10 Balance everything

And, and, and

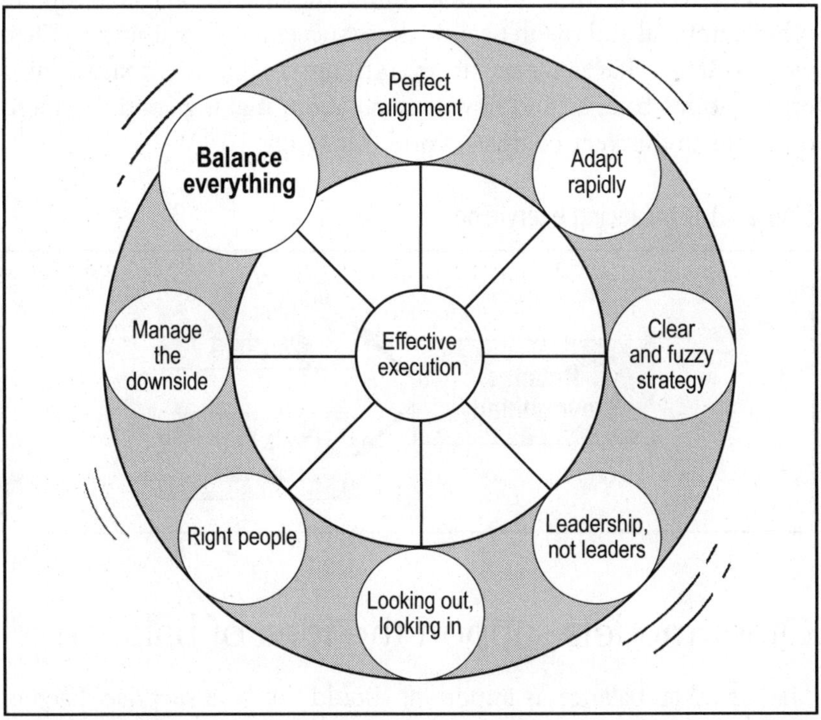

Perfect alignment
Adapt rapidly
Clear and fuzzy strategy
Leadership, not leaders
Looking out, looking in
Right people
Manage the downside
Balance everything
Effective execution

As we analysed each of the winning organisations, it became very clear that there is no simple '1, 2, 3' or 'A leads to B which leads to C' formula

The First XI

for success for any of them. They do many things well. They are not choosing to focus on only a small number of issues or variables. They focus on many items and yet they each have a clear focus.

This seems paradoxical. Yet the more we looked, the more consistent this paradoxical picture was. And you will be aware of this phenomenon from reading earlier examples and chapters. Winning organisations seem to balance everything in their world. It is not a case of A or B but A *and* B—*and* C *and* D and so on. So we came to the view that 'balance' was a key element in the 'winning framework' of winning organisations. And it was a case of balancing many things—'and, and, and'—not a case of balancing a few things. To capture this idea, we termed it *'balance everything'*. To First XI teams, it's not just a case of focusing on the offence, on the scoring; it's a case of also focusing on the defence, preventing the other team from scoring. It's necessary for First XI players to present themselves well off the field—to the media and the community—as well as being the best on the field. It's all part of the job these days for high-performing organisations.

In this chapter, which addresses the last element of the winning wheel framework, we'll first look at how the idea of balance occurs in other empirical and theoretical work on successful organisations. Then we'll address what is meant by 'everything'—what it is that winning organisations balance and how they go about making good, balanced decisions in this very complex world (see figure 10.1).

Figure 10.1: balancing everything

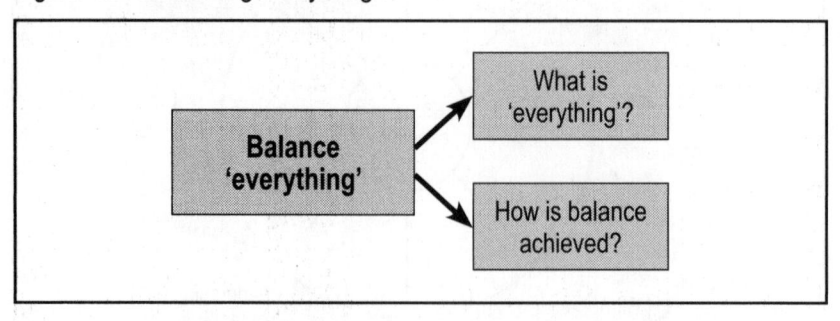

Other models support the idea of balance

The idea that 'balance' is important should not be a surprise. Each of the other major frameworks we considered in our foundations for this research includes or implies 'balance' as a key element (see chapter 3 for a brief discussion of each of these frameworks).

Built to Last and balance

Collins and Porras explicitly include 'balance' in their *Built to Last* framework under the heading 'No "Tyranny of the Or" (Embrace the "Genius of the And")'.

They say:

> You'll notice ... that we use the yin/yang symbol from Chinese dualist philosophy. We've consciously selected this symbol to represent a key aspect of highly visionary companies: They do not oppress themselves with what we call the 'Tyranny of the OR'—the rational view that cannot easily accept paradox, that cannot live with two seemingly contradictory forces or ideas at the same time ...
>
> ...
>
> highly visionary companies liberate themselves with the 'Genius of the AND' ...
>
> ...
>
> a highly visionary company doesn't want to blend yin and yang into a gray, indistinguishable circle ... it aims to be distinctly yin *and* distinctly yang—*both* at the same time, all the time.
>
> Irrational? Perhaps. Rare? Yes. Difficult? Absolutely. But... 'The test of a first-rate intelligence is the ability to hold two opposed ideas in the mind at the same time, and still retain the ability to function' (pp. 43–45).

They also use this concept of balance elsewhere in their framework. For instance, the following ideas are all about doing both or doing several things at once and concentrating on them both or all:

▶ 'preserve the core/stimulate progress'

▶ 'more than profit'

▶ 'try a lot of stuff and see what works'.

In Search of Excellence/7S and balance

Peters and Waterman also make it clear that balance is important in their 7S model for excellent companies in *In Search of Excellence*. They make it clear that each of the Ss affects all the others, that all are important and that all need to be aligned. In their model, it is a case of balancing all seven of the elements to become an 'excellent' organisation. So, even though 'balance' is not a specific idea in the model itself, it is implied by the framework and is implicit in the words used.

The E-S-C gap analysis and implementation framework and balance

Hubbard's (2000) E-S-C gap analysis and implementation framework (see chapter 3) also implies the concept of balance. In this framework, not only does the organisation need to align its strategy with the requirements of its external environment and its internal capabilities, but the elements of the framework used to align the strategy—leadership, people, culture, systems and structure—all need to be aligned. To be effective, the organisation has to balance (and align) all these elements to deliver the strategy and get the outcomes required.

The balanced scorecard and balance

It's obvious just from the name that Kaplan and Norton's (1996) framework for measuring performance expects a 'balanced' approach to organisational activity. The balanced scorecard implies that financial, customer and employee stakeholder interests all need to be served. It also demands that both a short-term and a long-term perspective are considered for the 'growth and learning' measures of the scorecard to be achieved. Such a balanced measurement approach can only make sense if the underlying activities of the organisation are planned to be balanced.

Paradox theory and balance

Groen and Hampden-Turner (2005) promote the idea that management should be viewed as a series of paradoxes, rather than a series of 'either/or' choices. They say:

> What distinguishes the capacity to learn rapidly, culminating in superlative performance, is the capacity to confront and to resolve *value paradoxes*...

> Certainty is in tension with Doubt. Unity is in tension with Diversity. Loyalty is in tension with Dissent. What happens is that the people, teams and organizations move *between these differences*, for example from systematically doubting to becoming more certain...

> We believe that superlative performance is driven by reconciliations and flow experiences *among many different paradoxes*...Brilliant *performances resolve these paradoxes* (pp. 34–38).

So we see that there is very strong empirical and theoretical support for the concept of 'balance' and its importance. Even more, the idea of balancing many elements, not just one or two items of key focus, is brought out consistently through these frameworks. However, we also see from Collins and Porras' comments earlier that doing this, executing this, is considered to be extremely difficult. It is easy to talk about and even conceptualise, but difficult to make happen. But that is exactly the challenge and that is what winning organisations manage to do! This is one of the key elements that makes an organisation a winning one.

What is 'everything'? And, and, and

The idea of 'everything' conjures up impossibilities—how can we possibly focus on 'everything'? What does 'everything' mean? 'Everything' really just means the 'many' things an organisation has to balance if it is to succeed over the long term. Achieving this balance is complex and difficult. We use the word 'everything' to convey this complexity.

We do not have a list of 'everything'. Clearly it will vary from one industry to another, one organisation to another, one level in an organisation to another. We summarise here what our research shows are the key factors that the winning organisations address. We have grouped these into a number of themes, below (see figure 10.2 overleaf). Organisations must:

▶ balance perspectives

▶ balance philosophies

▶ balance organisation levels

▶ balance operations/activities/functions

▶ achieve an overall balance.

Balance perspectives

Many organisations tend to have only one perspective or to primarily focus on only one perspective about what is important to the organisation. This makes it easier to focus on what to do and often reflects the (possibly erroneous) beliefs of the CEO or top management team about what is important.

Figure 10.2: balancing 'everything'

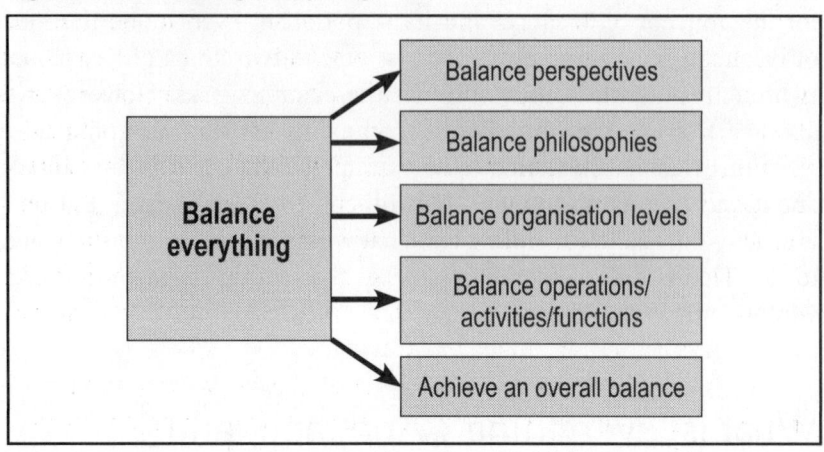

```
                    ┌─────────────────────────────────┐
                    │      Balance perspectives       │
                    └─────────────────────────────────┘
                    ┌─────────────────────────────────┐
                    │      Balance philosophies       │
                    └─────────────────────────────────┘
    ┌─────────┐     ┌─────────────────────────────────┐
    │ Balance │ ──▶ │   Balance organisation levels   │
    │everything│    └─────────────────────────────────┘
    └─────────┘     ┌─────────────────────────────────┐
                    │       Balance operations/       │
                    │       activities/functions      │
                    └─────────────────────────────────┘
                    ┌─────────────────────────────────┐
                    │    Achieve an overall balance   │
                    └─────────────────────────────────┘
```

However, our research did not find that organisational life was so simple! Instead, we found that winning organisations know that they must balance several different perspectives simultaneously if they are to succeed (see figure 10.3). These include balancing external and internal perspectives, stakeholder and shareholder perspectives and short-term and long-term perspectives. A focus on one or other of each of these pairs of perspectives leads to an unbalanced view, unbalanced actions and possibly disaster sometime in the future.

Figure 10.3: balancing perspectives

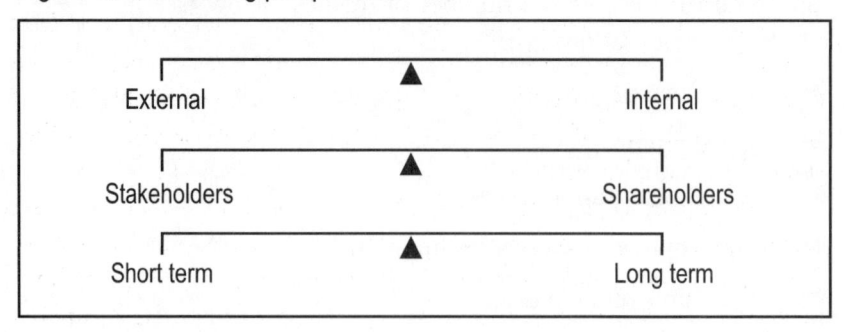

```
      External                ▲                Internal
      
      Stakeholders            ▲                Shareholders
      
      Short term              ▲                Long term
```

External and *internal perspectives*

Winning organisations are able to simultaneously consider both external and internal perspectives. We see being externally focused as one of the key elements in the winning framework (see chapter 7). But winning organisations are not externally focused *instead* of having an internal focus, they incorporate both views. In fact, most of the other elements in our framework are heavily internally oriented. The point we made in chapter 7 was that winning organisations are not just focused on becoming internally aligned and efficient; they are also concerned with fitting into their external world. They are very aware of that external world. That awareness and linking to the external world is quite different from the orientation of many normal organisations.

For instance, Woolworths is very concerned about its internal logistics management, but it is also aware of what new products consumers are interested in and what other forms of retailing are emerging. The Salvation Army is aware of other solutions being proposed for social problems. It is also concerned about balancing its role as church and as a charity.

We can think of 'external' and 'internal' in other ways too. Winning organisations are aware of the national market, which might be seen as the 'internal' market, but they are also very aware of what is going on in international or overseas markets, even when they are not international themselves. Woolworths is very aware of how Wal-Mart, the global leader in discount operations, is developing. Qantas is very concerned about efficient scheduling of its planes, but it is also concerned about what services are being offered to passengers by other airlines and what new technology developments are occurring internationally.

Stakeholder *and* shareholder *perspectives*

One of the biggest debates about organisations is where their 'responsibilities' lie. No-one denies that financial performance is important or that shareholders deserve a reasonable return on their investment. No-one denies that, without at least minimal financial performance, an organisation dies. However, it often dies from lack of cash flow, not lack of profits. This can occur regardless of how other stakeholders are being served.

Nevertheless, empirical evidence clearly shows that winning organisations balance a variety of perspectives and are not focused on financial returns alone. For instance, while Brambles argued throughout most of its life that it was heavily driven by financial returns ('crunch a quid'), we also know that Brambles:

▶ carefully chooses the organisations it wants to partner with
▶ seeks to develop strong customer relationships over time
▶ seeks to develop specially customised products for its customers
▶ has its top managers spend a lot of time with the regular people in the organisation, knowing that it is their performance that determines the outcome for the whole company

▶ supports its people in their charitable activities

▶ wants to be a leader in environmental policy and behaviour.

Brambles does not seek to 'rip off' its customers to increase its shareholder returns. It does not seek to exploit its people just to increase financial returns. So 'financial returns' or 'financial focus' is just one perspective (albeit a very important one in Brambles' case). Even for Brambles, by itself it does not accurately represent the required or desired behaviour.

The evidence that winning organisations use a stakeholder approach—a balanced scorecard approach to performance, not just a financial approach as is often advocated—is overwhelming. Table 10.1 provides examples of how winning organisations balance the various stakeholder groups.

Table 10.1: examples of stakeholders other than shareholders that are important to winning organisations

Organisation	Other important stakeholders
Brambles	Customers, partners, people
Harvey Norman	Franchisees, suppliers
Lend Lease	People, customers, partners, community
Macquarie	People
NAB	Customers
Qantas	Customers, partners, people, Australian people
Rio Tinto	Local communities, people, governments
The Salvation Army	Clients, church, governments, people
Telstra	Government, Australian community, regulators, suppliers
Westfield	End customers, customers, community, planning regulators
Woolworths	Customers, suppliers

Over the last few years it is evident that environmental issues and therefore the role of the community have become increasingly important to winning organisations. The community is emerging as a 'stakeholder' in the organisation, whether managers or shareholders like it or not. This is leading to the need for a much wider view of the organisation and the impact it has on the community than has previously been considered. Lend Lease introduced the idea in 2000 of a 'community day' for its people to give back to the communities in which it operates. Macquarie supports its people spending some of their time working for community organisations, over and above what it or the staff may donate in dollars.

A variation on this stakeholder and shareholder theme is that winning organisations are concerned with both financial and non-financial measures and outcomes. It could be argued that keeping stakeholders happy ultimately serves the bottom line. For instance, perhaps Macquarie and Harvey Norman focus on their people and pay them high rewards simply because 'it is all about money'. But even this is still a narrow argument. Macquarie people certainly do receive a lot of money for their efforts, but the solutions they come up with for customers have been equally valuable, or even more so, for them. Macquarie people only benefit if customers and shareholders benefit. The same argument applies for Harvey Norman people.

Another variation on the theme occurs through the gain-sharing concept, whereby future targeted gains are agreed to be shared with customers, employees, suppliers or partners. A shareholder-oriented organisation would keep all the gains for itself. A financially focused organisation would do the same. Gain sharing represents a way of linking the interests of more than one stakeholder group and, whatever the short-term results, the long-term ones are likely to be beneficial, and beneficial to all! Lend Lease, Qantas, Brambles and Woolworths are some of the winning organisations that use gain-sharing approaches with stakeholders.

Woolworths refers to the 'twin goals' of increasing customer satisfaction and shareholder value at the same time. It noted that 85 per cent of the gains from Project Refresh would go back to the customers and 15 per cent would go to shareholders. At the same time, as many of its people are also shareholders (and shoppers) its people gain in three ways—cheaper goods, better share returns and more jobs being available. That's actually 'triple goals'!

Rio Tinto's 'The way we work' and Lend Lease's 'Community of interests' are two other examples of winning organisations balancing the variety of stakeholder groups and not just focusing on shareholders.

In summary, of course shareholders are important, but they are just one of several stakeholder groups. Winning organisations balance the interests of them all according to their particular circumstances and situation.

Short-term and long-term perspectives

Another classic debate, especially for public companies, is the argument that, since the sharemarket is very focused on short-term results, listed companies need to focus on the short term and not on the long term. Despite the fact that finance research does not actually support it, this argument is put forward with increasing intensity. However, it is usually put by CEOs and organisations whose performance is poor, rather than by those whose performance is good.

Winning organisations don't have this view at all. They see that both a short-term and a long-term perspective is required. Both short-term and long-term results must be achieved. Consider these examples:

▶ Brambles spent 20 years getting CHEP established throughout Europe, yet it is said to have a short-term focus on this year's performance.

▶ Woolworths measures its performance weekly, yet its Project Refresh continuous improvement project is expected to run for more than 10 years.

▶ Westfield is continually redeveloping its shopping centres, but most of them continue to trade through the redevelopment so that the year's sales and profit targets can be reached.

▶ Harvey Norman is judged on current profit growth, but it expects to take 10 years for its venture into Ireland to meet a satisfactory return target.

In summary, winning organisations don't choose to focus on the internal *or* the external, shareholders *or* stakeholders, short term *or* long term. They focus on *all* of these, in order to produce a balanced result overall.

Balance philosophies

Winning organisations also balance a variety of different philosophies about the essential nature of what an organisation ought to be. There are endless possible philosophies that might be used. Our research found that winning organisations balanced entrepreneurial and conservative, stable and changing, loose and tight, clear and fuzzy, and objective and subjective philosophies (see figure 10.4).

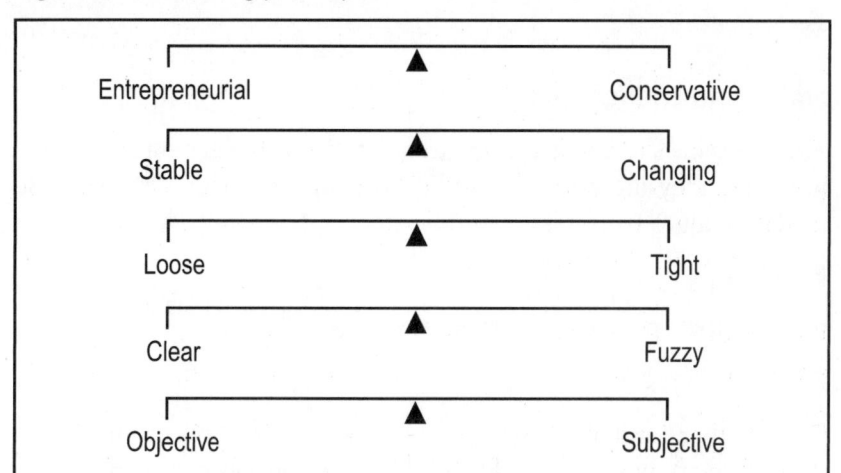

Figure 10.4: balancing philosophies

Entrepreneurial	▲	Conservative
Stable	▲	Changing
Loose	▲	Tight
Clear	▲	Fuzzy
Objective	▲	Subjective

Entrepreneurial and *conservative*

While the winning organisations have all been entrepreneurial in their development to some degree, even the most entrepreneurial and opportunistic also regard themselves as conservative! We reconciled this issue in chapter 9 (managing the downside) but, for most organisations, this is a classic 'either/or' choice—they believe that the organisation should be one or the other.

What we see for the winning organisations is that they are entrepreneurial in the sense of seeking new ideas, considering new opportunities, taking advantage of short-term events, developing new products and services and moving into new geographies. However, we also see that they do this within clearly defined strategies, laying off risks whenever they can, being conservative financially and being sure that they have the capabilities to undertake the new activities.

Telstra has invested billions of dollars to enter Asian markets, particularly the Chinese market, which represents a highly risky strategy for an organisation with limited international experience and success. It reduced its risk by investing on a joint venture basis with local partners that had good relationships in the Chinese markets, and also by structuring the deals to allow for a series of options to increase or decrease its investments, based on certain outcomes. Simultaneously, in its home market, Telstra has been conservative in resisting change to protect its strong positions in various market segments.

Macquarie encourages its staff to be creative and innovative in developing new products and services and business opportunities. Yet its Risk Management Division is seen to be critical to assessing all new business proposals and it takes a rigorous approach to risk assessment.

Stable and *changing*

Another paradox is that winning organisations are very stable in some ways, yet they are also constantly changing in others. Organisations tend to want to be stable around:

▶ what their strategy is

▶ who their people and leaders are

▶ what their culture is.

On the other hand, they are constantly seeking new opportunities that, if undertaken, will require change. They are constantly seeking:

▶ continuous improvement, which requires change

▶ to innovate

▶ to grow

▶ to expand product and service ranges.

Collins and Porras refer to the need to 'preserve the core/stimulate progress'. This is what we see here—the need to preserve, or hold stable, the core of the organisation while simultaneously seeking change in its activities and the methods of operation it uses. Winning organisations achieve both! Together! They have few CEOs and make few changes to their basic strategy, but they are constantly changing their organisational structures and their product and service ranges, the way they deliver the strategy and what markets they deliver it to.

Qantas maintains its high-quality service international profile, but seeks to reduce costs on domestic routes in the face of a low-cost competitor, Virgin Blue, and its own low-cost airline, Jetstar. It has also developed Jetstar and Jetstar Asia to capitalise on the increasing number of Australian tourists seeking low-cost international airfares to a wide variety of destinations that Qantas cannot economically service with its high-quality service/high-cost model. Qantas is competing with itself! But actually it is growing the market also, by giving access to air travel for many people who would previously not have considered it as an option.

Lend Lease, in discussing its problems with its attempt to globalise, noted that it had lost its entrepreneurial spirit and value, and was keen to get it back as it recovered.

Loose and *tight* philosophies

The term 'loose/tight' originates in the Peters and Waterman study. While only Macquarie uses this as a formal part of the wording of its values, 'loose/tight' is a highly appropriate descriptor of the behaviour of most of the winning organisations. The centre focuses on a small number of critically important variables ('tight'). The units, on the other hand, have the ability to innovate and experiment ('loose'), provided they meet the organisation's requirements on those items that are centrally controlled.

Most of the organisations push responsibility down the line. One example of this is autonomous business units that are not cross-subsidised and can largely determine their own future development (entrepreneurial) and make their own decisions (empowered, responsible). Macquarie, for instance, has over 90 separate business units, but the public sees it as one investment bank with a small number of listed subsidiaries. Macquarie says:

> Key to Macquarie's success is a distinctive management style that aims to provide individual businesses with a balance between operating freedom and controls on risk limits and observance of professional standards. This approach we term 'loose tight' is reflected in the Bank's organizational structure. It is designed to be non-hierarchical and encourages a sense of ownership and entrepreneurial endeavour by business managers. (2001 annual report)

In 2006 it said, 'This strategy is known as "freedom within boundaries"' (annual report).

On the other hand, organisations retain central control of a small number of key items. For the banks it is credit control and risk management. For entrepreneurial organisations it is budget and targets (which must be met). For all organisations it is culture and values. Units can be autonomous, but they need to conduct their activities within the value system of the whole organisation.

Clear and *fuzzy*

A variation on 'loose/tight' is 'clear and fuzzy', which we used to describe the strategies of the winning organisations (see chapter 5). We don't see completely clear strategies, as might be expected in textbook solutions. The lack of plain and simple vision and mission statements supports this view. Yet the strategies are quite clear in practice and, as they unfold over time, strategic change is incremental in virtually every case. The fuzziness is in the details of the variations and small increments. For instance, is a new business really related to the other businesses? How exactly does new business fit?

We see that there is an element of freedom (fuzziness) in strategic development, but within a constrained (clear) existing framework of current strategy and position. This is a deliberate choice, not an accident. Winning organisations want to be clear at the core and fuzzy at the edge. For instance, Brambles uses 'and' in the following statements of strategy to propose what are, traditionally, alternative focuses for strategy that would be regarded as fuzzy (our italics):

> CHEP's strategy is to...differentiate CHEP from its competitors through quality of service delivery, the application of technology, innovative products *and* the ability to offer a lower cost solution to customers. (2003 annual report)

> Brambles Industrial Services...generate growth through strong customer relationships *and* a particular focus on safety and tight cost controls. (2004 annual report)

Objective and *subjective*

Neither a coldly objective analytical philosophy nor a hot-blooded passionate one are enough by themselves. Both are needed for winning organisations. Cold, objective organisations can be right in their analysis and activities...but they are no fun and so who cares what they do? Passionate organisations are exciting and motivating, but may be badly organised and run out of money without proper analysis. Head and heart are *both* required.

Winning organisations are clear-headed and objective. Gathering 'facts' is critical for proper evaluation and assessment of their position or for a new proposal. But winning organisations also have fun and are passionate about what they do. As one Telstra executive said to us:

> People around here work very hard. But we also know how to have fun.

Brambles' waste management division might not be considered a lot of fun to work in. But Carew disagrees:

> Waste services, says Pemberton, was staffed by 'bright young things who went places...we were very cheeky young larrikins who enjoyed the excitement of it, the intellectual challenge of creating something new'. (Carew, 2000, p. 107)

People in winning organisations are committed and proud (see chapter 8). They want a cause to motivate them to work for the organisation.

Leaders in winning organisations are passionate about the cause of the organisation (see chapter 6) and engage their people.

In summary, it is not a case of choosing a single focus for the organisational philosophy. A holistic philosophy is necessary —entrepreneurial and conservative, stable and changing, loose and tight, clear and fuzzy, objective and subjective. All balanced together. It's a hard order to fill.

Balance organisation levels

Winning organisations also balance the importance of the different levels of the organisation. Careful consideration of the different levels and balancing of the information, activities and concerns at each level is necessary. Otherwise, the organisation can quickly become remote from its customers and make incorrect decisions due to acting on a biased sample of information. The levels that winning organisations balance include top and bottom, individual and team, and small business and large business (see figure 10.5).

Figure 10.5: balancing levels

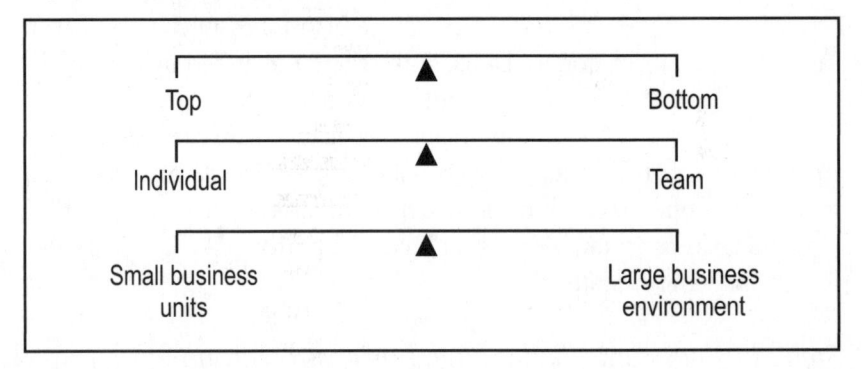

```
┌─────────────────▲─────────────────┐
  Top                           Bottom
┌─────────────────▲─────────────────┐
  Individual                    Team
┌─────────────────▲─────────────────┐
  Small business            Large business
  units                     environment
```

Top and bottom

There are many levels within an organisation—usually five to 10 or more from CEO to shop floor. Most people are involved at only one or two levels in the organisation and so that is their perspective on it. But the view from the top of the mountain is quite different from the views from the bottom. The organisation must be aligned and work at all levels for best results. Does the view at the top (the leadership group) really understand the views at the bottom (and in the middle)?

For most organisations, there is a dramatic difference between how different levels perceive it and its performance. Leadership is often out of touch with customer-facing and operational people. This means the analysis and consequent solutions proposed at the top may not be appropriate and therefore may not work, as they may not address the real issues that exist.

Winning organisations have mechanisms for ensuring that the levels of the organisation are connected and mixed. Leadership walks around, it communicates, it listens, it acts on what it hears, it provides channels from the bottom to the top and it reduces the levels of hierarchy to decrease this top/bottom issue.

Individual and *team*

At most organisations, there is either an individual *or* a team approach to the way the organisation behaves. Individual initiative can be frustrated in team-based organisations, while it can be difficult to get coordination in individually oriented organisations.

While winning organisations emphasise the role of the individual and individual responsibility, they also emphasise teamwork! And both individual performance and team performance are rewarded! High-quality individuals are desired, but prima donnas who can't work with or in a team need not apply. For instance, while Macquarie heavily rewards individuals, its reward structure also takes into account the individual's contribution to teams. Failure to be included in teams will, of course, limit the individual's ability to contribute.

This focus on both individuals and teams partly explains why the structure of the organisation constantly changes. As an individual moves from one position in the structure to another, it is not just that person's tasks as an individual that have to be covered—it is also their role in the various teams they are in.

Small business units and *a large business environment*

Not only do winning organisations encourage the development of autonomous business units (see chapter 2), they also seek to develop a small business philosophy, but within the environment, and with the benefits, of a large business framework. For instance, we see a clear focus on units rather than the whole organisation at:

- ▶ Macquarie and NAB (business units)
- ▶ Harvey Norman and Woolworths (each store)
- ▶ Westfield (each shopping centre must succeed)
- ▶ the Salvation Army (each church community is its own unit).

Since 2003, Qantas has also moved towards a business-unit focus with its 'Segmentation' theme. Brambles, Rio Tinto and Lend Lease have, since their globalisation strategies were introduced, moved towards global businesses rather than their previous more individual-unit focus.

Yet the organisations also see that their large size has advantages — for instance, through:

- buying power (Harvey Norman, Telstra, Woolworths)
- ability to replicate or improve (Westfield, Rio Tinto, Woolworths, Lend Lease)
- ability to provide customer benefits (Qantas, Macquarie, NAB, Telstra, the Salvation Army)
- scale (Rio Tinto, Brambles).

Balance operations/activities/functions

Another way in which balance occurs is between the variety of different operations, activities and functions that exist or take place within the organisation. Many normal organisations are predominantly focused on or dominated by a single function (for example, marketing, accounting or production), or they are dominated by a particular business or business unit. This often makes it very difficult for them to accurately evaluate information and opportunities that come from the dominated operations, activities or functions.

Winning organisations are able to avoid these problems. They seek balance across areas. For instance, Macquarie's risk management function is neither policeman nor supporter of the more entrepreneurial business units. It has a role and it plays its part. Lend Lease, Harvey Norman and Westfield seek to balance the streams of income they receive from their variety of business units, to avoid becoming too dependent on one unit or one business stream. The Salvation Army, Woolworths, Telstra, Brambles and Rio Tinto attempt to balance their business units so they are not dependent on any particular unit.

Overall balance

In the discussions above, we have given examples of particular situations that describe the specifics of an approach. However, more important than the individual items is the concept of overall balance, of balancing 'everything'. Balance is not simply A *or* B *or* C *or* D. It is A *and* B *and* C *and* D—*and* E *and* F *and* more!

Fred Hilmer gave his views as a non-executive director of how Westfield operates:

> According to an old saying, 'When presented with a choice between two good alternatives, take both!' (*The Detailed Westfield Story*, 2000, p. 131).

His overwhelming impression is that of balance—balance of many things: and, and, and. Westfield's success, and the spirit behind it, is a perfect example of 'taking both', of being able to combine seemingly opposite approaches to develop its own unique Westfield way. This entails being both:

▶ adventurous *and* careful

▶ big picture *and* detailed

▶ fast *and* measured

▶ here and now *and* in the future

▶ demanding *and* paternalistic

▶ exacting *and* expedient

▶ public *and* private

▶ extravagant *and* frugal

▶ firm *and* flexible.

When asked why other organisations didn't copy its approach to business, one Rio Tinto executive said,

> Others can copy parts of what we do but not the whole set.

In responding to the same question, a Macquarie executive said:

> There are a number of pieces that would have to be put into place simultaneously... [We are] similar to other investment banks. The difference we perceive is that we take it further and enforce it more rigidly. We articulate it, write it down and apply it more rigidly with very formal processes.

This observation came home to us in our interviews for this edition, as also being applicable at most of the organisations. It's not *what* they do that makes them unique, but how they do it. It's their effective execution.

When we analyse organisations like the Salvation Army, Telstra and NAB, they epitomise to us this concept of 'overall balance'.

One could be very critical and say they are not 'best' at much, but what comes through for each of them—and for the other winning organisations—is a comprehensive, solid performance in all areas, over long periods of time. They have managed to get the balance right, and that, as Collins and Porras said in the quote given at the start of this chapter, is an extremely difficult thing to do. That's why they are winning organisations!

How is balance achieved?

It's all very well to read about being 'balanced' and what to balance, but how is it achieved? What do winning organisations do to balance their perspectives, philosophies and levels of operations to get a balanced set of outcomes?

We found several important factors in winning organisations that addressed how balance is achieved (see figure 10.6). They are having:

▶ a culture that supports diversity of views

▶ an information system that provides diverse information

▶ leadership that values information

▶ a humble, self-critical leadership that is willing to admit mistakes

▶ the ability to make decisions and deliver results.

Figure 10.6: how is balance achieved?

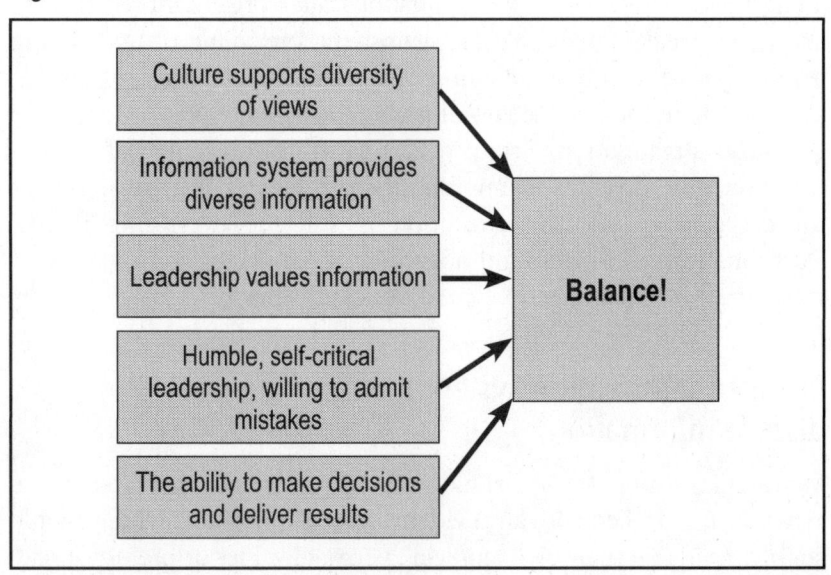

Have a culture that supports diversity of views

To make balanced decisions, a variety of perspectives, ideas and information must be available and must be discussed. The chance of any one individual or group being able to 'represent' this diversity is zero. One of the biggest issues for most cultures, especially 'cult-like cultures' is the difficulty of allowing different views to exist. So we have another paradox: the culture must be tight, but it must support a diversity of views. More than just allowing different views, the culture must value and support them, since without that support they will wither and die.

A Lend Lease executive said, 'This is the kind of place where you can speak up, whoever you are. You are expected to speak up and raise issues if you have them'.

A Woolworths executive said, 'What I like is going around the stores and having customers and employees come up to me and tell me what's wrong and what's right with the stores'.

A Telstra executive, commenting on the new Trujillo leadership style, said, 'Everyone can have a say, is expected to have a say, in an open forum. That's the way it used to be under Frank [Blount]'.

We see this also at Westfield, where wide groups of people are brought together before decisions are made. Everyone is expected to speak up and contribute; when a decision is made, everyone is expected to make that decision happen.

In most organisations that fail, or even those that decline, the pointers to decline or failure are there well before the decline is recognised. Why aren't these pointers seen? Examinations after organisational failures show that weak signals that go against the prevailing orthodoxy are assumed to be wrong or are ignored, until they become strong signals, at which point the decline is well under way.

Most organisations simply don't value diversity of views. Consequently, diversity cannot flourish. But it is not diversity for diversity's sake. Effective execution is still the overriding theme. Decisions must be made and alignment must occur. Yet a variety of views must be encouraged before a decision is made.

Have an information system that provides diverse information

Many organisations have people with diverse views, but often those views are not backed with any evidence. Decision making where people simply decide on their own 'gut feel', personal values or prejudice may well consider a wide variety of views, but many of these views will be ill-informed.

In our experience, few organisations in Australia really have good information about their markets, industries, competitors, environments or the future trends likely to affect them. It takes time and effort to develop such information. The information needs to be systematically collected. Neither of these conditions usually exists.

In practice, it is difficult to get appropriate and reliable information in Australia. We do not have a culture that values freedom of information. Much information is not made publicly available and many organisations are not listed and thus not required to provide useful information to the public arena. As a result, even if the culture supports a diversity of views, much of the information required in most organisations for making decisions is simply not there, so the basis for good decisions is extremely shaky.

Information can be built up. It can be collected. It takes time and effort, which of course means costs and responsibility. Macquarie set up its own economic research database in the 1980s, for its own internal use. Such was the paucity of good information, even on such basic issues as macroeconomic statistics, that, being entrepreneurial, Macquarie found that it could sell the data to others.

All the winning organisations develop good databases of information about their customers and markets, but they are jealously guarded, as they are a key source of competitive advantage.

Another way in which a diverse set of information can be encouraged and used to balance the issues an organisation has to respond to is to use the balanced scorecard method of performance measurement. Use of this technique can help to 'balance' the various approaches to performance. More recently, the triple-bottom-line technique has been developed to include specific consideration of social and (green) environment issues in organisational performance assessment, alongside economic indicators. In 2004, Woolworths introduced the triple bottom line to widen the sense of 'balance' to include environmental and social issues. Brambles has also introduced environmental impact reports as part of its performance assessment, again extending the sense of the balanced scorecard.

Have a leadership that values information

One of the reasons why such information is not gathered in many organisations is that leaders in Australia have preferred the 'she'll be right, mate', gut feel, intuitive approach to decision making rather than the considered analysis of factual, quantitative data.

In addition, information is power. In many organisations, depriving people of information means they cannot challenge the leadership (often of a single, autocratic leader). In such cases, leaders don't *want* information to be collected, as it may undermine their past decisions and give power to others. Use of this information by others can be personally embarrassing, so it is easier to avoid the risk by not having information widely available! You can't manage what you can't or don't measure.

In winning organisations, information is valued. It is used for decision making and it is shared widely, so that many people are able to use it and provide different—and informed—perspectives. Computing power has changed the viability of collecting information, particularly over the last five to 10 years. Much more information is available now, it is easier to access and easier and cheaper to process. All organisations need to take advantage of this change to improve their information base.

Have a leadership that is humble, self-critical and willing to admit mistakes

These characteristics are not associated with many leaders, though we did highlight them in chapter 6 (Leadership, not leaders) as important aspects of leadership in winning organisations. In our experience, many leaders and leadership teams in many organisations enjoy power. They believe that past successes are due to them and them alone. They believe they have 'earned' the perks that are available at the top of the organisation, either by past service or through simply being in the important positions they now hold. They quickly become remote from their people and how their organisations actually run. They forget how they got where they are.

These beliefs and attitudes are far removed from those of the humble leaders we encountered in our interviews in the winning organisations and in other material in our research. And their descriptions of previous leaders and leadership styles suggested that, for the most part, the same attitudes were held in the past (although there were exceptions!).

We were surprised by the degree to which:

▶ the leaders admitted errors made

▶ they did not employ PR spin to explain away inconsistencies or past errors

▶ they were critical of themselves and their predecessors

▶ they appeared to be willing to learn from past mistakes.

These qualities are critical if the organisation is going to be able to objectively assess the position it is in, learn from it and use that knowledge to go forward. This humble attitude enables leaders to objectively consider information from other sources. Others' ideas can be accepted. Not everything has to be invented here or be the idea of the CEO to succeed.

Simple though these ideas sound, in practice their combination is rare in our experience. Most leaders (and people) are threatened by assessment, by evaluation, by external critique. Many organisational leaders want to defend their past decisions and present positions, rather than accept new evidence. Many leaders don't consider the possibility that 'luck' or external factors might have caused success, even when these factors are often listed as the cause of 'failures' under their leadership.

Have the ability to make decisions and deliver results

Diversity is important but results are what organisations are about. Moving from diverse views through to making decisions to getting those decisions accepted and, most importantly, getting the results from those decisions 'on time and on budget' (or better) is what the game is about.

And this brings us back to our winning wheel framework! Winning organisations need to balance 'everything' and the nine elements of our framework are further evidence of the variety of issues that need to be balanced.

Winning organisations need:

▶ good leadership (chapter 6)

▶ the right people, who are committed to the organisation (chapter 8)

▶ to follow a clear strategy that is flexible at the margin (chapter 5)

▶ internal and external focus (chapter 7)

▶ to manage risks (chapter 9)

▶ to adapt rapidly to changes (chapter 4)

▶ to align everything (chapter 3)

▶ to balance everything (chapter 10)
▶ to execute effectively in order to deliver results (chapter 2).

That's a lot of things to balance!

Summary and key messages for leaders

The last element in our winning wheel framework is balance. Winning organisations balance everything. They have a variety of perspectives, a variety of philosophies, a variety of organisation levels and a variety of operations, activities and functions to balance in order to 'balance everything'. They do it by having a culture that supports diverse views, an information system that collects diverse information and a leadership that values that information and is willing to admit mistakes, yet which also makes decisions that deliver results.

The key messages for leaders are:

▶ Balance external and internal views.
▶ Balance shareholders and stakeholders.
▶ Balance the short term and long term.
▶ Balance entrepreneurialism and conservatism.
▶ Balance stability and change.
▶ Balance loose and tight policies.
▶ Balance clear and fuzzy strategy.
▶ Balance the objective and subjective.
▶ Balance the top and bottom of the organisation.
▶ Balance the individual and team.
▶ Balance small business units and the large business environment.
▶ Balance operations, activities and functions.
▶ Have a culture that supports diversity of views.
▶ Have an information system that provides diverse information.
▶ Value information.
▶ Be humble and self-critical.
▶ Be willing to admit mistakes.

11 How does 'Australia' make it different?

Our research would still have been useful if all it achieved was to pinpoint which are the winning organisations in Australia. However, a second key reason for undertaking the study was to answer the question: 'Is good business practice global, or is there something unique about business practice and context in Australia that makes succeeding here different?'

The answer to this question is both 'yes' and 'no'. Good practice is largely the same. Around 80 per cent of our findings are similar to those in the earlier and concurrent US-based studies (this is discussed further in chapter 12). However, there are some differences and they are significant. If you want to be selected in the First XI, you can't just be a 'home ground' player. You have to be able to adapt to the different circumstances where the game is played — different locations, different weather, different umpires — and still perform well.

In this chapter, we address the factors unique to the Australian business context that affect how to operate, if an organisation wants to be successful. These differences are (see also figure 11.1):

▶ the specific comparative advantages Australia has

▶ the immaturity of organisations' exposure to international competition

▶ the different motivations of Australians for working in organisations

- the consequent different leadership styles that are necessary for leading successful organisations in Australia
- the small market size of Australia
- the use of ideas from overseas
- the role and influence of government in developing organisations in the business environment.

Organisations going international tend to take their home-country culture and critical success factors with them. So even Australian-based organisations that are operating internationally need to understand what these factors are, as the 'DNA' of Australian organisation thinking is important background to how they are likely to operate internationally.

Figure 11.1: differences in the Australian business landscape

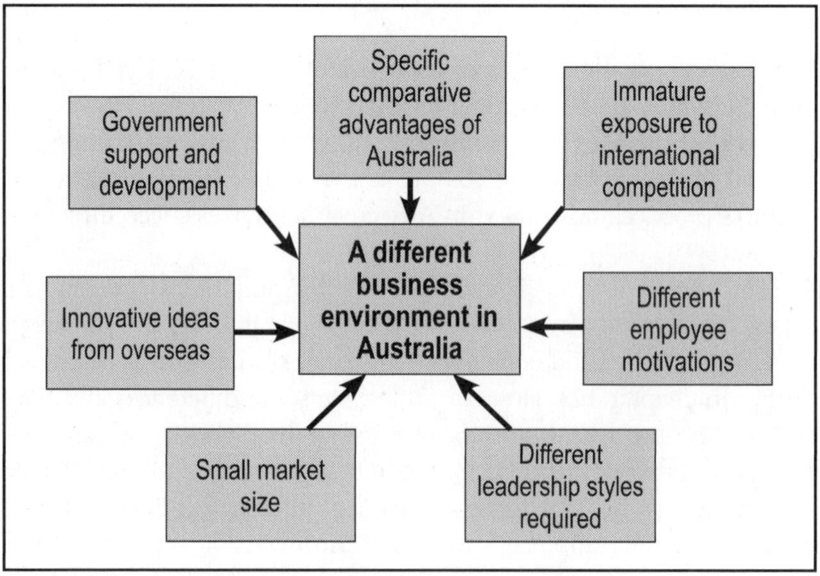

[Figure 11.1: A diagram showing "A different business environment in Australia" at the centre, with arrows pointing to it from six surrounding factors: Government support and development; Specific comparative advantages of Australia; Immature exposure to international competition; Innovative ideas from overseas; Different employee motivations; Small market size; Different leadership styles required.]

Specific comparative advantages of Australia

The nature of the Australian economy and the opportunities it presents obviously influence the types of businesses that develop here. Our large resource and agricultural base provides a natural foundation for the development of major Australian industries and organisations, whereas many of the developed economies do not have similar bases.

For many years, agricultural and mining industries have been the major source of exports for Australia and Australia is known as being a major international supplier of many such products. It is strange, therefore, that apart from Rio Tinto, no other winning organisation comes from this background. A possible reason for this is that much agriculture has been small scale, with monopoly cooperatives, sometimes government-owned, being used to market the products overseas. The rapid changes that are occurring in primary industries through industry deregulation and privatisation should produce winning organisations nominated from this sector in the future, as some larger, competitive organisations emerge. However, this has not been the case for our study.

Another interesting observation is that none of the winning organisations come from the manufacturing sector. The continued and rapid decline of this sector in the face of open economy competition from low-cost countries confirms this, but it does raise an interesting macroeconomic policy question about whether a developed economy can survive in the long term without a significant and vibrant manufacturing economy.

The immature international Australian business environment

The 'two organisation' concept: pre- and post-1980

When we were analysing each of the winning organisations, time after time in our interviews in our original research, we were told that we were really dealing with two organisations. The 'two organisations' idea relates to the changes that have occurred in the business landscape since the 1970s, particularly over the last 20 years, that have revolutionised winning Australian organisations' way of thinking. In particular, they highlighted the impact of the opening of the economy and the world to the internationalisation of business.

Interviewees often felt that we should only be looking at their organisation from around 1987–90 onwards. The period before this related to a completely different era. In their view, they were like two different organisations.

This is most obvious at Telstra and Qantas, which moved from being public sector organisations to privately listed companies. However, it also applies at Rio Tinto (through the Australianisation process) and

NAB and Macquarie (through banking deregulation), and we are sure it affects many organisations competing in Australia.

These changes over the last 25 to 30 years followed a 30-year stable period from 1945 to 1972, when economic growth and prosperity were the norm and the economy was protected economically, socially and geographically from major disruptive change. This is a very short time period in the history of a country, and even in the history of an organisation.

Illustration 11.1 covers some of the main changes that have occurred in the Australian business landscape, to give a quick view of the magnitude of these changes. Although each of these individual changes—while major in itself—seems absorbable, illustration 11.1 shows how dramatic the cumulative change has been. It is ironic to note that Labor governments have made most of these major changes, rather than the assumed-to-be-more-business-oriented Liberal governments.

Illustration 11.1: major changes to the business landscape in Australia

Year	Event
1971	Bretton Woods pegged exchange rates agreement collapse. Australian dollar linked to US dollar instead of UK pound.
1972	Conciliation and Arbitration Commission grants equal pay.
1973	25 per cent across-the-board tariff cut. Tariff Board replaced by philosophically different Industries Assistance Commission.
1974	Trade Practices Act introduced, which outlawed collusion, price fixing, cartels and other anti-competitive behaviour that was widespread, and particularly addressed the lack of competition across state boundaries. This Act led to subsequent competition reviews and regulation over the period through the establishment of organisations such as the Prices Justification Tribunal, Prices Surveillance Authority, Trade Practices Commission, National Competition Council and the Australian Competition & Consumer Commission.
1975	Jackson Committee Report on Manufacturing Industry Policy. This recommended the reduction of tariffs and quotas and encouragement of the development of a more efficient manufacturing industry.

How does 'Australia' make it different?

1976	Coombs Royal Commission Report. This recommended drastic changes to the public service to make it more efficient and more attractive to potential employees.
1981	Campbell Committee Enquiry into the Australian financial system. This recommended dramatic deregulation of the financial system and opening it to international systems.
1983	Abandoning of currency controls and floating of the Australian dollar. This meant currency risk was introduced as an element to be managed. It also opened up the ability for organisations to invest overseas, not just in Australia.
1983	Government/ACTU Accord introduced. The government agreed to consult with the ACTU on an agreed wages policy for the country that they would jointly take to the Conciliation and Arbitration Commission, to facilitate wage negotiations and reduce industrial disputes.
1984	New foreign exchange licences granted. Forty new licences made foreign exchange accessible and competitive.
1985	Banking system opened up. The granting of 16 new banking licences (10 were expected in the original 1983 announcement) allowed international banks from overseas and credit unions and building societies from within Australia to enter the banking system.
1985	Government/ACTU Accord Mark II. This traded off wages for increases in superannuation for most employees. It led to the first industrial awards that included superannuation as part of remuneration.
1986	Human Rights and Equal Opportunity Act and Affirmative Action (Equal Opportunity for Women) Act passed.
1987	Introduction of the option of Enterprise Bargaining Agreements—the first time individual organisations were encouraged to bargain with their employees for a deal that was different from that of their competitors. This forced managers to be responsible for managing their workforce to rules that they negotiated directly with them, rather than to rules imposed by the courts. This led to big increases in employment flexibility and changes in employment practices.
1987 onwards	The beginning of the government commercialisation and privatisation movement. This has resulted in the sale of many

Illustration 11.1 *(cont'd)*: major changes to the business landscape in Australia

1987 onwards government assets and organisations to private owners and the adoption of commercial principles by most others.
(cont'd)

1991 Industry Statement: all tariffs to be reduced to 5 per cent by 2000. This increased the urgency for change in most manufacturing industries.

1991 onwards Floating of government and mutual organisations on to the stock market. Beginning with the Commonwealth Bank first tranche in 1991 and Qantas first stage in 1993, this eventually made Australia the country with the largest proportion of individuals who own shares.

1993 Hilmer Report. It recommended that the principles of competition be applied in all areas, and highlighted areas, such as government monopolies, governments and professional services, where price competition or price justification was needed.

1993 Government/ACTU Accord Mark VII: enterprise bargaining introduced as the standard. This meant governments and unions accepted that bargaining should be the norm at the enterprise level rather than the exception.

1990s Rapid increase in compulsory superannuation payments as a proportion of payroll—resulting in people developing a sense of personal responsibility for their economic futures, and a rapid increase in interest in financial sophistication by working people.

1995 Australian Competition & Consumer Commission established. This merged the Trade Practices Commission and the Prices Surveillance Authority.

1996 Industry Commission becomes the Productivity Commission. This occurred when it absorbed the Bureau of Industry Economics and the Economic Planning Advisory Commission.

mid 90s onwards Emergence of the internet—providing the basis for fundamental changes in business practices, business models and rapid globalisation of ideas and information. This has had a bigger effect on Australia than on some other nations, firstly because Australians are very quick to adopt new technologies and secondly because it dramatically decreased the time within which

	new ideas became available to what was previously a country made remote by distance.
1997	First stage of Telstra privatisation. Sale of airports begins. Wallis Committee Enquiry into the Financial System report.
2000	Goods and Services Tax (GST) replaces varying sales and wholesale taxes. Y2K led to wholesale replacement and upgrading of IT in virtually all organisations for fear of IT failures on 1 January 2000.
2001	Collapse of Ansett Airlines, HIH Insurance and One.Tel, coupled with major international collapses, led to dramatic increase in focus on corporate governance regulations.
2001	China joins the World Trade Organisation.
2003	Free trade agreement with Singapore.
2004	ASEAN upgrades economic relationship with Australia.
2005	Free trade agreement with US and Thailand. Significant decreases in personal tax rates including halving of the capital gains tax rate.
2006	Australian Workplace Award industrial relations regulations passed. This meant employers could make individual agreements with employees, rather than be bound by common pay rates. Companies with less than 100 employees are free to fire people without giving reasons. Further significant effective decreases in income tax rates.
2006	Australian International Financial Reporting Standards adopted. The aim is to harmonise financial reporting on a global basis.
2007	Basel II: common global standards being introduced for banks for risk weighting criteria. The aim is to harmonise risk assessment by all major banks.

Sources: adapted from a compilation by Ray Cotsell, Mt Eliza Business School, July 2002; supplemented by Sajid Anwar, Adelaide University Graduate School of Business, July 2006.

Illustration 11.1 also shows the increasing affect of internationalisation over recent years, as the Australian economy is gradually opened up to international competition.

When we wrote the first edition, the 'immaturity' of the Australian economy to international experience was a major issue. In 2000, most organisations and industries had only 10 years of exposure to international competition of one sort or another. By 2005, they had 15 years' experience—that's a 50 per cent increase. By 2010, the internationalisation experience will have doubled since 2000. We think by 2010 the 'immaturity' we referred to will be almost gone. Most organisations now are either selling to China, buying from China, operating in China—or all three! India is also rapidly emerging as a major market and competitor. Free trade agreements with the US and other countries are allowing unheard-of levels of competition locally and access to new opportunities. We expect this trend to continue, locally and internationally.

Australian organisations face an international world—of threats and opportunities—and the successful organisations of the future will be international in their thinking and operations. This is quite different from the past. The 'two organisation' concept is correct and the old ways of operating within Australia only are dying in relevance. Consider your own organisation. How involved is it internationally or how affected is it by international competitors?

Initial lack of local competition

Locally, most industries in Australia have few major national competitors. Combined with the small market size, limited appeal to overseas companies, the legacy of state-based competitors and the agreed pricing regimes of 30 years ago (some of which still exist in practice), this has meant the typical Australian organisation has had limited real experience of a competitive environment. We are only beginning to have truly mature local competitors prepared to use the gamut of competitive tools and techniques available.

The long local boom from around 1994 to the time of writing has benefited those organisations that were able to adapt to these fundamental changes both in their visions of their futures and also in their organisational practices. Previously, size per se has been seen as preventing acquisitions. Local size is no longer a relevant benchmark in a globalising economy. Even the largest Australian organisations are no longer 'too big' to be acquired.

Rapid opening up to international competition

These changes have occurred both incrementally and quickly. Many organisations have still not really adjusted their thinking to where their future lies (international markets), what their future is dependent on (international issues and events) and the changing nature of what their people want (commitment, economic gain sharing, social relevance and environmental responsibility).

Since the 1980s, the Australian business context has had an 'awakening' to international forces. Some of these forces are very advantageous (for example, the growth of Asia as a market) while others are very disadvantageous (for example, the closure of large areas of manufacturing unable to compete with low-cost Asian competitors).

This reveals the very limited experience Australian organisations have generally had with international markets. Consequently, we see a lot of 'work in progress' or 'consolidation' in Australian organisations. It is notable that our winning organisations generally do have much more international experience than this. Qantas went overseas in 1935, Lend Lease in 1964, Brambles in 1971, Westfield in 1977, NAB in 1987 and several of the others have always had overseas connections. But Harvey Norman, Telstra and Woolworths have only just begun their own international experiences.

By 2010, the exposure of the Australian business environment to international markets will have virtually doubled! The winning organisations of the future will need to succeed in these markets. This will undoubtedly make a difference to the way most successful organisations will operate in the future.

Different motivations: the need for a 'cause', not a BHAG

The Telstra Cultural Archetype study identified Australians' need to identify a 'cause' in working for their organisations. This contrasts with the American desire to take up a challenge, as seen in the importance in the US of Big Hairy Audacious Goals (BHAGs), which Collins and Porras found to be one of the drivers of their 'visionary organisations'.

As we mentioned in chapter 1, to Australians, a BHAG is seen as confronting, not encouraging—a challenge that invites the possibility not of success but of failure! According to the Cultural Archetype study, Australians want to feel that what their organisation is doing is worth doing, is achievable and that their leaders can show them how it can be achieved.

This concept of a 'cause' has been discussed extensively in previous chapters (particularly chapters 5 and 6). We have seen that the concept of a 'cause' can be quite wide (see illustration 5.3). From our study, it seems likely that it is possible to develop a 'cause' in most or all industries. It depends on the ability of the leadership group to couch the idea, generate emotion around the value of that idea and coach their people towards achieving it.

The absence of vision and mission statements in the winning organisations and the general disdain we hear expressed towards these statements — despite, in our view, their validity as a tool of strategy — may be consistent with the idea of needing a cause. People don't believe vision or mission statements. Organisations are often unable to get their people to identify with the vision or mission.

Whatever the reason, the idea of having a 'cause' that people identify with is a different Australian cultural perspective. Motivating people is a critical part of success for winning organisations: having a cause is an important underlying component for that success. But don't develop a 'cause' statement — it will go the same way mission and vision statements have gone!

Different leadership styles: captain-coach leadership

The same study that identified the need for a cause also identified that the style of leadership required was different in Australia. Captain-coach leadership is required — leadership on the field with the troops rather than leadership from on high (see chapter 6).

This finding is also backed up by other work on Australian leadership (see illustration 6.4). The Karpin Report into Australian management skills reported that the key strengths were perceived to be:

- ▶ hard-working (68 per cent agreed)
- ▶ flexible and adaptable (48 per cent)
- ▶ innovative/inventive (41 per cent)
- ▶ technically sound (31 per cent)
- ▶ egalitarian (31 per cent).

On the other hand, the key weaknesses were seen to be:

- ▶ having a short-term view (49 per cent)
- ▶ a lack of strategic perspective (41 per cent)
- ▶ being inflexible/rigid (43 per cent)

- complacency (42 per cent)
- poor teamwork and empowerment (40 per cent)
- the inability to cope with differences (40 per cent)
- poor people skills (37 per cent).

Captain-coach style is quite different both from US BHAG-style leadership and, importantly, different from what is experienced at many large organisations in Australia, which is represented by the Karpin Report strengths and weaknesses above. In addition, our experience is that leadership is often remote, perceives itself as all-knowing and all-powerful and is unwilling to share information with the people. All this means there is often a very large gap between the desired style for Australia and both the actual style used and the desired style for US organisations.

For winning organisations, we identified several organisational characteristics that link into the general Australian psyche, and are different and require a different style of leadership. These are all consistent with a 'captain-coach' leadership style, where leaders and followers are similar in their aims and endeavours. While we discuss each idea separately below, they are in many ways integrally linked. They are (see figure 11.2 overleaf):

- the 'have a go' attitude
- challenging/changing the rules
- the 'can do'/Aussie battler attitude
- the idea of pioneering for Australia
- being determined/tenacious
- having a team orientation.

'Have a go' attitude

Most often observed in the traditional Australian cricketing cry to stolid batsmen, 'ave a go, yer mug', this attitude of Australians reflects the idea that being defensive has low value. Better to try and fail than not to try. Trying and making a fool of yourself is better than not trying at all.

We see this in Brambles' entry into the 'garbos' field of waste management. We also see it in the willingness of Harvey Norman, Lend Lease, Macquarie, the Salvation Army, Westfield, Lend Lease and Qantas to take on new challenges that neither they nor others have tried.

Figure 11.2: organisational characteristics that link to captain-coach leadership

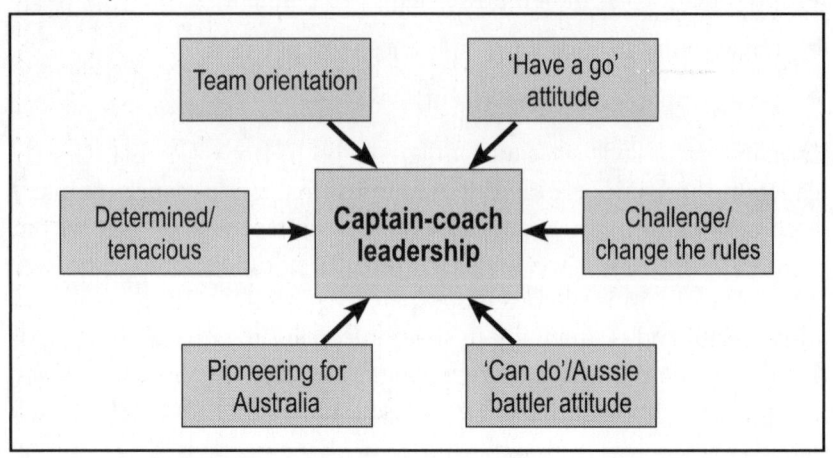

```
         Team orientation          'Have a go'
                                    attitude
                    ↘         ↙
  Determined/      Captain-coach      Challenge/
  tenacious    →    leadership    ←   change the rules
                    ↗         ↖
         Pioneering for      'Can do'/Aussie
         Australia            battler attitude
```

Along with the desire to try comes the need to be flexible and adaptable, which results from the small market size of Australia. In this sense, having a go is often necessary, as the existence of specialists or help from large scale organisations is unlikely to be available.

Challenging/changing the rules

The Karpin Report found that two of the three key strengths identified for Australian management were being flexible and adaptable, and being innovative/inventive. Honesty and high ethical standards were seen as low on the 'strength' list and—notably—low on the list of the characteristics of the 'ideal' manager.

Our anecdotal experience of Australians as well as Australian management is consistent with these findings—Australians are keen to challenge the rules or operate outside the rules if they don't suit them. (In fact, one of the ways of being 'flexible' and 'adaptable'—two identified key strengths—is to do just this!) We see many examples of this in the winning organisations (see illustration 11.2).

'Can do'/Aussie battler attitude: a new professionalism

In order to 'challenge/change the rules', people in organisations have to have the view that they can actually do what they propose. This is exemplified anecdotally in the 'little Aussie battler' stereotype. The idea here is that the 'battler' can achieve a lot, despite the handicap of not having the right background, training, equipment or resources.

Illustration 11.2: examples of winning organisations challenging or changing the rules

Brambles	Establishing Cleanaway required rethinking of how garbage was handled—from being a unique, one-off, small-scale action to being a standardised, repetitive, large-scale activity.
Harvey Norman	Introducing a new method of contracting with 'employees' as franchisees, which changed the rules about how 'employees' would behave and what they would be responsible—and rewarded—for.
Lend Lease	Introducing the 'community of interests' concept, which changed the aim from building the building for a profit to building a building that would satisfy a wide variety of stakeholder groups.
Macquarie Bank	Developing new financial products—for example, infrastructure trusts. These products package up assets that have previously been seen as requiring large-scale, wholesale financing, not retail financing.
NAB	Establishing flexible home loans when fixed loans were the only alternative.
Qantas	Operating a high-quality airline and a low-cost airline simultaneously, in the same market.
Rio Tinto	Establishing individual contracts with employees when all competitors were using industry-based, court-arbitrated awards.
The Salvation Army	Establishing new methods of treating social problems by being prepared to ignore political correctness or social norms and address real issues.
Telstra	Challenging competitors in the courts to slow the pace of market share loss, as required by the privatisation of the monopoly.
Westfield	Branding shopping centres rather than relying on branded retailers.
Woolworths	Establishing 'fresh food' as a point of difference, rather than packaged groceries.

Many Australian organisations feel this way when confronted with the might of European or North American or Japanese (and increasingly

Chinese) organisations as competitors. There is a belief, exemplified in our sports stars and sporting success, that Australians 'can do' it. This attitude by itself can assist us in 'punching above our weight'. Intriguingly, organisations such as the giant News Corporation and Macquarie Bank present themselves as 'little Aussie battlers' in their competition with global corporations.

However, winning Australian organisations venturing into international waters have a new professionalism. The macho, rough but enthusiastic images in the 1980s of organisations such as Fosters and Bond Corporation have given way to a highly professional approach. In 2006 Michael Cheney, president of the Business Council of Australia, said Australians no longer associated themselves with the term 'Aussie battler' and instead have an aspirational mindset, a legacy of a more confident and capable Australia. Cheney said that Australians are more accepting of risk, more confident of being able to meet challenges and are more interested in locking in the wealth and prosperity they have worked for, than being focused on basic needs and being inward looking.

Macquarie Bank was regarded as audacious in launching a bid for the London Stock Exchange in 2006, but it was not regarded as unprofessional. Qantas is highly regarded for its professionalism and regularly wins international awards. Westfield has consistently partnered, then acquired, international shopping centre developers and managers. Rio Tinto is one of the three big global miners (BHP Billiton is another one from Australia). Brambles is a world leader in both its CHEP and Recall products. The Salvation Army's two Australian territories are just two of the 12 self-funding territories of the 112 territories in the world. There's a genuine respect that is given to Australian businesspeople in the world now, compared with 20 years ago. This is not surprising, given the rapid change in our levels of international experience.

Pioneering for Australia

An idea that kept arising in our study was that, though the organisations were seeking their own success, there was also a degree of patriotism involved, a sense of 'doing it for Australia' and in some cases a sense of leading the way for Australia. This idea is of course consistent with those mentioned previously. Part of the 'cause' in some cases was 'doing it for Australia'. Part of the leadership style was demonstrating that Australians could do it. Having the ability to change the rules so that they suit Australian needs and the idea of the little Aussie battler

How does 'Australia' make it different?

are reinforced by this 'pioneering' ideal. Illustration 11.3 gives some examples of this idea.

Illustration 11.3: examples of 'pioneering' for Australia	
Brambles	Establishing CHEP pallet control and tracking system.
Harvey Norman	Large volume electrical and other product discount stores that are profitable.
Lend Lease	Establishment of property trusts, strata titles, project management and control systems, community-friendly, eco-efficient buildings.
Macquarie	An investment bank that innovates in Australia but competes internationally. Infrastructure trust funds and its model of acquiring assets and spinning them off into listed trusts.
NAB	Flexible home loans; cost control.
Qantas	Qantas as a brand representing 'Australia'.
Rio Tinto	Developing large-scale resource deposits for global export.
The Salvation Army	Forming business alliances for welfare objectives.
Telstra	Developing Australia's telecommunications infrastructure.
Westfield	Branding shopping centres. Redeveloping existing malls.
Woolworths	Establishing 'fresh food' as a point of difference.

Being determined/tenacious

In order to 'do' the task, to carry out the 'cause', to be successful despite being from a small country, these organisations have had to be very determined and very tenacious.

This characteristic is often understated by 'success stories'. Organisations that are recognised as successes are often assumed to have suddenly arrived, suddenly succeeded. In fact, as we demonstrate in the strategic cycle (see chapter 12), particularly through the consolidation stage, winning organisations work very hard for long periods with often little to show for it. They do not start as 'successes'. Indeed, they often start with handicaps! Illustration 11.4 lists some of the barriers that the winning organisations have had to overcome. Not one of them was guaranteed success when it began. All have had many barriers to overcome. Success in each case has taken many years.

Illustration 11.4: barriers overcome to achieve success by the winning organisations

Brambles	Starting as a small family business in Newcastle; introduced the pallet control system to Europe and the US.
Harvey Norman	Harvey and Norman were sacked by Alan Bond when Norman Ross was taken over in 1982, so they had to start again.
Lend Lease	Started up as a subsidiary of a Dutch building contractor.
Macquarie	As a foreign-owned merchant bank, it had to get a banking licence, of which there were very few.
NAB	Acquiring and managing international banks.
Qantas	Sold business to the government in 1947 when it could not raise capital to expand the fleet.
Rio Tinto	Survived long resources depression in 1980s and large-scale industrial action as it endeavoured to change the basis of employment.
The Salvation Army	Limited resources: reliance on donations from non-Salvation Army members.
Telstra	Developing commercial skills to compete in a competitive world.
Westfield	Lowy and Saunders started as penniless immigrants in Sydney in the early 1950s.
Woolworths	Shareholders refused to support it further in 1925; survived a merger proposal with Coles in 1936; survived acquisition by a corporate raider in 1980s.

Team orientation

A final aspect that affects leadership in an Australian winning organisation—and the driver for captain-coach leadership—is the desire for a team orientation. Mateship and egalitarianism are alive and well. Australians want to be part of a team—ideally a team of 'mates'—rather than be individuals working for themselves, taking chances for themselves and taking responsibility on themselves.

Australia's small market size and spread

Another feature that makes being in Australia different from operating in large economies such as the US, Germany, Japan, the European Union and China is the size of market available. The Australian market is miniscule compared with any of the major economies. Further, it is extremely spread out—a factor that non-Australians never really understand until they actually visit the country. Even though much of the population lives in what seems a small number of cities on the eastern seaboard, these cities are far apart compared with their equivalents elsewhere. Finally, unlike some successful small economies (for example, Singapore, Sweden, Switzerland and South Korea), it does not have a major market on its physical doorstep. Asia is hardly 'close' physically, even if its market size is rapidly expanding.

This small market size means that economies of scale are limited in Australia when compared with those available to international competitors in their home markets. This has an impact on many aspects of business operations, including the ability to conduct research and development economically, product run lengths, customer segmentation, supplier choices, physical operating plant size (for example, one car plant could probably provide all the cars we need in Australia, but which plant, and what about the need for choice?).

When markets were protected up until the mid 1980s, small market size was of little importance. Competitors could not enter and international cost comparisons were therefore of little relevance. In an open international market, this issue is of utmost importance. To be unable to operate at close to world cost levels leaves an Australian organisation vulnerable to significant cost differentials, as we have seen through the closing of a great deal of manufacturing in Australia over the last 10 to 20 years.

So the future for Australian organisations is not in competing on economies of scale or competing on cost. This is quite different from being an organisation in a large economy, where competing on low cost is a viable strategic option and where there are many niches available.

But Australia and its organisations cannot retreat to the past 'good times' of protected local markets. The rest of the world is not going backwards! Regardless of the rate at which the Australian market grows, it will never be a large-scale global market, so success for Australia's future winning organisations will not come about by being successful only in Australia. The future is in finding overseas markets, international niches and competing on differentiation.

Many Australian organisations are still focused on the local market. Even some of the winning organisations have only just made the transition to being international (for example, Woolworths and Harvey Norman), while NAB's recent retreat towards Australia is unsettling and Telstra is struggling to find overseas success.

In the future, being international will be essential to be a winning organisation. In order to be successful, winning organisations will have to compete with international competitors both overseas and in Australia. The element we identified in our winning framework of 'looking out' or being externally focused will grow in importance over time.

Big overseas influences on Australian organisation development

There are two aspects to the overseas influences on Australian organisation development. Firstly, the importance of organisations that do not originate in Australia. Secondly, how Australian organisations make use of innovations that originate overseas.

It is important to recognise that several of the 'Australian' winning organisations—Lend Lease, Macquarie Bank, Rio Tinto and the Salvation Army—had their origins overseas. Yet Australians are often critical of overseas organisations, arguing that we should develop our own.

This is another classic paradox. It's not 'either/or', but 'and'. Each of the above organisations may have begun overseas, but the real development that we are celebrating here is their Australian activities. So why can't this occur for other overseas-originating organisations? Why can't a local subsidiary of an international organisation become an Australian winner?

We think it is important to take the best from wherever Australia can get it and to develop it as much as possible within Australia and—now—expand that activity into other countries too. Focus should be on how value can be added to an organisation's Australian and Australian-originated and controlled activity, not on the organisation's origins. For instance, Brambles drew on best practice from all over the world in the development of its 'Perfect Plant' (see illustration 11.5).

Because relatively little research and development is affordable in Australia, due to the small market size, many innovative ideas are actually borrowed from overseas (see chapter 4). This is quite different

How does 'Australia' make it different?

from organisations in major economies (US, Germany, Europe, Japan), where research and development is an important function and can be afforded due to product run lengths and scale of economies.

Illustration 11.5: Brambles 'Perfect Plant' built from all over the world

Brambles 'Perfect Plant' is a world-class site that achieves a benchmarked perfect score (10/10) on all competencies required for global operational excellence to achieve:

- lowest operational cost in the world
- highest pallet quality
- best on-time delivery
- zero harm
- lowest plant stock globally.

Brambles' initial investigations identified that the perfect plant had the following processes in place:

- global plant systems
- organisational excellence
- global plant metrics
- equipment reliability
- lean manufacturing and supply chain
- Six Sigma process and product quality
- process technology and automation
- zero harm programs.

Brambles discovered large regional discrepancies in plant performance. It concluded that, if all regions operated with best-in-class cost, the plant costs for CHEP could be US$100 million lower.

Global competency matrix teams with a global team 'owner' were established to investigate global practices in each of the competency areas and to nominate global best practice from within the group. The 'Perfect Plant' was set up conceptually at first, and then in Orlando, Florida, to showcase global best practices identified by a flag from their country of origin.

The 'Perfect Plant' exists as a showcase of best practice and now Brambles is working through its four-step technology roadmap with 19 other CHEP plants to achieve unmanned, fully automated plants that employ best practice from the global group of CHEP businesses, aiming to achieve around US$20 million in annualised savings.

We do not see this changing. Overseas influences—from anywhere and everywhere—will be an increasing factor in the future. The reduction in trade barriers, the emergence of China and India as more open, capitalist economies (with Brazil and Russia following closely), the inherently small scale of the Australian market and the increasing use of the internet to transfer ideas rapidly around the globe all suggest this.

If Australian organisations are to be winners, they will need to be externally focused and able to rapidly adopt or adapt ideas from overseas. While being externally focused is also of increasing importance for organisations in large economies, the size of the home market available to these organisations will continue to provide them with opportunities to specialise domestically.

The significant government role in developing winning organisations

When we began this work, we sought nominations for winning organisations for all types of organisations, specifically including government enterprises and departments. We received very few nominations in this category and no organisation received sufficient nominations to be included in the final group for analysis. Of course, this does not necessarily mean they are not 'winning'—just that, if they are, not enough senior people seem to know about it and recognise it.

Intellectually, it was surprising and disappointing not to have a wider range of organisations to analyse. We are sure it does not mean that listed organisations necessarily make up the overwhelming proportion of winning organisations. What it does mean, as might be presumed from our final group, is that the performance of organisations outside that group is not well enough known for winners to be identified there. There are several reasons for this. First, government organisations do not focus on 'growth', sales or profits, so their performance is harder to assess on conventional financial measures. Second, government organisations often do not publicise their performance or practices, so we are often unaware of what they do. Third, generally they are local monopolies, making it difficult to know how they are performing compared with their peers or with equivalent competitors.

However, reflecting on the First XI winning organisations, we find that government influence is much more significant than it appears (see illustration 11.6 overleaf). Not only are two of them direct privatisations from the government, but the government pallet pool that was 'privatised' after World War II forms the core of what is now Brambles. Also, Lend Lease directly benefited from the government-sponsored Snowy Mountains Hydroelectricity Scheme. The Salvation Army, too, receives a large proportion of its funds for operations from various government departments.

In addition, other recently privatised government organisations, such as the Commonwealth Bank and Commonwealth Serum Laboratories (CSL), have performed extremely well since their privatisations. Due to having quite a short public history, they had little chance of being included in the study when we sought nominations in 1999. Also, Australia Post has dramatically improved its performance over the last 10 years. Though it is not scheduled for privatisation, more public scrutiny may identify Post as a potential winner in the longer term. The commercialisation and privatisation of utilities in Australia seems likely, in the longer run, to identify one or more organisations, as these industries settle and consolidate over time.

These examples are probably only the tip of the iceberg, as it is difficult to identify, assess and compare government organisations. Some of those that have not been privatised may also be 'winning' in their sectors. Hospitals and universities are some obvious examples of Australian organisations that have great reputations internationally, but they were not nominated by CEOs for our study. Australian sports development bodies and some administrative organisations are also highly regarded. It is intriguing to note the rise of soccer in Australia in 2005–06 when Frank Lowy, chair of Westfield, took control of Football Australia. In less than a year, Australia was in the World Cup, a feat not achieved for 32 years. Was this a fluke, or does it suggest what can be achieved when good businesspeople turn their attention to other areas?

In summary, organisations that originate in the government sector—and probably many that remain there—have been identified as winning organisations. Just because an organisation is in the public sector does not mean it is not doing a great job, as is assumed by many business people. Naturally, government organisations focus more on the quality of what they produce and on the specific (political) needs of their masters, but it does seem that this starting background provides an excellent foundation for commercial success if they are privatised.

Illustration 11.6: government development of winning organisations now and in the future?

Brambles	Bought the government pallet pool, which formed the basis for CHEP.
Lend Lease	Started work as a contractor to the government Snowy Mountains Hydroelectric Scheme.
Qantas	Most of its life has been a government-owned airline.
Rio Tinto	Development benefited from being classified as 'Australianised' by the government.
The Salvation Army	Fifty per cent of its revenue comes from government contracts.
Telstra	Owned by the government for its whole organisational life until recent privatisation.
Commonwealth Bank?	Has performed very well since being privatised in the mid 1990s and is developing a very good reputation.
CSL?	Has grown dramatically and is now a major international player in niche areas of medical supplies, such as blood.
Medical organisations?	Australian research organisations are well regarded internationally and Australian hospitals are considered to have very high standards.
Agricultural organisations?	Australia is a significant international supplier of many agricultural products.
Educational institutions?	Education is now one of Australia's major export industries and Australia has a high reputation for quality in some areas of research and education.
Arts organisations?	Several Australian organisations are world renowned (for example, Sydney Dance Theatre, Australian Ballet) and performers and directors are regularly in demand overseas.
Utilities?	This gradually nationalising industry may produce a leading player.
Sports organisations?	Australian sports academies (for example, cricket, cycling, swimming) and sports administrations (for example, Australian Football League, Cricket Australia) are well regarded internationally.

This is different from larger economy countries, where the role of government is less intrusive and support is less important. The role of government is likely to continue to be important for developing industries in Australia and providing the context for organisations in those industries to succeed—or not—internationally. Industries such as agriculture, medicine, universities, film and media are some other areas with significant government support where Australian organisations have developed international reputations. We do not see that continuing in the future without ongoing government support. Given the small market size of Australia, government support provides a way of making the local market 'bigger' and improving its chances of international success. Indeed, the danger is that the government will see 'success' as a reason for withdrawing support.

Summary and key messages for leaders

There are several differences in the Australian context that make slavish adoption of international 'success formulas' likely to have limited success. The business environment and sources of comparative advantage available are quite different in Australia from most larger economies. Australian organisations have had limited international experience in the past, making them poorly prepared for international activity and competition. Australians have different motivations in working for organisations than people working for US organisations. This also requires different styles of leadership for Australian organisations. Successful Australian organisations have often been quite dependent on, or influenced by, international origins or innovations. And the role of government is quite important in both the types of organisations that are successful and also the ways in which success is achieved in Australia. Finally, it is clear that future success for Australian-based organisations will only come with a strong measure of international activity.

The key messages for leaders of organisations in Australia from this chapter are:

- ▶ Being a winning organisation in the future will be dependent on international success.
- ▶ Different leadership styles are required for success in Australia.
- ▶ Employees have different motivations in Australia.

- ▶ Organisations in the government sector may be just as well placed to become 'winning' as those in the private sector.
- ▶ Look for differentiation and niche positions internationally, not low cost or scale.

The eight stages of the strategic cycle

Figure 12.1 shows the eight stages of the strategic cycle in Australia. They are:

- ▶ stage 1: focused—domestic regional
- ▶ stages 2 and 3: geographic spread and related expansion
- ▶ stages 4 and 5: diversification experiment and international experiment
- ▶ stage 6: consolidation
- ▶ stage 7: portfolio of international businesses
- ▶ stage 8: global.

Stage 1: focused—domestic regional

The organisation begins by starting its business. It usually has a single product or narrowly focused line of business, generally in one location or state of Australia. We call this the *focused—domestic regional* stage of the strategic cycle. We use the term 'domestic regional' to indicate it is within Australia (domestic) and localised (regional). However, when the word 'regional' is used by itself in business, it often tends to mean an international region (for example, Asia-Pacific). For instance, Woolworths and Harvey Norman both began retailing in Sydney. Woolworths focused on variety stores and Harvey Norman focused on discount electric goods. Each began with a single store.

Stages 2 and 3: geographic spread and related expansion

If the organisation is successful in its start-up phase and wants to grow, it usually expands by *geographic spread*—taking that activity across the country. This is generally done on a state-by-state basis, as the geographic spread of Australia makes this expansion quite difficult, especially given the small market size of the country. Woolworths began to spread across the country in 1927, while Harvey Norman is only just reaching 'national' coverage, having begun in 1988.

At some point the organisation begins to expand the products and services—and businesses—that it operates. Usually it chooses to expand into products and services that are related in some way—consistent with the fuzzy strategy concept—to its original products or line of business. We call this the *related expansion* stage of the cycle.

Strategy over time: the strategic cycle in Australia

Figure 12.1: the strategic cycle in Australia

1. Focused — Domestic–regional
2. Focused – geographically spread — Domestic–national
3. Related expansion
4. Diversification experiment
5. International experiment — Domestic–international
6. Growth ↔ Consolidation ↔ Growth
7. Portfolio of international businesses — International
8. Global products/businesses/part of global system — Global

Spread of activities

Organisation size

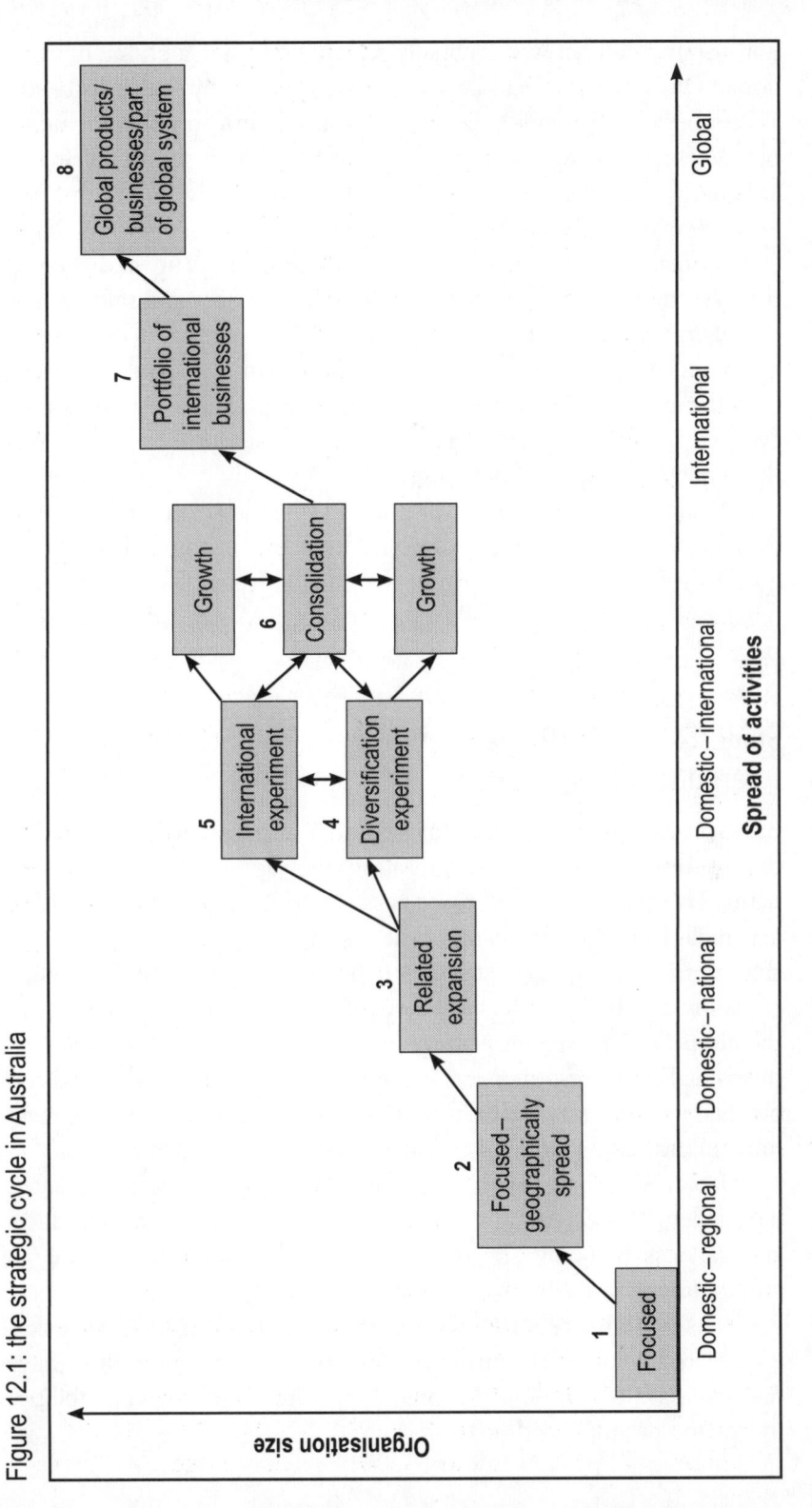

313

For instance, Telstra was originally set up to provide a phone in every home. Once that task had largely been completed by the early 1990s, Telstra began to provide a variety of products and services, including payTV, electronic white pages and classified advertising—all related in some way to telephone communications. The Salvation Army, too, now offers a variety of services to people needing assistance, such as employment, youth crisis, marriage enrichment, drug and alcohol recovery, disaster relief, intellectual disability services and safe houses. In Telstra's case, the expansion is focused on common or 'related' customers and their telephone-related needs. In the Salvation Army's case, the expansion is focused on having the capabilities to understand, evaluate, design and deliver assistance to people in need, even when those people are quite different groups.

We grouped stages 2 and 3 together because they are interchangeable in practice. Some organisations go into related expansion before they go into geographic spread. Some go into both simultaneously. Most organisations enter into both areas before they proceed to the next stages, however.

Stages 4 and 5: diversification experiment and international experiment

Based on achieving success in stages 2 and 3, and seeking further growth opportunities, the winning organisations then appear to take one of two paths. The more traditional route has been to diversify activities within Australia. In particular, many of the winning organisations diversified significantly during the 1980s, due to the closed nature of the Australian economy and high barriers of entry into other countries. We call this the *diversification experiment* stage of the cycle. For instance, Westfield diversified into resource exploration and services, and television ownership. Rio Tinto diversified into biotechnology and downstream mineral processing, and Telstra diversified into IT consulting.

However, as barriers to entry for other countries (and Australia) have fallen, the increasingly popular route is to take existing products and services that have been successful within Australia and to go 'international' with them. We call this the *international experiment* stage. As trade barriers have fallen and understanding of what makes for successful strategic management has increased, organisations have realised that there are international opportunities for their capabilities in existing products and services.

On the other hand, entering into other product and services areas, such as in the diversification experiment case, often does not build on those existing capabilities. For instance, Telstra entered the Hong Kong mobile phone market. NAB bought banks in the United Kingdom, Ireland and the United States. Westfield bought shopping centres in the US. Lend Lease undertook large-scale property developments in the UK and the US. Brambles established pallet joint ventures in Europe.

These stages are also interchangeable in practice. Over time, most of the organisations end up undertaking both types of experiment, separately or at the same time. If the initial international experiment works and the organisation is successful, it builds on this and continues to grow internationally.

Stage 6: consolidation

Regardless of which of these two routes (diversification or internationalisation) is taken, the risks seem to be greater than expected, as most organisations at some stage enter a consolidation period, to recover from errors and to learn from experiences before moving forward. We call this the *consolidation* stage. Steven Lowy of Westfield said:

> The company over time has had some serious failures and I think we are much better and stronger for that and more disciplined about the way we go about our activities because we do know what it is like and it is very uncomfortable to taste the alternative ... The challenges for us overseas are to continue our international expansion and to execute very well. I think the Australian corporate landscape is littered with companies that have not fully executed internationally and therefore suffered greatly. (*AFR BOSS*, July 2006)

Examples of getting out of the product and services diversification experiments include Rio Tinto, which sold out of biotechnology, and the Salvation Army, which sold its aged-care and printing activities. Examples of getting out of international experiments include NAB, which sold out of US and Irish banking, and Brambles, which sold its rail wagon operations in Europe.

Not all of the organisations have reached the consolidation stage. For instance, Woolworths and Harvey Norman have limited experience with overseas operations. The Salvation Army is restricted to Australia, as it is part of a global organisation that has its own operations in other countries. However, all winning organisations that have experienced the final two stages of the strategic cycle for any significant time have been through a consolidation phase. This suggests that it is much harder to succeed in diversification or international businesses than expected, even for First XI organisations.

Stage 7: portfolio of international businesses

Even where organisations have retained their activities overseas, international development is generally quite slow, indicating that it takes a long time to become 'established' in any overseas markets. Most of the organisations have only been in international markets to any significant degree since the mid 1980s. This is even true of Australia's established international players, such as News Corporation, CSR/Rinker, Foster's and Southcorp.

Most Australian organisations have limited international experience (see chapter 13); however, in the 2000s, the amount and variety of international experience is increasing very rapidly. We call this the *portfolio of international businesses* stage. The portfolio of businesses occurs mostly through acquisitions of international businesses. For instance, Brambles made many purchases to establish its international operations, which eventually consolidated into the CHEP, Cleanaway and Recall portfolio. NAB had several banks in Europe and the US, all of which were acquired and generally operated independently. Rio Tinto acquired many mines overseas, which it tended to run as individual business units. Telstra acquired companies in Hong Kong and New Zealand to develop its portfolio. Westfield has acquired many shopping centre portfolios and consolidated them into four businesses by country.

Some winning organisations have reached this stage before a problem occurs, requiring a return to the consolidation stage. However, organisations that have been in this stage for some time do, or have, experienced consolidation at some point. All organisations make mistakes!

Stage 8: global

Finally, the ultimate—*global*—stage may be reached. This stage is attained when organisations are operating in many countries (theoretically all countries) with largely similar products or services. The global stage requires different structures from a portfolio of international businesses, which will be independently managed or managed by region. However, global businesses require centralised global management to achieve global consistency across all business units—a completely different way of thinking and operating from a portfolio of international businesses, so a move from a portfolio of international businesses to a global business is not a simple step. Leigh Clifford, CEO of Rio Tinto, said:

> A lot of people confuse 'international' and 'global'. Being global is very different. You have to be in all time zones, you have to use videoconferences to align people. Your communications are compressed. You need hubs of people around the world. You need executives who can deal in different environments.

By 2006, only three winning organisations had reached this stage and even they had limited experience with it. Rio Tinto has been acting 'global' since it became a dual-listed company in 1995. It operates each particular mineral on a global basis (for example, coal and iron ore), regardless of where it is found, mined or marketed. The Rio Tinto Iron Ore CEO said:

> We are a 24-hour operation. Before bed, I look at my emails from London. In the morning I see what's happened in Canada and Brazil or other locations.

Brambles, through its merger with the support services activities of Guest Keen & Nettlefold plc (GKN), moved to a global stage of the CHEP pallet system business in 2001 and has also taken a global perspective for the variety of international Cleanaway and Recall business units (though its Australian operation, Brambles Industrial Services, remained an Australian portfolio of relatively independent business units). Subsequently, in 2005, Brambles decided to sell out of Cleanaway and Brambles Industrial Services, leaving it with only two of the three global businesses, but also a 'clean' global structure for the first time.

Lend Lease changed its strategy in 2000 to reflect the true global focus on two businesses—real estate development and property funds management—which it developed through acquisitions in 2000. Lend Lease's experience was a disaster, due to its inability to manage the new global organisation. It withdrew from its global strategy in early 2003 and returned to a portfolio of international businesses, which it felt better reflected the capabilities of the organisation. Lend Lease moved its headquarters back from London to Sydney in 2004 and cut out 60 per cent of the head office costs that had been incurred as it experimented with being a global organisation.

From this we can see then that even the winning organisations have had limited experience of this stage of development, though the word 'global' is used loosely in many strategic discussions. From the experiences of Rio Tinto, Brambles and Lend Lease, while no clear conclusions can yet be drawn, it seems likely that this stage will prove as difficult as the earlier 'international experiment' stage in the strategic cycle, even for winning Australian organisations.

Matching the winning wheel framework to the strategic cycle

While the principles we outline in this book apply at each stage of the strategic cycle, the specific capabilities and activities will be quite different at each stage. For instance, 'looking out' when moving from one state to another within Australia has quite a different meaning from 'looking out' when entering the international market or trying to develop a global business. The skills required of leadership in running a focused—domestic regional organisation will be quite different from what is required to run a global organisation. And so on.

Identification of the stage of the strategic cycle an organisation is in is important to enable the issues that arise within each element to be identified too. For instance, for a small *focused—domestic regional* business, addressing 'perfect alignment' is likely to involve aligning systems that are all in one office, handled by a very few staff. For *international experiment* businesses, 'perfect alignment' must consider how to align systems that must cover other countries, perhaps in other time zones, or covering other languages and other legal contexts. For *global* businesses, 'perfect alignment' means reintegrating all those individual country or product differences into one consistent set of systems.

This is particularly vital, considering the increasing internationalisation of business, the very limited international experience that most Australian organisations have—even the winning organisations—and the limited success at this stage that these organisations appear to be having.

A detailed example of the journey through the strategic cycle: Brambles

'Winning' looks different at different stages of the strategic cycle. In this section we'll follow the strategic evolution of one of the most highly developed of the winning organisations to explain in detail how the strategic cycle works for a particular organisation over a long period of time. Figure 12.2 (overleaf) provides a visual representation of the strategic cycle developments for Brambles over this period.

The strategic cycle for Brambles

In 1875, Walter Bramble began as a butcher in Newcastle, beginning the *focused—domestic regional* stage of the organisation. In 1916 W.E. Bramble & Sons was established when Walter's three sons entered the business, and it soon included a variety of small businesses (*related expansion* and *diversification experiment* stages), including transport and industrial services for large local companies such as BHP at Port Kembla and Wollongong (*geographic spread*).

Still based in Newcastle, in 1954 Brambles became a public company and the current organisation was born. Brambles was always seeking new outlets to diversify into.

In 1958, it bought the Commonwealth Handling Equipment Pool (CHEP) and established it as a major business unit. This moved Brambles from being a *domestic-regional* company to being a *domestic-national* company and substantially changed its product mix (*related expansion*). From 1961 to 1970, the company continued to expand into related businesses, such as interstate transport, customs and shipping agencies, steel fabrication engineering and industrial waste collection.

In 1971, it made acquisitions in Papua New Guinea and New Zealand, beginning its *international experiment*. It also continued to make many other acquisitions in the related product fields of transport and industrial services.

In 1974, the first major international expansion occurred when it formed a joint venture with GKN in the UK to start the CHEP pallet system there. Meanwhile, it continued to acquire a variety of industrial services companies in Australia, including Grace Bros transport group, within which was the box storage operation that eventually became Recall records management. Brambles then expanded the CHEP system across Europe, country by country (*portfolio of international businesses*).

International expansion continued. In 1984, Brambles acquired Groupe CAIB, Europe's largest specialised rail wagon rental service. This diversified Brambles both in products and markets, and turned it into a substantial multidomestic company, expanding the portfolio of international businesses. In 1986, Cleanaway expanded into the UK, following CHEP, further diversifying the international portfolio.

The First XI

Figure 12.2: the strategic cycle for Brambles

- Focused – transport
- Focused – geographically spread away from Newcastle
- Related expansion: CHEP, industrial services
- International experiment: many small M&As
- Diversification experiment: PNG and NZ
- Growth: CHEP to UK, then Europe and US
- Consolidation: Ensco sale, disposal of many small businesses
- Portfolio of international businesses: Europe, Australia, North America
- Global products/businesses/part of global system: CHEP, Cleanaway, Recall

Spread of activities: Domestic–regional | Domestic–national | Domestic–international | International | Global

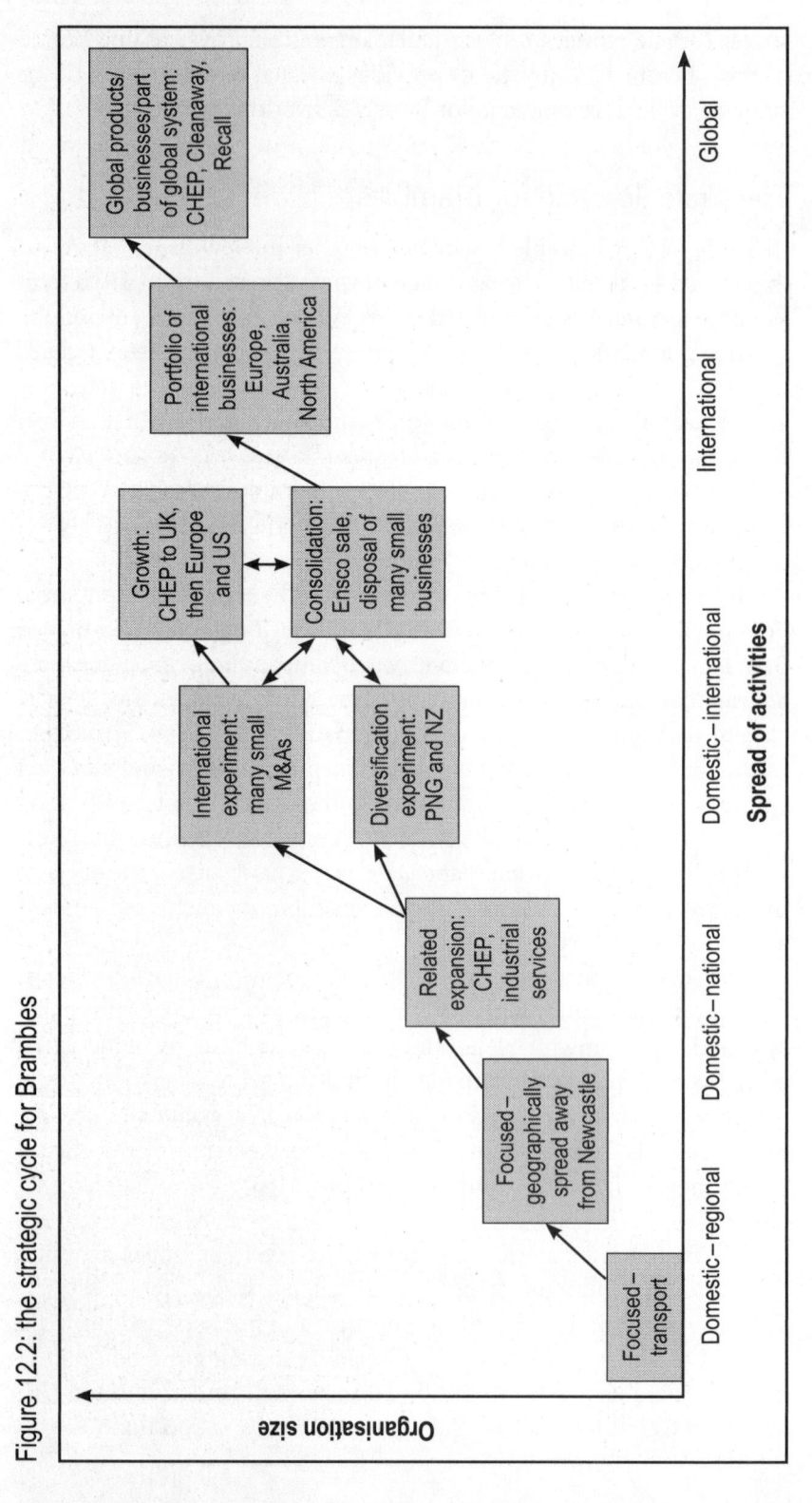

Organisation size

In 1989, Brambles took its international business portfolio from Europe into North America with CHEP (Canada and then the US the following year), Ensco environmental waste and some US equipment rental businesses. Brambles reorganised into three geographic areas—Australia, Europe and North America—to reflect the fact that the businesses were now all multidomestic.

Finally Brambles ran into a problem! *Consolidation* occurred in the early 1990s. Results declined from 1990 to 1997, when Ensco, which had been a disaster for Brambles due to changes in the environmental waste industry regulations, caused A$500 million to be written off. Several businesses were sold but records management, which trailed the other businesses in development, expanded rapidly into several different countries. Brambles also began to explore Asia and looked into airport privatisation in Australia as a potential new diversified business.

In 1999, the final phase began, with Recall records management being established as a *global* business headquartered in the US. CHEP also went global, followed by Cleanaway. Groupe CAIB was sold, as it was not seen as having the potential to go global. However, the Australian diversified products business, Brambles Industrial Services, was not sold, as it was extremely profitable and it was also the emotional core of Brambles—a good example of 'fuzzy' strategy!

In 2001, Brambles merged with its global CHEP partner, GKN, to bring the joint interests together into one company. Brambles held 57 per cent of the joint company. This move aimed to facilitate the joint venture moving 'as one' into further international markets.

However, the combined dual-listed companies did not perform well, running into problems almost immediately. Millions of CHEP pallets in Europe suddenly seemed to be 'lost' and profits began to fall. This did not require a change of strategic cycle stage, as it was primarily an implementation problem due, in part, to the joint venture structural arrangements of the past and excessive sales growth.

By 2004, CEO Sir CK Chow had left Brambles, and David Turner, the CFO who had come to Brambles from GKN, was promoted to restore the fortunes of the company. Rather than consolidate and revert to the portfolio of international businesses stage, Brambles has decided to focus on CHEP and Recall. In the 12 months from October 2005, Brambles sold its Cleanaway operations in Germany, the UK, Australia and Asia, as well as its Industrial Services businesses—the original source of Brambles' success—in the Northern Hemisphere, Australia and New Zealand.

In 2006, Brambles was an organisation in the *global* stage of the strategic cycle, with a narrow focus on two global businesses. This is quite different from its history of a wide range of independent businesses, or a portfolio of international businesses. But Brambles is at the stage that winning organisations aspire to be at—having a set of consistent products that are desired around the world.

Good growth comes from incremental related diversification

From the example we have just followed in detail it is clear that, in general, as the organisation grows it diversifies, but it does this incrementally or in a related manner. This idea was best expressed to us by a Macquarie executive who said:

> In terms of expanding the businesses we are in, we think in terms of 'adjacency' and whether we have the relevant competency or could get the relevant competencies. 'Adjacency' to us means expanding one step at a time, which reduces the risk.

With Brambles (and Lend Lease, Rio Tinto and others), each diversification was perceived to be 'related' to the businesses they were already in. Brambles' initial informal definition of its areas of business as 'dig, lift, load and haul' industrial services, the encouragement of managers seeing themselves running their own businesses, the focus on profit growth, not just growth, and the focus on services to customers and building customer relationships, all provided powerful levers not just for expansion, but for related expansion. The issue is to determine what is 'related' business.

Brambles' failure with US waste management company Ensco is one of the biggest by the winning organisations, costing Brambles around A$500 million. Yet Ensco was in a product area—industrial waste management—that Brambles was experienced in and Brambles had international experience. It looked 'related' to Brambles, and to most people. However, Ensco was the first hostile takeover Brambles had ever made and the evidence is that hostile takeovers have much lower success rates than friendly takeovers. It took three years from the time the idea was broached for Brambles to conclude the acquisition, due to both regulatory and competitive issues. During that time, cheaper rival technologies entered the market, so that Ensco's market position was no longer favourable, compared with the original business case. In addition, other competitors had entered the industry, which, by the time of acquisition, was heavily over capacity.

Experiences of winning organisations that have reached the global stage

Rio Tinto is the most developed of all the winning organisations in terms of the strategic cycle, having gone global in 1995 when it was reacquired by its parent. Of the other winning organisations:

▶ Lend Lease developed a global strategy in 2000, but ran into significant implementation problems and by early 2003 retreated to a portfolio of international businesses.

▶ Brambles developed a (mainly) global strategy in 2001, but ran into implementation problems and sold one of its three global businesses in 2005.

▶ The Australian territories of the Salvation Army are part of a global organisation, but its different units tend to behave independently in their own territories, so that the organisation acts as a series of national or regional independent businesses.

▶ NAB for some time in the 1990s called its strategy 'global', but in reality its operations only covered Australia, New Zealand, the US, the UK and Ireland, so it has never actually been more than a portfolio of international businesses.

▶ Macquarie Bank operated in 25 countries in 2006, but, although it encourages each business unit to be aware of the capabilities of its other business units, each unit acts independently. Therefore, it is in no way 'global', though it has a large number of international businesses.

This shows the limited experience, the confusion over the term 'global' and the relatively poor results that currently exist for global strategies of Australian winning organisations. There's a lot of work to be done here!

Another path to globalisation?

Many newer organisations are working out a different development path to globalisation from those of our winning organisations. Born into the new international era where local and national boundaries have been broken down through declining trade barriers, rapid and cheap communications, wide travel experiences, and cheap and plentiful technology, they take 'international' for granted. They see all businesses as needing to be international and they start by seeking international markets, not local markets. Some are called 'born globals', particularly those in industries with high capital needs, long development times, and uneconomic local and national markets (for example, the pharmaceutical, mining, video game, film and education industries).

What is clear is that future winning Australian organisations will need to have large international operations and quite a number are likely to develop global operations. What is also clear from the existing experience of the First XI is that this is a hard path and a path travelled by only a few Australian organisations. What is less clear is what that path—or paths—will look like for future global success.

Mapping the journeys

We have 'captured' the winning organisations at particular points in their individual development, even though we have studied them in detail over a 25-year study period and for longer spans where possible, and they have not all reached the ultimate 'global' stage—far from it!

While this book is about the commonalities among the organisations' journeys, they are clearly at quite different stages in their lives and the issues that each faces are quite different at any particular time. Table 12.1 maps the journeys by dating the move from one stage of the strategic cycle to entry to the next. The events we have used to define the change of stage of the cycle are included in appendix A. By comparing the dates of entry to a stage, you can see how the organisation has progressed, the stages it has remained in for long periods and where it has moved on quickly. The dates are only entry dates to stages, however. In fact, as the organisations enter new stages, they are simultaneously reinforcing previous stages. For instance, while Brambles was expanding into international and diversified markets, it was simultaneously building its original core, Brambles Industrial Services.

While there is an apparent simplicity in table 12.1, each organisation's development is much more complex. However, the patterns are clear:

▶ All 11 have passed the first three stages.

▶ Ten have undertaken an international experiment. (The Salvation Army has not done this because it is already part of an international organisation and its local units are restricted to Australian activities.

Strategy over time: the strategic cycle in Australia

Table 12.1: year of entry to each stage of the strategic cycle

Organisation	Focused	Geographical spread	Related expansion	International experiment	Diversification experiment	Consolidation	Portfolio of international businesses	Global
Brambles	1916	1937	1956	1970	1937	1995	1978	2001
Harvey Norman	1972	1988	1993	1997	1998		2004	
Lend Lease	1950	1962	1985	1964	1985	2002	2003	1999
Macquarie	1969	1983	1978	1983	1985	–	1989	
NAB	1918	1922	1954	1974	–	2001	1992	
Qantas	1921	1930	1935	1935	–	1947	2006	
Rio Tinto	1905	1949	1949	1964	1981	1983	1987	1995
The Salvation Army	1880	1882	1891	–	1983	2005		
Telstra	1901	1901	1954	2001	1994		2002	
Westfield	1956	1967	1961	1977	1981	1989	1988	
Woolworths	1924	1927	1958	1929	1964	1985	2005	
No. orgs covered this stage	11	11	11	10	9	8	10	3

325

However, in practice, the Salvation Army has access to international experience through its sister international business units.)

- Nine have diversified—the area with the biggest risk of failure. Qantas and NAB are exceptions, though arguments could be made that each of them has had some closely related, but minor, diversification activities as well.
- Eight have had to consolidate. In most cases the consolidation has been related to the diversification activity. Telstra and Harvey Norman, which have diversified, have not yet consolidated, though it could be argued that Telstra's write-downs of its international operations represents the effective consolidation of its activities. NAB and Qantas, which did not diversify, have nevertheless had to consolidate due to poor implementation of their strategy at one point.
- Only seven have developed a portfolio of international businesses with reasonable experience, but two others—Harvey Norman and Woolworths—have recently entered this stage.
- Only three have developed to the global business stage and, of those, one (Lend Lease) has abandoned it.

The strategic cycle is long and it is hard to progress from stage to stage. Our winning organisations are still on their journeys. Only three have reached the ultimate global stage in the strategic cycle and one has retreated from that. There's a long way to go, even for winning organisations that seem to be so successful from a local perspective.

Mistakes in the strategic cycle

The strategic cycle shows a stage of 'consolidation' that organisations all seem to go through. None of the winning organisations has simply proceeded in a forward direction without having to retreat from some business areas. They are not infallible. Mistakes occur. There are three types of 'mistakes' that appear—unrelated diversifications, overseas related diversifications and implementation problems.

Mistake 1: unrelated diversification

The more difficult mistake to understand is where the organisation diversifies into unrelated areas, despite its history of success in related businesses and despite the known history of the failure of unrelated diversification.

A good example of this is Westfield (see figure 12.3). After 20 years of success building shopping centres, in 1981 Westfield took a minority interest in an oil prospect and also entered another consortium in the heavy construction and civil engineering industry, specialising in resource and energy development. In 1983, it took another minority interest in an oil and gas pipeline. In 1986, it launched a 'cash-box' company—an investment company in which investors backed the management team, not knowing exactly what that management team might do with the money invested. They were an extremely popular idea at the time. Westfield Capital Corporation, as it was known, bought into media, retail and manufacturing companies and ended up owning Channel Ten in 1987, just before the sharemarket crash.

Figure 12.3: Westfield's unusual diversification period

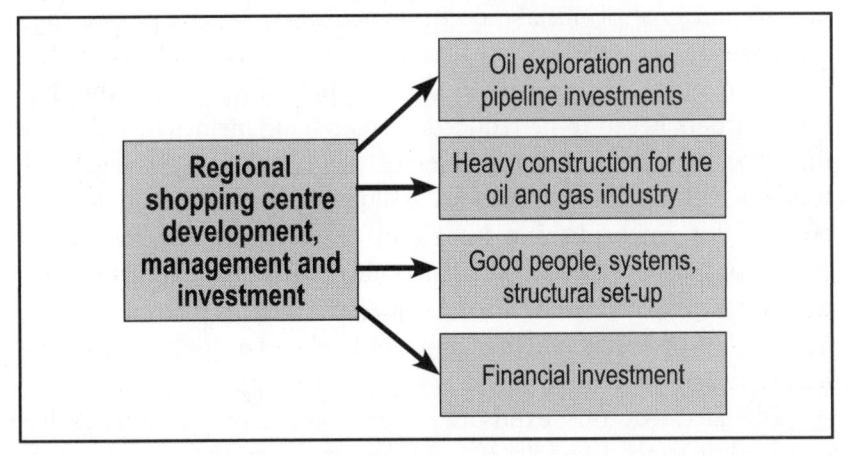

```
Regional                    →  Oil exploration and
shopping centre                pipeline investments
development,
management and              →  Heavy construction for the
investment                     oil and gas industry
                            →  Good people, systems,
                               structural set-up
                            →  Financial investment
```

Why did Westfield do this? It is easy to forget that at the start of the 1980s Australia was expected to experience a 'resources boom' and that in the mid 1980s, the sharemarket and general economic boom led people—even experienced managers—to believe in an unbelievably golden future. (The cash-box/sharemarket boom was of course repeated again with the dotcom boom of the late 1990s and the resources boom is also being repeated from 2004 to the time of writing.) At these times, managers begin to believe they can manage anything. Investing in good managers in an unknown industry is viewed as a way to 'free ride' on their potential or prospects for success.

Westfield appears to have been caught up in both of these fashionable trends—resources and cash boxes. By 1989 it had sold out of all these investments, making a huge loss ($500 million) on the media investment (which ironically has done very well since, under media industry management), though the resource industry investments did adequately well.

Since then, Westfield has remained focused on its shopping centres with only one other minor non-core activity—a minority joint venture investment in Intencity, a high technology leisure entertainment chain of retail shops.

It is worth noting the time period involved. While the 'consolidation' took only two years, the whole episode of unrelated expansion took almost 10 years. Strategic decisions, good or bad, have long-term effects of some magnitude. That's one good reason that alone indicates why strategy is important!

Mistake 2: related diversification overseas

The second type of mistake occurs when organisations pursue their own businesses, but go into unfamiliar overseas markets. Most Australian businesses focused on Australia until the 1980s. At this time trade barriers began to be reduced, discouraging inefficient industries in Australia, and the finance industry was opened up through such fundamental institutional reforms as floating the dollar, allowing the entry of foreign banks and freeing up interest rate and investment restrictions. This allowed and encouraged Australian organisations to begin to explore taking their businesses overseas as local markets become less protected and more competitive, and overseas markets are more accessible.

The fact that this exposure to international opportunities has occurred in only the last 20 years means that the experience of international Australian organisations is quite limited, even now. It is not surprising that many Australian organisations have found it difficult to succeed overseas, given this lack of history and experience.

NAB's failure in 2002 with HomeSide, a mortgage consolidator in the US, is another even more costly example. NAB wrote off almost $4 billion due to technical miscalculations in HomeSide's pricing model and lack of control of the subsidiary from head office. Coupled with NAB's (profitable) sale of Michigan National Bank in 2001 and its Irish banks in 2005, which meant a total retreat from the US, it is clear that, at the time of writing, NAB is in the 'consolidation' stage of the strategic cycle. That NAB first invested overseas in 1987 and in the US in 1995 indicates the difficulty of being successful overseas, even for winning organisations. It is a long, slow process.

Lend Lease bought a series of US property fund investment and management organisations in 2000 as part of its global real estate strategy. It should have been well aware of what it was buying and how to manage those organisations as it had experience of these activities in Australia and even overseas. However, its strategy did not work, primarily because of the size of the change (tripling in size in one year) and the spread of location of the activity (mostly in the US, though head office was in the UK and the main historical activity in Australia). Again, simply being 'related' activities and organisations did not seem to be sufficient.

Telstra's investment in Pacific Century Cyber Works (PCCW) in 2000 and in Clear and Reach in New Zealand in 2001, coupled with its more minor investments in Vietnam and other countries in the 1990s, have yet to demonstrate any significant return, even though these are businesses in which Telstra is intimately involved in Australia. Telstra is also in the 'consolidation' stage.

Qantas has periodically flirted with the strategy of being an 'around the world' airline on its own, but when times have been tough in the industry, it has withdrawn from many routes. Recognising its limited resources (and the constraints of its ability to undertake market development in the industry), it went through a period of focusing on Asia on its own in the late 1980s, then as part of the British Airways–Qantas alliance in the mid 1990s, then for the Oneworld alliance in the late 1990s and most recently in the formation of Jetstar Asia in Singapore in 2005. But Qantas withdrew from Asian routes during the 1997 and 2001 Asian crises. In Qantas' case it is relatively easy to withdraw, as it has little capital tied up. However, its signal of lack of commitment and the evident lack of profitability in overseas markets again suggest the difficulty of operating overseas, even in one's own industry.

Mistake 3: inability to implement the strategy

The third mistake that is made is not to do with the strategy or the stage of the strategic cycle; it is to do with the inability to make the (new) strategy work. This occurs as the organisation moves from one stage of the cycle to another and requires changes in the capabilities needed to match the new strategy. For the winning organisations, this has occurred mainly in relation to mistake 2—related diversification overseas—as evidenced in the earlier Lend Lease example. The key implementation problems appear to be the size of any change, any cultural differences and the degree to which the move is 'related'. Large acquisitions can be difficult to manage and control. Cultural differences are often underplayed in acquisitions where the focus is on related products and markets. Products and markets may not be sufficiently related either.

So why do these failures occur when these organisations have very successful track records at home and they are expanding in their own or related industries? From the previous examples, the experiences of the winning organisations indicate that the key reasons seem to be:

- lack of understanding of the social and business culture of the country in question
- lack of understanding of the specifics of the industry in that country
- having a poor understanding of the business partner in the joint venture (if applicable)
- paying too much or being too optimistic about the likelihood of being able to turnaround or change the company that has been acquired.

All this suggests caution is important in overseas expansion. (We addressed this in chapter 9 under risk management.)

Realignment during a major strategy change versus mistakes

As organisations move through the strategic cycle, the change in perception required for each new stage at the point where they make the transition from one stage to another has significant implications for some of the businesses in their current portfolios.

Perhaps the clearest example of this is Lend Lease. In 1998, Lend Lease said it was 'creating a global niche strategy as a property investment manager'. In 1999 it said it had 'two core areas of activity—financial services and real estate'. In 2000, Lend Lease's strategy was to be a 'global real estate company' with three activities:

- real estate investment and funds management
- project management and construction
- property development.

Here we see the gradual emergence of a truly global strategy and the consequent sale of its Australian-based financial services company,

MLC, in 2000. In this case, Lend Lease sold the company that was responsible for almost half of its total profits, to focus on strategy at a new level—global products—instead of remaining a multidomestic organisation. Good strategic thinking! Unfortunately, it didn't have the capabilities to implement the strategy.

Brambles similarly decided to focus on three global product businesses. This required the sale of its European rail wagon rental business—Groupe CAIB—which had also been responsible for a significant part of its profits. However, Brambles did not see this business 'fitting' into a global structure, so it had to sell, for strategic consistency.

Rio Tinto continues to go global following the merger of CRA with its UK parent RTZ in 1995, focusing on large-scale long-life mines. Its policy is to encourage the development of large mines where economies of scale allow it to be globally competitive. So quite a number of its smaller assets have been sold since 1995 as this realignment to a global product strategy takes place.

These are not 'mistakes'. They represent the internal effects of important strategy changes. They confirm the central role that strategy plays in organisational development—but they do result in substantial change in the business portfolio.

Organisations in transition: unbalanced? rebalancing?

In our research for this edition, it seemed clear that some of the organisations were not 'balanced'. Of course, as we have noted, this is inevitable. However, it's worth discussing what happened to the 'balance' in these organisations.

NAB is an organisation that became unbalanced in the early 2000s. However, this was not recognised—or acted on—by the top management until the 2004 forex scandal, the third disaster the organisation had incurred in relatively short time. NAB embarked on a three-year recovery program that, by the end of 2006, seemed to have them rebalanced. Although costly and traumatic, we can't help but wonder how quickly the changes have occurred, testimony to the recovery qualities of winning organisations.

Telstra, on the other hand, seemed to have become unbalanced under its imported management team. Rather than having good relationships with its stakeholders, it appeared to have upset almost all of them. One explanation is that Telstra management is 'right' in its views and everyone else is wrong, but this does not seem likely. We expect rebalancing to occur in the near future. However, Telstra's industry, unlike NAB's, is under fundamental technology change and Telstra's choices of technology and speed of implementation will be the most likely key indicators of whether it will retain its 'winning organisation' status.

Qantas is an organisation that has been constantly rebalancing since 2000 (or perhaps even since it became a commercial organisation in the early 1990s). The rebalancing has been away from its people, who were extremely well rewarded in the old airline industry world, and its customers, who had become accustomed to wonderfully high levels of service in a duopoly domestic world. Naturally customers—you and I—are not so happy about this! But we forget that the prices we can fly at now are well below those charged in the old world—and we have real choice. We can't have it both ways! The rebalancing has been in favour of shareholders, many of which are customers and employees. Shareholders did extremely well until 2001 and have done remarkably well since, considering the parlous state of the airline industry the world over, though not particularly well in an absolute sense.

Staged rebalancing is necessary as part of a continual improvement model to maintain perfect alignment. Recovering from errors that led to being unbalanced is also necessary. We believe that each year one or two of the winning organisations will be unbalanced and needing to recover. But it should be a small episode in the long history of a winning organisation.

Summary and key messages for leaders

A strategic cycle of eight stages exists for Australian organisations. They proceed through the cycle as part of their journey. The specific nature of an organisation's strategy varies over time, depending on the stage of the strategic cycle it is in, or wishes to be in. Only a few of the winning organisations have reached the ultimate stage of the strategic cycle—the global stage—suggesting that even the winning organisations have plenty of opportunities to grow.

The evidence suggests that quite long periods occur before organisations 'experiment' in their strategic cycle. When they have 'experimented', most of the organisations have made at least one significant mistake and have had to consolidate or retreat, particularly

Strategy over time: the strategic cycle in Australia

after international diversification experiments, before moving forward again.

The key messages for leaders from this chapter are:

▶ Understand the strategic cycle and which stage your organisation is in.

▶ Manage the organisation for that stage of the cycle; look ahead for the next stage and prepare for it.

▶ Enter each new stage incrementally and slowly.

▶ Be careful about undertaking strategic experiments, particularly diversification or international experiments.

▶ Understand that some mistakes will be made.

▶ Try to recover from mistakes quickly.

12 Strategy over time: the strategic cycle in Australia

Organisations develop and grow over time. The content of their strategy varies with this. What does an organisation's path of strategic development look like? Our study of the winning organisations suggests that there is a 'strategic cycle' that organisations go through, with each stage of the cycle requiring different clear and fuzzy strategies and related aligned capabilities, leadership and organisational processes.

In this chapter, we'll outline the eight stages of the strategic cycle of the development of winning organisations in Australia over time and we'll explore in detail each of the stages. We'll then provide a detailed example of the strategic cycle, using Brambles to show how one organisation has traversed the whole cycle. Following this we'll look at where each of the organisations were in 2006 and how they got there, to demonstrate both the evidence for the cycle and how it works for different organisations.

We'll also look at the types of mistakes that winning organisations make and try to understand why they are made and how winning organisations recover from them. Even First XI players fail to score, make errors and allow opponents to win occasionally. No organisation is infallible, but winning organisations don't fail very often and they recover quickly.

13 The First XI: where are they now?

The study we undertook, analysing 11 organisations over a 20-year study period, formally concluded in 2000. In this edition we revisit the First XI and consider what has happened to those organisations between 2001 and 2006. Five years does not sound a long time in the context of a 20-year study, but five years is a whole business cycle. During this period:

- ▶ the internet bubble burst
- ▶ the September 11, 2001 terrorist attacks took place, resulting in wars in Afghanistan and Iraq, which remain ongoing
- ▶ corporate collapses occurred in the United States and Australia, which led to significant increases in demands for corporate governance and reporting transparency
- ▶ the SARS health problem occurred
- ▶ free trade agreements, with implications for low-cost imports into Australia, developed
- ▶ demand for commodities from China and India increased rapidly
- ▶ oil prices soared.

All of these events had a major impact on local and international business, so the winning organisations have had difficult circumstances to negotiate. This chapter asks, in effect, are they still winning organisations?

The First XI

Keep in mind, however, that this study is about the principles of winning, rather than the First XI organisations themselves. Normally, over a five-year period, changes would occur in the actual make-up of the top team. Nevertheless, if the 11 we identified were indeed winners from 1981 to 2000, and the principles they followed are indeed enduring, we might expect them to have continued to win since then.

This chapter examines each organisation's progress between 2001 and 2006. (See appendix A for each organisation's key historical information for a fuller picture of each). We'll look at the overall picture for each organisation against the winning organisation framework. We'll then consider what the overall picture is for the winning organisations as a whole. Finally, we'll consider some issues that arose during the period that we did not consider in our original research.

The overall picture

We analysed the sharemarket performance of the portfolio from January 2001 to January 2006 (see figure 13.1). We reweighted the portfolio to reflect equal shares for each organisation (except the Salvation Army, of course) as at January 2001, so this graph is not directly comparable with figure 1.2 in chapter 1. Despite a number of well-publicised stumbles by First XI organisations, the portfolio recorded a 60 per cent gain over the five-year period. However, the S&P/ASX 200 Accumulation Index rose by 81 per cent — those stumbles mattered!

Figure 13.1: winning organisations' total sharemarket return, 2001–06

The First XI: where are they now?

There were three low performers in the First XI between 2001 and 2006:

- Telstra, whose total shareholder return (TSR) decreased by 23 per cent.
- Harvey Norman, whose TSR surprisingly decreased by 18 per cent.
- Lend Lease, whose TSR remained constant.

The TSR of the remaining organisations increased by 114 per cent. As you will see, the two negative TSR performers had excellent accounting returns and Lend Lease is clearly in recovery. Note, however, that in the overall research we are not measuring performance simply on a financial basis, but on a balanced scorecard basis.

It's important to remember that five years is a very short time over which to measure performance for a winning organisation. As you will see, organisations that have experienced a major problem have been significantly affected and do not have the time within a five-year period to recover sufficiently. We also note that some industries were affected by particular events during this period, outside of the impact of the organisation itself. For instance, the bursting of the internet bubble had a major impact on the global telecommunications industry, which significantly underperformed the sharemarket for the period. Similarly, the airline industry was dealt blow after blow during the period. On the other hand, the period was very kind to the mining industry, whose performance was high almost regardless of the quality of the organisation.

All of these issues indicate that five years is insufficient time to form a complete conclusion. Therefore, the five-year analysis needs to be seen as additional to the 20 years already considered. Let's take a look at each organisation individually to see what happened to them between 2001 and 2006.

Brambles

In 2000, Brambles was a diversified industrial services company dominated by three businesses that were developing global branding strategies—CHEP pallets, Cleanaway waste management and Recall record storage—together with its original Australian industrial services business, Brambles Industrial Services. In 2001, Brambles' UK joint venture partner, GKN plc, demerged its support services activities (which represented GKN's part of the overseas joint venture with Brambles), listed it separately on the stock exchange as Brambles Industries plc, and the operations and management of the two dual-listed companies were combined, under new CEO, Sir CK Chow. In effect, Brambles controlled the operations of both companies, but the CEO came from GKN. Brambles' then CEO, John Fletcher, left and became CEO of Coles Myer, a direct competitor of Woolworths. Indicative of the market's opinion of Fletcher's management ability, the Coles Myer share price made a dramatic rise on the day Fletcher's move was announced.

After the merger, Brambles began to implement its strategy of developing its businesses as global businesses and a global group, rather than just global brands and individual independent businesses, and divesting other businesses. In January 2002, Brambles introduced a mission statement (part of which read, 'to be the world's leading provider of innovative business solutions in support services ...') and began developing a new global operating model for each business. However, despite the optimism and laudable aims, overall the organisation's performance began to decline.

The major problem appeared in the CHEP pallet business. CHEP had been rapidly expanding through to 2001. In 2003, Brambles reported that 4 million pallets had been written off, 2.4 million pallets had been recovered and 1.1 million pallets had been found at European customers' premises. Management of the pallet pool—a key operational discipline at CHEP—had been poor.

Although Brambles painted an optimistic picture of itself in 2003, the large fall in its share price led to a turnaround process, which began in 2004. A new CEO was appointed, together with significant changes to the management team and board. In 2005, Brambles decided to merge the dual-listed companies into one, to sell Cleanaway and its Australian business unit, Brambles Industrial Services, and focus globally on CHEP and Recall. These sales were announced in 2006 and raised over US$3.6 billion, so that, by the end of the period, Brambles consisted of two global businesses—CHEP and Recall. Even the original diversified industrial services businesses in Australia and Europe that formed the heart of Brambles' historical success has been sold. Brambles' financial performance between 2001 and 2006 is shown in table 13.1.

Overall, Brambles had a troubled operational period from 2001 to 2004 as it tried to globalise its key business units, typical of that stage of the strategic cycle. Although it reported good accounting performance in terms of return on equity, share price returns were weaker, reflecting concern about its ability to manage the globalisation process. The hiring of a CEO from outside the company when it merged with GKN, the development of mission statements and some cultural change driven by the new CEO are outside the principles of the winning wheel. It is interesting to note that the outside CEO did not survive long.

Table 13.1: Brambles' financial performance, 2001–06

Year	Sales growth (%)	Profit after tax growth (%)	Return on equity (%)	Total shareholder return (%)
2001	12	–58	14	5
2002	129	221	35	–54
2003	–8	–33	24	17
2004	–6	–9	21	36
2005	6	75	13	49
2006	8	16	12	27*

*Ten months to 31 October 2006.

Brambles seems to have now gone through the difficult 'consolidation' period as it changed from one part of the strategic cycle to another. However, it has decided to continue with its global strategy and has been working hard to develop perfect alignment of units to that. Brambles also clearly had problems with effective execution in terms of the CHEP pallet issue. On the other hand, it was able to adapt rapidly to the performance and execution decline and chose a leader from within to lead the change required.

By the end of the period, Brambles seemed to be back on track, but, as the core of the original Brambles business had been sold in 2006, it is — once again — a significantly different organisation from that which it has been, although its core business — CHEP pallets — has been a major part of the organisation for over 50 years now.

Harvey Norman

During the period 2001–06, Harvey Norman carried on the same type of business that it had developed — discount retailing of home products — but it expanded overseas, into Slovenia (1999), Ireland (2003) and Malaysia (2003), and also expanded its existing New Zealand and Singapore operations. In 2003, it developed a new franchise product area—Mega Flooring Depot and it also expanded into Home Renovations.

In 2001, it diversified into a non–home based product line when it acquired Rebel Sport, a listed, brand-oriented, discount retail sports store, and installed a Harvey Norman franchisee to run it on Harvey Norman lines. This led to a big improvement in Rebel Sport's results. It rebranded the Joyce Mayne stores it had bought in 1998 as 'Domayne', in 1999, a downmarket version of Harvey Norman, and, in 2005, it relaunched Joyce Mayne as a country/regional brand similar to Harvey Norman. In 2006 it agreed to sell Rebel Sport at a large profit on the acquisition price. By the end of the period, it had 174 stores in Australia and 42 stores overseas. Harvey Norman is clearly well into the 'international experiment' stage of the strategic cycle.

During the five-year period, the company appeared to make little or no operational change, though chairman Gerry Harvey himself became a larger-than-life media figure due to his very quotable lines, his involvement in horse breeding and racing, and his development and support of ecological farming practices. Harvey Norman's financial performance from 2001 to 2006 is shown in table 13.2.

Table 13.2: Harvey Norman's financial performance, 2001–06

Year	Sales growth (%)	Profit after tax growth (%)	Return on equity (%)	Total shareholder return (%)
2001	32	–4	16	5
2002	68	21	15	–34
2003	22	25	16	16
2004	29	16	15	8
2005	10	1	14	–5
2006	15	20	17	26*

*Ten months to 31 October 2006.

Overall, within Australia, Harvey Norman has been the dominant retailer of its type and its methods and execution are considered to be outstanding. It has become an iconic company in Australia. As demonstrated, it has also been in the international expansion stage of the strategic cycle. While it has performed well in accounting terms overall, its profit growth has lagged its sales growth in most years and its total shareholder return has been poor.

We believe the low TSR reflects concerns about whether its overseas operations will be as successful as its Australian ones have been (effective execution?), the rather eclectic set of countries into which Harvey Norman has expanded (fuzzy strategy?) and its depth of management beyond the Harvey family (leadership, not leaders). The very thin financial statements and annual reports do not provide the expected level of transparency of corporate governance that is increasingly required (not looking out?) and this may also have had an impact on the TSR.

Lend Lease

From 1999 to 2001, Lend Lease developed a global real estate development and funds management strategy, primarily by buying a number of major US-based organisations, and tripled its size in terms of sales. However, no sooner was the global strategy formed, than performance started to decline.

The strategy appeared to be quite sound and an incremental expansion of Lend Lease's thinking—the problems were clearly ones of implementation. Its timing was wrong—it appeared to be ahead of its time in believing that the time for the 'securitisation' of the global real estate property industry had come. The collection of US companies purchased was wrong, as little synergy existed between them, the management of them was poorly handled and they did not return sufficient profit for the investment made. Further, Lend Lease underestimated the cultural differences between the US companies and its Australian management culture.

Lend Lease had moved its head office to the UK, yet most of its new businesses were in the US, while the heart and history of the business remained in Australia. As well, the management team was new, came from outside Lend Lease and was similarly geographically scattered. The organisation used few of its own management team to assist in the integration of the new acquisitions. Three rounds of management turnover in quick succession—including one round of Australian managers—did nothing to achieve the required performance. As a result, Lend Lease, an organisation that had been renowned for its openness, developed a reputation at its centre of being aloof and unresponsive.

In 2002, CEO David Higgins, the architect of the global strategy and a long-time Lend Lease employee, was replaced by UK outsider Greg Clarke, a man with no building industry experience, who began a turnaround strategy. Although initially buying in to the global strategy concept, Clarke quickly realised that Lend Lease did not have the capabilities to make the US-based global strategy work, so he began to dismantle the strategy, selling off most of the newly acquired US businesses and returning to the strategy of regional property developer, in which different business units were relatively independent—the heart of the previous Lend Lease corporate strategy. He also moved the head office back to Australia, quite a decision for an English CEO!

In 2004 Lend Lease made a hostile bid for General Property Trust (GPT), its Australian-based listed funds management affiliate, which, though closely aligned with and the manager of most of Lend Lease's property developments, was an independent public corporation. The bid was consistent with an emerging fashion in the listed property trust industry, in which previously low-risk, low-return property trusts were being used to develop into growth organisations. Concerned that GPT would be snared by another organisation, Lend Lease acted first. It believed that not notifying GPT's management about the bid was the right thing to do, as there were questions of independence and concerns about leaking of information. Hence the hostile bid (although most other organisations in a similar position would have had discussions first).

GPT's board resisted the bid, courted another bidder and, after a protracted bidding process, Lend Lease refused to pay the highest price. As a result, in 2005 GPT eventually broke ties with Lend Lease. Lend Lease's approach to the whole saga was regarded by the investment community with amazement. To launch a hostile bid on an organisation that it had established in 1971 and that had been a partner for over 30 years, and then to completely lose the relationship, seemed incomprehensible. Surprisingly, however, Lend Lease's share price rose after the failed bid, while GPT's has fallen, indicating the market has taken a different view from the analysts.

In 2006, Lend Lease moved from its regional structure to a clearer line-of-business structure with four businesses: retail, communities (the ideas and innovative end of the firm), project and construction management (the builders), and investment management (the internal replacement activity for what GPT had done). Thus, by the end of the period, Lend Lease had returned to its non-global international real estate–based property developer strategy. Its results indicated that it was on the way back (see table 13.3).

As table 13.3 shows, Lend Lease's financial performance had been fairly poor until 2005. Negative sales growth indicates the consolidation that occurred, though profit growth has been good since 2004. The return on equity has consistently improved and has reached acceptable to good levels. The share price fell dramatically but has been consistently recovering over the last two to three years. It seems that Lend Lease has survived a major execution error, made another major error under its new management team, yet is beginning to re-emerge as a solid performer once again.

Table 13.3: Lend Lease's financial performance, 2001–06

Year	Sales growth (%)	Profit after tax growth (%)	Return on equity (%)	Total shareholder return (%)
2001	–12	–65	4	–20
2002	9	50	6	–24
2003	–19	2	8	6
2004	–4	11	9	35
2005	–2	21	11	15
2006	29	24	15	12*

*Ten months to 31 October 2006.

In terms of winning organisation principles, Lend Lease is perplexing. On the one hand, its strategy was very clear and consistent with its developments over time. However, increasing in size by 300 per cent within one year, having a CEO based in the UK, its major businesses (and chair of the board) in the US and most of its management expertise in Australia was simply too much change to absorb in such a short period. Effective execution was just not possible!

Lend Lease did adapt rapidly to the error, taking less than two years to begin the change process. While hiring a CEO from outside caused some discontent, and is inconsistent with the principles of winning organisations, it is consistent with turnaround strategy. It may have been necessary to go outside, despite good leaders within the organisation, for market credibility. What is clear is that Lend Lease has recovered under Clarke's leadership. Clarke has respected and supported the hands-on Lend Lease culture. It appears that the execution of the global strategy was indeed a 'big mistake' of the type all organisations make occasionally and which is typical of this stage of the strategic cycle, but from which Lend Lease is recovering well.

Finally, although the GPT 'error' in 2004–05 had a significant effect on the market reputation of Lend Lease's management, the recovery of the share price indicates that there is more confidence in its operational development capabilities.

Macquarie Bank

The period 2001–06 was an enormous success on all fronts for Macquarie Bank. It went from being perceived as a relatively small investment bank with highly innovative and creative ideas to a diversified international provider of financial and investment banking services, a major Australian organisation and an aggressive and creative international player. It achieved much of this through a combination of organic growth of its internal divisions and through buying assets, repackaging those assets and selling them to other buyers. Indeed, Macquarie became renowned for its ability to repackage assets thought to be of limited value into specialised funds of considerable value to investors seeking particular asset-class investments.

By 2006, as well as the parent company, Macquarie Bank, there were 14 other listed 'Macquarie' investment vehicles in Australia and many other unlisted ones, including:

- Macquarie Airports
- Macquarie Capital Alliance Group
- Macquarie Communications Infrastructure Group
- Macquarie CountryWide Trust
- Macquarie Diversified Utility and Energy Trust
- Macquarie Goodman Group
- Macquarie Infrastructure Group
- Macquarie International Infrastructure Fund
- Macquarie Leisure Trust
- Macquarie Media Group
- Macquarie Office Trust
- Macquarie Power and Infrastructure Income Fund
- Macquarie Private Capital Group
- Macquarie Prologis Trust.

Macquarie became known for its audacious and creative bids for infrastructure assets in a wide variety of countries (for example, the

London Stock Exchange; Rome Airport; Chicago, Canadian and French toll roads; Eurotunnel; and Sydney Airport). In 2006 it had the unique experience of advising one Australian company (Alinta Gas) to make a hostile acquisition of another Australian company (AGL) that was chaired by its own deputy chair and one of its founders, Mark Johnson!

In 2000 Macquarie was represented in 15 countries. By 2006 it was represented in 24 countries. The share of operating income from international sources increased from 21 per cent to 48 per cent and over 25 per cent of its people are now employed outside Australia.

Macquarie's operating model continues to encourage and involve several of its business units working together on a deal or in a relationship, with fees flowing from one entity to another. Despite increasing attention given to the vertically integrated nature of the operations of its many different arms and the large fees it receives from deals via the fees paid to the various Macquarie units involved in a transaction, not to mention the development of organisations, such as Babcock and Brown, that are trying to copy Macquarie's tactics, Macquarie powered through the period with very few slip-ups, especially considering the audacious and innovative nature of the deals it proposed. Its financial performance for 2001–06 is shown in table 13.4.

Table 13.4: Macquarie Bank's financial performance, 2001–06

Year	Sales growth (%)	Profit after tax growth (%)	Return on equity (%)	Total shareholder return (%)
2001	24	23	27	34
2002	9	3	19	–35
2003	18	30	18	59
2004	30	44	22	36
2005	52	66	30	53
2006	17	15	26	11*

*Ten months to 31 October 2006.

It would be easy to think that the 'millionaires factory'—as Macquarie is widely known due to the extremely high total remuneration received by its executives—is focused purely on financial performance. However, Macquarie is also a leader in corporate social responsibility, in community work, in encouraging its staff to volunteer for charities, in developing in-house training and development, in risk assessment, and in aligning staff rewards with shareholder and customer outcomes. It is also quick to respond to criticism and to change if such criticism is justified.

Overall, Macquarie has overcome minor hurdles and is very well placed at the end of the period. It has applied all the elements of the winning wheel. Recent growth has been extraordinary—particularly benefiting from one-off transactions—and may be difficult to repeat in the short term.

National Australia Bank

In 2000, National Australia Bank was riding high as the pre-eminent Australian retail bank with an expanding portfolio of international banks in the US, UK and Ireland, which it saw as a 'global' banking strategy. The newly appointed CEO, Frank Cicutto, a long-term insider, and the purchase of highly regarded listed funds manager MLC, suggested NAB was well placed to continue performing well.

However, in 2001 NAB made a then-surprising, and quick, decision to sell its US mortgage operation, HomeSide, recording a loss on the sale, first reported at around $700 million, which grew to $3 billion. Particularly surprising was the revelation that NAB had made a basic error on acquisition valuation and, having discovered that error, realised it had overpaid. For a bank that prided itself on being conservative and that professed to have an ability to assess and integrate acquisitions well, this was a major issue.

While NAB conducted a full enquiry and some senior people retired early in decisions that seemed related to the HomeSide losses, the results of the enquiry were never satisfactorily aired and analysts felt that the true nature of the problem and who was responsible was rather murky.

In 2002, as part of a strategic review, NAB changed its strategy and retreated from its previous professed aim to globalise its activities. After considering but failing to go ahead with major acquisition opportunities in both the UK and Australia, it developed a program, 'Positioning for Growth', which in reality was mainly about cutting costs through the implementation of large-scale technological change. An across-the-board 10 per cent cut was attempted. As a consequence, a number of potential CEOs and senior managers left the organisation. In 2003 a fraud occurred in the Korean office with $77 million of bank certificates forged. Also that year, NAB badly handled a share raid on insurer AMP and made a loss on the transaction, while not coming close to gaining control over AMP and damaging its business reputation during the process. It also considered a major UK acquisition, but did not bid in the end.

In 2004, a foreign exchange trading scandal in NAB's Melbourne office was revealed. While the losses, originally said to be $180 million, were in the order of $300 million—small, relative to the HomeSide loss—they proved to be the catalyst for wide-ranging change at NAB, as they revealed major cultural and policy problems at the bank. UK banker John Stewart, who had been recently hired to run the UK banking operations, replaced Cicutto as CEO. Many senior executives were replaced and the board, which was at loggerheads over who was responsible for the debacle, was also largely replaced.

In effect, NAB began a turnaround under largely new, largely external management in 2004, a phase that was expected to last for three years. During the period it had two complete management changes, one complete board change and four chairs of the board (Mark Rayner, Charles Allen, Graham Kraehe and Michael Cheney). Interestingly, despite the major errors in the period, NAB continued to report high levels of accounting profits, but its share price, reputation for conservative risk management and business profile suffered. In 2006 it was named bank of the year in Australia, further evidence that it is building momentum to return to its former glory. NAB's financial performance for 2001–06 is shown in table 13.5.

Table 13.5: National Australia Bank's financial performance, 2001–06

Year	Sales growth (%)	Profit after tax growth (%)	Return on equity (%)	Total shareholder return (%)
2001	58	–36	9	15
2002	–7	62	15	4
2003	–26	17	16	–1
2004	9	–10	14	2
2005	20	34	17	19
2006	NA	NA	NA	23*

*Ten months to 31 October 2006.

Where did NAB go wrong? It seems that, during the late 1990s, the culture at NAB had become ultra-conservative, risk averse and responsibility averse. It had become somewhat unbalanced, failing to 'look out' sufficiently and did not admit its mistakes as well as it might have. NAB felt that the economy would turn down and was preparing for a recession scenario that did not eventuate. At the same time, the culture changed, demanding short-term profits—perhaps to shore up the reduced business from tightening lending criteria or to provide funds for one of the major acquisitions that was contemplated. In at least some parts of the bank, the conservative banking culture was over-ridden and unexpected risks were taken.

The failure to properly address the HomeSide disaster—internally and particularly externally—may have allowed or even encouraged other areas of the bank to avoid addressing the hard issues of operational management. NAB's previous success and recognition seemed to have gone to its head (ignoring elements of the winning wheel—failure to admit mistakes, not looking out) and it was not until events compounded that true recognition and acceptance finally occurred.

However, by 2006 NAB's share price had hit a record high and it was beginning to show progress in sales, profits and returns, suggesting the turnaround was in the process of being successful. The accounting return on equity results also demonstrate that NAB did well throughout, regardless of these disasters, suggesting that the publicity surrounding the crises—significant though they were—was greater than their real effect on the bank. NAB has performed adequately at worst, and seemed in 2006 to be rapidly returning to being a strong performer.

Qantas

In contrast to Macquarie, Qantas could not have faced a more difficult five-year period. Yet, like Macquarie, Qantas has come through this period in a great position, as it continued to focus its activities and strategy almost exclusively on the airline industry.

The September 11 terrorist plane attacks in 2001, the resulting Afghanistan and Iraq wars, the 2003 SARS health epidemic, the domestic airfare wars and the 2002 and 2005 Bali bombings subjected the international airline industry to 'constant shock syndrome' and many airlines became marginal, failed or required government support. Security costs tripled and Qantas has spent over $1 billion per annum during the period on this.

The gradual international development of 'open skies' agreements between governments allowed airlines to begin to fly where and when they wanted between two countries. Qantas' business model of a high-price, high-service airline has also been under severe attack from the eruption of low-cost, point-to-point airlines that followed the success of the famous Southwest Airlines model in the US. Compounding this, the effects of over capacity in the industry and the surge in fuel prices between 2004 and 2006, which made fuel the number one cost for the airline, doubling its percentage in the cost structure, all meant that revenue per seat declined during the period.

These issues were offset only by the positive domestic effects of the collapse of Ansett in 2001, which enabled Qantas to dominate its home market until low-cost airline Virgin Blue took up the slack and offered a different, highly competitive domestic model. Despite this very hostile environment, Qantas remained one of a very small number of airlines that has been consistently profitable despite being in an industry that has lost more than US$42 billion since 2001.

After appointing insider Geoff Dixon as CEO in 2001, Qantas launched Australian Airlines as a new international airline in 2002, focusing on the Asian in-bound holiday market, based in Cairns. It started Jetstar as a domestic low-cost airline in 2004, to serve the part of the market that Qantas, with its much higher cost structure, could not serve. It started Jetstar Asia in 2005 as an international low-cost airline flying from Singapore, a joint venture with Temasek Holdings, a Singapore Government investment company. In late 2005, Jetstar Asia acquired ValuAir, another low-cost airline based in Singapore. In 2006, it decided to close down Australian Airlines, whose cost structure was too high to compete as a true low-cost airline and develop a Jetstar Group, operationally equivalent in status to the Qantas Group in the organisational structure, which would cover low-cost international travel as well as domestic. It also decided to set up a separate freight group, Express Freighters Australia, expanding its activity in that part of the airline business.

The success of Jetstar has been very important to Qantas. No other quality airline in the world had been able to develop a low-cost airline within its group. Experts were sceptical that Qantas would succeed with Jetstar, yet indications are that Jetstar is doing well and it is consequently replacing Qantas services on a variety of lower volume routes within Australia and from 2006 onwards, internationally. Jetstar operations also give Qantas management insights into how to reduce its own costs. However, Qantas is constrained by legacy systems and dealing with many unions. Qantas' financial performance for the period 2001–06 is shown in table 13.6 (overleaf).

Table 13.6: Qantas' financial performance, 2001–06

Year	Sales growth (%)	Profit after tax growth (%)	Return on equity (%)	Total shareholder return (%)
2001	12	–19	19	11
2002	8	2	15	10
2003	4	–19	9	–10
2004	0	87	16	19
2005	11	18	18	15
2006	9	–30	8	9*

*Ten months to 31 October 2006.

Throughout the five-year period, Qantas focused on reducing costs, reflecting both the unprofitability of the industry, the pressure from the low-cost airlines domestically and internationally, and the escalating price of fuel and security costs. Its corporate 'Sustainable Future' program, established in 2003, generated $1.5 billion of cost savings (as targeted) and a new target of a cumulative $3 billion by 2008 has been set. Reflecting its overall success, Qantas paid bonuses in cash to employees in 2004 and 2005 of $1000 per employee and in 2006 of $500 per employee.

The danger for Qantas is that the focus on costs could generate significant passenger dissatisfaction among passengers used to high-quality service. However, Qantas reports the highest levels of customer satisfaction on record, somewhat at odds with our own anecdotal experiences. However, apart from using private jets, business passengers have little choice domestically at the moment and the attempt by another group to launch a business class–only airline — OzJet — failed within six months.

Qantas was successful in keeping Singapore Airlines, Air New Zealand and other international airlines out of the domestic market, as well as the Australia–US routes, which are considered to be a key market for Qantas' profitability. Qantas attempted to form an alliance with Air New Zealand for flights across the Tasman, to reduce the heavy competition that had emerged in that market. The Australian and New Zealand competition regulators rejected the first attempt. A second attempt was abandoned in 2006 after the Australian regulators again rejected it.

By the end of the period, Qantas was beginning to use offshore operations as a new way of reducing costs, an approach that was vehemently opposed by its local unions. Nevertheless, the vast majority of Qantas staff (approximately 85 per cent) were shareholders, reflecting an alignment of interests between employees and shareholders.

Overall, in terms of the winning wheel framework, Qantas has been concerned with looking out, adapting rapidly, managing the downside, perfect alignment and balancing everything in order to achieve effective execution. It has been rebalancing its operations to ensure that shareholders make a return (compared with losses for most other airline shareholders), but at prices that customers can afford (with customers showing every sign of favouring lower costs over higher quality). Customers who were used to high domestic quality on Qantas have not been happy during these five years, but this is a natural consequence of the rebalancing that is occurring. Staff are also less happy as they face outsourcing, overseas sourcing and less generous conditions, but these changes have been necessary as Qantas gets its costs down to be competitive with lower cost airlines. Qantas has executed extremely well and, by developing Jetstar, is well placed whether the industry continues down the path of low-cost preference or returns to quality. In this respect, it is in a very unusual position.

Rio Tinto

During the period 2001–06, Rio Tinto consolidated its strategic position as one of the very few truly global exploration, mining and refining companies. Indeed, it is one of the top two in the world. It focused on developing 'first class orebodies into large, long life and efficient operations, capable of sustaining competitive advantage through business cycles' ('The way we work', p.2). Rio Tinto only undertook downstream processing when that contributed to its sustainable competitive advantage. It also emphasises sustainable development as a key part of its operating philosophy, an area that increased in emphasis over the period.

Effectively, Rio Tinto continued with the strategy it had been following at the end of our previous research period. It operated in iron ore, aluminium, copper, diamonds, energy and industrial minerals. Its long-term perspectives were reflected in:

▶ the opening of the Hail Creek coking coal mine, which it had discovered over 30 years earlier

- its commercialisation of the HIsmelt iron ore smelting plant in 2005 after over 20 years of research and development
- its recognition in 2001 and 2002 by the Dow Jones Sustainability Index as the sustainability leader in basic resources sector
- its decision not to mine uranium in the Jabiluka area, which is on Aboriginal land adjacent to a World Heritage-listed national park
- its focus on long-term customer relationships in export markets— 40 years in the case of Japan and more than 30 years in China.

For Rio Tinto, 2001–06 was marked by a major upturn in commodities prices, which resulted in rapidly rising profits and share price, particularly during 2004–06. For Rio Tinto, these five years were a period when it was able to reap the benefits of the long cycle of its industries and it did extremely well. The organisation grew at double the rate of the mining industry as a whole and outperformed the industry in terms of shareholder return over the period.

Rio Tinto introduced an important corporate program, 'Improving Performance Together', aimed at ensuring best practice flowed across all its units (learning from the best within Rio Tinto) and for a 'one Rio' consistent global company, to consolidate the global strategy that had been in full swing for over five years. Its financial performance for 2001–06 is shown in table 13.7.

Table 13.7: Rio Tinto's financial performance, 2001–06

Year	Sales growth (%)	Profit after tax growth (%)	Return on equity (%)	Total shareholder return (%)
2001	5	–28	15	30
2002	7	–40	9	–6
2003	9	132	15	13
2004	20	119	28	8
2005	43	58	35	80
2006	NA	NA	NA	17*

*Ten months to 31 October 2006.

At the end of the period, Rio Tinto was one of the world's largest global miners. Its practices are consistent with all the winning wheel elements—in particular, clear strategy; effective execution; looking out, looking in; managing the downside; and perfect alignment. Its financial success depends on commodity prices, which fluctuate wildly over time, but, because its focus is on low-cost mines and long-term contracts, it is always likely to be well placed. Rio Tinto is also a global leader in sustainable development, another emerging issue for the future.

The Salvation Army

The two Australian 'territories' of the Salvation Army are part of a global organisation that combines an evangelical Christian church with extensive social services. The Salvation Army as a whole operates in 106 countries. The Southern Territory operation in Australia had 6500 people working for it in 2006, of whom 600 were officers.

The Salvation Army underwent significant change between 2001 and 2006. As a church, it suffered from the secularisation of society, along with all other formal, established churches in Australia. Despite this, its 'brand' as a charity was one of the most highly regarded in the country and the Australian territories of the Salvation Army were regarded as two of the best in the world.

Its greatest growth during the period came from a rapid expansion of its retail Family Stores (renamed Salvo's Stores in 2006), which grew from 112 stores in 2001 to 175 in 2005, with planned growth to 250 stores by 2010. These stores take donated goods and resell them via a retail network, at cheap prices designed to be affordable for needy families.

Its other major area of expansion was in employment services. When the federal government outsourced management of unemployed people, the Salvation Army already had some operations in this area and it won major contracts with the government, trading as Employment Plus.

The Bali bombings in 2002 and 2005, and the Asian tsunami in 2005 were significant, unexpected events to which the Salvation Army made major contributions. Internationally, due to having churches and programs in the areas, it had 5000 people on the ground for the tsunami and was able to respond immediately. The development in 2004 of a Problem Gambling Centre in Sydney was another new initiative, although this was a planned one. It was the first of its kind in Australia, typically reflecting the Salvation Army's early recognition of a difficult new problem in the community and finding a practical solution for it.

During the five-year period, the Salvation Army continued to maintain low administration costs, of only 11.5 to 13 cents in the dollar being incurred. This measure became a key way in which charities competed for donations, as people wanted to maximise the percentage of their donation that actually ended up with the beneficiaries of the charity.

During the period, the Salvation Army spent considerable time changing operation processes to improve efficiencies and established an organisation-wide 'Future Now' program to address this. For instance, it outsourced a number of operations, developed integrated web operations and improved its information technology capabilities. It also sold its printing operations in Melbourne in 2004, which it had maintained for over 100 years. The operations were no longer viable in a highly competitive environment.

Financially, 2001–06 was not good for the Salvation Army, as it was deluged by requests for assistance. Its financial performance is shown in table 13.8. A loss of $4.8 million in 2004 forced the organisation to cut social programs and services. The biggest strategic decision made was the decision to sell 15 of its 19 aged-care homes in 2005, in the face of increasing regulatory demands, longer living, higher technology costs, government subsidies not keeping pace with costs and the development of standardised models by larger, more commercially oriented operators. Interestingly, the Army was able to maintain its pastoral care role in the accommodation even after the sale.

Table 13.8: the Salvation Army's financial performance, 2001–06

Year	Sales growth (%)	Profit after tax growth (%)
2001	15	−1
2002	21	−74
2003	5	132
2004	11	119
2005	12	58
2006	NA	NA

At the end of the period, the Salvation Army remained a very highly regarded organisation, but one facing significant challenges as the need of underprivileged members of the community for social services far outweighs the sources of support that are available. It has struggled as a church to remain relevant (looking out, looking in), yet its social relevance is its very strength as a charity. The Salvation Army continues to adapt rapidly, effectively execute and balance everything.

Telstra

Telstra experienced a tumultuous period from 2001 to 2006, partly due to industry changes, partly due to its own strategy and implementation, and partly due to the conflicted position of its 51 per cent owner, the Australian Government, which wanted large returns as owner, high-quality, reasonably priced community services for its voters and also to sell the company!

During the period, Telstra's strategy changed markedly. Telstra initially sought to take advantage of the rapid growth of the international market. It saw this as a way to use its technological capability, to match international competition consolidation and also as a way to escape from the influence of local regulatory issues. Its strategy was around a 'full-service integrated model' of telecommunications, offering all services to its domestic market, with international growth.

Telstra had already expanded internationally into Hong Kong and New Zealand in 2000 via acquisition and joint venture (the start of the international experiment stage of its strategic cycle). In 2002 it acquired the rest of CSL, a mobile operator in Hong Kong, CLEAR in New Zealand, and Level3 Communications in Hong Kong. However, these operations did not bring the expected success. In essence, Telstra failed to develop a significant or profitable international presence and, while maintaining its Hong Kong and New Zealand operations, it has not pushed further in this direction.

In 2003, as it refocused on Australia, its strategy became 'Australia's connection to the future, to develop, design and deliver communications solutions to every customer'. This also indicated a change in strategy from telecommunications to 'communications solutions'. For example, its:

- rebranding of White Pages directories as Sensis—one of the major profit drivers of Telstra through the period
- restructuring in 2002 of payTV joint venture Foxtel, such that it finally reached profitability in 2006
- increase in importance of internet business Bigpond, which was raised to a division in 2005
- acquisitions in 2005 of KAZ information technology consulting services and Damovo, a small business systems telecommunications franchise
- acquisition of the *Trading Post* in 2004, a classified advertisements newspaper

- proposed attempt to purchase Fairfax, a major national newspaper chain, in early 2004
- 3G joint venture with competitor Hutchinson Telecommunications in 2003.

Between 2001 and 2006, Telstra's board of directors became increasingly independent of government opinion. In July 2005, it sacked CEO Ziggy Switkowski and appointed Sol Trujillo, a US executive with international telco industry experience in the US and Europe, including as a CEO, but an outsider to Telstra. Trujillo rapidly undertook a wide structural, cultural and strategic review. He brought in a group of mainly US executives who had worked with him previously. They spoke very frankly and aggressively about Telstra's position, what Telstra needed from the government and how the government was not helping Telstra to deliver what the government, as customer, wanted. This was unheard-of rhetoric from a government-owned organisation, but quite normal for a CEO of a major listed company! This approach is consistent with US culture and the 'challenge' approach to leadership, but not with the 'cause'-based captain-coach leadership style of Australian organisations. As well, Telstra had again gone outside for its new leadership, which is also inconsistent with winning organisation practice.

Under Trujillo, Telstra developed a vision, mission and 'cultural priorities' statement in 2006. The mission was:

> to do for customers what no one else has done: create a world of 1 click, 1 touch, 1 button, 1 screen, 1 step solutions that are simple, easy and valued by individuals, businesses, enterprises and government.

Telstra now saw itself as a telecommunications and information solutions company, though it would seem that the new mission resembles a US-style BHAG, as Telstra's—and the industry's—operations are so far from achieving this set of objectives.

The period was dominated by Telstra's difficult ownership and dominant market power positions. On the one hand, the federal government wanted Telstra to deliver high financial returns, but on the other expected it to continue to provide universal high coverage to vast uneconomic geographic areas at low prices to (voting and lobbying) customers.

As well, the government was committed to 'T3'—the sale of the third and last part (51 per cent) of Telstra. However, other political parties, who wanted Telstra to remain in public ownership, opposed this and as the Opposition parties controlled the Senate, it seemed

Telstra could not be sold, regardless of the government's wishes. The general public, too, were not in favour of the sale of Telstra, fearing it would lead to less service and higher prices without government control. On the other hand, Telstra management supported Telstra's complete privatisation, so that it could have more control of the organisation. In 2005, the government unexpectedly gained control of the Senate and the full sale of Telstra suddenly appeared politically possible. Throughout the period the discussion had been around what might happen if Telstra was sold. By November 2006, the government had completed the sale of its 51 per cent share in Telstra—34 per cent to retail and institutional investors, and 17 per cent to a government-controlled Future Fund.

Telstra also took an increasingly antagonistic and hard-line approach to the industry regulator, the Australian Competition and Consumer Commission (ACCC). It refused to compromise with the ACCC or with competitors that needed access to its monopoly fixed-line network and was involved in a series of legal cases, mostly as defendant. Its competitors and the regulator believed Telstra to be charging prices that were not justified and that made competition extremely difficult. It was also forced to set up the Country Wide division to address continued complaints of slow regional access and poor service levels.

Despite its poor public image, Telstra's accounting returns were extremely high during the period. Growth fell, however, as its main product, phone calls on the fixed-line network, were replaced by a more competitive mobile market that was also becoming cheaper due to technology developments. Its total shareholder return was poor during the period, particularly after Trujillo was appointed—the share price fell from $5.06 to around $3.50, a fall of 30 per cent. Some attributed this to Trujillo's approach, while others claimed it simply meant that the true value of Telstra was now being appreciated as the conflicted government position became obvious. Telstra's financial performance for 2001–06 is shown in table 13.9 (overleaf).

At the end of the period, Telstra's position was turbulent. It appeared to be 'unbalanced' (in 'balance everything' terms). It had just become privately controlled, albeit at a much lower price than the government had originally expected, potentially resolving the ownership conflict. However, Telstra's antagonism to the government, to its industry competitors, to the regulator, to some of its major customers (not looking out, not managing the downside) and its brash new external US-style management, challenge-style leadership, rather than captain-coach style, means that it is not well regarded in the community, despite its significant cash flows, extensive community relations programs and emergency service role. On the other hand, the first operational fruits of Trujillo's period were beginning to appear and the share price had increased significantly since the sale. The situation appeared unstable and might expect to be resolved significantly in the near future, though the direction of the resolution is less clear.

Table 13.9: Telstra's financial performance, 2001–06

Year	Sales growth (%)	Profit after tax growth (%)	Return on equity (%)	Total shareholder return (%)
2001	16	10	30	−13
2002	−9	−10	26	−16
2003	4	−6	22	15
2004	−2	20	27	7
2005	7	8	30	−15
2006	3	−26	25	11*

*Ten months to 31 October 2006.

Westfield

Westfield largely sailed through the period 2001–06 doing 'more of the same'. It remained almost entirely focused on shopping centre acquisition and, most importantly, redevelopment of its existing 120 centres. During this time it continued to concentrate on only three other countries—New Zealand (11 centres); the United States (59 centres), where it became by acquisition the largest shopping centre owner; and the United Kingdom (seven centres), which it had entered in 2000 and where it was rapidly expanding its presence. As a result, Westfield became the largest listed retail property group in the world.

During the five-year period it moved from friendly acquisitions to a number of hostile acquisition bids, but it was never rushed to make a deal in such cases and sometimes walked away. It frequently buys an interest in a portfolio, then subsequently acquires more or the rest over time.

Prior to 2004, Westfield had argued that having separate listed organisations for the individual focuses of developer, manager and shopping centre owner allowed each organisation to specialise in what it did well, without compromise. However, in 2004, following the trend set by other major property developers and following its failure to raise sufficient funds by itself to make a major international acquisition, Westfield decided to merge its three listed entities—Westfield Holdings (developer and manager), Westfield Trust (the real estate owner of its Australian, New Zealand and UK shopping centres) and Westfield America Trust (the real estate owner of its US shopping centres). Westfield argued this was to enable it to access the finances needed for larger international acquisitions.

While the merger was supported by shareholders and the combined company has done well in accounting terms since, Westfield's run of 44 consecutive years of profit increases came to an end, due to a write-down on the acquisitions. Its financial performance for 2001–06 is shown in table 13.10.

Table 13.10: Westfield's financial performance, 2001–06

Year	Sales growth (%)	Profit after tax growth (%)	Return on equity (%)	Total shareholder return (%)
2001	−11	14		27
2002	−14	38	16	−19
2003	16	23	18	7
2004	18	201	8	20
2005	54	420	29	15
2006	NA	NA	NA	7*

*Ten months to 31 October 2006.

The Lowy family continued to dominate the senior management roles throughout the period, with Frank Lowy's sons Peter and Steven both managing directors of the Westfield Group. David left public company management but became non-executive deputy chairman of Westfield Holdings Ltd. Frank Lowy remained chairman and public figurehead. In 2003 he established the Lowy Institute for International Policy, a research institute in international policy and development. Privately, Frank Lowy became chairman of the failing Soccer Federation of Australia in 2005. Within a year he had led the redevelopment of it as Football Federation Australia, had recreated the national soccer competition as the A-League, had hired wizard Dutch coach Guus Hiddink to successfully steer Australia into the World Cup for the first time in 32 years and had bought control of Sydney Football Club, which became A-League champion in the first year. Not bad for a person of 75 years!

Overall, Westfield continued to exhibit all the characteristics of the winning wheel that had enabled it to be selected in the First XI and seemed well placed to continue to expand in the future.

Woolworths

Like Westfield, Woolworths was a star performer during the period 2001–06. CEO Roger Corbett became a media leadership 'star' as Woolworths was widely admired for the way it outperformed close rival Coles Myer throughout the period.

Woolworths developed a mission statement during the period: 'To deliver a better shopping experience—each and every time'. This confirms the 'cause' that Woolworths had developed and operated for many years, which we highlighted in the first edition. It planned to deliver this experience by its 'passion for retail, attention to detail, working hard ... focused on continuously refreshing and improving our business and our people'—all elements we identified in the winning wheel as critical for First XI winning organisations.

Perhaps the biggest and most influential activity for Woolworths during the period was the launching of 'Project Refresh' in 2000—an internal continuous improvement process originally centred on supermarket operations (to revitalise the 'Fresh Food People' campaign begun in the late 1980s). It was seen as a long-term development process with huge cost-savings aims (perfect alignment). These aims have been beaten each year (effective execution). For instance, in 2000, the expected annual savings were $110 million within three years; however, between 2000 and 2006, the cumulative savings were $3.6 billion. The majority of these savings are passed on to the customer, with the remainder allocated to shareholders—and Woolworths has more employee shareholders than any other company in Australia! This aligns employee and shareholder rewards. Over the period, Project Refresh has also turned into a supply chain management project. In 2006, Woolworths expected that the cumulative savings by 2008 would be $8 billion, representing 3.8 per cent of sales.

Woolworths also developed petrol retailing during the five-year period, transforming the petrol retailing industry (a clear and fuzzy strategy move away from food). It first entered the industry in Dubbo in 1996, but grew little until 2003. By 2005 it had expanded to 456 stations, including the Woolworths/Caltex alliance sites. Its success had been copied by rival Coles Myer, which formed an alliance with Shell, so that together they obtained over 50 per cent of the petrol sales in Australia.

In addition, Woolworths continued its process of transforming the liquor industry (further clear and fuzzy strategy). It had acquired Dan Murphy liquor stores (a large-scale, low-cost, high-volume, wide-range Victorian retailer) in 1998. After minor acquisitions in Sydney, Adelaide and Perth in 2000 and the national rollout of the Dan Murphy name and concept, it acquired Queensland's Australian Leisure and Hospitality (ALH) hotel chain in 2005 as a means to gain liquor distribution in Queensland. In so doing, it developed a national supermarket-style liquor retail operation. Once again, this move was copied by Coles Myer, which sought to develop its own competing chains, a recognition of Woolworths' success. Less well understood was the hotel acquisitions, which brought with them a large number of gaming machines, such that Woolworths was effectively a major player in the gaming industry by the end of the period.

Woolworths also acquired 67 Franklins supermarket stores and Tandy electrical stores in 2001, and Foodland supermarkets (mainly in New Zealand) in 2005. In that same year, it pushed the government to allow it to enter the retail pharmaceutical industry to break the pharmacists' monopoly five-year agreements with the government (clear and fuzzy strategy again), but was unsuccessful.

Internally, the company also spent a great deal of time on training and development. It formed the Woolworths Academy with the Macquarie Graduate School of Management in 2004 and employed and enrolled 1100 school-based trainees (right people, leadership not leaders).

In 2005, it formed the Woolworths Australian Communities Foundation as a platform for community-based support (looking out) and began to look further offshore, forming a relationship with India's Tata Group to develop consumer electronics stores in India, beginning in 2006 (international experiment).

By 2006, 35 000 of Woolworths' 145 000 people were shareholders, clearly a vote of confidence in the company, aligning people and shareholder perspectives. Its financial performance over the period was simply outstanding and, as indicated above, it had been developing in all respects according to a balanced approach to the organisation. The only issue was that, during the period 2003–06, it lost four ACCC cases, being found to have pressured competitors or suppliers unfairly, which is inconsistent with its stated values of 'Integrity: we're proud of our record of doing the right thing'. However, some of these cases were from some time in the past and Woolworths did change its practices following each case to ensure those practices are not repeated (admit mistakes). Woolworths' financial performance for 2001–06 is shown in table 13.11.

Table 13.11: Woolworths' financial performance, 2001–06

Year	Sales growth (%)	Profit after tax growth (%)	Return on equity (%)	Total shareholder return (%)
2001	10	18	46	37
2002	17	22	42	4
2003	8	16	49	7
2004	6	13	47	32
2005	12	15	37	16
2006	20	26	29	26*

*Ten months to 31 October 2006.

Overall, by 2006 Woolworths was widely regarded by the investment community as one of Australia's best-performing companies. Woolworths appears to use and align all the elements of the winning wheel. Profits have grown every year except one since 1993 and earnings have doubled approximately every five years. The dividend is expected to grow by at least 10 per cent every year. The appointment in September 2006 of long-term employee and previous manager of Project Refresh and Big W, Mike Luscombe as CEO, with a four-month transition period working with Roger Corbett, suggests that Woolworths will continue in the same vein.

Summary: where are they now?

Perhaps not surprisingly, the picture of the First XI organisations is more mixed over the five-year period 2001–06, than over the 20-year period we used to prove their worth. Keep in mind, however, that although all winning organisations make mistakes, they do recover from them quickly.

Macquarie Bank, Rio Tinto, Woolworths, Westfield and Qantas have done extremely well during the period and have largely continued with all aspects of their operations and strategy. Qantas is perhaps the exception. It operates in a difficult industry, where it appears that the global business model of success is changing from that of full-service, high-cost airlines to low-cost airlines. Qantas' ability to acquire Impulse (and retain it successfully as part of Qantaslink), develop Jetstar domestically and internationally, experiment with Australian Airlines, remain profitable throughout a horrific period while coping with huge increases in the costs of security and fuel, and balancing of competing and conflicting stakeholder needs, reflects great organisation management.

Harvey Norman and Telstra have done very well in accounting terms, but their share prices have not shown the growth of the others. In each case, it seems likely that, if the uncertainty around a firm's strategic direction and implementation can be resolved, the underlying operating and financial results are strong and this should eventually be reflected in the share price. In Telstra's case, however, the global share price performance of telecommunications businesses has been well below average over the period. Although Harvey Norman's share price has performed poorly, it has cemented its place in the Australian retail industry as the innovative leader. Moreover, Telstra has many good activities and people, but at the time of writing it is at odds with many of its stakeholders, a position it must correct to remain a winning organisation.

The Salvation Army continues to have a great reputation as an operational deliverer of efficient and effective welfare and it is always listened to. Financially it has found the going harder, but this is mainly due to the demands on it rather than its own operations. The main challenge it faces is remaining relevant as more and more professional organisations move into the not-for-profit sector.

Brambles, Lend Lease and National Australia Bank experienced major setbacks between 2001 and 2006. Notably, all three described themselves as 'global' organisations with global strategies, but two of them came unstuck through an inability to organise and implement this global strategy. This suggests that implementing a global strategy is extremely difficult and should be approached with great caution. However, all recovered during the period—evidence of their ability to make rapid turnarounds and recover from even major errors. Had we taken a 20-year view, the events in this five-year period would have less significance, unless they were repeated. We conclude, therefore, that our First XI team, while making some significant but not fatal mistakes, has continued to manage as winning organisations.

Remember, however, that this book is about principles and practices of winning organisations more than the specific organisations. Were we to choose 11 winning organisations in 2006, only half of the original team would likely be included, but this would be true of any top national team over a five-year period. There would be new players in the team from a broad range of industry sectors—including the public sector. Nevertheless, the original First XI continue to perform at very high levels and to demonstrate most of the winning principles and practices most of the time. Five years on, they remain worthy of the title 'winning organisations'.

Emerging issues

In the course of our analysis of the period 2001–06, we found several issues had emerged that were different from those in our previous analysis. They were:

- ▶ corporate-wide continuous improvement or change programs
- ▶ sustainable development
- ▶ corporate governance processes.

These issues can be integrated into the winning wheel framework, but we think they are useful to highlight in their own right, as they reflect the emergence of some significant changes in organisation practice. Not all of the First XI organisations included these issues as a major part of their activities or thinking, but enough did to suggest that these are important trends for winning organisations in the future.

Corporate-wide change programs

Many of the winning organisations referred publicly to their corporate-wide change programs, indicating that they believe these are important activities. A feature of the corporate-wide change programs is that they have 'names', as a way to give them a focus, to better communicate them across the organisation as significant integrated activities that have wide impact and to provide an opportunity for individuals to align to the corporate goals. They are also expected to run for some years, making them strategically important.

Corporate-wide change programs are not new. Nevertheless, this process of naming them, reporting them publicly and giving them external significance is new. Organisations design change programs

The First XI: where are they now?

that are customised to the particular needs of that organisation. Some of the programs undertaken by the First XI during 2001–06 are shown in illustration 13.1.

Illustration 13.1: corporate-wide change programs in the winning organisations

Brambles:

- CommunityReach—designed to support its employees in their charitable activities (2002).
- Brambles Value Added (BVA rather than the conventional Economic Value Added)—designed to focus on creating economic value, rather than accounting profit (2003).
- CARE (consistency, accuracy, reliability, efficiency)—designed to focus on system alignment, consistency and costs (2003).
- Perfect Order—designed to develop system alignment and consistency within the Recall business (2003).
- Perfect Trip (CHEP)—designed to develop system alignment and consistency within the CHEP business (2004).
- Clean Run (Cleanaway)—designed to develop system alignment and consistency within the Cleanaway business (2004).
- Impact (Group)—continuous improvement through Six Sigma and lean process methodologies (2005).

Qantas:

- Sustainable Future—designed to reduce operating costs by $1.5 billion over two years and prepare Qantas for future challenges by striving to become the industry leader in all facets of the business (2003). It was upgraded in 2006 to saving $3 billion by 2008.
- Sharing the Spirit—designed to bring the Australian people together during the Olympics period, but has continued since to represent the ways in which Qantas assists many groups in its communities (2004).
- Be Safe—designed to prevent injuries (2003).

National Australia Bank:

- Positioning for Growth—designed to restructure the organisation, cut costs and improve productivity through the use of new information technology systems (2002).

> **Illustration 13.1 *(cont'd)*: corporate-wide change programs in the winning organisations**
>
> **Rio Tinto:**
>
> - Improving Performance Together—designed to create value through capital efficiency, higher volumes, higher revenues and improved productivity, leading to lower costs and operational excellence (2004).
>
> **The Salvation Army:**
>
> - Future Now—designed to translate the broader reasons for the Salvos' existence into day-to-day activities (2003).
>
> **Telstra:**
>
> - Six Sigma—a methodology designed to improve operating processes (2003).
> - The Transition—designed to reposition Telstra as one of the leading telecommunications companies in the world (2006).
>
> **Woolworths:**
>
> - Project Refresh—designed as a continuous-improvement program covering all aspects of supermarket operations (2000). Extended to cover information technology, human resources, organisational redesign and the cost of doing business.
> - Project Refresh Level II—designed to focus on supply chain improvement for expanded operations (2003); the two programs together aim to save costs of $8 billion by 2008.

These programs suggest this is now a widespread way of addressing corporate-wide improvements, particularly in efficiencies, cost savings and in trying to energise people in the organisation to align to a higher goal. We expect to see more of these programs in organisations in the future.

Sustainable development

Over the five-year period, organisational reporting moved from the balanced scorecard approach that we adopted, to begin to include examination of the impact of organisations on the wider environment. This has led to major organisations beginning to consider the 'sustainability' of their operations.

'Sustainability' may be defined as the way an organisation meets the needs of its stakeholders without compromising its ability also to meet their needs in the future (Hockerts, 1999). It includes social aspects of the organisation's activities (for example, effects on local communities, countries, governments, suppliers, employees and their families), as well as the more publicised environmental effects (for example, water, energy, emissions, waste, biodiversity). Sustainability is emerging in the 2000s as the next component of the stakeholder model of an organisation, a model that already includes customers, employees, suppliers and shareholders. 'Sustainability' does not mean the sustained growth of the profits or sales of the organisation, as the term is sometimes used.

Not surprisingly, some of the winning organisations are leaders in the area of sustainability reporting, which is clearly going to be the way of thinking in the future. Rio Tinto has been a leader in this area for some time, partly because resources organisations are at the forefront of environmental effects. Rio Tinto executives regard sustainability as 'embedded' in the organisation's DNA, as part of its emphasis on 'The way we work' principles, which have existed for many years. During the period 2001–06, Rio Tinto made several major changes to its processes of handling sustainability issues. It:

▶ added environmental performance to the reward system (2002)

▶ aligned its business with the principles of sustainable development (2002)

▶ appointed cross-functional teams to implement a sustainable development framework appropriate to local circumstances (2003)

▶ supported over 2000 socioeconomic programs covering health, education, agriculture and business development (2004)

▶ stated that it can make an important contribution to the economic prosperity and social wellbeing of its host societies and the stewardship of the environment (2005)

▶ started reporting against the Global Reporting Initiative checklist (a global triple-bottom-line framework) (2005).

Summarising its progress and position in 2005, the chairman stated in the annual report:

> a key part of the strategy is to make social and environmental responsibility integral to our planning and decision making. We

> always seek to align our interests with those of the communities and environments where our operations are based. Rio Tinto regards corporate social responsibility as a vital determinant of commercial success...we remain committed to the principles of sustainable development. We see a clear responsibility to help to address the challenges posed by climate change, to manage issues related to biodiversity and to maintain effective product stewardship across the value chain of our products. I believe Rio Tinto has become a leader in our industry in these areas but we still have some way to go.

Brambles is another organisation that significantly changed its approach to sustainable development. This is of particular note, since Brambles is an industrial services firm rather than a manufacturer. It:

- ▶ made environmental reporting a major issue (2001)
- ▶ revised its policy and raised its standards, seeing legal compliance as the minimum standard, with the expectation that each business would seek to achieve industry-best environmental practice and minimum waste generation (2002).

Lend Lease has always been at the high-quality end of property development. For some years it has focused on establishing sustainable and ecologically desirable building practices and, like Rio Tinto, Lend Lease executives consider sustainability to be embedded in its normal way of working, via the 'community of interests' and 'sustainable communities' approaches that are part of its philosophy. During the period, Lend Lease:

- ▶ developed its new Sydney head office as a five-star greenhouse office building, which emits 30 per cent less carbon dioxide than a typical office building (2004)
- ▶ developed a specific sustainability 'vision': 'Our vision is to be a sustainable organisation' (2005)
- ▶ developed a 'sustainability covenant' with the Environmental Protection Authority, declaring both will work together to protect and contribute to a more sustainable environment (2005).

Qantas was working on its first sustainability report, which was expected to be released in late 2006. Qantas believes that it includes sustainability thinking in its normal ways of operating, but it had not formalised this at the time of writing, except for the development of a group environment policy.

The First XI: where are they now?

Woolworths has also joined this trend. In 2000, Woolworths announced that it was committed to pursuing best environment practice, particularly through waste minimisation and recycling programs. In 2005, it produced its first sustainability report.

Westfield has begun a pilot experiment in sustainability. At the Sydney Central Plaza international food court, it started a program involving retailer training, and workshops to reduce water and energy use, transport costs and waste management, as well as focusing on the social issues of staff satisfaction and productivity. This program will also be part of its new Sydney CBD development linking Centrepoint, Imperial Arcade and Skygarden where a 25 per cent reduction in energy and water usage is targeted.

The Salvation Army's whole 'cause' is about sustainability — of the family and the individual. We should note that, in our interview at head office, if no-one moved in the room for a short period of time, the lights went off, to be reactivated when movement occurred!

In the 'social' area of sustainability, most of the First XI have developed foundations to donate money and resources back to community organisations and activities. For instance:

▶ Macquarie Bank formed the Macquarie Bank Foundation in 1984. In 2006 it contributed over $11 million to over 500 organisations worldwide. The foundation funds a diverse set of community needs in the areas of health, welfare, education, the arts and the environment.

▶ Qantas developed Sharing the Spirit as a way to cover the wide range of sponsorships and community support that it provides. It covers the arts, community, sports, youth, environment and charity donations. In 2006 Qantas began a 'Workplace Giving' program for its employees. Many employee groups develop their own charitable activities, donating their time and providing hands-on assistance.

▶ Telstra is one of the largest corporate sponsors in Australia via the Telstra Foundation, sponsoring sport, business, arts, health and community initiatives.

▶ Westfield started the Lowy Institute in 2003 to contribute to national policy debate. Westfield also contributes significantly in areas around its shopping centres, but it has not developed a foundation as such.

▶ Woolworths developed the Woolworths Australian Communities Foundation in 2004, which is focused on children, rural and regional Australia, education and employment, and grassroots giving.

These mostly new examples of environmental and social sustainability programs indicate that winning organisations are involved in this fundamental change to business practices and we can expect to see more focus given to this by winning organisations in the near future.

Corporate governance processes

Due to the large corporate crashes in the early 2000s of organisations such as Enron, Worldcom and others in the US, and of HIH, One.Tel and Westpoint in Australia, the issue of corporate governance processes has become prominent. As a result, organisations are now expected to have clear, transparent and equitable practices for their corporate decision making. All groups interested in the organisation—current investors, potential investors and stakeholders affected by the practices of the organisation—not just the incumbent management and board of directors, who generally control the voting process for the board of directors and the appointment of senior managers, need to be able to understand corporate governance practices. This will allow them to make decisions about their involvement in the organisation with much better knowledge of how it operates and allow them to see that reasonable governance practices are being followed.

In the US, the Sarbanes-Oxley Act, which was passed in 2002 following a series of high-profile organisation failures and scandals, requires members of the board of directors to take personal liability for the reported results of their organisations. In Australia, while there has not been a similar change in government legislation, the stock exchanges have required changes in governance practices for listed companies, focusing in particular on:

▶ the make-up of the board, requiring a majority of non-executives

▶ having separate chair and CEO roles

▶ separating the remuneration and audit committees from executive control

▶ providing information on executive compensation programs, with a non-binding vote on executive compensation for listed organisations now required at the annual general meeting.

Transparent and equitable corporate governance is an issue that has a wide impact and it is not an issue in which the winning organisations have particularly led. Indeed, Harvey Norman and Westfield have both been outspoken in their opposition to some of the ideas, arguing that committed executives who know the business are better placed to make business decisions than part-time board members with little or no knowledge. Further, in some of the collapsed or poorly performing organisations all the new corporate governance requirements would have been met, yet the organisation still collapsed or continues to perform poorly. Research evidence also shows little or no relationship between corporate governance structures and corporate performance outcomes.

While it is clear that corporate governance is an important issue for winning organisations (as part of looking out, perfect alignment, leadership not leaders), at the time of writing there is much focus on the 'form' and 'structure' of this issue, rather than on what really matters—that is, behaviour, attitudes and outcomes (elements of effective execution). We see this as a typical example of focusing on the wrong issue. Therefore, while the form and structure of corporate governance receives a great deal of prominence, winning organisations do not regard this as an issue of critical importance to performance, and hence have no consistent position on it.

Summary and messages for leaders

Individually, the winning organisations faced a wide variety of different circumstances between 2001 and 2006. The results of this show that performance over a five-year period is too short to assess long-term winning, but our assessment of the individual organisations suggests all are still worthy of the title, despite some of them having made major mistakes during the period.

We have also seen the development of some emerging issues that were not present in our original analysis. The issues of corporate-change programs, of environmental and social sustainability and of transparent corporate governance processes are particularly consistent with the winning wheel element of 'looking out, looking in' and are rapidly adapted to by winning organisations.

The key messages for leaders are:

- ▶ think about performance in a balanced way over the long term

- adapt rapidly to mistakes
- look outward to ensure you are aware of changing and new trends
- remain balanced.

14 Comparing our findings with other studies

What we have tried to do in this study is to identify some of Australia's winning organisations and, more importantly, the practices that they use—as a group—that seem to be the key reasons for their high performance. By watching and studying the First XI players, we try to understand what they do better than we do. We try to learn from them, to copy their practices and then to better them—so we can get into the First XI ourselves.

In this chapter we try to see how the elements in our winning wheel framework are similar to or different from those elements identified in other major studies. As highlighted in chapter 11, there are context differences in Australia that make operating in this country different, so we would expect some differences in practices for winning organisations here compared with overseas. However, the principles of success seem likely to be very similar across the world—everyone wants to grow, to be profitable, to have happy customers and employees, to have efficient processes and so on. So we would also expect a large degree of similarity in the principles identified.

Throughout the book we have referred to other work that has been done to identify high-performing organisations and the practices that they use. In this chapter we'll compare our findings with theirs in detail. What commonalities exist? What are the differences? And why might this be so?

We focus on the three major holistic, empirical studies that have identified specific organisations as winners—*In Search of Excellence*, *Built to Last* and *Good to Great*. These studies have been well received by senior executives and have had a major impact on the way they operate their organisations. We'll also consider the findings of a wider study of studies of high-performance organisations. Finally, we'll consider how the issues highlighted for 'winning' organisations and the pursuit of success link to the general issues that must be managed in running any organisation.

Other studies of 'winning' organisations

Two US studies were the forerunners and inspirations for our work. Since our research began in 1999, another US study has been published using a similar methodology and been similarly influential in business thinking. The three studies are:

- ▶ *In Search of Excellence* (1982)—Peters and Waterman
- ▶ *Built to Last* (1994)—Collins and Porras
- ▶ *Good to Great* (2001)—Collins.

These studies have each had a major impact on the business community, for several reasons:

- ▶ Their use of business community experience and expertise to identify winning organisations.
- ▶ The use of hard quantitative analysis and rigorous assessment to support intuitive sense.
- ▶ Their findings accord with what experienced business people think and feel makes 'sense' for successful business practice—but that they could not and cannot prove.
- ▶ In identifying specific organisations and their specific practices, they have provided role models to observe and discuss.
- ▶ These role model organisations are well known in the community, so that businesspeople are not dependent simply on what 'experts' say is good practice. They can assess it for themselves.

The first study: *In Search of Excellence*

In Search of Excellence was the first study to seek out winning organisations and identify them and their collective practices. Prior to this, business literature was heavily dependent on individual—and independent—case studies.

In Search of Excellence was initiated because of dissatisfaction at US consulting firm McKinsey & Co. with the 'problems of management effectiveness' in the face of the invasion of Japanese companies competing with what appeared to be a different—and superior—model. At the time, the oil crisis was in full flow and many industries and organisations were struggling to find a model of how to cope with the quite different circumstances they faced—that is, low or negative growth, high inflation, high capital costs and dislocated cost structures. McKinsey set up project teams to consider the issues. The company talked to many people and found that:

> All were uncomfortable with the limitations of the usual structural solutions... skeptical about the usefulness of any known tools, doubting they were up to the task of revitalizing and redirecting billion-dollar-giants. (Peters and Waterman, 1982, p. 4)

The practices that were identified in this seminal study were instrumental in changing US thinking about how to compete. The essentials of the study are provided in illustration 14.1 (overleaf).

This study publicised the now-famous McKinsey 7S technique of analysis as well as the eight key findings. A close look at these key findings and the elements of the 7S would suggest that many of these are still critical for success in current organisations. The study stimulated the 'excellent' consulting industry that, for at least the next 10 years, focused on trying to apply these techniques to organisations that wished to become 'excellent'.

In Search of Excellence has been criticised for focusing too much on high-technology companies, for not making its methodology clear enough and because some of the companies have had trouble since being identified. However, more than 20 years on, it is notable that most of these companies are still going strongly and have remained high performers for long periods. Of the 14 highlighted, 11 were ranked in the top 200 in the Fortune 500 in 2002. This was still the case in 2006, with five in the top 30 and only two disappearing from the list (Bechtel and Digital Equipment). These companies are all well known and generally admired, though each has naturally endured challenges over such a long period. But remember, the aim of these studies is to focus on the *principles* that are being used to achieve success, not just on the organisations.

The key limiting feature has been the purely US focus of the work. Do its findings also apply in other countries? Which are the best organisations in other countries? (The study actually started with wider aims and identified 13 winning European organisations, but it was unable to gather enough information to be confident in its European work, so it abandoned that aspect of the project.)

Illustration 14.1: *In Search of Excellence*

Study Date: 1977 to 1979

Methodology:

Asked an informed group of observers of the business scene to identify good companies.

Limited industries studied, for convenience. Excluded 13 European firms.

Applied six quantitative financial tests for a 20-year period—company had to be in the top half of its industry in at least four of six growth and returns measures over a 20-year period.

Used an expert rating of innovativeness over the 20-year period.

Found 43 companies that passed the tests. Interviewed 21 in depth.

Surveyed 25 years of literature prior to the survey period for each company.

Findings focused on 14 that exemplified the eight traits identified.

Key findings:
- A bias for action.
- (Be) Close to the customer.
- (Foster) Autonomy and entrepreneurship.
- Productivity through people.
- Hands-on, value driven.
- Stick to the knitting.
- Simple (structural) form, lean (head office) staff.
- Simultaneous loose/tight properties (decentralised and centralised).
- 7S model for implementation (strategy, style, staff, skills, shared values, structure and systems).

Excellent companies (top 14 out of 43 in total):
- Bechtel
- Boeing
- Caterpillar Tractor
- Dana
- Delta airlines
- Digital Equipment
- Emerson Electric
- Fluor
- Hewlett-Packard
- IBM
- Johnson & Johnson
- McDonald's
- Procter & Gamble
- 3M

Visionary companies: *Built to Last*

Built to Last was stimulated when two Stanford University academics, Collins and Porras, wanted to explore what was meant by 'vision' and 'visionary companies'. They had two primary objectives:

1. To identify the underlying characteristics and dynamics common to highly visionary companies (and that distinguish them from other companies) and to translate those findings into a useful conceptual framework.

2. To effectively communicate these findings and concepts so that they influence the practice of management and prove beneficial to people who want to help create, build and maintain visionary companies.

(Collins and Porras, 1994, p. 12)

Built to Last has a more 'academic' feel about its research than does *In Search of Excellence*. This study lays out its methodology very clearly at the back of the book, perhaps reflecting the university origins of its researchers. It also has the very strong methodological advantage of using comparison companies, which maximises the chance of focusing on differences, rather than simply 'good' practices. (We were unable to do this in our study as we could not find comparison companies for all of the First XI, due to the thinness of the Australian market.)

Like *In Search of Excellence*, its findings begin with business opinion, but a clearly structured approach was used. The study focused on the complete history of the company, rather than the recent period. There were no interviews with the companies. Illustration 14.2 (overleaf) outlines the essentials of the study. As you consider these findings, you will likely find that many of them are relevant to good practice in your organisation. In 2006, all of these organisations were in the top 300 in the Fortune 500 by size, nine were in the top 50 and all are well known and well regarded.

Like *In Search of Excellence*, *Built to Last* is heavily US-centric, with only one non-US company in the study. There is considerable overlap between the two studies, with 10 of the 17 US companies being in both studies. The overlap would have been greater except that some companies did not qualify for both. For instance, *In Search of Excellence* limited the industries it studied, while *Built to Last* eliminated companies started after 1950.

The *In Search of Excellence* study is not mentioned in *Built to Last* until near the end of the book, where a very brief comparison is made. This is surprising, since the interest and debate generated by the earlier book must certainly have encouraged the research for *Built to Last*.

Illustration 14.2: *Built to Last*

Study Date: 1988 to 1994

Methodology:

Surveyed a representative sample of 700 US CEOs seeking five nominations of organisations that were 'highly visionary'.

Identified the 20 most frequently mentioned.

Eliminated those founded since 1950, reasoning that their 'vision' might be due to a single great idea or a single leader. Left with 18 companies.

Selected a good comparison company for each company.

Studied both firms since their inception to understand their evolution and to understand the difference between the good and the visionary company.

Identified nine key factors.

Key findings:

- Clock building, not time telling (that is, build the organisation, don't focus on what to do with it).
- No 'tyranny of the or'.
- (Success is) More than profits.
- Preserve the core/stimulate progress.
- Big Hairy Audacious Goals (BHAGs).
- Cult-like cultures.
- Try a lot of stuff and keep what works.
- Home-grown management.
- Good enough never is.

Excellent companies:

- American Express
- Boeing
- Citicorp
- Ford
- General Electric*
- Hewlett-Packard*
- IBM*
- Johnson & Johnson*
- Marriott*
- Merck
- Motorola
- Nordstrom
- Philip Morris*
- Proctor & Gamble*
- Sony
- Wal-Mart
- Walt Disney*
- 3M*

(* Also included in the *In Search of Excellence* sample.)

Whereas *In Search of Excellence* was focused on innovative, growing and profitable organisations, *Built to Last* was focused on 'visionary' organisations. These organisations also turned out to be very good stock market performers, though this was not a criterion for choosing them.

A prequel: *Good to Great*

Collins subsequently wrote another book, *Good to Great*, which was triggered by his concern that the 'great' companies in *Built to Last* were always great, that they had not 'improved' from being good performers to being 'great':

> the vast majority of good companies remain just that—good, but not great...Can a good company become a great company and, if so, how? Or is the disease of 'just being good' incurable? (Collins, 2001, p. 3)

Good to Great aimed to address this issue. It was published well after our study was under way. Collins says that this study is essentially a prequel to *Built to Last*, since it identifies companies that had not being doing well but that have been able to turn their performance around. He describes these companies as 'nondescript, even dowdy companies, in unglamorous industries'. Illustration 14.3 (overleaf) outlines the essentials of this study. The findings as described are difficult to understand, so we have 'translated' them (in the brackets associated with each finding).

Good to Great, like our work, also had a list of what *not* to do—managerial myths. These myths included having or relying on:

▶ celebrity leaders

▶ particular (usually variable) managerial reward systems

▶ extra time spent on strategic planning

▶ technology leadership or technology-driven change

▶ mergers and acquisitions

▶ named programs or tag lines to signify corporate transformation programs

▶ being in the right industry.

Collins also says:

> I don't principally think of my (sic) work as about the study of business...Rather, I see my work as being about discovering what creates enduring great *organizations* of *any* type. [Our italics.] (Collins, 2002, p. 15)

Illustration 14.3: *Good to Great*

Study Date: 1996 to 2000

Methodology:
Analysis of Fortune 500 companies from 1965 to 1995.

Looking for companies that had nondescript stock returns for 15 years, followed by at least 15 years in which stock returns outperformed the market by three times.

Sought comparison companies where possible.

Key findings:
- Level 5 leadership (self-effacing, quiet, reserved, shy leadership).
- First who, then what (get the people right first, then decide on strategy).
- (Be committed and) Confront the brutal facts (yet never lose faith).
- The hedgehog concept (focus on one thing that people are passionate about).
- Culture of discipline (disciplined people don't need a hierarchy).
- Technology accelerators (pioneer selected technologies).
- The flywheel and the doom loop (grand restructures and dramatic change programs will not give the leap required—continuous incremental change is needed).

Excellent companies:
- Abbott Laboratories
- Circuit City
- Fannie Mae
- Gillette
- Kimberley-Clark
- Kroger
- Nucor
- Pitney Bowes
- Philip Morris*
- Walgreens
- Wells Fargo

(*Included in both *In Search of Excellence* and *Built to Last*.)

As with *Built to Last*, a key limitation of the study is its US focus. Another limitation in our view is that the approach is quite different from the other two studies, as the sample was chosen by quantitative analysis of stock market returns with no input from executives at the start. Organisations had to have 15 years of 'nondescript' stock market returns followed by 15 years of outperforming the stock market by three times. Hence these organisations are high financial performers over a 15-year period and not necessarily balanced organisations built for long-term success. Not surprisingly, there is only one common organisation between the three studies—Phillip Morris—the other organisations are not particularly well known outside the US. However, Collins' reputation, the focus on the detail of specific, real organisations and the nature of the findings has similarly captured the interest of executives.

Collins' implication is that these organisations have the potential to be the 'great' organisations of the future. In this sense, he regards *Good to Great* as a prequel to *Built to Last*. As with the other studies, the organisations featured here are mostly listed in the top 200 of the Fortune 500, but none are in the top 40, perhaps indicative of the 'good' rather than 'great' nature of the companies.

Good to Great companies may well be of relevance to Australian organisations because, as we have shown, only limited 'vision' was identified in our winning organisations and many organisations are 'good' but not 'great'. Also, the sense of what to do to become great is intuitively quite attractive for an organisation that sees itself as good.

How do our findings on business practices compare with others?

So how do our findings compare with these others on winning business practice? Let's look at how our study compares with the three American works, first individually and then comparing all four studies' findings together.

The First XI versus In Search of Excellence

Table 14.1 (overleaf) shows the findings of *The First XI* and *In Search of Excellence*. The two studies agree on the importance of people, of strategy (having a clear one), of customers and of focusing on execution to deliver results.

Table 14.1: *The First XI* versus *In Search of Excellence*

The First XI	In Search of Excellence
Effective execution	A bias for action
	Hands-on, (value driven)
Perfect alignment	(Hands-on), value driven
Adapt rapidly	Encouraging autonomy and entrepreneurship
Clear and fuzzy strategy	Stick to the knitting
Leadership, not leaders	–
Looking out, looking in	Close to the customer
Right people	Productivity through people
Manage the downside	–
Balance everything	Loose/tight
–	Simple form, lean staff

Strangely, *In Search of Excellence* does not include a chapter on leadership. Instead, the authors include 'style', which meant leadership style, as one of the 7S elements summarising how to implement excellence. We think omitting a chapter on leadership was an oversight, as everything within the study implies that leadership is important. However, there is a strong emphasis on the 'strong, charismatic, dominant leader' as the driver of the organisation, which is different from our findings. Peters and Waterman said:

> We must admit that our bias at the beginning was to discount the role of leadership heavily... Unfortunately what we found was that associated with almost every excellent company was a strong leader (or two) who seemed to have had a lot to do with making the company excellent in the first place. (p. 26)

Our study highlights managing risk and the concept of 'everything' more than *In Search of Excellence* does. Our study also has a wider focus on 'external' than merely the customer concept of *In Search of Excellence*. *In Search of Excellence*, on the other hand, includes a finding about structure (simple form, lean staff), whereas we find structure not to be particularly important (constantly changing and not particularly associated with success). Perhaps this reflects the fact that a trigger for the *In Search of Excellence* study was dissatisfaction with current structural solutions.

Comparing our findings with other studies

Overall, apart from the leadership chapter oversight, there is nothing our findings conflict with in a major way in the *In Search of Excellence* study. There is considerable agreement between the findings. Given the 20 year time difference between the studies, this is itself interesting and encouraging.

The First XI versus *Built to Last*

Table 14.2 compares *The First XI* and *Built to Last*. The studies agree on the role of leadership, a clear and fuzzy strategy, adapting rapidly, balance, alignment and execution.

Table 14.2: *The First XI* versus *Built to Last*

The First XI	Built to Last
Effective execution	Try a lot of stuff and keep what works More than profits
Perfect alignment	Cult-like cultures
Adapt rapidly	Try a lot of stuff and keep what works Good enough never is
Clear and fuzzy strategy	Preserve the core/stimulate progress
Leadership, not leaders	Clock building, not time telling Home-grown management
Looking out, looking in	–
Right people	–
Manage the downside	–
Balance everything	No 'tyranny of the or' More than profits
–	Big Hairy Audacious Goals (BHAGs)

Strangely, *Built to Last* omits the role of people. Yet everything in the study implies the importance of people (for example, 'cult-like culture' and 'home-grown management'). This seems an oversight. On the other hand, it includes BHAGs, which we found to be culturally inappropriate. This is probably because the study was looking for 'visionary' companies, whereas we did not have that specification. Our study includes 'looking out, looking in' and 'manage the downside', which are not covered by *Built to Last*.

Overall, apart from BHAGs and the apparent 'people' oversight, there is a large degree of agreement between the two studies. Our study covers all the issues that *Built to Last* covers and we also include elements that were not covered in that study. Nothing else we found is in conflict with *Built to Last*.

The First XI versus *Good to Great*

Table 14.3 compares *The First XI* and *Good to Great*. The studies agree on the importance of leadership, of people, of strategy, of alignment and of delivering results.

Table 14.3: *The First XI* versus *Good to Great*

The First XI	Good to Great
Effective execution	A culture of discipline
Perfect alignment	The flywheel and the doom loop
Adapt rapidly	Technology accelerators
Clear and fuzzy strategy	The hedgehog concept
	(First who), then what
Leadership, not leaders	Level 5 leadership
Looking out, looking in	Confront the brutal facts
	(yet never lose faith)
Right people	(First who), then what
Manage the downside	–
Balance everything	–

Our study's factors of 'manage the downside', 'looking out', 'adapt rapidly' and 'balance' are not covered by *Good to Great*. In contrast, there is nothing in that study that is not covered by our work, though the role of technology is a specific issue raised that we do not particularly address (but we do agree that technology per se is not critical).

Once again, overall there is little disagreement, though this study highlights fewer and rather unusual factors. This may simply be due to the fact that it is seeking a different type of company (a 'good' company seeking to become a 'great' company) and using a different process from the other three studies. The findings may be more relevant for improving organisations rather than identifying 'winning' ones.

The First XI versus all three studies

While we have done a one-to-one comparison for each major study, comparing all four simultaneously may make it clearer where the differences are.

Table 14.4 (overleaf) shows the findings of all four studies. It shows:

- ▶ The agreement on leadership, on people and on strategy. We would have been shocked if these studies did not have anything to say about these three elements.

- ▶ Agreement around the concepts of adapting rapidly, alignment, balance and execution.

- ▶ Our concept of managing the downside, managing risk, is new, as it is not present in any of the other studies.

- ▶ Our emphasis on 'looking out' rather than simply focusing on customers is a wider external perspective.

- ▶ Anything that is not in our findings is not common across any other two studies, so our work does not appear to have missed any major elements.

A recent summary of studies of high-performance organisation studies

In 2005, Kirby summarised 10 studies of high-performance organisations. Interestingly, the study did not include *Good to Great*—nor did it include our study, probably because all but one of the studies were US-based (the other was Indian)! We cover some of the studies included in this article in appendix B. However, none of them, apart from *In Search of Excellence* or *Built to Last*, used the same methodology of interviewing executives at the companies first and none of the other studies had had any real business impact. Many of the studies have been conducted between 2001 and 2006, further confirming the interest in understanding and learning from high-performing organisations.

Kirby drew a number of conclusions:

- ▶ 'Winning' is long term and must last at least 10 years.

- ▶ 'Winning' in a study depends on the criteria used to define winning.

The First XI

- The criteria for 'winning' vary from study to study, making comparisons of findings difficult.
- Causality is still hard to be confident about—are the factors found in winning organisations the *causes* of success or do organisations that are successful engage in practices as a *result* of that success?

Table 14.4: *The First XI* versus all three studies

The First XI	In Search of Excellence	Built to Last	Good to Great
Effective execution	A bias for action Hands-on (value driven)	Try a lot of stuff and keep what works More than profits	A culture of discipline Confront the brutal facts (yet never lose faith)
Perfect alignment	(Hands-on), value driven	Cult-like cultures	The flywheel and the doom loop
Adapt rapidly	Encouraging autonomy and entrepreneurship	Try a lot of stuff and keep what works Good enough never is	Technology accelerators
Clear and fuzzy strategy	Stick to the knitting	Preserve core/ stimulate progress	The hedgehog concept First who, then what
Leadership, not leaders	–	Clock building, not time telling Home-grown management	Level 5 leadership
Looking out, looking in	Close to the customer	–	Confront the brutal facts (yet never lose the faith)
Right people	Productivity through people	–	First who, then what
Manage the downside	–	–	–
Balance everything	Loose/tight	No 'tyranny of the or' More than profits	–
–	Simple form, lean staff	–	–
–	–	Big Hairy Audacious Goals (BHAGs)	–

Kirby also posed a number of questions:

▶ Do findings from studies of high-performance organisations apply in the future, when the context is changing so rapidly?

▶ How variable are findings for different cultures, countries and industries?

Despite the concerns she raised, Kirby concluded that the studies are beginning to reinforce each other and that progress towards a full understanding of what constitutes 'winning' is being made. We agree with this. Our work is not perfect, but there is, as yet, no agreed definition of 'winning' or of the 'right' way to find out about it.

More importantly, there are now 25 years of overlapping and reinforcing findings for 'normal' organisations, rather than those seeking a particular form of success in a particular context or industry. Most of the findings are similar. We should focus on the findings and worry less about the methodologies.

Other studies

A variety of other studies have also sought to identify winning practices, but they have not identified the organisations from which these practices are drawn, nor have they identified how those organisations were chosen or what their performance was. See appendix B for details.

'Winning' criteria versus criteria for managing any organisation

Our analysis in this chapter of the three major studies compares those factors that have been found for winning organisations. We should not confuse them with the factors that need to be managed for all organisations.

What the winning wheel framework provides is the issues that differentiate long-term high-performing organisations from their competitors. There are many factors that need to be managed well, but only some of those make the difference between good organisations—those that do most things well—and winning organisations—those that are noted by their peers as being the best organisations.

Figure 14.1 provides some examples of the types of issues that organisations in different situations may have to address. 'Normal' organisations—those that are somewhere between the 'survivor' and 'good performer' classifications in the figure—have to concentrate on doing the basics right. What are the basics? We'd suggest the following:

▶ developing a business strategy that has a clear, but not unique view of what the organisation wants to be

▶ developing most of the capabilities to make that strategy work satisfactorily most of the time

▶ developing functions and systems that are aligned (not perfectly but satisfactorily) and get the job done most of the time

▶ having some idea of how the organisation is performing by possessing a reasonable system of measuring performance.

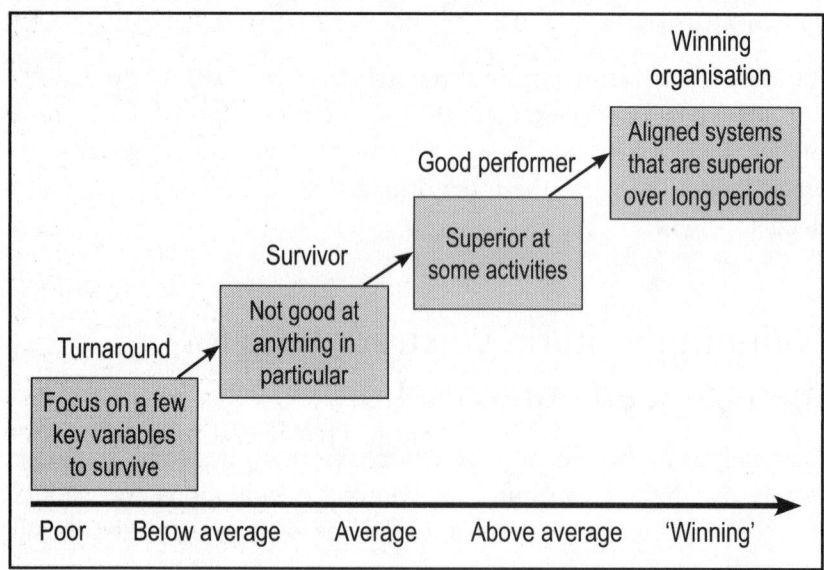

Figure 14.1: issues for organisations at different positions of competence

Most organisations, even at the 'basic' level, will have gaps that they need to address, with lots to be done if the organisation wants to improve. Of course, a 'normal' organisation may not want to improve, in which case those gaps will remain or expand or change, but major gaps will continue to exist.

Winning organisations take all of the above for granted. They have all of these all the time, indicating the higher level of skills, capabilities and competitive advantages they have developed to be high performers. But we don't mention them in this book. We take them for granted. In chapter 15, we'll consider how such a 'normal' organisation might try to move itself up the ladder, to reach First XI levels of competence and performance.

Summary

The elements found across the major studies assessed here have a large degree of consistency. This is not surprising! The elements of running successful organisations are well known for the most part. They just aren't practised, or organisations simply don't want to rise to the levels of winning organisations.

However, our findings, being specifically for the Australian context, build on the others and provide subtle but important variations. Winning organisations in Australia need:

▶ To execute effectively in a disciplined way to deliver the results that they target.

▶ To perfectly align everything they do to their strategy and to do so consistently.

▶ To adapt rapidly over time by trying a lot of things and empowering people to take action.

▶ Clear strategy, which is fuzzy at the edges, to enable them to take advantage of relevant opportunities.

▶ Good leadership, not a good individual leader—leadership that provides a cause for the people to work for.

▶ To be looking out, to be externally focused on the wide world around them.

▶ The right people for the organisation's strategy and values, people who are committed to the organisation and proud to work for it.

▶ To manage the downside risk, to be conservative, to share risk.

▶ To balance everything, using both tight and loose controls.

15 Starting your organisation on a winning journey

This book aims not just to outline the practices of the winning organisations, but also to enable those practices to be emulated by other organisations and, in so doing, improve managerial practice in Australian-based organisations. Reading it, we know you will have said to yourself, 'If only my organisation was like this/did this, we could be a lot more successful'.

Now it's your turn! Your organisation *can* change its practices and become more like a winning organisation. But someone has to get it started. Ideally, this 'someone' would be the leaders or top managers (leadership, not leaders), as they are the ones with the power to make things happen. However, most readers are not the CEOs (there is only one of these in each organisation!). That's not a reason to give up—you can help make this happen:

▶ If you are in the top management team, give the book to the others in the team and start a dialogue with them about it.

▶ If you run a unit of the organisation, start the application of the winning wheel framework for your unit (particularly if you have profit responsibility for that unit, not just expense or revenue responsibility).

It's often much easier to lead by example and there are a lot of things that can be done by a business unit that has high organisational impact with individual and team commitment on a negligible budget. However, to avoid disappointment and frustration managers need to be realistic about what can be achieved in a particular time frame, which is often a reflection of the size of the organisation, current levels of performance and maturity.

So this chapter is different. It is about what *you* can do to get your organisation started on its First XI journey, to try to make it into the first team, the top group (which is, after all, where most people would like to be if they had the chance). In this chapter we'll show you how to make allowance for the level of maturity and size of your organisation, and to allow for its stage in the strategic cycle. We'll then explain—step by step—how you can get started. We'll work through how to achieve quick successes and then work towards the longer term outcomes needed to become a First XI organisation.

The first steps

Every journey has to start by first understanding exactly what your organisation is trying to achieve, and what its current position and performance levels are. An organisation needs to have a clear understanding of:

- its business or corporate strategy
- the key capabilities it has that can be used to create a sustainable competitive advantage in the marketplace
- its external and internal operating environments
- how it is performing, using a balanced scorecard framework
- where it is in the strategic cycle
- how mature it is.

These are not issues for winning organisations. These are basic descriptors of the position of every organisation. Without these as a foundation of knowledge, there is little you can do.

Defining the current strategic position

Let's start with the *strategy* of the organisation. Hubbard (2004) recommends five basic questions be asked to elicit the business strategy of the organisation:

1   Does the organisation want to grow (and grow profitably)?
2   What specific products and services does it wish to offer?

3 What customers and geographic markets does it wish to offer them to?

4 What generic strategy (low cost, differentiation, or focus) does it plan to use to develop sustainable competitive advantage (and, if not low cost, what is the specific basis of the differentiation or focus)?

5 What position does it want to achieve or get to in the industry?

For example, the business strategy derived from the answers to these questions for, say, an organic produce grower might be:

- to grow rapidly (and profitably)
- to offer organic fruit and vegetables
- for the produce to be sold in Australian supermarket chains
- differentiation on the basis of being 100 per cent organic
- to be the highest quality, most reputable organic grower in Australia.

In terms of the *capabilities* of the organisation, it needs to know what it does to meet all of the following tests:

- Is it valuable to customers?
- Is it better than most competitors?
- Is it difficult to imitate or replicate?

This indicates what the organisation has (or plans to develop) to give it a sustainable competitive advantage. For instance, using the above hypothetical organic produce grower, it might have the following strategic capabilities:

- quality approval
- growers with professional and research backgrounds
- links to academic institutions that specialise in organic fruit and vegetables
- quick delivery.

The organisation then needs to understand *the state of its industry* — how fast it is growing and why, and how profitable it is and why. For instance, using the same example, the organic produce industry might be growing rapidly, be extremely fragmented and be easy to enter, with low profitability due to the high power of buyer organisations.

Finally, the organisation needs to know its *current performance level* in terms of:

- financial performance
- market/customer performance
- internal efficiency performance
- long-term growth and development initiatives.

For instance, the organisation might be making good financial returns and growing strongly, have low market share but be valued by its customers, be extremely efficient with its processes and productivity, but have no future aims or no new product developments in the pipeline.

At this point, it will be in good shape to assess its *overall strategic position* and, effectively, know what it needs to improve. In the hypothetical case of the organic produce grower, the organisation has a clear strategy with matching capabilities, but its industry is suffering from fragmentation, so overall returns are low. It will need to develop good relationships with its powerful buyers, find ways to become more powerful in the industry (perhaps through acquisitions) and develop new products so that it can grow in the future.

The organisation also needs to consider its *position in the strategic cycle, its size and its level of organisational maturity* to understand its own views of the world and what it can and can't do. Clearly, a start-up domestic-local organisation has a different context to an underperforming national-diversified organisation—though both may want to become winning organisations! The way the questions will be answered will depend on the answer to the strategic cycle analysis. For instance, our hypothetical organic produce grower is a focused domestic-national organisation. It has grown beyond the regional level and is expanding across Australia, but it has no international experience.

The *size* of the organisation will affect its opportunities and constraints. For instance, our organisation is family owned and quite small, limiting its prospects on what it can do and who can own it.

Organisational maturity

By organisational 'maturity', we refer to the maturity of the organisation's systems and processes. We consider there to be five levels of maturity:

- *Level 1*—Systems are ad hoc and unsystematic. Success depends on individual effort, skills and experience. If a particularly talented individual leaves, there is a chance that the whole business will fall over unless someone with similar skill levels replaces them. In other words, the organisation is unsustainable because processes are undefined and cannot be easily replicated due to the dependence on individuals.

- *Level 2* — Some systems and processes are documented, which enables successful activities to be repeated, as long as they are similar to past activities, because success is very much based on previous experience.
- *Level 3* — Standard processes are in place for documenting procedures and management systems, and processes are widely integrated into the decision-making processes of the organisation.
- *Level 4* — Decisions are made using formal management processes. This includes resource and decision planning, context setting, risk identification and management, and monitoring of outcomes for feedback.
- *Level 5* — Continuous improvement is possible due to the capture of quantitative information and feedback from decision implementation. New ideas and technologies can be systematically trialled and the risk associated with them managed because of the stringent systems and processes in place. Decision reviews provide information that is immediately used to improve current systems and processes, thereby supporting continuous improvement.

Organisations move from level 1 to level 5 as they develop. If your organisation is at level 1, the focus should be on systematising your processes and moving away from a reliance on the individual. If your organisation is at level 2, you may be able to look outside, but the focus should be on standardising your processes first. If your organisation is at level 3, it has the 'basics' and can begin to expand its focus, but continue to consider the First XI principles while improving the organisation. If your organisation is at level 4 or 5, it should be quite comfortably on its way to becoming a winning organisation.

This framework can be used at any level in the organisation — the organisation itself, the business unit or even the team. It is particularly important if you want to institute change, that you are realistic about your organisation's maturity level. If you aren't, the change initiatives you want to institute are likely to be far too ambitious. It's much better to start off with small initiatives that have a greater likelihood of success. Doing so will build the confidence of you, your team members and your superiors. After all, you are more likely to be given budget for more ambitious initiatives once you have demonstrated successes. Team members are also more likely to engage in other initiatives if they have achieved success in previous endeavours.

Working out where to start on the winning wheel

Having established the organisational foundations—the basics—you can now start the journey of improvement. The first thing to do is work out, overall, how your organisation or unit performs against the nine elements of the winning wheel. You can start very easily. Clearly define the organisation or unit you are asking the questions about—that is, are you assessing the whole organisation or just your unit? Be precise about the definition; make sure that everyone in the team is thinking of the same unit when making their assessments. For instance, you may be talking about the Australian subsidiary of the global corporation, rather than the whole global corporation. It makes a difference!

Table 15.1 allows you to establish the performance of the organisation according to the winning wheel framework. Using the statements in table 15.1 have your team score the organisation's performance on a 10-point scale, where 1 = very poor and 10 = excellent. We suggest you weight the elements equally because they all need to be present. You may, however, have a different view about the particular weights in your particular environment, but don't weight them to match your current best position. Weight them as you think is most appropriate for a winning organisation. Add the individual scores to find the group score and to even out individual differences and outliers. Compare the scores, the range and the average. How did you do?

This should be a quick exercise to identify any major imbalances around the wheel. A significant number of participants is needed to complete the exercise. More important, however, is that the participants are experienced in your organisation, take an organisational view, rather than a functional or personal view, and consider the 'normal' response to each question, not the odd or unusual response. While it may be best to have the top managers complete the survey, it may also be useful to have other experienced people at different levels in the organisation do it too, as their perspectives may well be different, which may be very useful.

Starting your organisation on a winning journey

Table 15.1: how is my organisation/unit doing?

Element	Score (out of 10)
We execute effectively on time and within budget	
We have perfect alignment of our systems and processes	
We adapt rapidly, using continuous improvement and innovation	
We have a clear but slightly fuzzy strategy	
We have a good leadership team	
We are outwardly oriented, not just inwardly oriented	
We have the right people in the organisation	
We manage risk well	
We have a balanced view to our activities and decisions	
Total score (out of 90)	

Table 15.2 gives an idea of what a set of individual responses might look like. There is some variability on the individual elements, but there is also quite a lot of agreement about both high and low areas of performance.

Table 15.2: how is my organisation/unit doing? — group scores

Element	A	B	C	D	E	F
We execute effectively on time and within budget	7	8	7	7	6	8
We have perfect alignment of our systems and processes	6	9	9	9	9	8
We adapt rapidly, using continuous improvement and innovation	5	4	3	5	6	4
We have a clear but slightly fuzzy strategy	8	8	7	8	7	8
We have a good leadership team	9	8	7	7	7	9
We are outwardly oriented, not just inwardly oriented	5	5	6	7	6	7
We have the right people in the organisation	3	7	7	6	8	7
We manage risk well	6	6	7	5	7	6
We have a balanced view to our activities and decisions	4	8	8	8	8	6
Total score (out of 90)	53	63	52	62	64	63

Seeking more detail

The above process is *very* easy. You may want to extend it by asking more detailed questions about each of the elements in the winning wheel framework. At the end of each chapter for each element of the winning wheel we have provided a summary of key messages for leaders. We recommend that you adopt these statements (or adapt them to your organisation, if necessary) and ask the people in your team to rank your performance on them on the same scale of one to 10. Our experience from our own database and survey exercise is that this should only take around 20 to 30 minutes—a very small investment of time for what it may reveal if people are honest in their responses. Appendix C provides a sample of some of the questions we use in our database. If you would like to compare the responses with the database we have compiled since 2001, we would be happy to discuss this with you and your organisation, and we would certainly be interested in adding your data to ours to increase our sample. Our contact details are provided in the 'About the authors' section at the beginning of the book.

Avoid the trap of making this exercise too precise. Also, avoid trying to clarify specifically what is meant by each of the statements. These are general, overview impressions (which are often quite accurate!). You may want to investigate the scores at a later stage, but right now you need to get buy-in from your people. You just need some information to get started and what you should really be interested in is not the absolute number, but the general ranking. Remember also that each person's perceptions are their reality and, rather like brainstorming, this is not the place where you should debate anything, even if their perceptions of performance against specific criteria do not align with yours.

Table 15.3 provides an example, using 'looking out, looking in' as the element of the winning wheel framework. We have adapted the 'key messages for leaders' for a hypothetical example of a small business group operating only in one local area (Victoria). The statements have been formed for a firm that is performing well in all areas of its balanced scorecard and is at the focused–domestic regional level of the strategic cycle, with level 3 organisational maturity.

Once you have done this for all nine elements, you can quickly chart the results for everyone to see, either using a simple hand-drawn diagram or more sophisticated graphing tools. The 'spider web' approach to communicating the results is recommended for its simplicity and its visual impact (see figure 15.1 on page 400).

Starting your organisation on a winning journey

Table 15.3: organisational assessment of 'looking out, looking in'—for a small, focused–domestic regional organisation at level 3 maturity

Winning practice	Rank on a scale of 1 (strongly disagree) to 10 (strongly agree)
1 We think 'customer'.	
2 We develop products and services based on intensive market research.	
3 We develop and manage ongoing customer relationships.	
4 We work with other organisations on a partnership basis to expand resources and reduce risk.	
5 We manage government and regulators as part of our normal business activities.	
6 We work with suppliers on an ongoing basis.	
7 We are future-focused with a whole-of-industry perspective.	
8 We are looking outside Victoria for trends in our industry.	
9 We source ideas from other geographic areas outside Victoria, including overseas.	
10 We have a sense of community responsibility as part of our day-to-day operations.	
Total out of 100	
Average score (total divided by 10)	

Once you have done this with your team, you should agree with them about the elements you want to focus on first. What to do first is, of course, a critical question and one that needs to be considered in light of a number of factors, in agreement with your team. The exercise will typically have highlighted two or three elements where your team considers the organisation's performance to be below desired or expected, or 'good', levels, as you might define them, so you can look at them in more detail. If the results are deficient across more areas, you will have a lot more work to do! For instance, in figure 15.1 'adapt rapidly' stands out as the low-performing element, with 'looking out, looking in' the next lowest.

Figure 15.1: organisational performance assessment of the 'winning wheel' using a spider's web graph (1 to 10 scale)

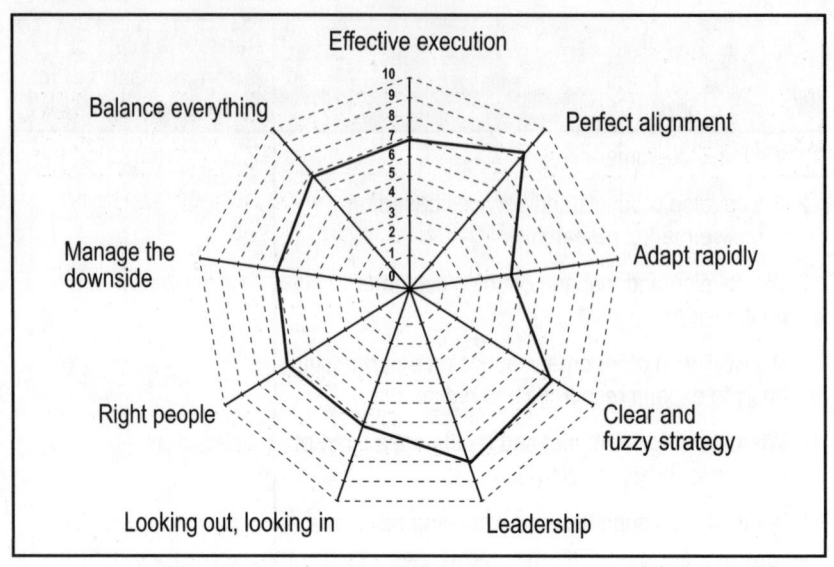

[Spider's web graph with axes: Effective execution, Perfect alignment, Adapt rapidly, Clear and fuzzy strategy, Leadership, Looking out, looking in, Right people, Manage the downside, Balance everything]

The next step is to consider each of the practices relating to each element chosen, to ask:

> For our group, what would doing this practice well look like? What would we need to have in place to characterise each sub-element as doing each of these things well.

You may also want to involve other people in this process, such as managers from other groups in your organisation and key partners who you work closely with. You can also look back at some of the practices used by the First XI for insights. Table 15.4 provides some examples of issues from the 'looking out, looking in' element of the winning wheel.

By following this process, your goals or desired outcomes are likely to be grounded in reality in a way that matches the size, strategic cycle position and organisational maturity level of your organisation. Importantly, this approach also provides the opportunity for your team to have a sense of ownership and engagement from the process, and be able to contribute their knowledge of systems and process from other organisations they may have worked for.

Once you have defined what doing each of these things 'well' would look like for your organisation, you need to decide what needs to be done to achieve it. Figure 15.2 (on page 403) provides an example of how this might work for the 'looking out, looking in' element for our hypothetical organisation above. It takes the practices from table 15.4

Starting your organisation on a winning journey

and develops example activities for them to show what would need to be done to achieve success in those practices.

Table 15.4: what does 'doing it well' look like?

Winning practice	For our group, what would doing this practice well look like?
Think 'customer'	• Involve our customers in the development of new products and services. • Survey our customers annually for feedback on our practices, which can be integrated into next years operating plans. • Make it easy for our customers to return products. • Train all our people in things like how to answer the phone, how to handle dissatisfied customers and so on.
Develop products and services based on intensive market research	• Have well-defined processes for developing new products that involve our current and potential customers. • Have systems to capture changes in market trends to inform product development. • Use objective market information to select which new product development initiatives to undertake from the options available.
Develop and manage ongoing customer relationships	• Know who best customers are by volume and value. • Know when changes in the purchasing patterns of best customers occurs so we can follow up the cause with them quickly.
Work with other organisations on a partnership basis to expand resources and reduce risk	• Have a number of joint projects currently being implemented. • Identify some organisations we would like to work with and understand what value we can offer them and what value they can offer us.
Manage government and regulators as part of our normal business activities	• Make sure staff understand the specific regulatory requirements we need to fulfil and the records that need to be maintained to comply. • Meet with regulators on a regular basis to stay up-to-date with any prospective changes. • Have membership of appropriate industry bodies and participate in and support their activities.

Table 15.4 *(cont'd)*: what does 'doing it well' look like?

Winning practice	For our group, what would doing this practice well look like?
Work with suppliers on an ongoing basis	• Meet regularly with suppliers to advise them of our future business predictions. • Have preferred suppliers for a number of inputs. • Provide feedback to suppliers on their performance.
Future focused with a whole-of-industry perspective	• Track changes in trends for our products and services. • Take time out to explore future possibilities for the organisation and question our (continued) relevance. • Understand who our current competitors are. • Understand who future competitors might be.
Looking outside Victoria for trends in our industry	• Send staff overseas for appropriate activities such as trade shows. • Have a system for getting ideas from all levels of staff. • Subscribe to relevant industry journals.
Source ideas from other geographic areas outside Victoria, including overseas	• As above.
Sense of community responsibility as part of our day-to-day operations	• Understand the community affiliations and responsibilities of staff and publicly recognise and support this.

The next step is to identify the issues you are going to focus on now, in the near term and in the future. Some of the criteria you could use to make this evaluation include budget, time, resources available, complexity of what needs to be done and the impact on the business. How you choose to rank each activity required to do each practice well is up to you, but in the first instance, agreement on high, medium and low priorities is a good way of coming up with a short list of possible activities.

Essentially, what you are looking to uncover through this process are any *high-impact* activities that are *easy and low cost to implement*, as these are the activities you should be aiming to put into practice first.

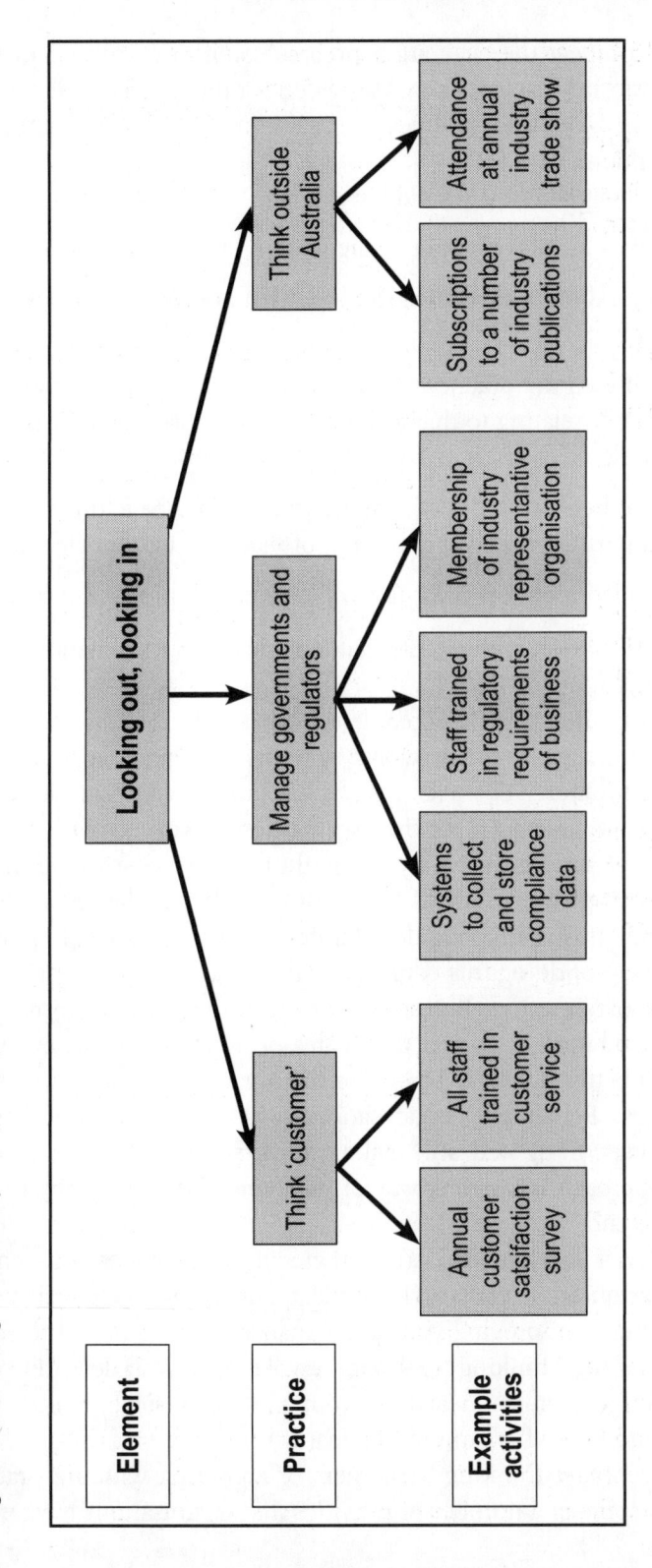

Starting your organisation on a winning journey

Figure 15.2: linking elements, practices and desired activities

Element	Practice	Example activities

Looking out, looking in

- Think 'customer'
  - Annual customer satisfaction survey
  - All staff trained in customer service
- Manage governments and regulators
  - Systems to collect and store compliance data
  - Staff trained in regulatory requirements of business
  - Membership of industry representative organisation
- Think outside Australia
  - Subscriptions to a number of industry publications
  - Attendance at annual industry trade show

403

You can repeat the evaluation process using more precise evaluation criteria to rank activities and agree on an implementation program if you have a lot of possibilities, using the first pass to eliminate some of your options.

At this point you should have:

▶ looked at each element in the winning wheel

▶ focused on two or three elements that are well below desired levels

▶ identified the practices (developed from the 'key messages for leaders' relating to that element) within those elements that should be focused on

▶ identified a number of activities that should be addressed to support the effective execution of that practice and element

▶ decided what the priorities will be for each practice execution.

You might finish with a table that includes such information as shown in table 15.5.

When the table is complete you should be able to prioritise the importance of the activities in terms of impact, cost and ease of implementation. For example, there are three example practices inserted in table 15.5 for the organisation (if you take a look back at table 15.4 and figure 15.1 you should be able to see where they have been derived from). If this organisation only has the resources to do one thing this year, it should definitely get its regulatory requirements in order. Not doing this could potentially have a high negative impact on the organisation, but as addressing this is low in terms of both implementation costs and the degree of difficulty of implementation, it has a better potential pay-off to the organisation than the other two activities. Remember, organisations will rarely have the resources to do everything and still make money so you need to be realistic. This approach is a strong way of justifying and getting buy-in for the recommended course of action.

Even if you don't undertake them all, the activities you define will generate questions that can be used later on to evaluate whether you are achieving or improving your performance. For example, the activities identified for 'Thinking "customer"', will inform your definition of what thinking 'customer' means for your particular stage in the strategic cycle and level of organisational maturity.

Essentially, thinking 'customer', or any other winning practice, is the outcome of a number of activities that organisations have in place.

Table 15.5: implementation plans for improving performance

Winning practice—practices from 'looking out, looking in'	For our group, what would doing this well look like?	What needs to be done to put this in place?	What is the impact on the business?	What is the cost of implementation?	What is the degree of difficulty of implementation?
Manage governments and regulations	Have systems to collect and store compliance data	Decide what records we have to keep and develop standard operating procedures for data collection and storage	High—if we are audited our business could be fined or closed if we don't have the necessary records on hand	Low to medium—once we have set up the way we want to keep records we could get a temporary staff member in to get this job done (assumes no major investment is required)	Low
	Have regular meetings with regulatory authorities	Identify the correct person or group and set up a meeting	Low to medium—if we inform them of what we are doing they may have some time-saving solutions and ideas, and be flexible and supportive as we put compliance systems in place	Low—staff time and possibly travel costs	Low

Table 15.5 (cont'd): implementation plans for improving performance

Winning practice—practices from 'looking out, looking in'	For our group, what would doing this well look like?	What needs to be done to put this in place?	What is the impact on the business?	What is the cost of implementation?	What is the degree of difficulty of implementation?
	Have an annual customer satisfaction survey	Decide what information we actually want from our customers so that we can use it to inform future activities	Medium—this will create buy-in but we will need to make sure we can demonstrate how we will use the information to create benefits for them	Medium—some staff time and workshops to work out what we want to do. Possibly outsource this depending on scale of survey we want to undertake	Low to medium— (depends on current goodwill with customers) and if we do it ourselves or use a consultant (depending on the experience we have at this kind of thing)
Think outside Australia	For example, subscriptions to a number of industry publications				
	For example, attendance at annual industry trade show				
Think 'customer'	For example, annual customer satisfaction survey				
	For example, all staff trained in customer service				

Starting your organisation on a winning journey

What you should be aiming for is being able to conclude that the organisation thinks 'customer' because you have evidence about the activities it does that supports that conclusion.

In summary, the process you need to follow is:

1. Choose a unit of analysis—whole organisation or business unit, and make sure your team is 'thinking' this unit.
2. Analyse your current strategy, capabilities and performance in the context of your organisation's size, maturity and position in the strategic cycle.
3. Choose the team to be involved in the assessment and goal-setting process.
4. Work out, in approximate order, where your team believes your organisation is in terms of the nine elements of the winning wheel framework. Adjust the 'key messages for leaders' at the end of each chapter into statements relevant to your specific organisation so you can plot the results on your own 'winning wheel' and get a quick indication of relative performance against all the elements.
5. Identify two or three elements that you can focus on in more detail, where your performance is perceived to be below that of performance on other elements.
6. Develop descriptors of what doing 'well' would look like for each of the practices that make up the elements you are focusing on.
7. Evaluate the activities identified by your team for improving performance.
8. Come up with a short list of possible activities.
9. Rank the activities in terms of implementation order and plan the implementation.
10. Develop metrics for measuring performance of these activities such as time frame, budget, milestones, key performance indicators and so on.
11. Get the plan approved.
12. Evaluate how you perform over the next period. Evaluation also includes adjusting the plan if necessary and setting new goals.

This is clearly a rigorous process and it will take time. The key is to break it down into achievable activities to build the organisation's confidence and success. Don't forget, the practices of the First XI have been developed over at least 25 years of operations. Even the First XI continuously re-evaluate, change and improve what they are doing to better their performance. Remember, regardless of your organisation's size, position in the strategic cycle or level of maturity, there are improvements you can make.

Summary and key messages for leaders

Becoming a winning organisation is a long journey. Using a systematic approach, all organisations and business units can implement activities that will contribute to improvement. As more and more improvements are made, the organisation moves ever closer to being a winning organisation.

The key messages for leaders are:

▶ Understand your strategy and strategic position before you start.
▶ Work with your people to identify winning wheel elements that your organisation should concentrate on improving.
▶ Be realistic and incremental in starting the process.
▶ Focus on getting quick wins from high-impact, easy-to-implement, low-cost activities first.
▶ Get started!

We think this book provides you with the elements to enable your organisation to become a 'winning' organisation in Australia *and* with examples of Australian operating organisations that follow these practices. Now it is up to you! 'Winning' is hard work, but it is rewarding. Will your organisation be nominated by your peers for inclusion in this book in 10 years' time?

Appendix A

Winning organisation brief biographies

Brambles

Year and place founded

1916, Newcastle, NSW

CEOs

1916	Walter Bramble
1941	Alan Bramble
1946	Milton Bramble
1948	Tom Price
1962	Warwick Holcroft
1981	Oliver Richter
1983	Gary Pemberton
1993	John Fletcher
2001	Sir CK Chow
2004	David Turner

Founding concept

Walter Bramble started as a Newcastle butcher and developed a carrying business as a feeder service to the railway terminal.

Key events

1916   WE Bramble & Sons established as Walter's three sons were now in the business

1917   Motor vehicle distribution added to list of activities

1920   First contract outside Newcastle district to haul rabbits

1925   Motor distributorships extended to Essex, Hudson and Rolls Royce cars

1937   Diversified to Port Kembla to excavate blast furnace site

1954   Public listing

1956   Together with Heckett Engineering (United States), provided a unique service to recover metallic slag for BHP at Port Kembla

1958   Acquired Commonwealth Handling Equipment Pool (CHEP) from the federal government

1959   Moved head office to Sydney

1969   CHEP split into pallets, containers and equipment divisions; acquired Truran Earthmovers and Southern Plant Hire

1970   Won Bougainville Copper cartage project; acquired Fenwick, Purle Waste Disposals and Industrial Waste Collections

1971   Acquired M & W Chard (Papua New Guinea) and Goroka Toad Transport (PNG)

1972   Acquired Port Jackson & Manly Steamship, Armoured Escorts and Broman Divers

1973   Acquired Industrial Waste Collection; joint venture with Oceaneering International into deep-sea diving; sold Steelmark and Manly ferries

1974   CHEP UK 20:80 joint venture established with Guest Keen & Nettlefold, a diversified United Kingdom manufacturer

1978   CHEP Benelux launched with Groupe CAIB; CHEP Europe established

1979   CHEP Canada formed with Canadian Pacific

1980   Bought Redland Purle (UK) with Guest Keen & Nettlefold

1983   Acquired Grace Bros Transport Group

Appendix A: winning organisation brief biographies

1984   Acquired 49.9 per cent of Groupe CAIB

1986   Increased ownership in Groupe CAIB to 90 per cent; Cleanaway's 10-year contract with Greater London Council began; acquired American Pallet Systems

1988   Acquired Metransa (Spain—transport)

1989   GKN–Brambles Enterprises began—GKN acquired 50 per cent of CHEP Canada and American Pallet Systems; reorganised into regional businesses; entered the US waste management industry by initial purchases in Ensco; bought Choctaw (US crane rental), Sky Reach (US equipment rental), Wreckair (Australian equipment rental), United Transport (Australia—transport), Gardner Perrott (Australia—transport) and TMF (France—transport)

1990   Bought FMS (France—forklifts), Fostrans and Cochez (France—cranes), Lastra (Holland—cranes), Econofreight (UK—heavy freight), Toman (Austria—cranes)

1992   Acquired Ensco, Security Archives (UK)

1994   Acquired NILO (Netherlands—industrial services) and Leto Recycling (Netherlands); started records management in Canada and acquired more businesses in the US

1995   Wrote off Ensco; sold Grace Removals and Wallace Tugs; started operations in Taiwan, Malaysia and Singapore; acquired more US records businesses; established CHEP in Mexico and Chile

1996   Sold Australian general freight; sold Oceaneering, Fostrans and Cochez

1997   Cleanaway acquired Mabeg (Germany)

1998   Cleanaway acquired SKP (Germany); CHEP acquired Gespalets (Spain); Industrial Services acquired Cockburn Corporation (Australia), Recall Records management acquired Eco-Arc (France), CTD (Spain) and Arcavia and Serint (Italy); CHEP set up in Greece, Brazil and Hong Kong; sold Cargowaggon, Atlantic Waste and Seroul

1999   Recall established as global brand

2001   Merger of businesses with GKN under a dual-listed structure (Brambles held 57 per cent of merged structure); divested

FMS (France), Car Transport (Italy), Brambles Equipment (Australia), Brambles Security and Ensco (US); Cleanaway acquired Wastemaster and entered China; Recall made acquisitions in US, South America, Europe, Asia and Australasia. Globalisation process begins

2002   Recall completed 14 acquisitions and entered Denmark, Hong Kong, Norway, Mexico and India; Brambles Industrial Services divested several non-profitable businesses

2003   Recall made 18 acquisitions in the US, UK, Sweden and Finland; Brambles Industrial Services made several divestments

2004   CHEP reorganised into two regions; Recall made three acquisitions in Australia and Asia

2005   Brambles Industrial Services divested a number of non-core businesses

2006   Sold Brambles Industrial Services and all Cleanaway companies by nationality; sold Interlake and Eurotainer; consisted now of only CHEP and Recall

Harvey Norman

Year and place founded

1961, Sydney, NSW

CEOs

1961 Gerry Harvey and Ian Norman

1982 Gerry Harvey

1994 Michael Harvey

1998 Katie Page

Founding concept

Norman Ross Discounts was a discount electrical retailer that expanded to 42 stores in New South Wales and Queensland. Harvey Norman was begun immediately after the takeover of Norman Ross. The concept of Harvey Norman is a franchise of owner-operated stores where the owner's expertise and dedication to personal service is backed up by the financial muscle, buying power and management services ability of a larger organisation. The concept expanded from electrical goods to a wide range of household goods including lighting, manchester and bedding, furniture, computers, bathroom hardware, carpet and flooring, and home improvement.

Key events

1972 Norman Ross listed on the stock exchange

1982 Norman Ross acquired by Waltons Bond and Gerry Harvey and Ian Ross had their positions terminated. They immediately started up Harvey Norman in opposition, using the new franchise concept

1987 Harvey Norman listed on the stock exchange

1988 Entered Queensland

1992 Entered the Australian Capital Territory

1993 First computer superstore; entered Victoria

1997 Entered New Zealand and Western Australia

1998 Acquired Vox chain of stores, the Loughran Group (Tasmania) and the Joyce Mayne Group (NSW)

1999 Entered South Australia and Tasmania; acquired a minority interest in Pertama, a listed electrical retailer in Singapore

2000 Acquisition of 22 Vox stores, to be operated by Harvey Norman franchisees

2001 Acquired Rebel Sport (and Glue); relaunched Joyce Mayne as Domayne

2002 Entered Slovenia

2003 Entered Ireland; started Mega Flooring Depot—a new franchising concept—and Home Renovations

2004 Joint venture in UK to open Space furniture store; entered Malaysia

2005 Launched Joyce Mayne for country and regional stores

2006 Sold Rebel Sport

Lend Lease

Year and place founded
1951, Sydney, NSW

CEOs
1951 Dick Dusseldorp

1978 Stuart Hornery

1994 John Morschel

1995 David Higgins

2002 Greg Clarke

Founding concept
Civil & Civic was sponsored by its Netherlands parent, Bredero's United Companies, a significant building organisation, to seek building opportunities in Australia, with a focus on project management, design, engineering and construction.

Key events
1950 Dick Dusseldorp visited Australia to assess the market opportunities

1951 Civil & Civic contractors formed

1958 Lend Lease Corporation formed with Civil & Civic as largest shareholder. MLC encouraged the formation of the new company and provided funding for Lend Lease's first project, North Shore Medical Centre; first productivity agreement established with the Building Trades' Union in New South Wales and the Australian Capital Territory; Lend Lease listed

1959 First (unlisted) National Buildings Trust established; Lend Lease Development formed

1961 Acquired Civil & Civic from Bredero's

1962 Opened in Perth and first project in Adelaide commenced

1963 Employee presentations of results commenced; Australian wages staff superannuation commenced 20 years before the rest of the industry

1964 Operations commenced in New Zealand

The First XI

1965   First project in Tasmania

1970   Operations extended to the US

1971   General Property Trust formed and the first public trust in Australia floated

1972   Memorandum of Understanding signed with Australia Council of Trade Unions (ACTU) extending the 1958 productivity agreement Australia-wide

1973   Commenced operations in Singapore; formation of Prime Property Fund, one of the first commingled real estate accounts for US pension funds; profit sharing for Lend Lease Australian employees introduced

1977   International Income Property (IIP) launched in the US

1981   ACTU/Lend Lease Foundation set up to encourage people to acquire skills

1982   Successful partial takeover (50 per cent) of MLC

1983   Lend Lease Foundation established to promote the 'well-being of Lend Lease employees and their families'

1984   IIP listed on Australian stock exchanges; Lend Lease Association, Lend Lease Youth Council and Lend Lease Apprentice Council formed; Work Skill Australia formed with Lend Lease as an inaugural sponsor

1985   MLC became wholly owned; Lend Lease Interiors began

1986   Equal Opportunity management program introduced; MLC multi-manager, multi-style investment philosophy introduced

1987   Childcare facilities introduced for Sydney employees

1988   Dusseldorp Skills Forum formed; Australian Trust launched

1989   Australian Prime Property Fund (APPF) commenced

1990   All Australian employees received profit share; Capita Group merged with MLC; Mayne Nickless Payroll Services acquired

1991   Commenced operations in Europe; Board committee for Environment and Occupations Health and Safety set up; Australian Water Services formed

1992   First global property fund launched

Appendix A: winning organisation brief biographies

1993 Yarmouth acquired in the US; Thailand and Jakarta offices opened

1994 Integrated Systems Solutions Corporation Australia (ISSC) information technology joint venture formed with IBM; Sinar Mas joint ventures signed in Indonesia

1995 Hong Kong office opened

1997 MLC sold its building society; acquired ERE and merged with the Yarmouth Group

1998 SITEL Asia Pacific launched (joint venture between Lend Lease and the SITEL Group); acquisition of Southern European retail services company, Larry Smith Group; acquisition of 50 per cent of Kiwi Property Group (Kiwi Income Property Trust and Kiwi Development Trust); Plum Financial Services launched (joint venture between MLC and The Vanguard Group)

1999 Launched global strategy by acquiring Boston Financial Group, and five AMRESCO businesses and merging Lend Lease Projects and Bovis to form Bovis Lend Lease

2000 Formation of European real estate securities firm—Lend Lease Houlihan Rovers; launch of Lend Lease Diversified Real Estate Fund; sale of MLC

2001 Lend Lease Real Estate Investments introduced mutual fund for US-based investors to invest in European real estate; acquired residential community developer Delfin

2002 Global strategy reversed—went back to regional business units; appointed construction manager of World Trade Centre Ground Zero site

2003 Sold US Real Estate Investments Equity Advisory businesses, Lend Lease Agribusiness, a 23 per cent stake in IBM Global Services Australia, Lend Lease Mortgage Capital, Holliday Fenoglio Fowler, Housing and Community Investing, and CapMark Services

2004 Unsuccessful bid for General Property Trust led to divorce of the two organisations; established own investment management operation in-house; relocated head office from London to Sydney; built first five-star eco-efficient commercial office building in Australia for its new headquarters

Macquarie Bank

Year and place founded

1969, Sydney, NSW

CEOs

1969   Christopher Castleman

1971   David Clarke and Mark Johnson (joint)

1977   David Clarke

1983   Tony Berg

1993   Allan Moss

Founding concept

Originally Hill Samuel Australia, the Australian arm of an English merchant bank, providing a range of financial services and products of the highest quality in terms of service, knowledge and skill.

Key events

1969   Hill Samuel Australia established

1978   First Australian project finance division set up

1978   Authorised as a foreign exchange dealer

1980   Introduced Australia's first cash management account

1983   First international office opened in New Zealand

1985   Granted a trading bank licence; changed name to Macquarie Bank

1989   Opened offices in London and Munich

1991   Opened US office in Denver

1995   Established offices in Hong Kong

1995   Offices in China established

1996   Funds management joint venture with Arab-Malaysian merchant bank Berhad in Malaysia

1996   Listed on Australian Stock Exchange

1996   Opened Singapore office

Appendix A: winning organisation brief biographies

1997 Advisory services joint venture with Goldman Sachs in New Zealand

1998 Alliance with Standard Bank in South Africa

1999 Joint ventures with JBWere (equities clearing), Sanham Ltd (South Africa—fund manager), Kookmin Bank (Korea); opened office in Canada

2000 Acquired Bankers Trust (Australia); opened office in Brazil; joint venture with Industrial Bank of Japan; Macquarie Infrastructure Group one of the world's largest owner of toll roads; offices in 15 countries

2001 Offices in 22 countries; started Macquarie Airport Group and bought Sydney and Bristol airports in joint ventures

2002 Offices in 24 countries

2003 Launched three new infrastructure funds in Australia, road infrastructure fund in Korea, energy trading (UK), oil and gas finance (US); expanded into Dublin, Geneva, Houston, San Diego, Memphis and Labuan; equity derivatives alliances in South Africa and South Korea

2004 Acquired SE Water (UK); acquired ING's Asian equities business; alliance with Nedbank in South Africa; set up Korea's first wholly owned investment trust manager; established infrastructure funds in Canada, US, South Africa

2005 Formed Macquarie Goodman Group; acquired 92 Australian radio stations; completed largest initial public offering (IPO) in Philippines' history; awarded Malaysia stockbroking licence; joint venture with Thai Military Bank; acquired 70 per cent of Brussels Airport; acquired NTL Broadcast (UK); acquired Canadian aged-care provider; entered Brazilian cotton market; launched fully integrated hedge fund facility

2006 IPOs of Macquarie Media Group, Macquarie Capital Alliance Group, Macquarie Global Infrastructure, listed MEAG in Singapore, Macquarie International Infrastructure, Macquarie Korean Infrastructure Fund; established brokerage and corporate finance business in Mumbai; stockbroking joint venture with Thai Military Bank; joint ventures with Abu Dhabi Commercial Bank; bought Smarte Carte, Icon Parking and Indiana toll road

National Australia Bank

Year and place founded

1858, Melbourne, Vic.

CEOs

1979   JD Booth

1985   Nobby Clark

1990   Don Argus

1999   Frank Cicutto

2004   John Stewart

Founding concept

To service the banking needs arising from the Victorian gold rush in the 1850s.

Key events

1918   Acquired Colonial Bank of Australasia

1922   Acquired Bank of Queensland

1947   Acquired Queensland National Bank

1954   Diversified into non-banking with a 40 per cent shareholding in Custom Credit (finance)

1955   Acquired Ballarat Banking Group

1962   Commenced savings bank operations

1969   Established Chase-NBA Group with Chase Manhattan Overseas Banking Corporation

1971   Acquired control of Custom Credit

1973   Entered insurance business through establishment of National and General Insurance; acquired 100 per cent of Custom Credit

1974   Established Bank of South Pacific for PNG

1981   Merged with Commercial Banking Company of Sydney

1984   Acquired 50 per cent of AC Goode (stockbroking) and 100 per cent of Chase-NBA (merchant banking)

Appendix A: winning organisation brief biographies

1985   National Australia Financial Management (personal financial services) established; listed on Tokyo stock exchange; established merchant bank in New Zealand; acquired a finance company in NZ

1987   Acquired three subsidiaries of Midland Bank plc—Clydesdale Bank of Scotland, Northern Bank (Northern Ireland) and Northern Bank (Ireland—renamed the National Irish Bank)

1990   Acquired Yorkshire Bank plc; closed AC Goode

1992   Acquired Bank of New Zealand

1995   Acquired Michigan National

1997   Acquired County Natwest Investment Management; acquired Homeside (US residential mortgage loan originator)

2000   Acquired MLC (funds management) and transferred National Australia Funds Management operations into MLC

2001   Sold Michigan National

2002   Sold HomeSide

2004   Melbourne forex scandal revealed; sold Irish banks

2006   Sold BNZ Investment Management, MLC's Asian life insurance and Custom Fleet leasing

Qantas

Year and place founded

1920, Winton, Qld

CEOs

1952 Cedric Turner

1966 RJ Ritchie

1975 Keith Hamilton

1984 RJ Yates

1985 John Menadue

1989 John Ward

1993 James Strong

2000 Geoff Dixon

Founding concept

Queensland and Northern Territory Aerial Services Ltd was established by Paul McGinness and Wilmot Hudson Fysh, who purchased a plane to service the outback of northern Queensland and the Northern Territory.

Key events

1921 Headquarters moved to Longreach

1922 First flight from Charleville to Cloncurry

1929 Outback network extended to Brisbane

1930 Headquarters moved to Brisbane

1934 Name changed to Qantas Empire Airways

1935 First overseas flight from Brisbane to Singapore, carrying mail

1938 Headquarters moved to Sydney

1946 Network extended to India, New Guinea and Pacific Islands

1947 Sold out to Commonwealth Government as could not raise capital to compete in an environment where all airlines were government owned and controlled; government designated

Appendix A: winning organisation brief biographies

Qantas Australia's overseas flag-carrier and it began services to London and Japan

1949 Domestic airline services handed over to government-owned Trans Australian Airlines

1954 Started service to San Francisco and Vancouver

1958 Services extended to New York to establish an around-the-world airline

1967 Name changed to Qantas Airways

1979 Boeing 707s phased out and became world's only all-747 airline; introduced world's first business class

1989 Acquired 19.9 per cent of Air New Zealand

1992 Acquired Australian Airlines

1993 25 per cent of Qantas sold to British Airways

1995 Privatisation sale completed

1997 Sold out of Air New Zealand

1999 Joined Oneworld global airline alliance

2000 Acquired Impulse Airlines and folded into Qantaslink regional services

2002 Launched international subsidiary airline, Australian Airlines

2004 Jetstar launched domestically and Jetstar Asia launched as joint venture with Temasek Holdings

2006 Australian Airlines operations folded into Jetstar, which became a new Group equivalent to Qantas; Jetstar started international routes; formed Express Freighters Australia

Rio Tinto

Year and place founded

1905, Broken Hill, NSW

CEOs

1962   Maurice Mawby

1974   Rod Carnegie

1986   John Ralph

1994   Leon Davis

2000   Leigh Clifford

Founding concept

As Zinc Corporation in 1905, applying new technology to treat previously useless tailings at Broken Hill. As CRA in 1961, the exploration for and development of Australian resources. As Rio Tinto in 1995, the global exploration, mining and processing of mineral resources.

Key events

1905   Zinc Corporation formed

1911   Head office moved to London

1949   Merged with Imperial Smelting to form Consolidated Zinc, with a subsidiary designed to explore for minerals in Australia

1955   Weipa bauxite reserves discovered

1960   Kaiser Aluminum & Chemical Corporation became a partner to develop Comalco as an integrated aluminium company

1961   Merged with Rio Tinto to form Conzinc Riotinto of Australia (CRA) for the Australian interests and RTZ for the non-Australian interests

1962   Mount Tom Price iron ore reserves discovered; Hamersley Holdings formed in partnership with Kaiser Steel

1964   Bougainville copper reserves discovered

1966   Hamersley Holdings floated (10 per cent available to the public)

Appendix A: winning organisation brief biographies

1971   Bougainville Copper floated (10 per cent available to the public)

1972   Hamersley's second mine—Paraburdoo—began production

1978   Australian government policy of 'naturalisation' accepted by CRA; sold alumina production to Comalco and acquired Comalco's 50 per cent interest in Dampier Salt

1979   Acquired Kaiser Steel out of Hamersley; hostile takeover of Broken Hill South began—CRA finished up with Kembla Coal & Coke, Cobar Mines (gold), Electrolytical Refining and Smelting (silver, lead and zinc), Kanmantoo Mines (copper) and Metal Manufactures (steel—minority interest)

1981   Acquired Biotechnology Australia; closed Mary Kathleen Uranium

1982   Discovered heavy industrial minerals at Horsham (since divested)

1985   Purchased Martin Marietta US aluminium facilities

1986   Became majority Australian-owned

1987   Discovered gold at Kelian (Indonesia) and coal at East Kalimantan (Indonesia)

1988   Started aluminium wheel plant at Bell Bay, Tasmania (since divested); merged lead and zinc assets with those of North Broken Hill into a new company, Pasminco (now Zinifex); sold Metal Manufactures

1989   Bougainville shut down through militant attacks; Channar iron ore mine began; purchased BP's coking coal assets

1990   Discovered Century zinc deposit (since divested); acquired Kalimantan Gold (Indonesia); finalised research work on HIsmelt iron ore process

1993   Sold An Mau Steel, manufacturing investments in Asia; acquired control of Coal & Allied

1995   Merged with RTZ to form Rio Tinto, a dual-listed company

1996   Renamed Rio Tinto and restructured along six global business lines—iron ore, industrial minerals, copper, aluminium, energy and gold, and other minerals—with many acquisitions and divestments

The First XI

2000   Acquired 100 per cent of Comalco, North, Ashton Mining and some Australian coal businesses

2002   HIsmelt decision to expand into commercial operation

2003   Hail Creek coal mine opened; sale of Kaltim Prima Coal

2004   Sold several small non-core businesses; completed construction of new alumina refinery in Queensland

2005   Purchased 50 per cent of Hope Downs iron assets; continued aggressive expansion of iron ore mines in Pilbara; completed construction of HIsmelt commercial plant

The Salvation Army

(Southern Territories Division information listed here)

Year and place founded

1880, Adelaide, SA

CEOs

1977   Arthur Linnett

1982   Eva Burrows

1986   Donald Campbell

1989   Bramwell Tillsely

1991   Dinsdale Pender

1993   John Clinch

1996   Norman Howe

1998   Douglas Davis

2002   Ross Kendrew

2004   Ivan Lang

2006   James Knaggs

Founding concept

The Salvation Army was founded by a Methodist Minister, William Booth, and his wife Catherine in 1865 to provide the poor of the East End of London with a church in which they would feel welcome. This soon saw the introduction of feeding, accommodation and other social services. It quickly became a London-wide 'Christian Mission' and then became popular throughout the UK. In 1878 it was renamed 'the Salvation Army', doctrines were written, a flag designed and the first brass band introduced as 'a walking organ'. Women were accepted as ministers of religion from the beginning and the decision not to incorporate the sacraments was made.

Key events

1880   The Salvation Army in Australia commences in Botanic Gardens, Adelaide

1882   Majors James and Alice Barker arrive in Melbourne

The First XI

1883	First social institution commenced in Carlton for released prisoners from Melbourne Gaol
1891	First free labour exchange in Australia introduced
1900	The Salvation Army 'Limelight' department produces a film of the Federation ceremonies
1915	Red Shield welfare officers go with Australian troops to the front lines
1921	The Salvation Army in Australia divides into two territories
1939	General George Carpenter, an Australian, elected as the world leader
1945	Flying Padre services introduced in the Northern Territory and Queensland
1969	The first Red Shield Appeal using national publicity launched
1983	First Employment 2000 agency opened in Western Australia; later spreads throughout Australia to assist the long-term unemployed
1986	General Eva Burrows elected as General (second Australian and second woman general)
1995	Employment Plus is launched as part of the government's 'Job Network' program
1996	Assistance given to one million people
2000	Cost for the provision of services passed $250 million; Red Shield Welfare Officers went with Australian peacekeeping troops to East Timor (100 years of Salvo/troop services celebrated)
2002	Red Shield Appeal passed $50 million for first time and 'wills and bequests' passed $40 million for the first time
2003	Won tender for Employment Plus
2004	Closed Citadel Press
2005	Sold 15 of 19 aged-care centres; invested in Youthworx
2006	Family Stores chain rebranded as 'Salvo's Stores'

Appendix A: winning organisation brief biographies

Telstra

Year and place founded

1901, Melbourne, Vic.

CEOs

1975 John Curtis

1981 William Pollock

1986 Mel Ward

1992 Frank Blount

1999 Ziggy Switkowski

2005 Sol Trujillo

Founding concept

The Postmaster-General's Department was established by the Commonwealth Government in 1901 to plan, establish, maintain and operate the telephone system for Australia.

Key events

1901 At Federation, control of the telephone system was vested in the new Commonwealth Government and exercised via the Postmaster-General's Department

1912 First public automatic telephone exchange in Australia opened at Geelong

1930 First overseas calls available

1954 Telex services opened between Melbourne and Sydney

1956 Subscriber trunk dialling (STD) first introduced between Dandenong and Melbourne

1959 First broadband microwave system opened between Melbourne and Bendigo

1969 Datel service introduced to provide data transmission

1975 Telecommunications Act established the Australian Telecommunications Commission as a separate body from the Post Office

1981 First mobile phones introduced

1989	Telecommunications market deregulation began with deregulation of telecommunications equipment sales
1991	Deregulation of the national long distance and international telephone call markets
1992	Acquired the Overseas Telecommunications Corporation; mobile market opened to competition
1993	Name changed to Telstra
1994	PayTV services commenced
1997	Market fully opened to competition; government floats one-third of Telstra
1999	Government sold more shares to the public, reducing government ownership to 51 per cent
2000	Joint venture with Pacific Century Cyber Works to enter the Asian market; created Telstra Saturn (NZ); joint venture with KPN—formed as Station 12
2001	Established Reach and CSL in Hong Kong
2002	Acquired the rest of CSL; acquired the rest of CLEAR to form TelstraClear; acquired Level3 Communications; Foxtel restructured; Telstra Country Wide formed; White Pages rebranded as Sensis
2003	Reach write-down; formed joint venture for 3G mobiles with Hutchinson Telecommunications
2004	Acquired the *Trading Post*
2005	BigPond became a division; acquired KAZ and Damovo
2006	Government sells controlling stake to public with Future Fund holding minority (17 per cent) share; launches national 3G wireless mobile broadband (Next G); buys 51 per cent of Sou Fun, a Chinese internet website business

Westfield

Year and place founded

1956, Sydney, NSW

CEOs

1958   Frank Lowy and John Saunders (joint)

1987   Frank Lowy

1987   David Lowy

1997   Steven, Peter and David Lowy (joint)

2000   Steven and Peter Lowy (joint)

Founding concept

Commercial property development leading to specialisation in the creation, development and management of retail shopping centres.

Key events

1956   Westfield Investments founded

1959   Westfield Place opens in Blacktown, Sydney, with one supermarket, two department stores and 12 shops

1960   Westfield Development Corporation listed on Sydney Stock Exchange

1961   Shore Motel opened

1966   Burwood (Sydney) opened—the first centre to be branded 'Westfield Shoppingtown'

1967   First centre in Queensland opened

1969   Opened first centre in Victoria

1977   Entered US shopping mall market with acquisition of Trumbull Shopping Park, Connecticut

1979   Westfield Holdings and Westfield Property Trust formed and listed

1987   Westfield Capital Corporation listed on Australian Stock Exchange

1988   Westfield Holdings split into Westfield Australia and Westfield International; Westfield International listed on London stock exchange

1989   Westfield International privatised

1994   Acquired CenterMark shopping centre portfolio in the US — 19 regional and super-regional malls

1995   Entered Malaysia with a joint venture with Rodamco NV

1996   Westfield America Trust listed on the Australian stock exchange

1997   Appointed manager of St Lukes Group, New Zealand's premier shopping centre company; Westfield America listed on the New York stock exchange

1998   Westfield America acquired major shopping centre portfolio of TrizecHahn in US; Westfield Trust acquired major share in St Lukes Group

2000   Entered UK through joint ventures with Hermes and MEPC; brands all US shopping centres; Westfield Trust and St Lukes Group amalgamated

2001   Acquired 24 per cent of Rodamco (US)

2002   Acquired 22 shopping centres from Rodamco and Richard Jacobs Group; acquired management and development rights to Continental Airlines Terminal E Houston

2003   Acquired AMP Shopping Centre Trust

2004   Merged all three Westfield companies into one; four new joint ventures with Deutsche Diversifed Fund; acquired Skygarden, Imperial Arcade in Sydney and the rest of Auckland One

2005   Acquired 15 Federated Department Stores at 11 Westfield centres in the US, Chicago Ridge, 50 per cent of Penrith Plaza, 50 per cent of Woden Plaza and 50 per cent of White City (UK)

2006   Acquired 100 per cent of Stratford City (UK)

Woolworths

Year and place founded

1924, Sydney, NSW

CEOs

1924   Percy Christmas

1929   Percy Christmas and George Creed (joint)

1930   Percy Christmas

1945   Theo Kelly

1971   Owen Price

1974   Bill Dean and Paul Simons (joint)

1981   Tony Harding

1988   Harry Watts

1993   Reg Clairs

1998   Roger Corbett

2006   Mike Luscombe

Founding concept

When a business opportunity opened up in the basement of Percy Christmas and Stanley Chatterton's S.E. Chatterton frock salon in Sydney, they decided to use the new open display method of selling to establish a cash and carry store modelled on the American Woolworth company.

Key events

1924   Opened first Sydney store

1927   Opened Brisbane store

1928   Opened Perth store

1929   Established the London buying office; opened in New Zealand

1933   Opened Melbourne store; had 23 stores in Australia and eight in New Zealand

1955   First self-service store; 200 stores in Australia and 55 in New Zealand

The First XI

1958	Entered the food market by acquiring 32 BCC stores in Queensland
1960	First Woolworths supermarket; first retailer to operate Australia-wide by entering the Northern Territory
1961	Expansion into apparel by acquisition of 70 Rockmans stores
1964	First regional shopping centre at Newcastle, including first Big W store
1965	Acquired Fitzpatrick's Food Supplies, a leading Singapore retail/wholesale organisation
1967	Acquired Cox Bros and Foys department stores
1969	Acquired 26 Nancarrows food stores
1970	Acquired 75 Crofts Food Stores
1978	Sold New Zealand interests
1981	Acquired Dick Smith Electronics, Philip Leong, Purity Group and Roelf Vos group (supermarkets)
1985	Acquired 126 Australian Safeway Stores to become the largest food retailer in Australia; acquired 59 Chandlers electrical stores; opened Dick Smith in the US; closed Homemakers chain of 12 stores
1989	Industrial Equity acquired Woolworths (it had had a minority interest since 1986)
1993	Woolworths refloated on the stock exchange
1996	Acquired Cannons Group, including Australian Independent Wholesalers; opened first Marketplace shopping centre development; introduced petrol retailing
1997	First Metro stores
1998	Alliance with Commonwealth Bank to provide co-branded financial services; acquired Dan Murphy liquor stores.
2000	Project Refresh began; sold Rockmans and Chisholm Manufacturing; acquired 11 wine outlets in Sydney, 16 Booze Brothers liquor outlets in Adelaide and Liberty Liquor in Perth; relaunched 'fresh food'
2001	Acquired 67 Franklins supermarkets, Tandy consumer electronics and 38 per cent of GreenGrocer.com; sold Crazy Prices

2003 Established Project Refresh Level II; announced joint venture with Caltex to expand petrol outlets; acquired 22 Super Cellars and Le Grog liquor stores in Adelaide

2005 Acquired Australian Leisure and Hospitality Group, and Foodland's 22 New Zealand supermarkets

2006 Opened first electronics store in India in joint venture with Tata Group

Appendix B

Minor studies

International studies

Many other studies (apart from *In Search of Excellence*, *Built to Last* and *Good to Great*) have attempted to identify winning practices. However, most have not focused on specific examples of winning organisations, nor have they identified the selection criteria for such organisations. Nevertheless, their findings—from a variety of theoretical and practical perspectives—offer further support for many of the concepts we have discussed, and offer interesting food for thought in considering the issue of high performance.

Dertouzos, Lester and Solow (1989) conducted a survey of US manufacturing firms. They found six key similarities in firms that were doing well. They were:

- ▶ focus on continuous improvement in cost, quality and delivery
- ▶ closer links with customers
- ▶ closer relations with suppliers
- ▶ effective use of technology for strategic advantage
- ▶ less hierarchical and compartmentalised organisations for greater flexibility
- ▶ human resource policies that promote continuous learning, participation and flexibility.

This study encouraged organisations to look outside themselves for help in continuously improving. The emphasis on flexibility and less hierarchical structures were also important new findings at the time.

Kotter and Heskett (1992) studied 207 firms in 22 industries over 11 years, focusing on success in financial terms. Coming from an organisational behaviour background, they concluded that organisations should have demanding leadership from managers at all levels of the organisation, which emphasises cultures that balance all stakeholder groups. Although US-based, this study did include British Airways, ICI, Nissan and SAS as winning organisations.

Miles and Snow (1994) put together a formula for success. Based on their extensive research, teaching, study and consulting experience, but not based on a particular set of firms or study, they argued that keys to success were:

▶ tight fit

▶ responding to external change

▶ creating a stable network

▶ investing in people to achieve this.

Their study highlighted alignment, people and external focus—all key elements in our framework.

Pfeffer (1998) reviewed hundreds of studies in organisational change and human resource practice conducted over a 30-year period, and concluded that the following seven practices that 'seem to characterise' handling people well is the way to success. These practices are:

▶ providing secure employment

▶ selective hiring of new people

▶ self-managing teams and decentralised decision making as the basis for organisational design

▶ comparatively high remuneration contingent on organisation performance

▶ extensive training

▶ reduced status distinctions and barriers

▶ extensive sharing of financial and performance information.

Coming from an organisational behaviour background, Pfeffer passionately argues the business case for a focus on people as the driver of business success. This highlights the 'people' element in our framework and others.

De Geus (1997) reported on Shell's 1983 study of long-surviving organisations—that is, organisations that were older than Shell (which began in the 1890s) and relatively as important in their industries. The report found 40 companies that met the criteria, of which 27 were examined in detail. De Geus found that four factors were common across the sample. The organisations were:

- sensitive to their environment
- cohesive, with a strong sense of identity
- internally tolerant/decentralised decision-makers/able to build constructive relationships internally and externally
- conservative financially.

This is a very process-oriented list. De Geus made the interesting point that none of the organisations still operated in their core businesses, as they had to adapt to survive and often their core business simply did not exist any more. The factors identified imply an external sensitivity more than an internal focus and a conservative bent rather than an aggressive bent.

Katzenbach (2000) studied 25 organisations, including the non-profits NASA and the US Marine Corps, that were recommended by experts and had superior records in financial and market terms. Katzenbach concluded that high-performance organisations chose one of five—mutually exclusive—routes to success. Their focus was on one of:

- mission and vision
- process and measurement
- entrepreneurial spirit
- individual achievements
- group recognition and celebration.

Our study sees all of these as important (provided we interpret 'mission and vision' as 'clear strategy'), rather than as either/or choices.

Joyce, Nohria and Roberson (2003) studied 160 companies across 40 different industries, choosing one high performer, one low performer, one improver and one decliner in each industry, based on total shareholder returns over a 10-year period. They found '4+2' factors were important. The common ('primary') four were:

- strategy
- execution
- culture
- structure.

The winners also had two of four 'secondary' areas:
- talent
- leadership
- innovation
- mergers and partnerships.

Apart from structure and mergers and partnerships, our study agrees with all these issues, though we do not see them as 'primary' and 'secondary'.

Finally, Jain (1998) reported on an Indian study of 20 organisations that were selected from 56 nominations based on growth rates over four years and that allowed interviews. In our view, this is far too short a period, but it is useful to see that researchers in other countries are working on these issues too.

Australian studies

In addition to the international studies, there have been several Australian pieces of research that have considered 'success' from a variety of perspectives.

Best practice studies

The Australian Manufacturing Council (1994) published a survey of 1400 manufacturing sites, which identified leading practices for manufacturers. Its findings for best practices were:

- having effective people practices: creating cooperation and trust by commitment to teamwork, training, effective communication and employee morale
- building a shared vision
- benchmarking for best practice
- having a customer focus

- effectively utilising technology
- having a shared responsibility for total quality.

This study highlights leadership (through shared vision), people, strategy, an external focus and continuous improvement.

Rimmer et al. (1996) studied the organisations chosen to participate in the first two rounds (1991–92) of the Australian Government's 'best practice' program, to try to understand what the common practices were among those organisations. Some of these organisations were in fact divisions of firms rather than whole organisations and 35 of the 43 firms were manufacturers. The organisations were not necessarily high performers, but were seeking to be high performers. Rimmer et al. concluded that the following elements were important:

- having a consistent and cohesive strategy that is fully resourced
- having empowered, work-based teams of trained people
- having a focus on process improvement
- having integrated and comprehensive formal measurement and control systems
- people management
- forming links and relationships with outside organisations.

Their findings are similar to the Australian Manufacturing Council findings above. Once again strategy, people, leadership (through people management), continuous improvement and external focus are important factors. This study also includes reporting systems as a key element.

Quality movement studies

In the 1990s, as discussed previously, Australian business focused on improving quality to catch up to changes that had been made overseas. The Australian Quality Council established a framework that is now called the Australian Business Excellence Framework (ABEF). Proponents of this framework believe that organisations can be measured against the criteria and a point score used to assess their level of overall quality as well as what gaps need to be addressed. The main areas of the framework (and by implication the keys to success) are:

- Leadership and innovation (180 pts)

- People (160 pts)
- Processes, products and services (160 pts)
- Customer and market focus (150 pts)
- Business results (150 pts)
- Strategy and planning processes (100 pts)
- Data, information and knowledge (100 pts).

Hausner (1999) demonstrated a strong correlation between high ABEF scores and a wide-ranging definition of performance. He concluded that senior executive leadership, analysis and use of data and information, and having measures of success and planning processes were key drivers of this relationship.

Bell (2002), an ABEF assessor, published '10 principles of business excellence for increased market share'. They are:

- senior executives as role models
- focus on achievement of goals
- (focus on) customer perception of value
- to improve the outcome, improve the system
- improved decisions
- (decrease) variability
- enthusiastic people
- learning, innovation and continual improvement
- corporate citizenship
- value for all stakeholders.

There is considerable alignment with our study results here. Leadership, people, strategy, processes (perfect alignment, adapt rapidly) and outcomes (effective execution) are clear. Balance everything is implied. Looking out, looking in, and manage the downside are not specifically identified.

While based on his experience as an ABEF evaluator, Bell does not give any specific organisation examples to illustrate these principles. Interestingly, they do not correspond clearly to Hausner's findings. This suggests that the key differentiators for success are not the same as the set of factors that need to be managed by all organisations.

Appendix B: minor studies

Samson and Challis (1999) published a set of principles for success 'based on a global study of the world's best organisations'. Their principles are:

- alignment
- distributed leadership
- integration
- being out front (leading the industry)
- being upfront (being honest)
- resourcing the medium term
- being time focused
- embracing change
- (having a) learning focus
- being disciplined
- (having good) measurement and reporting
- (delivering) customer value
- (focus on creating) capabilities
- (linking) micro to macro.

This work focuses primarily on processes. For instance, strategy and people are not mentioned and 'leadership' is seen as 'distributed'. Unfortunately, in this work there is very limited reference to Australian organisations or particular practices, despite the Australian origins of its authors.

Finally, a series of 'most admired' surveys are now collated annually by magazines, such as *Business Review Weekly*, and consultants. These tend to highlight only the currently perceived 'good' organisations in the short term. However, they do reflect the increasingly intense interest in this subject.

Appendix C

Winning organisations in Australia — selected survey questions

Between 2001 and 2006 we developed a database of over 140 questions based on our research findings. By surveying 'normal' Australian organisations we are developing a sense of where 'normal' organisations fit against the 'winning wheel' practices. Following is a sample of some of the questions. We would be very pleased to add your organisation to our database and build our knowledge of the 'normal' Australian experience and situation. Our contact details are provided in 'About the authors' at the beginning of the book.

Effective execution

Your organisation:

1. Does what it says
2. Gets the job done on time
3. Gets the job done within budget
4. Has clear processes that are accepted
5. Doesn't cross-subsidise businesses or units

Perfect alignment

Your organisation:

1. Aligns its principal systems with each other

2 Aligns its culture to strategy
3 Aligns reward systems to strategy
4 Aligns performance measurement systems to strategy
5 Aligns its recruitment to strategy

Adapts rapidly
Your organisation:
1 Expects to do things quickly
2 Is set up to be able to do things quickly
3 Responds to external demands quickly
4 Responds to internal expectations quickly
5 Has a culture of continuous improvement

Clear and fuzzy strategy
Your organisation:
1 Has a clear strategy
2 Allows for some strategic flexibility
3 Can identify a 'cause' more than just a strategy
4 Strategy hooks people emotionally
5 Ensures that the strategy is clearly understood throughout the organisation

Leadership, not leaders
Your organisation:
1 Develops a leadership team
2 Focuses leadership behaviour on building the business
3 Leaders mix frequently with people at all levels
4 Leaders are valued by people at all levels
5 Leaders encourage people at all levels

Appendix C: winning organisations in Australia—selected survey questions

Looking out, looking in

Your organisation:

1. Thinks about customers in decision making
2. Works with other organisations on a partnership basis to expand resources
3. Manages government and regulators as part of the normal activity
4. Works with suppliers on an ongoing relationship basis
5. Has a sense of community responsibility as part of the organisation's normal activity

Right people

Your organisation:

1. Ensures people fit the strategy
2. Ensures people fit the culture
3. Invests in people through training and development
4. Promotes from within
5. Provides good feedback

Managing the downside

Your organisation:

1. Understands the variety of risks that can critically affect the long-term results
2. Uses techniques to manage those risks
3. Lays off risks to other parties involved in the activity
4. Is conservative in thinking and actions
5. Uses project management techniques

Balance everything

Your organisation:

1. Balances external and internal views
2. Balances shareholders and stakeholders

The First XI

3 Balances the short term and long term
4 Balances entrepreneurialism and conservatism
5 Balances the individual and team

Bibliography

In addition to the annual reports of the winning organisations for the period 1980 onwards, published case studies, major press and stockbroker analysis, websites and other public information, the following sources were used:

Ashkenasy, N & Trevor-Roberts, E 2001, 'Leading in Australia: the egalitarian visionary suits our style', *Mt Eliza Business Review*, Summer–Autumn, pp. 33–39.

Australian Manufacturing Council 1994, *Leading the way*, Australian Manufacturing Council.

Bell, G 2002, *The competitive enterprise*, McGraw-Hill.

Bossidy, L, Charan, R & Burck, C 2002, *Execution: the discipline of getting things done*, Crown.

Business Council of Australia, 2006, *New concepts in innovation: the keys to a growing Australia*, Business Council of Australia.

Carew, E 2000, *Brambles: working its way around the world*, Brambles.

Carnegie, R, Butlin, M, Barratt, P, Turnbull, A & Webber, I 1993, *Managing the innovating enterprise*, Business Council of Australia.

Collins, J 2001, *Good to great*, HarperBusiness.

—— 2001, 'Level 5 leadership: the triumph of humility and fierce resolve', *Harvard Business Review*, January, pp. 67–76.

Collins, J & Porras, J 1994, *Built to last: successful habits of visionary companies*, Century.

Condon, M 2002, 'Why the genius in Harvey Norman still keeps going', *The Sunday Age*, 24 March, p. 13.

De Geus, A 1997, *The living company*, Harvard Business School.

Dertouzos, M, Lester, R & Solow, R 1989, *Made in America: regaining the productive edge*, Harper.

The detailed Westfield story: the first 40 years, <www.westfield.com.au>.

Groen, B & Hampden-Turner, C 2005, *The titans of Saturn*, Marshall Cavendish.

Harley, R 2003, 'Re-imagining the mall', *AFR BOSS*, 10 October 2003.

Hausner, A 1999, 'Australian quality awards for business excellence', *The Quality Magazine*, August, pp. 47–50.

Hockerts, K 1999, *Greener Management International*, vol. 25, pp. 29–49.

Hubbard, G 2000, *Strategic management: thinking, analysis and action*, Prentice Hall.

—— 2004, *Strategic management: thinking, analysis and action*, 2nd edn, Pearson.

Hubbard, G, Pocknee, G & Taylor, G 1996, *Practical Australian strategy*, Prentice Hall/Australian Institute of Management.

Jackson, M 2002, 'Rapid response', *Management Today*, August, p. 5.

Jain , A 1998, *Corporate excellence*, Excel Books.

Jaques, E 1989, *Requisite organisation*, Cason Hall.

Javidan, M, Dorfman, PW, Sully de Luque, M & House, RJ 2006, 'In the eye of the beholder: cross cultural lessons in leadership from project GLOBE', *Academy of Management Perspectives*, February, pp. 67–88.

Joyce, W, Nohria, N & Roberson, B 2003, *What really works: the 4+2 formulas for sustained business success*, HarperCollins Business.

Kaplan, R & Norton, D 1996, *The balanced scorecard*, Harvard Business School.

Katzenbach, JR 2000, *Peak performance: aligning the hearts and minds of your employees*, Harvard Business School Press.

Kavanagh, J 2001, 'Superstar performers', *Business Review Weekly*, November 1–7, pp. 62–66.

Kirby, J 2005, 'Toward a theory of high performance', *Harvard Business Review*, July–August, pp. 30–39.

Kotter, J & Heskett, J 1992, *Corporate culture and performance*, Free Press.

Lewis, G, Morkel, A, Hubbard, G, Davenport, S & Stockport, G 1994, *Australian strategic management*, Prentice Hall.

Margo, J 2000, *Frank Lowy: pushing the limits*, HarperCollins.

Miles, R & Snow, C 1994, *Fit, failure and the hall of fame*, Free Press.

Murray, J 1999, *The Woolworths way*, Focus.

Peters, T & Waterman, R 1982, *In search of excellence: lessons from America's best-run companies*, Harper & Row.

Pfeffer, J 1998, *The human equation*, Harvard Business School.

The Qantas story, <www.qantas.com.au>.

Rimmer, M, Macneil, J, Chenhall, R, Langfield-Smith, K & Walls, L 1996, *Reinventing competitiveness: achieving best practice in Australia*, Pitman.

Samson, D & Challis, D 1999, *Patterns of excellence*, Prentice Hall.

'Talking Shop', *AFR BOSS*, 7 July 2006.

Telstra 1994, *Quality in Australia: the Telecom archetype study*, Telstra.

Viljoen, J 1991, *Strategic management*, Longman.

Welch, J 2001, *Jack: what I've learned leading a great company and great people*, Headline.

Wilson, R 1999, 'Global values—global difference', Centre for Tomorrow's Company conference, London, July 1999.

Young, P 1996, 'The coaching paradigm: developing the next generation of excellent managers', *The Practising Manager*, October, pp. 50–52.

Index

3M 11
7S model 49–50, 51, 53, 73–74, 265, 375

adaptation, rapid 81–111, 129–130
—causes of 82
—continuous improvement and 93–100
—factors behind 83, 84
—fuzzy strategy for 129–130
—innovation and 100–110
alignment 47–80
—communication 71–72
—culture 54–55, 74–76
—leadership 68–70, 76–77
—over time 78
—people 66–68
—perceptions 72–73
—strategy 53–54, 73–74
—structure 70–71
—systems 58–66
—values 55–56
American Airlines 61
A.T. Kearney 12
attitude 204–206, 297–298
Australian businesses 287–288
—advantages of 288–289
—competition 294–295

—determination and 301
—differences 288
—environmental changes 290–293
—pioneering 300–301
Australian Manufacturing Council 3
Australian market 303–304
Australian Workplace Agreements (AWAs) 63–64, 67

balance 263–286
—achieving 281
—*Built to Last* and 265
—7S model and 265
—operations/activities/functions 279
—organisation levels 277–279
—overall 279–281
—paradox theory and 266
—perspectives 267–272
—philosophies 272
balanced scorecard approach 7, 25–26, 266
beliefs *see* values
Big Hairy Audacious Goals (BHAGs) 11, 116, 117, 295
Blount, Frank 68, 149, 159
Bossidy, Larry 25

Brambles 15, 23, 40, 43–44, 56, 59, 99, 108, 228, 276, 305, 318–322, 337–339, 409–412
—Ensco and 322
—financial performance 339
—innovation at 107–108
—'Manly Manifesto' 99
—operating systems 59
—'Perfect Plant' 305
—strategic cycle 318–322
—values statement 56
breakthrough ideas 11–12
Built to Last viii, 3, 4, 5, 101–102, 147, 377–379, 383, 384, 385, 386
Business Council of Australia 101–102, 300

Carew, Edna 39, 44, 67, 99, 103, 186, 228, 276
Carnegie et al. 100–101, 104, 107
causes 133–134, 295–296
CEOs 76–77, 78, 138, 139–140, 141, 148–151
change programs 364–366
Cheney, Michael 300
CHEP (Commonwealth Handling Equipment Pool) 129, 176, 181, 251, 305, 317, 319, 321, 338
Chow, Sir CK 321, 338
Christmas, Percy 69, 90
Cicutto, Frank 346
Clairs, Reg 120, 151
Clarke, Greg 152, 341
Cleanaway 41, 107, 129, 176, 193, 316, 317, 319, 321, 338
Clifford, Leigh 317
Collins, J 14, 143, 163, 380
Collins J and Porras J 3–4, 5–6, 8, 9, 11, 13, 14, 22, 49, 75, 95, 95, 116–117, 123, 133, 142–143, 149, 209, 265, 267, 274, 281, 295
communication, aligning 71–72
community responsibility 194–198
consolidation 315–316
continuous improvement 94–100

control
—speed and 85–88
Corbett, Roger 72, 120, 141, 152, 360
corporate governance processes 370–371
CRA 31, 32, 107, 147, 184, 214
cross-subsidisation, 41–43, 45
culture 54–55, 74–76, 226–233, 282
—commitment 226–227
—diversity of views 282
—humility 230–231
—passion 227
—patriotism 231–232
customer relationship management (CRM) 177–179

decision making 60–62, 146–147, 285–286
Detailed Westfield Story, The 86, 153, 178, 179, 219
development, sustainable 366–367
Dixon, Geoff 76, 349
Dusseldorp, Dick 72

effective execution 21–45
efficiency 28–32
enterprise bargaining 62
environmental
—issues 270
—practices 198–199
environment, team 218

Ferguson, Rob 85
Fletcher, John 186, 338
flexibility
—operational 92–93
—strategic 88–92
focus, external 172–185
—community responsibility 194–197
—customer relationship management (CRM) 177–179
—customers 173–175
—customised products/services 176–177
—other organisations 179–185
—market research 175–176

Index

focus, future 186–190
fuzzy strategy 127–131

General Electric 25, 43
Gibb, Malcolm 40
Global Challenge, The 3
global expansion 316–317
globalisation 323–324
Good to Great ix, 379–381, 384, 385, 386
government and regulators 183–185, 306–309
Groen, B and Hampden-Turner, C 266
Guest Keen and Nettlefold plc (GKN) 44, 149, 181, 220, 251, 317, 319, 338

Harvey Norman 15, 23, 30, 28, 29–30, 42, 44, 339–341, 413–414
—cross-subsidisation and 42
—financial performance 340
—Joyce Mayne and 340
—operational efficiency and 29–30
HomeSide 70, 328
Hubbard, G 3, 49–50, 51, 266, 392
—E-S-C gap 266
—strategic implementation model 49–50, 51
Huizinga, Herman 85
humility 230–231

ideas 102–103, 192–193
incentive schemes 64, 65
innovation 100–110
—Australia and 101–102
—borrowing ideas 102–103
—process 104–107
—product and service 107–110
—sources of 102
In Search of Excellence viii, 4, 5, 8, 43, 265, 374–376, 381–383, 385, 386
international expansion 190–194, 314–315, 316

Jackson, Margaret 87
Jaques, Elliot 67
Jetstar 44, 54, 88

Karpin Report, The 298
Kavanagh, J 12
Kelly, Theo 86–87
key performance indicators (KPIs) 37–38, 221, 258, 386
Kirby, J 386

leaders 145–146, 148–150, 160–161, 166–168, 296–297, 298
leadership 68–70, 137–169, 283–284
—aligning 68–70
—Australian capabilities 144
—boards and 142
—captain-coach 138, 145, 296–302
—communication and 154–156
—from within 148–150
—humility in 284–285
—'Level 5 leadership' 143
—levels of 139–140
—passionate 152–153
—programs 161–165
—'right for the time' 158–159
—styles 164–165
—team-based 141
Leading the Way 3
Lend Lease 15, 23, 31, 35, 56, 58, 59, 72, 92, 105, 107, 125, 126, 152, 178, 188, 189, 195, 228–229, 330–331, 341–344, 415–417
—beliefs 125, 126
—board 58
—'community of interest' 105
—community responsibility and 195–196
—financial performance 343
—General Property Trust and 107, 342
—management control systems and 34–35
—MLC and 91–92, 331
—operating systems 59

Lend Lease (cont'd)
—technical efficiency and 31
—values statement 56
—'walking the talk' 152
Lowy, David 359
Lowy, Frank 28, 68, 84, 141, 315, 359–360
Lowy, Peter 141
Lowy, Steven 141, 315
Luscombe, Mike 96–97

Macquarie 15, 23, 37, 39–40, 43–44, 55, 56, 59, 89–91, 121, 129, 141, 145–147, 155, 245–246, 344–346, 418–419
—culture of 55
—financial performance 345
—Korea and 91
—leadership at 155
—operating systems 59
—values statement 56
—'What we stand for' 120
management control systems 34–36
management information systems (MIS) 60
management studies 437–443
Margo, J 84, 85
marketing 13–14
McKinsey & Co. 375, 376
Menadue, John 30, 76
mission statements 120–122, 356
mistakes 38–40
MLC 91–92, 181, 331, 346
Moss, Alan 141
Murray, J 69, 86, 151

National Australia Bank (NAB) 15, 23, 52, 56–57, 59, 60–61, 70, 68, 76, 177–178, 328, 346–348, 420–421
—Customer Account Management System (CAMS) 177–178
—financial performance 347
—forex trading and 347
—HomeSide 70, 328

—MLC and 346
—operating systems 59
—values statement 56–57

operating systems 59–60
organisational
—assessment 399, 400
—management 3
—maturity 394–396
—structure 13
organisation levels 277–279
Organisation of the Petroleum Exporting Countries (OPEC) 31
overseas influences 304

partnerships 180–183
Pemberton, Gary 41, 67
people 201–234, 257–258
—attitude versus qualifications 205–206
—'best' 206–208
—career development 216–217
—culture and strategy 203–204
—environment and 202
—investing in 211
—right 201–234
—selection 208–211
—supporting 217–218
—training 211–216
performance 7, 220–226, 404–406
—cube 7
perspectives 267–272
Peters, T and Waterman, R 22, 49–50, 51, 53
philosophies 272–277
pioneering organisations 300–301
plan-do-check-act cycle 94–95
privatisation 62–63
process innovation 104–107
project management 253–255
promotion from within 219–220

Qantas 15, 30, 31, 35–36, 42, 44, 53, 54, 61, 76–77, 87, 88, 147–148, 178, 184, 190, 229–230, 348–351, 422–423
—Australian Airlines and 44, 53
—*Australian Way, The* 148

—Bali bombings and 88
—CEOs 76–77
—Compass and 36
—cross-subsidisation and 42
—financial performance 350
—Impulse Airlines and 36, 54
—international security processes and 88
—Jetstar 44, 54, 88
—management control systems and 35–36
—September 11 and 61, 77
—'Sustainable Future' program 99, 188

return on equity (ROE) 25
reward systems 62–66
Richter, Oliver 41
Rio Tinto 15, 24, 25–26, 30, 31, 32, 64, 124–125, 158–159, 184, 190, 218, 317, 351–353, 422–426
—financial performance 352
—leadership at 158–159
—technical efficiency and 30, 31
—'The way we work' 15, 25, 124–125, 196
risk management 235–260
—techniques 244–260
—types of 238–244

Salvation Army 15, 29, 42, 55, 57–59, 120–121, 123–124, 177, 353–354, 427–429
—cross-subsidisation and 42
—culture 55
—financial performance 354
—mission statement 120–121
—operating systems 59
—operational efficiency and 29
—values statement 57, 123–124
—Youthworx 177
Saunders, John 28, 68, 84, 141
September 11, 2001 61, 77, 335, 348
speed
—control and 85–88

Standards Australia 259–260
Stewart, John 76, 76
strategic cycle 311–333
—Brambles and 318–322
—mistakes in 326–330
—stages of 318
—winning wheel framework and 318–322
strategic implementation 49–50, 51, 53
strategic position, defining 392–394
strategy 113–136, 330–331
—cause and 133–134
—change and 126
—clear 117–121
—clear and fuzzy 131–133
—confusion over 116–117
—conveyance of 118–119
—development 135
—fuzzy 127–131
—growth as a driver of 122–123
—importance of 131–132
—lack of 130–131
—levels of 114–115
—mission/vision statements and 121–122
—realignment during change 330–331
—setting 132–133
—values and 123–126
—what is 114–117
Strong, James 76, 147–148
structure, aligning 70–71
success factors 8–9
suppliers 182–183
survey questions 445–448
systems 58–66

Telstra 15, 32, 33, 44, 57–59, 68, 75, 87–88, 93, 126–127, 145, 146, 155, 159–160, 176, 183–184, 227–228, 355–358, 429–430
—cultural change and 75
—financial performance 358
—leadership and 145, 146, 155
—mission statement 356

Telstra (cont'd)
- —operating systems 59
- —responsibility and 33
- —structure 93
- —T3 356–357
- —technical efficiency and 32
- —TELCATS (Telecom Customer Attitudes to Service) 176
- —values statement 57
- —Vision 2000 126–127

three strikes rule 40–41
transition periods 331–332
Trujillo, Sol 68, 76, 356
Turner, David 321

values 55–58, 124–127
variable remuneration 64
Viljoen, J 3

Ward, John 76
Welch, Jack 42
Westfield 15, 28, 60, 64, 68, 74, 99, 108, 141, 175, 218–219, 249–251, 327–328, 358–360, 431–432
- —development process of 85–86
- —diversification and 327–328
- —financial performance 359
- —General Property Trust and 249
- —separating assets 108–109
- —Shoppingtown Promise 175
- —'Ten commandments for customer relations' 175
- —US and 74

Wilson, Robert 26
winning
- —criteria 387–389
- —practices 401–402

winning organisations 1–19, 336–337, 391–408
- —assessing 5–10
- —Big Hairy Audacious Goals (BHAGs) and 11
- —breakthrough ideas 11–12
- —how to become a 391–408
- —mission statements 10–11
- —sharemarket performance 336–337

winning wheel framework 14–18, 318–322, 396–398
Woolworths 15, 23–24, 30, 34, 57, 59, 69, 72, 86–87, 90, 96–97, 120, 141, 151, 210, 219, 254–255, 269, 360–362, 433–435
- —Big W 86–87
- —Caltex and 360
- —Dan Murphy's and 361
- —financial performance 362
- —food retailing and 90
- —mission statement 120
- —Murray, J 69
- —operating systems 59
- —Project Mercury 255
- —Project Refresh 96–97
- —responsibility and 34
- —results and 23–24
- —strategy and 119–120
- —values statement 57

Youthworx 177

Zampatti, Carla 85

amazing
P E O P L E

**Amazing people
will inspire and transform
YOUR leaders,
YOUR people and
YOUR organisation to
achieve exceptional results!**

Leadership

Communication

Teamwork

Coaching

Organisational Development.

Amazing People are in the business of helping individuals, organisations and communities do whatever it is they do better, in order that they may get more of what they want, in a way that is sustainable, fair, fun and ethical to all concerned.

We provide quality training and organisational development services incorporating Experience Based Learning.

Amazing People's success is due to their experience, commitment and focus on program design and delivery targeted to achieve the training results our clients require.

Amazing People

Ph +61 (02) 4367 5977
Fax +61 (02) 4367 5988

390 The Entrance Rd
Erina Heights NSW 2260

info@amazingpeople.com.au
www.amazingpeople.com.au

Inspire and Transform the World

© Macklin Holdings Pty Ltd   ABN : 52 058 772 875

NIDA

WE SHOW BUSINESS
HOW TO MANAGE THE SPOTLIGHT

For over ten years, NIDA Corporate Performance courses have enabled business executives to access similar skills that actors use to make their work performance more engaging.

ACT LIKE YOU MEAN BUSINESS

Actors can control their voice, breath, body language, expression and pitch in order to manage an audience and control perception. NIDA's unique courses extend these skills to the business environment, where they can be applied to improve confidence, negotiation ability, leadership, communication and presentation skills.

NIDA runs a variety of public programs throughout the year, and can also customise training to be specific and relevant to your requirements. Enquiries for private training are also welcome.

TRAINING FOR EVERY STAGE OF YOUR CAREER

National Institute of Dramatic Art
EXCELLENCE, INNOVATION & ACCESS IN ARTS EDUCATION

CORPORATE PERFORMANCE
Tel **61 2 9697 7560** Fax 61 2 9697 7681
CP@NIDA.EDU.AU | WWW.**NIDA**.EDU.AU

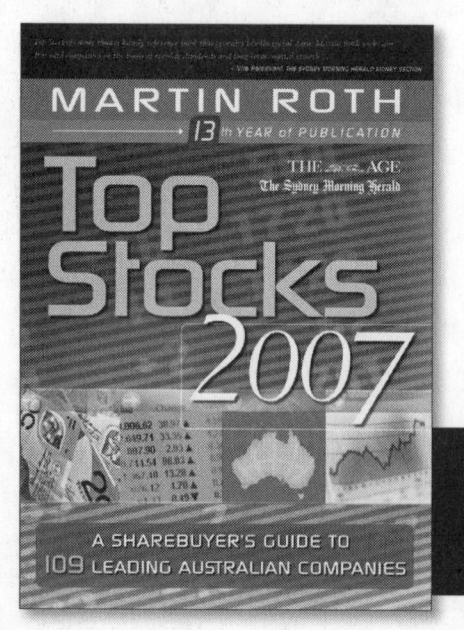

Top Stocks 2007
RRP $29.95

With 1700 companies listed on the Australian Stock Exchange it can be difficult knowing where to begin or who to invest in. Martin Roth, author of *Top Stocks 2007*, rates the leading companies, providing all the vital information and statistics to help you decide whether to take a gamble or play it safe.

Premium edition *Top Stocks* 2007 WITH BONUS CD also available. RRP $39.95

Available at all good bookstores or to order direct call 1300 656 059

THE AGE | The Sydney Morning Herald